A·N·N·U·A·L E·D·IT·I

Criminal Justice   *05/06*

Twenty-Nineth Edition

EDITOR

Joseph L. Victor

Mercy College, Dobbs Ferry

Joseph L. Victor is professor and chairman of the Department of Law, Criminal Justice, and Safety Administration at Mercy College. Professor Victor has extensive field experience in criminal justice agencies, counseling, and administering human service programs. He earned his B.A. and M.A. at Seton Hall University and his Doctorate of Education at Fairleigh Dickinson University.

Joanne Naughton

Mercy College, Dobbs Ferry

Joanne Naughton is assistant professor of Criminal Justice at Mercy College. Professor Naughton is a former member of the New York City Police Department, where she encountered most aspects of police work as a police officer, detective, sergeant, and lieutenant. She is also a former staff attorney with The Legal Aid Society. She received her B.A. and J.D. at Fordham University.

McGraw-Hill/Dushkin

2460 Kerper Blvd., Dubuque, IA 52001

Visit us on the Internet
http://www.dushkin.com

Credits

1. **Crime and Justice in America**
   Unit photo—© Getty Images/PhotoDisc
2. **Victimology**
   Unit photo—© Getty Images/PhotoLink/Jack Star
3. **The Police**
   Unit photo—© Getty Images/Brand X
4. **The Judicial System**
   Unit photo—CORBIS/Royalty-Free
5. **Juvenile Justice**
   Unit photo—© Getty Images/PhotoLink/Jack Star
6. **Punishment and Corrections**
   Unit photo—© Getty Images/Brand X

Copyright

Cataloging in Publication Data
Main entry under title: Annual Editions: Criminal Justice. 2005/2006.
1. Criminal Justice—Periodicals. I. Victor, Joseph L., *comp.* II. Naughton, Joanne Title: Criminal Justice.
ISBN 0–07–310194–X   658'.05   ISSN 0272–3816

Twenty-Nineth Edition

Cover image Corbis/Royalty Free and Brand X/Getty Images
Printed in the United States of America   1234567890QPDQPD987654   Printed on Recycled Paper

Editors/Advisory Board

Members of the Advisory Board are instrumental in the final selection of articles for each edition of ANNUAL EDITIONS. Their review of articles for content, level, currentness, and appropriateness provides critical direction to the editor and staff. We think that you will find their careful consideration well reflected in this volume.

Preface

In publishing ANNUAL EDITIONS we recognize the enormous role played by the magazines, newspapers, and journals of the public press in providing current, first-rate educational information in a broad spectrum of interest areas. Many of these articles are appropriate for students, researchers, and professionals seeking accurate, current material to help bridge the gap between principles and theories and the real world. These articles, however, become more useful for study when those of lasting value are carefully collected, organized, indexed, and reproduced in a low-cost format, which provides easy and permanent access when the material is needed. That is the role played by ANNUAL EDITIONS.

During the 1970's, Criminal Justice emerged as an appealing, vital, and unique academic discipline. It emphasizes the professional development of students who plan careers in the field, and attracts those who want to know more about a complex social problem and how this country deals with it. Criminal Justice incorporates a vast range of knowledge from a number of specialties, including law, history, and the behavioral and social sciences. Each specialty contributes to our fuller understanding of criminal behavior and of society's attitudes toward deviance.

In view of the fact that the criminal justice system is in a constant state of flux, and because the study of criminal justice covers such a broad spectrum, today's students must be aware of a variety of subjects and topics. Standard textbooks and traditional anthologies cannot keep pace with the changes as quickly as they occur. In fact, many such sources are already out of date the day they are published. *Annual Editions: Criminal Justice 05/06* strives to maintain currency in matters of concern by providing up-to-date commentaries, articles, reports, and statistics from the most recent literature in the criminal justice field.

This volume contains units concerning crime and justice in America, victimology, the police, the judicial system, juvenile justice, and punishment and corrections. The articles in these units were selected because they are informative, as well as provocative. The selections are timely and useful in their treatment of ethics, punishment, juveniles, courts, and other related topics.

Included in this volume are a number of features designed to be useful to students, researchers, and professionals in the criminal justice field. These include the table of contents, which summarizes each article, and features key concepts in bold italics; *a topic guide* for locating articles on specific subjects; a list of relevant *World Wide Web* sites; a comprehensive section on crime statistics; and a *glossary*. In addition, each unit is preceded by an overview that provides a background for informed reading of the articles, emphasizes critical issues, and presents key points to consider.

We would like to know what you think of the selections contained in this edition of *Annual Editions: Criminal Justice*. Please fill out the postage-paid article rating form on the last page and let us know your opinions. We change or retain many of the articles based on the comments we receive from you, the reader. Help us to improve this anthology—annually.

Joseph L. Victor
Editor

Joanne Naughton
Editor

Contents

UNIT 1
Crime and Justice in America

The concepts in bold italics are developed in the article. For further expansion, please refer to the Topic Guide and the Index.

UNIT 2
Victimology

The concepts in bold italics are developed in the article. For further expansion, please refer to the Topic Guide and the Index.

UNIT 3
The Police

The concepts in bold italics are developed in the article. For further expansion, please refer to the Topic Guide and the Index.

UNIT 4
The Judicial System

The concepts in bold italics are developed in the article. For further expansion, please refer to the Topic Guide and the Index.

UNIT 5
Juvenile Justice

Unit Overview   **150**

30. **Sentencing Guidelines and the Transformation of Juvenile Justice in the 21st Century,** Daniel P. Mears, *Journal of Contemporary Criminal Justice,* February 2002
The past decade witnessed dramatic changes to **juvenile justice** in America, changes that have altered the focus and administration of juvenile justice in the twenty-first century.   **152**

31. **A Century of Revolutionary Changes in the United States Juvenile Court Systems,** Charles Lindner, *Perspectives,* Spring 2004
Today's **juvenile court** is so different from the original setting, and more similar to the criminal courts than at any prior time in the past century. This turnabout is causing many to ask whether a separate juvenile court is needed any longer. The author points out that juvenile court is replicating the adult criminal court's move toward harsher and more punitive **sentences**.   **159**

32. **DARE Program: Sacred Cow or Fatted Calf?,** Julia C. Mead, *The New York Times,* February 1, 2004
Numerous studies across the country cast doubt on **DARE**'s effectiveness. Its graduates are no less likely to use **drugs** than other children, the studies have concluded, and the lack of any frank discussion of DARE's shortcomings, along with its widespread popularity are seen as part of the problem.   **166**

33. **The Peer Court Experience,** James P. Gray, *Perspectives,* Summer 2003
Nationally, the **peer court** (also known as youth court or teen court) movement is stong; as of July 2003, there were 900 youth **court** programs in 46 states. This article by a superior court judge provides insight into one of them, describing what happens when a real **juvenile** court case is brought before a jury of high school students.   **168**

34. **Isn't She a Little Young?,** Corrie Pikul, *Salon.com,* July 26, 2004
A new public service ad campaign in Virginia uses billboards and bar coasters to remind men that sex with a minor is against the law. What worries the Virginia Department of Health is **teen pregnancy** and how it relates to sex with minors. One of the goals of the campaign is to get men to start talking to each other about the reality of **statuatory rape**.   **172**

UNIT 6
Punishment and Corrections

The concepts in bold italics are developed in the article. For further expansion, please refer to the Topic Guide and the Index.

The concepts in bold italics are developed in the article. For further expansion, please refer to the Topic Guide and the Index.

Topic Guide

This topic guide suggests how the selections in this book relate to the subjects covered in your course. You may want to use the topics listed on these pages to search the Web more easily.

On the following pages a number of Web sites have been gathered specifically for this book. They are arranged to reflect the units of this *Annual Edition.* You can link to these sites by going to the DUSHKIN ONLINE support site at *http://www.dushkin.com/online/.*

ALL THE ARTICLES THAT RELATE TO EACH TOPIC ARE LISTED BELOW THE BOLD-FACED TERM.

World Wide Web Sites

The following World Wide Web sites have been carefully researched and selected to support the articles found in this reader. The easiest way to access these selected sites is to go to our DUSHKIN ONLINE support site at *http://www.dushkin.com/online/*.

AE: Criminal Justice 05/06

The following sites were available at the time of publication. Visit our Web site—we update DUSHKIN ONLINE regularly to reflect any changes.

General Sources

American Society of Criminology
http://www.bsos.umd.edu/asc/four.html

This is an excellent starting place for study of all aspects of criminology and criminal justice, with links to international criminal justice, juvenile justice, court information, police, governments, and so on.

Federal Bureau of Investigation
http://www.fbi.gov

The main page of the FBI Web site leads to lists of the most wanted criminals, uniform crime reports, FBI case reports, major investigations, and more.

National Archive of Criminal Justice Data
http://www.icpsr.umich.edu/NACJD/index.html

NACJD holds more than 500 data collections relating to criminal justice; this site provides browsing and downloading access to most of the data and documentation. NACJD's central mission is to facilitate and encourage research in the field of criminal justice.

Social Science Information Gateway
http://sosig.esrc.bris.ac.uk

This is an online catalog of thousands of Internet resources relevant to social science education and research. Every resource is selected and described by a librarian or subject specialist. Enter "criminal justice" under Search for an excellent annotated list of sources.

UNIT 1: Crime and Justice in America

Campaign for Equity-Restorative Justice
http://www.cerj.org

This is the home page of CERJ, which sees monumental problems in the justice systems and the need for reform. Examine this site and its links for information about the restorative justice movement.

Crime Times
http://www.crime-times.org/

This interesting site, listing research reviews and other information regarding biological causes of criminal, violent, and psychopathic behavior, consists of many articles that are listed by title. It is provided by the Wacker Foundation, publisher of *Crime Times.*

Sourcebook of Criminal Justice Statistics Online
http://www.albany.edu/sourcebook/

Data about all aspects of criminal justice in the United States are available at this site, which includes more than 600 tables from dozens of sources. A search mechanism is available.

UNIT 2: Victimology

National Crime Victim's Research and Treatment Center (NCVC)
http://www.musc.edu/cvc/

At this site, find out about the work of the NCVC at the Medical University of South Carolina, and click on Related Resources for an excellent listing of additional Web sources.

Office for Victims of Crime (OVC)
http://www.ojp.usdoj.gov/ovc

Established by the 1984 Victims of Crime Act, the OVC oversees diverse programs that benefit the victims of crime. From this site you can download a great deal of pertinent information.

UNIT 3: The Police

ACLU Criminal Justice Home Page
http://www.aclu.org/CriminalJustice/CriminalJusticeMain.cfm

This "Criminal Justice" page of the American Civil Liberties Union Web site highlights recent events in criminal justice, addresses police issues, lists important resources, and contains a search mechanism.

Law Enforcement Guide to the World Wide Web
http://leolinks.com/

This page is dedicated to excellence in law enforcement. It contains links to every possible related category: community policing, computer crime, forensics, gangs, and wanted persons are just a few.

Violent Criminal Apprehension Program (VICAP)
http://www.state.ma.us/msp/unitpage/vicap.htm

VICAP's mission is to facilitate cooperation, communication, and coordination among law enforcement agencies and provide support in their efforts to investigate, identify, track, apprehend, and prosecute violent serial offenders. Access VICAP's data information center resources here.

UNIT 4: The Judicial System

Center for Rational Correctional Policy
http://www.correctionalpolicy.com

This is an excellent site on courts and sentencing, with many additional links to a variety of criminal justice sources.

Justice Information Center (JIC)
http://www.ncjrs.org

Provided by the National Criminal Justice Reference Service, this JIC site connects to information about corrections, courts, crime prevention, criminal justice, statistics, drugs and crime, law enforcement, and victims.

National Center for Policy Analysis (NCPA)
http://www.public-policy.org/~ncpa/pd/law/index3.html

Through the NCPA's "Idea House," you can click onto links to an array of topics that are of major interest in the study of the American judicial system.

www.dushkin.com/online/

U.S. Department of Justice (DOJ)
http://www.usdoj.gov
The DOJ represents the American people in enforcing the law in the public interest. Open its main page to find information about the U.S. judicial system. This site provides links to federal government Web servers, topics of interest related to the justice system, documents and resources, and a topical index.

UNIT 5: Juvenile Justice

Gang Land: The Jerry Capeci Page
http://www.ganglandnews.com
Although this site particularly addresses organized-crime gangs, its insights into gang lifestyle—including gang families and their influence—are useful for those interested in exploring issues related to juvenile justice.

Institute for Intergovernmental Research (IIR)
http://www.iir.com
The IIR is a research organization that specializes in law enforcement, juvenile justice, and criminal justice issues. Explore the projects, links, and search engines from this home page. Topics addressed include youth gangs and white collar crime.

National Criminal Justice Reference Service (NCJRS)
http://virlib.ncjrs.org/JuvenileJustice.asp
NCJRS, a federally sponsored information clearinghouse for people involved with research, policy, and practice related to criminal and juvenile justice and drug control, provides this site of links to full-text juvenile justice publications.

Partnership Against Violence Network
http://www.pavnet.org
The Partnership Against Violence Network is a virtual library of information about violence and youths at risk, representing data from seven different federal agencies—a one-stop searchable information resource.

UNIT 6: Punishment and Corrections

American Probation and Parole Association (APPA)
http://www.appa-net.org
Open this APPA site to find information and resources related to probation and parole issues, position papers, the APPA code of ethics, and research and training programs and opportunities.

The Corrections Connection
http://www.corrections.com
This site is an online network for corrections professionals.

Critical Criminology Division of the ASC
http://www.critcrim.org/
Here you will find basic criminology resources and related government resources, provided by the American Society of Criminology, as well as other useful links. The death penalty is also discussed.

David Willshire's Forensic Psychology & Psychiatry Links
http://members.optushome.com.au/dwillsh/index.html
This site offers an enormous number of links to professional journals and associations. It is a valuable resource for study into possible connections between violence and mental disorders. Topics include serial killers, sex offenders, and trauma.

Oregon Department of Corrections
http://www.doc.state.or.us/links/welcome.htm
Open this site for resources in such areas as crime and law enforcement and for links to U.S. state corrections departments.

to offer you the most usable and useful information that will support and expand the value of your Annual Editions. You can reach us at: *http://www.dushkin.com/annualeditions/.*

We highly recommend that you review our Web site for expanded information and our other product lines. We are continually updating and adding links to our Web site in order

UNIT 1

Crime and Justice in America

Unit Selections

Key Points to Consider

- Do you worry when paying bills and making purchases online that someone may be stealing your identity?

- Is the American criminal justice system up to the task of fighting corporate crime?

- With the advantage of 20-20 hindsight, what steps do you think could have been taken prior to September 11, 2001, that might have prevented the attacks?

 **Links: www.dushkin.com/online/**
These sites are annotated in the World Wide Web pages.

Campaign for Equity-Restorative Justice
http://www.cerj.org
Crime Times
http://www.crime-times.org/
Sourcebook of Criminal Justice Statistics Online
http://www.albany.edu/sourcebook/

Crime continues to be a major problem in the United States. Court dockets are full, our prisons are overcrowded, probation and parole caseloads are overwhelming, and our police are being urged to do more. The bulging prison population places a heavy strain on the economy of the country. Clearly, crime is a complex problem that defies simple explanations or solutions. While the more familiar crimes of murder, rape, assault, and drug law violations are still with us, international terrorism has become a pressing worry. The debate also continues about how best to handle juvenile offenders, sex offenders, and those who commit acts of domestic violence. Crime committed using computers and the Internet also demands attention from the criminal justice system.

Annual Editions: Criminal Justice 05/06 focuses directly upon crime in America and the three traditional components of the criminal justice system: police, the courts, and corrections. It also gives special attention to crime victims in the victimology unit and to juveniles in the juvenile justice unit. The articles presented in this section are intended to serve as a foundation for the materials presented in subsequent sections.

The unit begins with "What Is the Sequence of Events in the Criminal Justice System?," this is an article that reveals that the response to crime is a complex process, involving citizens as well as many agencies, levels, and branches of government. Then, in "The Road to September 11," Evan Thomas chronicles the missed clues and missteps in a manhunt that is far from over. New crime fighting tactics in the United States may prove beneficial in other countries, says Gene Stephens in "Global Trends in Crime." The FBI's new computer crime squads are discussed in "The FBI's Cyber-Crime Crackdown."

In "Toward a Transvaluation of Criminal 'Justice': On Vengeance, Peacemaking, and Punishment," Christopher R. Williams focuses on the anger, hate, and violence that he says permeate the system of criminal justice. The role of top manage-

ment in tolerating corporate crime and the tendency of prosecutors to overcomplicate it are looked at in "Enough is Enough."

Although law enforcement has made great progress regarding corruption, brutality, and racism, Americans do not seem to have noticed according to Lawrence Sherman in "Trust and Confidence in Criminal Justice." Then, in his article, "Dirty Bomber? Dirty Justice," Lewis Z. Koch discusses the Justice Department's position regarding accused terrorist, Jose Padilla. Concluding this unit, Ellen Perlman writes in "Evidence of Failure" that public crime labs are performing poorly, leading to serious errors in the administration of justice.

What is the sequence of events in the criminal justice system?

The private sector initiates the response to crime

This first response may come from individuals, families, neighborhood associations, business, industry, agriculture, educational institutions, the news media, or any other private service to the public.

It involves crime prevention as well as participation in the criminal justice process once a crime has been committed. Private crime prevention is more than providing private security or burglar alarms or participating in neighborhood watch. It also includes a commitment to stop criminal behavior by not engaging in it or condoning it when it is committed by others.

Citizens take part directly in the criminal justice process by reporting crime to the police, by being a reliable participant (for example, a witness or a juror) in a criminal proceeding and by accepting the disposition of the system as just or reasonable. As voters and taxpayers, citizens also participate in criminal justice through the policymaking process that affects how the criminal justice process operates, the resources available to it, and its goals and objectives. At every stage of the process from the original formulation of objectives to the decision about where to locate jails and prisons to the reintegration of inmates into society, the private sector has a role to play. Without such involvement, the crim-

inal justice process cannot serve the citizens it is intended to protect.

The response to crime and public safety involves many agencies and services

Many of the services needed to prevent crime and make neighborhoods safe are supplied by noncriminal justice agencies, including agencies with primary concern for public health, education, welfare, public works, and housing. Individual citizens as well as public and private sector organizations have joined with criminal justice agencies to prevent crime and make neighborhoods safe.

Criminal cases are brought by the government through the criminal justice system

We apprehend, try, and punish offenders by means of a loose confederation of agencies at all levels of government. Our American system of justice has evolved from the English common law into a complex series of procedures and decisions. Founded on the concept that crimes against an individual are crimes against the State, our justice system prosecutes individuals as though they victimized all of society. However, crime victims are involved throughout the process and many justice

agencies have programs which focus on helping victims.

There is no single criminal justice system in this country. We have many similar systems that are individually unique. Criminal cases may be handled differently in different jurisdictions, but court decisions based on the due process guarantees of the U.S. Constitution require that specific steps be taken in the administration of criminal justice so that the individual will be protected from undue intervention from the State.

The description of the criminal and juvenile justice systems that follows portrays the most common sequence of events in response to serious criminal behavior.

Entry into the system

The justice system does not respond to most crime because so much crime is not discovered or reported to the police. Law enforcement agencies learn about crime from the reports of victims or other citizens, from discovery by a police officer in the field, from informants, or from investigative and intelligence work.

Once a law enforcement agency has established that a crime has been committed, a suspect must be identified and apprehended for the case to proceed through the system. Sometimes, a suspect is apprehended at the scene; however, identification of a suspect sometimes requires an extensive investigation. Often, no one is identified or apprehended. In some instances, a suspect is arrested and later the police determine that no crime was committed and the suspect is released.

Prosecution and pretrial services

After an arrest, law enforcement agencies present information about the case and about the accused to the prosecutor, who will decide if formal charges will be filed with the court. If no charges are filed, the accused must be released. The prosecutor can also drop charges after making efforts to prosecute (*nolle prosequi*).

A suspect charged with a crime must be taken before a judge or magistrate without unnecessary delay. At the initial appearance, the judge or magistrate informs the accused of the charges and decides whether there is probable cause to detain the accused person. If the offense is not very serious, the determination of guilt and assessment of a penalty may also occur at this stage.

Often, the defense counsel is also assigned at the initial appearance. All suspects prosecuted for serious crimes have a right to be represented by an attorney. If the court determines the suspect is indigent and cannot afford such representation, the court will assign counsel at the public's expense.

A pretrial-release decision may be made at the initial appearance, but may occur at other hearings or may be changed at another time during the process. Pretrial release and bail were traditionally intended to ensure appearance at trial. However, many jurisdictions permit pretrial detention of defendants accused of serious offenses and deemed to be dangerous to prevent them from committing crimes prior to trial.

The court often bases its pretrial decision on information about the defendant's drug use, as well as residence, employment, and family ties. The court may decide to release the accused on his/her own recognizance or into the custody of a third party after the posting of a financial bond or on the promise of satisfying certain conditions such as taking periodic drug tests to ensure drug abstinence.

In many jurisdictions, the initial appearance may be followed by a preliminary hearing. The main function of this hearing is to discover if there is probable cause to believe that the accused committed a known crime within the jurisdiction of the court. If the judge does not find probable cause, the case is dismissed; however, if the judge or magistrate finds probable cause for such a belief, or the accused waives his or her right to a preliminary hearing, the case may be bound over to a grand jury.

A grand jury hears evidence against the accused presented by the prosecutor and decides if there is sufficient evidence to cause the accused to be brought to trial. If the grand jury finds sufficient evidence, it submits to the court an indictment, a written statement of the essential facts of the offense charged against the accused.

Where the grand jury system is used, the grand jury may also investigate criminal activity generally and issue indictments called grand jury originals that initiate criminal cases. These investigations and indictments are often used in drug and conspiracy cases that involve complex organizations. After such an indictment, law enforcement tries to apprehend and arrest the suspects named in the indictment.

Misdemeanor cases and some felony cases proceed by the issuance of an information, a formal, written accusation submitted to the court by a prosecutor. In some jurisdictions, indictments may be required in felony cases. However, the accused may choose to waive a grand jury indictment and, instead, accept service of an information for the crime.

In some jurisdictions, defendants, often those without prior criminal records, may be eligible for diversion from prosecution subject to the completion of specific conditions such as drug treatment. Successful completion of the conditions may result in the dropping of charges or the expunging of the criminal record where the defendant is required to plead guilty prior to the diversion.

Adjudication

Once an indictment or information has been filed with the trial court, the accused is scheduled for arraignment. At the arraignment, the accused is informed of the charges, advised of the rights of criminal defendants, and asked to enter a plea to the charges. Sometimes, a plea of guilty is the result of negotiations between the prosecutor and the defendant.

If the accused pleads guilty or pleads *nolo contendere* (accepts penalty without admitting guilt), the judge may accept or reject the plea. If the plea is accepted, no trial is held and the offender is sentenced at this proceeding or at a later date. The plea may be rejected and proceed to trial if, for example, the judge believes that the accused may have been coerced.

If the accused pleads not guilty or not guilty by reason of insanity, a date is set for the trial. A person accused of a serious crime is guaranteed a trial by jury. However, the accused may ask for a bench trial where the judge, rather than a jury, serves as the finder of fact. In both instances the prosecution and defense present evidence by questioning witnesses while the judge decides on issues of law. The trial results in acquittal or conviction on the original charges or on lesser included offenses.

After the trial a defendant may request appellate review of the conviction or sentence. In some cases, appeals of convictions are a matter of right; all States with the death penalty provide for automatic appeal of cases involving a death sentence. Appeals may be subject to the discretion of the appellate court and may be granted only on acceptance of a defendant's petition for a *writ of certiorari*. Prisoners may also appeal their sentences through civil rights petitions and *writs of habeas corpus* where they claim unlawful detention.

Sentencing and sanctions

After a conviction, sentence is imposed. In most cases the judge decides on the sentence, but in some jurisdictions the sentence is decided by the jury, particularly for capital offenses.

In arriving at an appropriate sentence, a sentencing hearing may be held at which evidence of aggravating or mitigating circumstances is considered. In assessing the circumstances surrounding a convicted person's criminal behavior, courts often rely on presentence investigations by probation agencies or other designated authorities. Courts may also consider victim impact statements.

The sentencing choices that may be available to judges and juries include one or more of the following:

- the death penalty
- incarceration in a prison, jail, or other confinement facility
- probation—allowing the convicted person to remain at liberty but subject

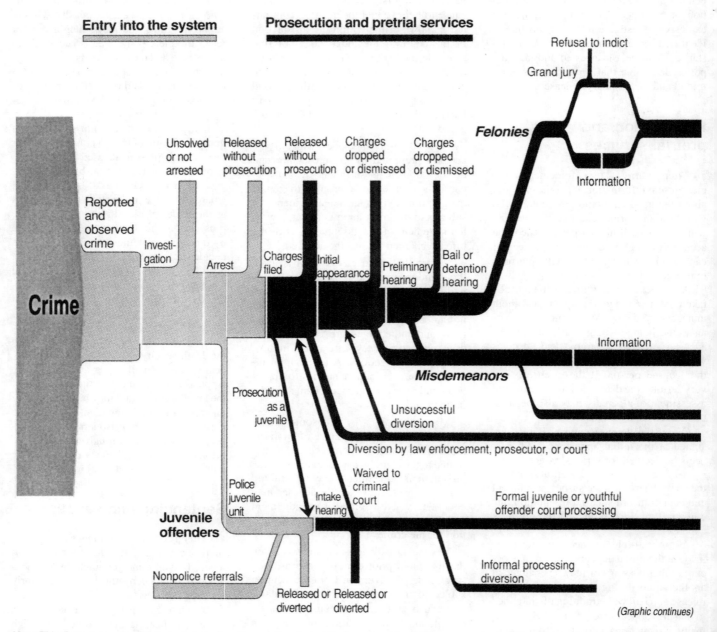

<u>**Entry into the system**</u>

Prosecution and pretrial services

Note: This chart gives a simplified view of caseflow through the criminal justice system. Procedures vary among jurisdictions. The weights of the lines are not intended to show the actual size of caseloads.

to certain conditions and restrictions such as drug testing or drug restrictions such as drug testing or drug treatment

- fines—primarily applied as penalties in minor offenses
- restitution—requiring the offender to pay compensation to the victim. In some jurisdictions, offenders may be sentenced to alternatives to incarceration that are considered more severe than straight probation but less severe

than a prison term. Examples of such sanctions include boot camps, intense supervision often with drug treatment and testing, house arrest and electronic monitoring, denial of Federal benefits, and community service.

In many jurisdictions, the law mandates that persons convicted of certain types of offenses serve a prison term. Most jurisdictions permit the judge to set the sentence length within certain limits, but some have determinate sentencing laws that stipulate

a specific sentence length that must be served and cannot be altered by a parole board.

Corrections

Offenders sentenced to incarceration usually serve time in a local jail or a State prison. Offenders sentenced to less than 1 year generally go to jail; those sentenced to more than 1 year go to prison. Persons admitted to the Federal system or a State prison system may be held in prison with

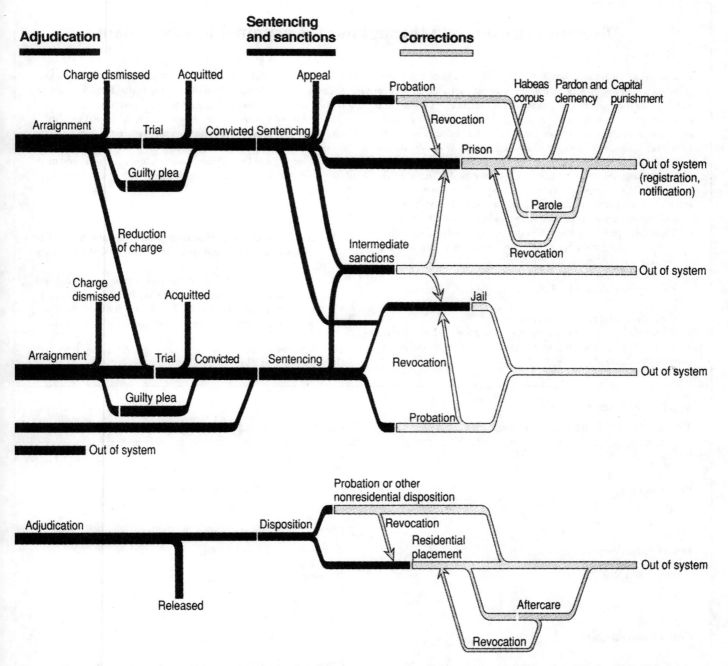

Source: Adapted from *The challenge of crime in a free society*. President's Commission on Law Enforcement and Administration of Justice, 1967. This revision, a result of the Symposium on the 30th Anniversary of the President's Commission, was prepared by the Bureau of Justice Statistics in 1997.

varying levels of custody or in a community correctional facility.

A prisoner may become eligible for parole after serving a specific part of his or her sentence. Parole is the conditional release of a prisoner before the prisoner's full sentence has been served. The decision to grant parole is made by an authority such as a parole board, which has power to grant or revoke parole or to discharge a parolee altogether. The way pa-

role decisions are made varies widely among jurisdictions.

Offenders may also be required to serve out their full sentences prior to release (expiration of term). Those sentenced under determinate sentencing laws can be released only after they have served their full sentence (mandatory release) less any "goodtime" received while in prison. Inmates get goodtime credits against their sentences automatically or

by earning them through participation in programs.

If released by a parole board decision or by mandatory release, the releasee will be under the supervision of a parole officer in the community for the balance of his or her unexpired sentence. This supervision is governed by specific conditions of release, and the releasee may be returned to prison for violations of such conditions.

Discretion is exercised throughout the criminal justice system

Discretion is "an authority conferred by law to act in certain conditions or situations in accordance with an official's or an official agency's own considered judgment and conscience."[1] Discretion is exercised throughout the government. It is a part of decisionmaking in all government systems from mental health to education, as well as criminal justice. The limits of discretion vary from jurisdiction to jurisdiction.

Concerning crime and justice, legislative bodies have recognized that they cannot anticipate the range of circumstances surrounding each crime, anticipate local mores, and enact laws that clearly encompass all conduct that is criminal and all that is not.[2]

Therefore, persons charged with the day-to-day response to crime are expected to exercise their own judgment within limits set by law. Basically, they must decide—
- whether to take action
- where the situation fits in the scheme of law, rules, and precedent
- which official response is appropriate.[3]

To ensure that discretion is exercised responsibly, government authority is often delegated to professionals. Professionalism requires a minimum

level of training and orientation, which guide officials in making decisions. The professionalism of policing is due largely to the desire to ensure the proper exercise of police discretion.

The limits of discretion vary from State to State and locality to locality. For example, some State judges have wide discretion in the type of sentence they may impose. In recent years, other states have sought to limit the judge's discretion in sentencing by passing mandatory sentencing laws that require prison sentences for certain offenses.

Notes

1. Roscoe Pound, "Discretion, dispensation and mitigation: The problem of the individual special case," *New York University Law Review* (1960) 35:925, 926.
2. Wayne R. LaFave, *Arrest: The decision to take a suspect into custody* (Boston: Little, Brown & Co., 1964), p. 63–184.
3. Memorandum of June 21, 1977, from Mark Moore to James Vorenberg, "Some abstract notes on the issue of discretion."

Bureau of Justice Statistics (*www.ojp.usdoj.gov/bjs/*). January 1998. NCJ 167894. To order: 1-800-732-3277.

Who exercises discretion?

These criminal justice officials...

...must often decide whether or not or how to—

These criminal justice officials...	must often decide whether or not or how to—
Police	Enforce specific laws Investigate specific crimes; Search people
Prosecutors	File charges or petitions for adjudication Seek indictments Drop cases Reduce charges
Judges or magistrates	Set bail or conditions for release Accept pleas Determine delinquency Dismiss charges Impose sentence Revoke probation
Correctional officials	Assign to type of correctional facility Award privileges Punish for disciplinary infractions
Paroling authorities	Determine date and conditions of parole Revoke parole

Recidivism

Once the suspects, defendants, or offenders are released from the jurisdiction of a criminal justice agency, they may be processed through the criminal justice system again for a new crime. Long term studies show that many suspects who are arrested have prior criminal histories and

those with a greater number of prior arrests were more likely to be arrested again. As the courts take prior criminal history into account at sentencing, most prison inmates have a prior criminal history and many have been incarcerated before. Nationally, about half the inmates released from State prison will return to prison.

The juvenile justice system

Juvenile courts usually have jurisdiction over matters concerning children, including delinquency, neglect, and adoption. They also handle "status offenses" such as truancy and running away, which are not applicable to adults. State statutes define which persons are under the original jurisdiction of the juvenile court. The upper age of juvenile court jurisdiction in delinquency matters is 17 in most States.

The processing of juvenile offenders is not entirely dissimilar to adult criminal processing, but there are crucial differences. Many juveniles are referred to juvenile courts by law enforcement officers, but many others are referred by school officials, social services agencies, neighbors, and even parents, for behavior or conditions that are determined to require intervention by the formal system for social control.

At arrest, a decision is made either to send the matter further into the justice system or to divert the case out of the system, often to alternative programs. Examples of alternative programs include drug treatment, individual or group counseling, or referral to educational and recreational programs.

When juveniles are referred to the juvenile courts, the court's intake department or the prosecuting attorney determines whether sufficient grounds exist to warrant filing a petition that requests an adjudictory hearing or a request to transfer jurisdiction to criminal court. At this point, many juveniles are released or diverted to alternative programs.

All States allow juveniles to be tried as adults in criminal court under certain circumstances. In many States, the legislature *statutorily excludes* certain (usually serious) offenses from the jurisdiction of the juvenile court regardless of the age of the accused. In some States and at the Federal level under certain circumstances, prosecutors have the *discretion* to either file criminal charges against juveniles directly in criminal courts or proceed through the juvenile justice process. The juvenile court's intake department or the prosecutor may petition the juvenile court to *waive* jurisdiction to criminal court. The juvenile court also may order *referral* to criminal court for trial as adults. In some jurisdic-

tions, juveniles processed as adults may upon conviction be sentenced to either an adult or a juvenile facility.

In those cases where the juvenile court retains jurisdiction, the case may be handled formally by filing a delinquency petition or informally by diverting the juvenile to other agencies or programs in lieu of further court processing.

If a petition for an adjudicatory hearing is accepted, the juvenile may be brought before a court quite unlike the court with jurisdiction over adult offenders. Despite the considerable discretion associated with juvenile court proceedings, juveniles are afforded many of the due-process safeguards associated with adult criminal trials. Several States permit the use of juries in juvenile courts; however, in light of the U.S. Supreme Court holding that juries are not essential to juvenile hearings, most States do not make provisions for juries in juvenile courts.

In disposing of cases, juvenile courts usually have far more discretion that adult courts. In addition to such options as probation, commitment to a residential facility, restitution, or fines, State laws grant juvenile courts the power to order removal of children from their homes to foster homes or treatment facilities. Juvenile courts also may order participation in special programs aimed at shoplifting prevention, drug counseling, or driver education.

Once a juvenile is under juvenile court disposition, the court may retain jurisdiction until the juvenile legally becomes an adult (at age 21 in most States). In some jurisdictions, juvenile offenders may be classified as youthful offenders which can lead to extended sentences.

Following release from an institution, juveniles are often ordered to a period of aftercare which is similar to parole supervision for adult offenders. Juvenile offenders who violate the conditions of aftercare may have their aftercare revoked, resulting

in being recommitted to a facility. Juveniles who are classified as youthful offenders and violate the conditions of aftercare may be subject to adult sanctions.

The governmental response to crime is founded in the intergovernmental structure of the United States

Under our form of government, each State and the Federal Government has its own criminal justice system. All systems must respect the rights of individuals set forth in court interpretation of the U.S. Constitution and defined in case law.

State constitutions and laws define the criminal justice system within each State and delegate the authority and responsibility for criminal justice to various jurisdictions, officials, and institutions. State laws also define criminal behavior and groups of children or acts under jurisdiction of the juvenile courts.

Municipalities and counties further define their criminal justice systems through local ordinances that proscribe the local agencies responsible for criminal justice processing that were not established by the State.

Congress has also established a criminal justice system at the Federal level to respond to Federal crimes such as bank robbery, kidnaping, and transporting stolen goods across State lines.

The response to crime is mainly a State and local function

Very few crimes are under exclusive Federal jurisdiction. The responsibility to respond to most crime rests with State and local governments. Police protection is primarily a function of cities and towns. Corrections is primarily a function of State governments. Most justice personnel are employed at the local level.

From the *Report to the Nation on Crime and Justice*, January 1998. Published by the U.S. Department of Justice, Office of Justice Programs, Bureau of Justice Statistics. Reprinted by permission.

The Road to September 11

It was a long time coming. For a decade, America's been fighting a losing secret war against terror. A NEWSWEEK investigation into the missed clues and missteps in a manhunt that is far from over.

He was more than a little suspicious. At the Airman Flight School in Norman, Okla., the stocky aspiring pilot with the heavy French accent acted oddly. He was abrupt and argumentative, refusing to pay the whole $4,995 fee upfront (he shelled out $2,500 in cash instead). He had been dodgy in his e-mails. "E is not secure," explained Zacarias Moussaoui, 33, who preferred to use his Internet alias, "zuluman tangotango." A poor flier, he suddenly quit in mid-May, before showing up at another flight school in Eagan, Minn. At Pan Am Flying Academy, he acknowledged that the biggest plane he'd ever flown was a single-engine Cessna. But he asked to be trained on a 747 flight simulator. He wanted to concentrate only on the midair turns, not the takeoffs and landings. It was all too fishy to one of the instructors, who tipped off the Feds. Incarcerated because his visa had expired, Moussaoui was sitting in the Sherburne County Jail when some other pilot trainees drove their hijacked airliners into the World Trade Center and the Pentagon.

It's not that the U.S. government was asleep. America's open borders make tracking terrorists a daunting exercise. NEWS-WEEK has learned that the FBI has privately estimated that more than 1,000 individuals—most of them foreign nationals—with suspected terrorist ties are currently living in the United States. "The American people would be surprised to learn how many of these people there are," says a top U.S. official. Moussaoui almost exactly fits the profile of the suicide hijackers, but he may or may not have been part of the plot. After Moussaoui's arrest on Aug. 17, U.S. immigration authorities dutifully notified the French (he was a passport holder), who responded 10 days later that Moussaoui was a suspected terrorist who had allegedly traveled to Osama bin Laden's training camps in Afghanistan. Ten days may seem like a leisurely pace for investigators racing against time to foil terrorist plots, but in the real world of international cooperation, 10 days, "c'est rapide," a French official told NEWSWEEK. Fast but, in the new age of terror, not fast enough.

As officials at the CIA and FBI sift through intelligence reports, they are berating themselves for missing warning signs on the road to Sept. 11. Those reports include intercepted messages with phrases like "There is a big thing coming," "They're going to pay the price" and "We're ready to go." Unfortunately, many of those messages, intercepted before the attack, did not reach the desks of intelligence analysts until afterward. In the bureaucracy of spying, 24-hour or 48-hour time lags are not unusual. None of the intercepted traffic mentioned the Pentagon or the World Trade Center. Some hinted at a target somewhere on the Pacific Rim. Nonetheless, an intelligence official told NEWSWEEK: "A lot of people feel guilty and think of what they could have done."

ALL ACROSS THE WORLD LAST WEEK, intelligence services were scrambling to catch the terrorists before they struck again. The scale of the roundup was breathtaking: in Yemen, a viper's nest of terror, authorities hauled in "dozens" of suspected bin Laden followers. In Germany, police were searching for a pair of men believed to be directly involved in the hijacking plot. In France, more than half a dozen were being held for questioning, while in Britain, Belgium and the Netherlands—and Peru and Paraguay—police raided suspected terror hideouts. In the United States, where the FBI has launched the greatest manhunt in history, authorities detained about 90 people. Most of them were being held for minor immigration charges, but investigators were looking for mass murderers. The gumshoes swept up pieces of chilling evidence, like two box cutters stuffed into the seat of a Sept. 11 flight out of Boston—another hijacking target? Boston was jittery over threats of an attack last Saturday. An Arab in a bar was overheard to say that blood would flow in Boston on Sept. 22, and U.S. intelligence intercepted a conversation between Algerian diplomats talking about "the upcoming Boston tea party on Sept. 22." It turned out that some women really were holding a tea party that day. Some federal officials were spooked when manuals describing crop-duster equipment—to spray deadly germs?—were found among Moussaoui's possessions. But a top U.S. official told NEWSWEEK, "I'm not getting into the bunker and putting on a gas mask. We're used to seeing these threats." (Nonetheless, crop-dusters were barred from flying near cities.)

The vast dragnet was heartening, unless one considers that after two American embassies were bombed in 1998, a similar crackdown swept up a hundred potential suspects from Europe to the Middle East to Latin America—and bin Laden's men were still able to regroup to launch far more devastating attacks. Catching foot soldiers and lieutenants will not be enough to stop even greater cataclysms. Last week the authorities were searching for a single man who might have triggered the assault on Washington and New York. In past attacks by bin Laden's Qaeda organization, "sleeper" agents have burrowed into the target country to await their orders. FBI officials now believe that the mastermind was Mohamed Atta, the intense Egyptian who apparently piloted the first plane, American Airlines Flight 11, into the North Tower of the World Trade Center. ("Did he ever learn to fly?" Atta's father, Mohamed al-Amir Atta, said to NEWS-WEEK. "Never. He never even had a kite. My daughter, who is a doctor, used to get

him medicine before every journey, to make him combat the cramps and vomiting he feels every time he gets on a plane.") Though intelligence officials believe they have spotted the operation's paymaster, identified to NEWSWEEK as Mustafa Ahmed, in the United Arab Emirates, Atta was the one hijacker who appeared to have the most contacts with conspirators on other aircraft prior to the attacks, and he was the one who left a last testament. According to a top government source, it included this prayer: "Be prepared to meet your God. Be ready for this moment." Atta's role "doesn't fit the usual pattern," said one official. "It looks like the ringleader went down with the plane."

You could date the arrival of the international jihad in America to the rainy night of Nov. 5, 1990, when a terrorist walked into a Marriott and killed Meir Kahane. The cops bungled the case.

The ultimate ringleader may be somewhere in the mountains of Afghanistan, hiding from U.S. bombs and commandos—but also no doubt plotting his next atrocity. In history's long list of villains, bin Laden will find a special place. He has no throne, no armies, not even any real territory, aside from the rocky wastes of Afghanistan. But he has the power to make men willingly go to their deaths for the sole purpose of indiscriminately killing Americans—men, women and children. He is an unusual combination in the annals of hate, at once mystical and fanatical—and deliberate and efficient. Now he has stirred America's wrath and may soon see America's vengeance. But the slow business of mopping up the poison spread by bin Laden through the Islamic world was almost pitifully underscored after the attack by a plea from FBI Director Robert Mueller. The nation's top G-man said the FBI was looking for more Arabic speakers. A reasonable request, but perhaps a

little late in the game. It's hard to know your enemy when you can't even speak his language.

For most Americans, life was instantly and forever changed on Sept. 11, 2001. But the terror war that led up to the attack had been simmering, and sometimes boiling over, for more than 10 years. It can be recalled as a tedious bureaucratic struggle—all those reports on "Homeland Defense" piling up unread on the shelves of congressmen, droning government officials trying to fatten their budgets with scare stories relegated to the back pages of the newspaper. Or it can be relived—as it truly was—as a race to the Gates of Hell. Before the world finds out what horrors lie beyond, it's worthwhile retracing a decade-long trail of terror to see how America stumbled. The enemy has clearly learned from experience. In December 1994, the Armed Islamic Group (GIA), an Algerian-based terrorist band that would go on to play a prominent role in bin Laden's global army, hijacked an Air France Airbus with 171 passengers aboard. The plan: to plunge into the Eiffel Tower. The problem: none of the hijackers could fly. The Air France pilot landed instead in Marseilles, where French police stormed the plane. It was not too long afterward that the first terrorists began quietly enrolling in flight schools in Florida.

THE UNITED STATES HAS BEEN A LITTLE slower on the uptake. Money has not really been the obstacle. The counterterrorism budget jumped from $2 billion to $12 billion over a decade. The United States spends $30 billion a year gathering intelligence. Nor has bin Laden been in any way ignored. For the past five years, analysts have been working through the night in a chamber, deep in the bowels of CIA headquarters, known as the Bin Laden Room. Some experts argued that the CIA was too focused on bin Laden—that, in an effort to put a face on faceless terror, the gaunt guerrilla fighter had been elevated to the role of international bogeyman, to the neglect of shadowy others who did the real killing. Now, as the Washington blame game escalates—along with the cries for revenge—intelligence officials are cautioning that terror cells, clannish and secretive, are extremely difficult to penetrate; that for every snake beheaded two more will crawl out of the swamp; that swamps can never be drained in land that drips with the blood of martyrs; that even the most persuasive interrogations may not crack a suspect who is willing to die.

All true. But the inability of the government to even guess that 19 suicidal terrorists might turn four jetliners into guided missiles aimed at national icons was more than a failure of intelligence. It was a failure of imagination. The United States is so strong, the American people seemed so secure, that the concept of Homeland Defense seemed abstract, almost foreign, the sort of thing tiny island nations worried about. Terrorists were regarded by most people as criminals, wicked and frightening, but not as mortal enemies of the state. There was a kind of collective denial, an unwillingness to see how monstrous the threat of Islamic extremism could be.

In part, that may be because the government of the United States helped create it. In the 1980s, the CIA secretly backed the mujahedin, the Islamic freedom fighters rebelling against the Soviet occupation of Afghanistan. Arming and training the "Mooj" was one of the most successful covert actions ever mounted by the CIA. It turned the tide against the Soviet invaders. But there is a word used by old CIA hands to describe covert actions that backfire: "blowback." In the coming weeks, if and when American Special Forces helicopters try to land in the mountains of Afghanistan to flush out bin Laden, they risk being shot down by Stinger surface-to-air missiles provided to the Afghan rebels by the CIA. Such an awful case of blowback would be a mere coda to a long and twisted tragedy of unanticipated consequences. The tale begins more than 10 years ago, when the veterans of the Mooj's holy war against the Soviets began arriving in the United States—many with passports arranged by the CIA.

Bonded by combat, full of religious zeal, the diaspora of young Arab men willing to die for Allah congregated at the Al-Kifah Refugee Center in Brooklyn, N.Y., a dreary inner-city building that doubled as a recruiting post for the CIA seeking to steer fresh troops to the mujahedin. The dominant figures at the center in the late '80s were a gloomy New York City engineer named El Sayyid Nosair, who took Prozac for his blues, and his sidekick, Mahmud Abouhalima, who had been a human minesweeper in the Afghan war (his only tool was a thin reed, which he used as a crude probe). The new immigrants were filled not with gratitude toward their new nation, but by implacable hatred toward America, symbol of West-

ern modernity that threatened to engulf Muslim fundamentalism in a tide of blue jeans and Hollywood videos. Half a world away, people who understood the ferocity of Islamic extremism could see the coming storm. In the late '80s, Pakistan's then head of state, Benazir Bhutto, told the first President George Bush, "You are creating a Frankenstein." But the warnings never quite filtered down to the cops and G-men on the streets of New York.

The international jihad arrived in America on the rainy night of Nov. 5, 1990, when Nosair walked into a crowded ballroom at the New York Marriott on 49th Street and shot and killed Rabbi Meir Kahane, a mindless hater who wanted to rid Israel of "Arab dogs" ("Every Jew a .22" was a Kahane slogan). The escape plan was amateur hour: Nosair's buddy Abouhalima was supposed to drive the getaway car, a taxicab, but the overexcited Nosair jumped in the wrong cab and was apprehended.

In the mid-'90s Ramzi Yousef took flying lessons and talked of crashing a plane into the CIA or a nuclear facility. At the time the FBI thought the plans grandiose. Now they look like blueprints.

With a room full of witnesses and a smoking gun, the case against Nosair should have been a lay-down. But the New York police bungled the evidence, and Nosair got off with a gun rap. At that moment, Nosair and Abouhalima may have had an epiphany: back home in Egypt, suspected terrorists are dragged in and tortured. In America, they can hire a good lawyer and beat the system. The New York City police hardly noticed any grander scheme. A search of Nosair's apartment turned up instructions for building bombs and photos of targets—including the Empire State Building and the World Trade Center. The police never bothered to inventory most of the evidence, nor were the documents translated—that is, until a van with a 1,500-

pound bomb blew up in the underground garage of the World Trade Center on Feb. 26, 1993. The (first) World Trade Center bombing, which killed six people and injured more than 1,000, might have been a powerful warning, especially when investigators discovered that the plotters had meant to topple the towers and packed the truck bomb with cyanide (in an effort to create a crude chemical weapon). But the cyanide was harmlessly burned up in the blast, the buildings didn't fall and the bombers seemed to be hapless. One of them went back to get his security deposit from the truck rental.

The plotters were quickly exposed as disciples of Sheik Omar Abdel-Rahman, the "Blind Sheik" who ranted against the infidels from a run-down mosque in Jersey City. The Blind Sheik's shady past should have been of great interest to the Feds—he had been linked to the plot to assassinate Egyptian President Anwar Sadat in 1981. But the sheik had slipped into the United States with the protection of the CIA, which saw the revered cleric as a valuable recruiting agent for the Mooj. Investigators trying to track down the Blind Sheik "had zero cooperation from the intelligence community, zero," recalled a federal investigator in New York.

ONE WORLD TRADE CENTER PLOTTER who did attract attention from the Feds was Ramzi Yousef. Operating under a dozen aliases, Yousef was a frightening new figure, seemingly stateless and sinister, a global avenging angel. Though he talked to Iraqi intelligence and stayed in a safe house that was later linked to bin Laden, Yousef at the time appeared to be a kind of terror freelancer. Yousef's luck ran out when the apartment of an old childhood friend, Abdul Hakim Murad, burst into flames. Plotting with Yousef, Murad had been at work making bombs to assassinate the pope and blow up no fewer than 11 U.S. airliners. Murad's arrest in January 1995 led investigators to capture Yousef in Pakistan, where he was hiding out. Murad and Yousef were a duo sent by the Devil: Murad had taken pilot lessons, and the two talked about flying a plane filled with explosives into the CIA headquarters or a nuclear facility. At the time, FBI officials thought the plans were grandiose and farfetched. Now they look like blueprints.

The capture of Yousef was regarded as a stirring victory in the war against terrorism, which was just then gearing up in Washington. But Yousef's arrest illustrates the difficulties of cracking terrorism even when a prize suspect is caught. At his sentencing, Yousef declared, "Yes, I am a terrorist, and I am proud of it." He has never cooperated with authorities. Instead, he spent his days chatting about movies with his fellow inmates in a federal maximum-security prison, Unabomber Ted Kaczynski and, until he was executed, the Oklahoma City bomber Timothy McVeigh.

By the mid-'90s, counterterror experts at the FBI and CIA had begun to focus on Osama bin Laden, the son of a Saudi billionaire who had joined the Mooj in Afghanistan and become a hero as a battlefield commander. Bin Laden was said to be bitter because the Saudi royal family had rebuffed his offer to rally freedom fighters to protect the kingdom against the threat of Saddam Hussein after the Iraqi strongman invaded Kuwait in 1990. Instead, the Saudi rulers chose to be defended by the armed forces of the United States. To bin Laden, corrupt princes were welcoming infidels to desecrate holy ground. Bin Laden devoted himself to expelling America, not just from Saudi Arabia, but—as his messianic madness grew—from Islam, indeed all the world.

Tony Lake, President Bill Clinton's national-security adviser, does not recall one single defining moment when bin Laden became Public Enemy No. 1. It was increasingly clear to intelligence analysts that extremists all over the Middle East viewed bin Laden as a modern-day Saladin, the Islamic warrior who drove out the Crusaders a millennium ago. Setting up a sort of Terror Central of spiritual, financial and logistical support—Al Qaeda (the Base)—bin Laden went public, in 1996 telling every Muslim that their duty was to kill Americans (at first the *fatwa* was limited to U.S. soldiers, then broadened in 1998 to all Americans). From his home in Sudan, bin Laden seemed to be inspiring and helping to fund a broad if shadowy network of terrorist cells. On the rationale that no nation should be allowed to harbor terrorists, the State Department in the mid-'90s pressured the government of Sudan to kick out bin Laden. In retrospect, that may have been a mistake. At least in Sudan, it was easier to keep an eye on bin Laden's activities. Instead, he vanished into the mountains of Afghanistan, where he would be welcomed by extremist Taliban rulers and enabled to set up training bases for terrorists. These camps—crude collections of mud huts—appear to have provided a sort of Iron John bonding experience for thou-

sands of aspiring martyrs who came for a course of brainwashing and bombmaking.

With the cold war over, the Mafia in retreat and the drug war unwinnable, the CIA and FBI were eager to have a new foe to fight. The two agencies established a Counter Terrorism Center in a bland, windowless warren of offices on the ground floor of CIA headquarters at Langley, Va. Historical rivals, the spies and G-men were finally learning to work together. But they didn't necessarily share secrets with the alphabet soup of other enforcement and intelligence agencies, like Customs and the Immigration and Naturalization Service, and they remained aloof from the Pentagon. And no amount of good will or money could bridge a fundamental divide between intelligence and law enforcement. Spies prefer to watch and wait; cops want to get their man. At the White House, a bright national-security staffer, Richard Clarke, tried to play counterterror coordinator, but he was given about as much real clout as the toothless "czars" sent out to fight the war on drugs. There was no central figure high in the administration to knock heads, demand performance and make sure everyone was on the same page. Lake now regrets that he did not try harder to create one. At the time, Clinton's national-security adviser was too preoccupied with U.S. involvement in Bosnia to do battle with fiefdoms in the intelligence community. "Bosnia was easier than changing the bureaucracy," Lake told NEWSWEEK.

Bitter after the Saudis allied themselves with the American infidels against Saddam, bin Laden, his messianic madness growing, devoted himself to destroying the United States.

AN EMPIRE BUILDER WITH A MESSIANIC streak OF his own, FBI Director Louis Freeh was eager to throw G-men at the terrorist threat all over the world. When a truck bomb blew up the Khobar Towers, a U.S. military barracks in Saudi Arabia,

Freeh made a personal quest of bringing the bombers to justice. As Freeh left office last summer, a grand jury in New York was about to indict several conspirators behind the bombing. But, safely secluded in Iran, the suspects will probably never stand trial. The Khobar Towers investigation shows the limits of treating terrorism as a crime. It also reveals some of the difficulties of working with foreign intelligence services that don't share the same values (or rules) as Americans. Freeh's gumshoes got a feel for Saudi justice when they asked to interview some suspects seized in an earlier bombing attack against a U.S.-run military compound in Riyadh. Before the FBI could ask any questions, the suspects were beheaded. An attempt by the FBI to play the role of Good Cop to the Saudis' Bad Cop was thwarted by American sensitivities. After the bombing, FBI agents managed to corner Hani al-Sayegh, a key suspect in Canada. Cooperate with us, the gumshoes threatened, or we'll send you back to Saudi Arabia, where a sword awaits. No fool, the suspect hired an American lawyer. The State Department was convinced that sending the man back to Saudi Arabia would violate international laws banning torture. Their leverage gone, the Feds were unable to make the suspect talk.

The CIA did have some luck in working with foreign security services to roll up terror networks. In 1997 and 1998, the agency collaborated with the Egyptians—whose security service is particularly ruthless—to root out cells of bin Laden's men from their hiding places in Albania. But just as the spooks were congratulating themselves, another bin Laden cell struck in a carefully coordinated, long-planned attack. Within minutes of each other, truck bombs blew up the U.S. embassies in Tanzania and Kenya, killing more than 220. The failure of intelligence in the August 1998 embassy bombings is a case study in the difficulty of penetrating bin Laden's network.

For some of the time that bin Laden's men were plotting to blow up the two embassies, U.S. intelligence was tapping their phones. According to Justice Department documents, the spooks tapped five telephone numbers used by bin Laden's men living in Kenya in 1996 and '97. But the plotters did not give themselves away. Bin Laden uses couriers to communicate with his agents face to face. His Qaeda organization is also technologically sophisticated, sometimes embedding coded messages in innocuous-seeming Web sites. Intelligence experts have worried for some time that the supersecret-code breakers at the National Security Agency are going deaf, overwhelmed by the sheer volume of telecommunications and encryption software that any consumer can buy at a computer store.

If high-tech espionage won't do the job, say the experts, then the CIA needs more human spies. It has become rote to say that in order to crack secretive terrorist cells the CIA needs to hire more Arabic-speaking case officers who can in turn recruit deep-penetration agents—HUMINT (human intelligence) in spy jargon. Actually, the CIA had a sometime informer among the embassy bombers. Ali Mohamed was a former Egyptian Army officer who enlisted in the U.S. Army and was sent to Fort Bragg, N.C., in the early 1980s to lecture U.S. Special Forces on Islamic terrorism. In his free time, he was a double agent. On the weekends he visited the Al-Kifah Refugee Center in Brooklyn, where he stayed with none other than El Sayyid Nosair, the man who struck the first blow in the holy war by murdering Rabbi Kahane. Ali Mohamed went to Afghanistan to fight with the Mooj, but after the 1993 World Trade Center bombing, he flipped back, telling the Feds about bin Laden's connection to some of the bombers. He described how the Islamic terrorist used "sleepers" who live normal lives for years and then are activated for operations. What he did not tell the spooks was that he was helping plan to bomb the U.S. embassies in Africa. Only after he had pleaded guilty to conspiracy in 1999 did he disclose that he had personally met with bin Laden about the plot. He described how bin Laden, looking at a photo of the U.S. Embassy in Nairobi, "pointed to where the truck could go as a suicide bomber."

The story of Ali Mohamed suggests that the calls by some politicians for more and better informants may be easier to preach than practice. The CIA's skills in the dark arts of running agents have atrophied over the years. The agency was purged of some of its best spy handlers after the 1975 Church Committee investigation exposed some harebrained agency plots, like hiring the Mafia to poison Fidel Castro. During the Reagan years, the agency was beefed up, but a series of scandals in the late '80s and the '90s once more sapped its esprit. America's spies were once proud to engage in "morally hazardous duty," said Carleton Swift, the CIA's Baghdad station chief in the late 1950s. "Now the CIA has become a standard government bureaucracy instead of a bunch of special guys."

A number of lawmakers are calling to, in effect, unleash the CIA. They want to do away with rules that restrict the agency from hiring agents and informers with a record of crimes or abusing human rights. Actually, case officers in the field can still hire sleazy or dangerous characters by asking permission from their bosses in Langley. "We almost never turn them down," said one high-ranking official. But that answer may gloss over a more significant point—that case officers, made cautious by scandal, no longer dare to launch operations that could get them hauled before a congressional inquisition.

THE WEAKNESSES OF THE CIA'S DIRECtorate of Operations, once called "the Department of Dirty Tricks," can be overstated. When the CIA suspected that the Sudanese government was helping bin Laden obtain chemical weapons, a CIA agent was able to obtain soil samples outside the Al Shifa pharmaceutical plant that showed traces of EMPTA—a precursor chemical used in deadly VX gas. The evidence was used to justify a cruise-missile attack on the factory in retaliation for the embassy bombings. At the same time, 70 cruise missiles rained down on a bin Laden training camp in Afghanistan.

The Clinton administration was later mocked for this showy but meaningless response. Clinton's credibility was not high: he was accused of trying to divert attention from the Monica Lewinsky scandal. In classic American fashion, the owner of the pharmaceutical plant in Sudan hired a top Washington lobbying firm to heap scorn on the notion that his plant was being used for chemical weapons. But Clinton's national-security adviser at the time, Sandy Berger, still "swears by" the evidence, and insists that the cruise missiles aimed at bin Laden's training camps missed bin Laden and his top advisers by only a few hours.

The Clinton administration never stopped trying to kill bin Laden. Although a 1976 executive order bans assassinations of foreign leaders, there is no prohibition on killing terrorists—or, for that matter, from killing a head of state in time of war. In 1998, President Clinton signed a "lethal finding," in effect holding the CIA harmless if bin Laden was killed in a covert operation. The agency tried for at least two years to hunt down bin Laden, working with Afghan rebels opposed to the Taliban regime. These rebels once fired a bazooka at bin Laden's convoy but hit the wrong

vehicle. "There were a few points when the pulse quickened, when we thought we were close," recalled Berger.

By the final year of the Clinton administration, top officials were very worried about the terrorist threat. Berger says he lay awake at night, wondering if his phone would ring with news of another attack. Administration officials were routinely trooping up to Capitol Hill to sound warnings. CIA Director George Tenet raised the specter of bin Laden so many times that some lawmakers suspected he was just trying to scare them into coughing up more money for intelligence. The Clinton Cassandras emphasized the growing risk that terrorists would obtain weapons of mass destruction—chemical, biological or nuclear. But the threat was not deemed to be imminent. Bin Laden was generally believed to be aiming at "soft" targets in the Middle East and Europe, like another embassy. The experts said that a few bin Laden lieutenants were probably operating in the United States, but no one seriously expected a major attack, at least right away.

The millennium plots should have been a wakeup call. Shortly before the 2000 New Year, an obscure Algerian refugee named Ahmed Ressam was caught by a wary U.S. Customs inspector trying to slip into the United States from Canada with the makings of a bomb. Ressam was a storm trooper in what may have been a much bigger plot to attack the Los Angeles airport and possibly other targets with a high symbolic value. A petty criminal who lived by credit-card fraud and stealing laptop computers, Ressam was part of a dangerous terrorist organization—GIA, the same group that hijacked the Air France jet in 1994 and tried, but failed, to plunge it into the Eiffel Tower. A particularly vicious group that staged a series of rush-hour subway bombings in Paris in the mid-'90s, GIA is a planet in Al Qaeda's solar system. Ressam later told investigators that he had just returned from one of bin Laden's Afghan training camps, where he learned such skills as feeding poison gas through the air vents of office buildings. Some of Ressam's confederates in the millennium plots were never picked up and are still at large. The Canadian Security Intelligence Service is believed to have fat files on the GIA, but like many secret services, the CSIS does not share its secrets readily with other services, at home or abroad. Some U.S. investigators believe that bin Laden was using Canada as a safe base for assaults on the United States. U.S.

border authorities now believe that several of the suicide hijackers came across the border via a ferry from Nova Scotia in the days before the attack on the World Trade Center.

In hindsight, the Ressam case offered clues to another bin Laden trademark: the ability of Al Qaeda-trained operatives to hide their tracks. While renting buildings in Vancouver, Ressam and his confederates frequently changed the names on the leases, apparently to lay a confusing paper trail. A kind of terrorist's how-to manual ("Military Studies in the Jihad Against the Tyrants") found at the home of a bin Laden associate in England last year instructs operatives to deflect suspicion by shaving beards, avoiding mosques and refraining from traditional Islamic greetings. Intelligence officials now suspect that bin Laden used all manner of feints and bluffs to throw investigators off the trail of the suicide hijackers. Decoy terrorist teams and disinformation kept the CIA frantically guessing about an attack somewhere in the Middle East, Asia or Europe all last summer. Embassies were shuttered, warships were sent to sea, troops were put on the highest state of alert in the Persian Gulf. The Threat Committee of national-security specialists that meets twice a week in the White House complex to monitor alerts sent out so many warnings that they began to blur together. One plot seemed particularly concrete and menacing. At the end of July, authorities picked up an alleged bin Laden lieutenant named Djamel Begal in Dubai. He began singing—a little too fast, perhaps—about a plan to bomb the American Embassy in Paris. Was the threat real—or a diversion?

The United States is heavily dependent on foreign intelligence services to roll up terror networks in their own countries. But typically, intelligence services prefer to keep an eye on suspected terrorists rather than prosecute them.

To persuade a foreign government to turn over information on a terrorist suspect, much less arrest him, requires heavy doses of diplomacy. The task is not made easier if different branches of the American government squabble with each other. Last October, the USS Cole, a destroyer making a refueling stop in the Yemeni port of Aden, was nearly sunk by suicide bombers in a small boat. (An earlier attempt, against a different American warship docking in Yemen, fizzled when the suicide boat, overloaded with explosives, sank as it was leaving the dock. Bin Laden,

nothing if not persistent, apparently ordered his hit men to try again.) FBI investigators immediately rushed to the scene, where they were coolly received by the Yemeni government. The G-men became apprehensive about their own security and demanded that they be allowed to carry assault rifles. The U.S. ambassador, Barbara Bodine, who regarded the FBI men as heavy-handed and undiplomatic, refused. After an awkward standoff between the G-men and embassy security officials in the embassy compound, the entire FBI team left the country—for three months. They did not return until just recently.

It now appears that the same men who masterminded the Cole bombing may be tied to the devastating Sept. 11 assault on the United States. Since January 2000 the CIA has been aware of a man named Tawfiq bin Atash, better known in terrorist circles by his nom de guerre "Khallad." A Yemeni-born former freedom fighter in Afghanistan, Khallad assumed control of bin Laden's bodyguards and became a kind of capo in Al Qaeda. According to intelligence sources, Khallad helped coordinate the attack on the Cole. These same sources tell NEWSWEEK that in December 1999, Khallad was photographed by the Malaysian security service (which was working with the CIA to track terrorists) at a hotel in Kuala Lumpur. There, Khallad met with several bin Laden operatives. One was Fahad al-Quso, who, it later turned out, was assigned to videotape the suicide attack on the Cole (not all of Al Qaeda's men are James Bond: al-Quso botched the job when he overslept). Another was Khalid al-Midhar, who was traveling with an associate, Nawaf al-Hazmi, on a trip arranged by an organization known to U.S. intelligence as a "logistical center" and "base of support" for Al Qaeda.

American intelligence agencies intercepted a number of messages pointing to an imminent terrorist assault. But none was analyzed until after the deadly September 11 attacks.

Those two names—al-Midhar and al-Hazmi—would resonate with intelligence officials on Sept. 11. Both men were listed among the hijackers of American Airlines Flight 77, the airliner that dive-bombed the Pentagon. Indeed, when one intelligence official saw the names on the list of suspects, he uttered an expletive. Just three weeks earlier, on Aug. 21, the CIA asked the INS to keep a watch out for al-Midhar. The INS reported that the man was already in the country; his only declared address was "Marriott Hotel" in New York. The CIA sent the FBI to find al-Midhar and his associate. The gumshoes were still looking on Sept. 11.

AT LEAST ONE OTHER NAME FROM THE list of hijackers had shown up in the files of Western intelligence services: Mohamed Atta. He is an intriguing figure, both because of his role as the apparent senior man among the suicide hijackers, and because his background offers some disturbing clues about the high quality of bin Laden's recruits. The stereotype of an Islamic suicide bomber is that of a young man or teenage boy who has no job, no education, no prospects and no hope. He has been gulled into believing that if he straps a few sticks of dynamite around his waist and presses a button, he will stroll through the Gates of Paradise, where he will be bedded by virgins. Atta in no way matches that pathetic creature. He did not come from a poor or desperate fundamentalist family. His father, Mohamed, described himself to NEWSWEEK as "one of the most important lawyers in Cairo." The Atta family has a vacation home on the Mediterranean coast. Their Cairo apartment, with a sweeping view of downtown, is filled with ornate furniture and decorated with paintings of flamingos and women in head scarves.

If anything, Atta seemed like a prodigy of Western modernism. His two sisters are university professors with Ph.D.s. Atta won a bachelor's degree in Cairo in 1990 and went to Germany for graduate work in urban studies.

His thesis adviser in Hamburg, where he studied at the Technical University, called Atta "a dear human being." Only in retrospect does it appear ominous that in his thesis dedication he wrote "my life and my death belong to Allah, master of all worlds." Atta went to bars and rented videos ("Ace Ventura," "Storm of the Century"), but he also grew a beard and began to dress more in Islamic style. He spoke often of Egypt's "humiliation" by the West.

While polite, he also could be haughty. He scorned women, refusing to shake their hands.

That was the only worry of Atta's proud father. "I started reminding him to get married," Atta senior recounted to NEWS-WEEK, as he chain-smoked cigarettes ("American blend"). "Many times I asked him to marry a woman of any nationality—Turkish, German, Syrian—because he did not have a girlfriend like his colleagues. But he insisted he would marry an Egyptian. He was never touching woman, so how can he live?" In October 1999, "we found him a bride who was nice and delicate, the daughter of a former ambassador," said Atta senior. But Atta junior said he had to go back to Germany to finish his Ph.D. Actually, he was going to Florida to enroll in flight school.

During his years as a student in Hamburg, Atta would disappear for long periods of time—possibly, to meet with his handlers. U.S. intelligence believes that Atta met in Europe this year with a midlevel Iraqi intelligence official. The report immediately raised the question of Saddam Hussein's possible role in the Sept. 11 atrocity, but intelligence officials cautioned against reading too much into the link. Atta was in close communication with his superiors. On Sept. 4, one week before the bombing, he sent a package from a Kinko's in Hollywood, Fla., to a man named Mustafa Ahmed in the United Arab Emirates. "We don't know for sure what was in the package," said a senior U.S. official. "But Mustafa could be the key to bin Laden's finances. We're taking a hard look at him." (Several of the hijackers also wired money to Ahmed.) There are indications that Atta prepared very carefully for the attack, casing the airport in Boston and flying coast to coast on airliners. He may have had a backup plan: NEWSWEEK has learned that Atta had round-trip reservations between Baltimore and San Francisco in mid-October.

Atta's father refuses to accept his son's role as a suicide bomber. "It's impossible my son would participate in this attack," he said, claiming that he was a victim of a plot by Israeli intelligence to provoke the United States against Islam. "The Mossad kidnapped my son," said Atta. "He is the easiest person to kidnap, very surrendering, no physical power, no money for bodyguards. They used his name and identity… Then they killed him. This was done by the Mossad, using American pilots." Atta's rant was wild and sad—yet it was matched by the vituperations of the viru-

lently anti-American Egyptian press, which spun fantastic plots featuring Mossad agents as the villains.

Atta appears to have been inseparable from another hijacker, Marwan al-Shehhi, up to the moment they parted ways at Logan airport on the morning of Sept. 11. The FBI believes that al-Shehhi piloted the second jetliner, United Airlines Flight 173, into the South Tower of the World Trade Center. Al-Shehhi and Atta roomed together in Florida and were tossed out of Jones Flying Service School for unprofessional behavior. (Instructors complained about their "attitude.") They signed up together for a one-month membership at a gym, the Delray Beach Health Club. They went to Las Vegas, where the FBI believes that several hijackers kept girlfriends. They ate American, but told the employees at Hungry Howie's to hold the ham when they ordered their favorite pizza, a pie with all the toppings called "The Works."

As investigators piece together the lives of the hijackers, details that once seemed innocuous now loom large. Ziad Samir Jarrahi, a Lebanese man, took martial-arts lessons at a Dania, Fla., gym. "What he wanted to study was street-fighting tactics—how to gain control over somebody with your hands, how to incapacitate someone with your hands," gym owner Bert Rodriguez told NEWSWEEK. Did Jarrahi use those tactics in the last, desperate struggle in the cockpit of Flight 93, which crashed in a field outside Pittsburgh? Top law-enforcement officials reported that the voice recorder from Flight 93 picked up sounds of Arab and American voices shouting as the plane went down. Some very brave passengers stormed the cockpit in a last-ditch effort to seize control of the plane. Did they encounter Jarrahi and his newly honed fighting skills?

THE AVAILABLE EVIDENCE SUGGESTS A death match. When the hijackers struck, at about 9:35 a.m., air-traffic controllers listening in on the frequency between the cockpit and the control center in Cleveland could hear screams, then a gap of 40 seconds with no sound, then more screams. Then, sources say, a nearly unintelligible voice said something like "Bomb onboard." The controllers tried to raise the captain but received no response. Then radar showed the plane turning sharply—toward Washington, D.C. A voice in thickly accented English said, "This is your captain. There is a bomb onboard. We are returning to the airport."

In the passenger cabin, there was bloodshed and fear. At least one passenger was dead, probably with his throat slashed. In the back of the plane, however, five men, all burly athletes, were plotting a rush at the hijackers. "We're going to do something," Todd Beamer told a GTE operator over the air phone. "I know I'm not going to get out of this." He asked the operator to say the Lord's Prayer with him. "Are you ready, guys?" he asked. "Let's roll." The cockpit voice recorder picked up someone, apparently a hijacker, screaming "Get out of here! Get out of here!" Then grunting, screaming and scuffling. Then silence.

Such stories of heroic struggle will be—and should be—told and retold in the years to come. But now investigators are groping with uncertainty, asking: Who else is still out there? And will they strike again? A congressional delegation to CIA headquarters last week reported that mattresses were strewn on the floors. The race is still on, round the clock. Some investigators were trying to follow the money. They learned that in the week before the Sept. 11 attack, the hijackers began sending small amounts of money back to their paymasters in the Middle East. "They were sending in their change," an intelligence source told NEWSWEEK. "They were going to a place where they wouldn't need money." The hijackers apparently didn't need all that much to begin with: law enforcement estimates that the entire plot, flight lessons and all, cost as little as $200,000. That is 10 times more than was spent on the first World Trade Center bombing, but still a low-enough sum so the money could be moved in small denominations among trusted agents. Still, Al Qaeda is reputed to be expert at money laundering. Last week the pressure was on banks all over the world to open up their books (and on the banking lobby in the United States to drop its opposition to new laws that would make it easier for investigators to follow the money). The trail is likely to lead in some diplomatically awkward directions. Moderate Arab regimes are said to try to buy off terrorists. Much of bin Laden's money has come from wealthy Saudis who ostensibly give to Islamic charities. Some of those charities resemble the "widows and orphans" funds the Irish Republican Army uses to finance its bombmaking.

The money trail led investigators last week to a suspect whose background and motives could be the stuff of nightmares. Nabil al-Marabh, a former Boston taxi driver of Kuwaiti descent, is suspected of funneling thousands of dollars in wire transfer through Fleet Bank to the Middle East. The money was allegedly sent to a former Boston cabby implicated in a terrorist plot in Jordan that was foiled at the time of the millennium celebrations. At the same time, investigators say, al-Marabh may have exchanged phone calls with at least two of the Sept. 11 hijackers. Al-Marabh, who like a number of terrorists seems to have used Canada as a sometime sanctuary, was hard to track down. Canadian authorities first informed U.S. Customs about al-Marabh in July, and investigators opened a money-laundering probe. Last week the FBI raided an apartment in Detroit, where al-Marabh had been living. They found instead three men who had once worked as caterers at the Detroit airport (and kept their airport ID badges). In the apartment was a diagram of an airport runway and a day planner filled with notations in Arabic about "the American base in Turkey," the "American foreign minister" and the name of an airport in Jordan. The FBI arrested the men, but al-Marabh was at the time getting a duplicate driver's license at the state department of motor vehicles.

Not just any license. Al-Marabh's license would permit him to drive an 18-wheel truck containing hazardous materials. As it turned out, two of his housemates had also been going to school to learn how to drive large trucks. Carrying what, exactly? And heading where?

This story was written by EVAN THOMAS *with reporting from* MARK HOSENBALL, MICHAEL ISIKOFF, ELEANOR CLIFT *and* DANIEL KLAIDMAN *in Washington*, PEG TYRE *in New York*, CHRISTOPHER DICKEY *in Paris*, ANDREW MURR, JOSEPH CONTRERAS *and* JOHN LANTINGUA *in Florida*, KAREN BRESLAU *in San Francisco*, SARAH DOWNEY *in Minneapolis*, STEFAN THEIL *in Hamburg*, TOM MASLAND *in Dubai and* ALAN ZARENBO *in Cairo*

Global Trends in Crime

Crime varies greatly around the world, statistics show, but new tactics have proved effective in the United States. To keep crime in check in the twenty-first century, we'll all need to get smarter, not just tougher.

By Gene Stephens

Crime in the United States is bottoming out after a steep slide downward during the past decade. But crime in many other nations—particularly in eastern and parts of western Europe—has continued to climb. In the United States, street crime overall remains near historic lows, prompting some analysts to declare life in the United States safer than it has ever been. In fact, statistics show that, despite terrorism, the world as a whole seems to be becoming safer. This is in sharp contrast to the perceptions of Americans and others, as polls indicate they believe the world gets more dangerous every day.

Current Crime Rates Around the World

Although the United States still has more violent crime than other industrialized nations and still ranks high in overall crime, the nation has nevertheless been experiencing a decline in crime numbers. Meanwhile, a number of European countries are catching up; traditionally low-crime societies, such as Denmark and Finland, are near the top in street crime rates today. Other countries that weren't even on the crime radar—such as Japan—are also experiencing a rise in crime.

Comparing crime rates across countries is difficult (see sidebar "The Trouble with Crime Statistics"). Different definitions of crimes, among other factors, make official crime statistics notoriously unreliable. However, the periodic World Crime Survey, a UN initiative to track global crime rates, may offer the most reliable figures currently available:

• **Overall crime (homicide, rape, major assault, robbery) and property crime**. The United States in 1980 clearly led the Western world in overall crime and ranked particularly high in property crime. A decade later, statis-

tics show a marked decline in U.S. property crime. By 2000, overall crime rates for the U.S. dropped below those of England and Wales, Denmark, and Finland, while U.S. property-crime rates also continued to decline.

• **Homicide**. The United States had consistently higher homicide rates than most Western nations from 1980 to 2000. In the 1990s, the U.S. rate was cut almost in half, but the 2000 rate of 5.5 homicides per 100,000 people was still higher than all nations except those in political and social turmoil. Colombia, for instance, had 63 homicides per 100,000 people; South Africa, 51.

• **Rape**. In 1980 and 1990, U.S. rape rates were higher than those of any Western nation, but by 2000, Canada took the lead. The lowest reported rape rates were in Asia and the Middle East.

• **Robbery** has been on a steady decline in the United States over the past two decades. As of 2000, countries with more reported robberies than the United States included England and Wales, Portugal, and Spain. Countries with fewer reported robberies include Germany, Italy, and France, as well as Middle Eastern and Asian nations.

• **Burglary**, usually considered the most serious property crime, is lower in the United States today than it was in 1980. As of 2000, the United States had lower burglary rates than Australia, Denmark, Finland, England and Wales, and Canada. It had higher reported burglary rates than Spain, Korea, and Saudi Arabia.

• **Vehicle theft** declined steadily in the United States from 1980 to 2000. The 2000 figures show that Australia, England and Wales, Denmark, Norway, Canada, France, and Italy all have higher rates of vehicle theft.

The Trouble with Crime Statistics

Accurate crime data are difficult to obtain. One reason is that most crime is not reported to police in many countries. Another reason is that police can increase or decrease the amount of crime detected and reported by their discretionary decisions at the administrative and/or street levels.

A third reason is that definitions of crime vary. Social scientists generally see crime as being what we say it is. Therefore, crime is defined by the local culture. For instance, an incident may be defined as assault by one person while being seen as "playing around" by another. Further complicating crime statistics, an officer may choose to arrest a participant in a domestic disturbance (reported as assault) or simply serve as a peacemaker and then leave (not reported).

Other obstacles to accurate crime data include intentional underreporting and manipulating of data so the statistics look good. Such conduct has been discovered in police agencies in New York, Philadelphia, Atlanta, and elsewhere.

There's also the problem that crime reported to police is not even considered to be the best measure of criminal activity. Unreported crime, termed by criminologists as "the dark figure of crime," is common: Roughly one in three crimes is actually reported to the police, according to self-reported-crime surveys by the U.S. Bureau of Justice Statistics. Asked why they didn't report crimes to police, some respondents answered, "It was too personal," "Nothing could be done," "It wasn't worth the effort," or "The offender might retaliate."

However, if you keep in mind the problems inherent in collection and reporting of crime rates, it is still worth the effort to examine the statistics. Their insight, though incomplete, can shed light on crime trends that speak to certain nations' successful crime-reduction tactics and other nations' need to do more.

—Gene Stephens

Overall, the United States has experienced a downward trend in crime while other Western nations, and even industrialized non-Western nations, are witnessing higher numbers. What's behind the U.S. decreases? Some analysts believe that tougher laws, enforcement, and incarceration policies have lowered crime in the United States. They point to "three-strikes" legislation, mandatory incarceration for offenses such as drug possession and domestic violence, and tougher street-level enforcement. The reason many European countries are suffering higher crime rates, analysts argue, is because of their fewer laws and more-lenient enforcement and sentencing.

Other analysts argue that socioeconomic changes—such as fewer youth in the crime-prone 15- to 25-year-old age group, a booming economy, and more community care of citizens—led to the drop in U.S. crime. They now point out that the new socioeconomic trends of growing unemployment, stagnation of wages, and the growing numbers in the adolescent male population are at work in today's terror-wary climate and may signal crime increases ahead.

Still other analysts see community-oriented policing (COP), problem-oriented policing (POP), and restorative justice (mediation, arbitration, restitution, and community service instead of criminal courts and incarceration) as the nexus of recent and future crime control successes.

Just which crime-fighting tactics have effected this U.S. crime trend is a matter of debate. Three loose coalitions offer their views:

Getting tough works. "There is, in fact, a simple explanation for America's success against crime: The American justice system now does a better job of catching criminals and locking them up," writes Eli Lehrer, senior editor of *The American Enterprise*. Lehrer says local control of policing was probably what made a critical difference between the United States and European countries where regional and national systems predominate. He holds that local control allowed police to use enforcement against loitering and other minor infractions to keep the streets clean of potential lawbreakers. He acknowledges that "positive loitering"—stickers or a pat on the back for well-behaved juveniles—was the other side of the successful effort. In addition, more people have since been imprisoned for longer periods of time, seen by "get-tough" advocates as another factor in safer streets today.

Demographics rule. Some criminologists and demographers see the crime decrease as a product of favorable socioeconomic population factors in the mid- through late-1990s. High employment rates, with jobs in some sectors going unfilled for lack of qualified candidates, kept salaries growing. Even the unemployed went back to school to gain job skills. By the end of the decade the older students filled the college classrooms, taking up the slack left by the lower numbers in the traditional student age group. In such times, both violent and property crimes have usually dropped, as economic need decreased and frustration and anger subsided.

"Get-tough" theorists hold that 200 crimes a year could be prevented for each criminal taken off the streets, but criminologist Albert Reiss counters that most offenders work in groups and are simply replaced when one leaves.

If demographic advocates are right, then the next few years could see a boom in street crime in the United States due to a combination of growing unemployment, stagnant wages, and state and local governments so strapped for funds that social programs and even education are facing major cutbacks.

Community-based approaches succeed. Whereas the "get-tough" advocates mention community policing as a factor in the crime decrease, this third group sees the service aspects (rather than strict enforcement) of COP combined with the emerging restorative-justice movement as

Crime Trends among Selected OECD Nations

Number of crimes per 100,000 population

	Total crimes		Homicides		Violent Assaults		All Thefts		Drug Offenses	
	1995	2000	1995	2000	1995	2000	1995	2000	1995	2000
Australia	4,167	7,475	3.5	3.6	560	737	3,532	6,653	n/a	n/a
Canada	9,163	8,054	5.1	4.3	165	146	4,883	4,070	208	286
Denmark	10,334	9,460	1.1	4.0	165	24	3,365	3,638	291	249
England, Wales *	7,206	9,823	2.6	2.8	17	405	6,822	6,175	42	261
Finland	7,930	8,697	0.8	0.7	38	38	2,745	2,623	177	260
France	6,317	6,446	4.4	3.7	123	182	4,137	3,990	136	177
Germany	8,179	7,625	4.9	3.4	117	142	4,797	3,703	194	297
Japan	1,486	1,985	1.0	1.1	14	24	1,253	1,683	21	22
Korea	1,181	1,635	1.5	2.0	443	69	197	379	5	8
Norway	9,167	10,087	2.2	2.7	57	77	4,541	4,677	539	984
Spain	2,313	2,213	2.4	2.9	23	22	1,789	1,768	107	252
United States	5,278	4,124	8.2	5.5	418	324	4,814	3,763	582	572

* England and Wales data for 1996 and 1998

Most of these countries in the Organization for Economic Cooperation and Development experienced an increase in total crimes from 1995 to 2000. The United States experienced a decrease in all crimes listed, yet still remains the leader in reported homicides. Its neighbor to the north, Canada, experienced a decline in all areas of crime except drug offenses.

Source: Interpol International Crime Statistics, Interpol, 200 quai Charles de Gaulle, 69006 Lyon, France. Web site www.interpol.int/Public/Statistics/ICS/.
U.S. drug offense data from FBI's annual *Crime in the United States Uniform Crime Reports*.

being the catalyst for success in crime prevention and control.

Most criminologists believe street crime is a product of socioeconomic conditions interacting on young people, primarily adolescent males. Usually their crimes occur in interaction with others in gangs or groups, especially when law-abiding alternatives (youth athletic programs, tutors, mentors, community centers, social clubs, after-school programs) are not available. Thus, any chance of success in keeping crime rates low on a long-term basis depends on constant assessment of the community and its needs to maintain a nurturing environment.

COP and POP coordinate community cohesion by identifying problems that will likely result in crime and by simply improving the quality of life in the neighborhoods. The key: partnerships among police, citizens, civic and business groups, public and private social-service agencies, and government agencies. Combined with an ongoing needs analysis in recognition of constantly changing community dynamics, the partnerships can quickly attack any problem or situation that arises.

A restorative-justice movement has grown rapidly but stayed below the radar screen in the United States. In many communities, civil and criminal incidents are more likely to be handled through mediation or arbitration, restitution, community service, and reformation/reintegration than in civil or criminal courts. The goal, besides justice for all, is the development of a symbiotic relationship and reconciliation within the community, since more than 90% of all street offenders return to the same community.

Lessons for the Future of Crime Prevention and Control

All schools of thought on why street crime is decreasing have a commonality: proactive prevention rather than reactive retribution. Even the method to achieve this goal is not really in question—only the emphasis.

Since the 1980s, progressive police agencies in the United States have adhered to the "Broken Windows" and "Weed and Seed" philosophies taken from the work of criminologists James Q. Wilson and George L. Kelling. Broken windows are a metaphor for failure to establish and maintain acceptable standards of behavior in the community. The blame, according to Wilson and Kelling, lay primarily in the change in emphasis by police from being peace officers who maintain order to law-enforcement officers who seek to capture criminals. They argue that, in healthy communities, informal but widely understood rules were maintained by citizens and police, often using extralegal ("move on") or arrest for minor infractions (vagrancy, loitering, pandering). It was, then, this citizen-police partnership that worked to stem commu-

International Law Enforcement Academies

The success of U.S. cities and states in lowering crime rates over the past decade has sparked the interest of law enforcement agencies around the globe in American police operations. At the same time, the attacks of September 11, 2001, and the resulting war on terrorism have made the United States acutely aware of its need for eyes and ears around the world, as well as for partners in the quest to make the earth safer. One of the ways to build symbiotic relationships among the world's police agencies is through International Law Enforcement Academies (ILEAs).

ILEAs "develop an extensive network of alumni, who will become the leaders and decision makers in their respective countries, to exchange information with their U.S. counterparts and assist in transnational investigations," according to the U.S. State Department. Started in 1995, ILEAs have already provided training for more than 8,000 officials from 50 countries, including Hungary, Thailand, Botswana, and Costa Rica.

One ILEA of note is the Moscow Police Command College. Coordinated by the Department of Criminology and Criminal Justice at the University of South Carolina and held in Columbia, South Carolina, MPCC has graduated five classes of command-level officers primarily from Moscow. Emphasis in this program is on the principles and implementation of community-oriented policing and victim assistance, as well as police leadership in the community. Moscow police stand to gain much from this new training, since they are dealing with crime that hardly existed under the iron fist of communism: Violence and organized crime, not just economic opportunity, are a product of Russia's free market.

—*Gene Stephens*

nity deterioration and disorder, which, unattended, would lead to crime.

"Weeding" involved using street-sweeping ordinances to clean the streets of the immediate problems (drunks, drug addicts, petty thieves, panhandlers). "Seeding" involved taking a breather while these offenders were in jail and establishing "opportunity" programs designed to make the community viable and capable of self-regulating its behavioral controls (job training, new employers, day care, nurseries in schools, after-school programs, tutors and mentors, civic pride demonstrations, tenant management of housing projects). In the early years, the "weed" portion was clearly favored; in the early 1990s, "seed" programs based on analysis of the specific needs of the individual community were developed and spread—about the time the crime rates began to plunge.

The Weed and Seed programs in the United States imparted the following lessons:

• Proactive prevention must be at the core of any successful crime-control strategy.

• Each community must have an ongoing needs assessment carried out by a police-citizen partnership.

• A multitude of factors—from laws and neighborhood standards to demographics and socioeconomic needs—must be considered in the assessment process.

• Weed and seed must be balanced according to specific needs—somewhat differently in each community.

• When crime does occur, community-based restorative justice should be used to provide restitution to victims and community while reforming and then reintegrating the offender as a law-abiding citizen of the community.

New Approaches for the Emerging Crime Landscape

Twenty-first-century crime is going to require new approaches to prevention and control. Street crime dominated the attention of the justice system in the twentieth century, but recent excesses of corporations, costing stockholders and retirees literally billions of dollars, do not fit into the street-crime paradigm. Nor do political or religious-motivated terrorism, Internet fraud, deception, theft, harassment, pedophilia, and terrorism on an information highway without borders, without ownership, and without jurisdiction. New attention must—and will—be paid to white-collar crimes, infotech and biotech crimes, and terrorism.

Surveys find that a large majority of corporations have been victims of computer-assisted crimes. Polls of citizens find high rates of victimization by Internet offenses ranging from identity theft to fraud, hacking to harassment. U.S. officials have maintained since the late 1990s that it is just a matter of time until there is a "Pearl Harbor" on the Internet (such as shutting down medical services networks, power grids, or financial services nationwide or even worldwide).

Following the attacks by terrorists on September 11, 2001, and later strikes abroad, doomsday scenarios have abounded, with release of radioactive or biological toxins being the most frightening. Attempts to shoot down an Israeli commercial airliner with a shoulder-held missile launcher further increased anxiety.

Clearly these crimes against victims generally unknown to the attacker and often chosen randomly cannot be stopped by community policing alone, although vigilant community partners often can spot suspicious activity and expose possible criminals and terrorists. Early response to this dilemma was to pass more laws, catch more offenders, and thus deter future incidents. This is the same response traditionally taken to street crime—the one being abandoned in preference to proactive prevention methods (COP and restorative justice). Clearly, prevention has to be the first and most important strategy for dealing with the new threats.

Two major approaches will evolve over the next few years. First, national and international partnerships will be necessary to cope with crimes without borders. In 2000, a task force of agents from 32 U.S. communities, the federal government, and 13 other nations conducted the largest-ever crackdown on child pornography exchanged internationally over the Internet. Coordinated by the U.S. Customs Service, the raid resulted in shutting down an international child-pornography ring that used secret Internet chat rooms and sophisticated encryption to exchange thousands of sexually explicit images of children as young as 18 months. It is this type of coordinated transnational effort that will be necessary to cope with infotech and biotech crime and terrorism.

Second, the focus of prevention must change from opportunity reduction to desire reduction. Crime-prevention specialists have long used the equation, Desire + Opportunity = Crime. Prevention programs have traditionally focused on reducing opportunity through target hardening. Locks, alarms, high-intensity lighting, key control, and other methods have been used, along with neighborhood crime watches and citizen patrols.

Little attention has been paid to desire reduction, in large part because of the atomistic approach to crime. Specifically, an offender's criminal behavior is viewed as a result of personal choice. Meanwhile, criminologists and other social scientists say crime is more likely to be a product of the conditions under which the criminal was reared and lived—yet there were no significant efforts to fix this root of the problem. Instead, the criminal-justice system stuck to target hardening, catching criminals, and exacting punishment.

Quashing conditions that lead to a desire to commit crime is especially necessary in light of the apparent reasons terrorists and international criminals attack: religious fervor heightened by seeing abject poverty, illiteracy, and often homelessness and hunger all around while also seeing others live in seeming splendor.

The opportunity to reduce crime and disorder is at hand. The strategies outlined above will go a long way toward that lofty goal, as will new technologies. A boom in high-tech development has brought about new surveillance and tracking gadgetry, security machines that see through clothing and skin, cameras and listening devices that see and hear through walls and ceilings, "bugs" that can be surreptitiously placed on individuals, and biometric scanners that can identify suspects in large crowds. On the other hand, these are also the technologies that could take away our freedom, particularly our freedom of speech and movement. Some in high government positions believe loss of privacy and presumption of innocence is the price we must pay for safety.

For many it is too high a price. One group that urges judicious use of technology within the limitations of civil liberties protected by the U.S. Constitution is the Society of Police Futurists International (PFI)—a collection primarily of police officials from all over the world dedicated to improving the professional field of policing by taking a professional futurist's approach to preparing for the times ahead. While definitely interested in staying on the cutting edge of technology and even helping to guide its development, PFI debates the promises and perils of each new innovation on pragmatic and ethical grounds. Citizens need to do the same.

About the Author Gene Stephens will be a featured guest speaker at the 2003 World Future Society annual conference in San Francisco. He is a distinguished professor emeritus of the Department of Criminology and Criminal Justice, University of South Carolina. He is also the criminal justice editor of THE FUTURIST. His address is 313 Lockner Court, Columbia, South Carolina 29212. Telephone 1-803-777-7315; e-mail stephens-gene@sc.edu; Web site www.thefuregene.com.

Originally published in the May/June 2003 issue of *The Futurist*. Used with permission from the World Future Society, 7910 Woodmont Avenue, Suite 450, Bethesda, MD 20814. Telephone: 301/656-8274; Fax: 301/951-0394; http://www.wfs.org. © 2003.

The FBI's CYBER-CRIME CRACKDOWN

ON ONE SIDE, TEEN HACKERS AND CORRUPT EMPLOYEES; ON THE OTHER, THE FBI'S COMPUTER CRIME-FIGHTING UNITS. LET THE BATTLES BEGIN.

BY SIMSON GARFINKEL

To protect the classified information stored on her desktop computer, Special Agent Nenette Day uses one of the most powerful tools on the planet—an air gap.

Day points to an IBM ThinkPad resting on the table behind her desk. "That computer is hooked up to the Internet," she says. "But if you break into it, have a good time: there's no secret work on it."

Two meters away on her desk sits Day's other computer—a gray-and-chrome minitower emblazoned with a red sticker proclaiming that its hard drive is classified SECRET. "This," she says protectively, "holds my e-mail." Day readily talks about the ThinkPad, describing how she got it as part of a big purchase by the Federal Bureau of Investigation (FBI) a few years ago and explaining that it's now somewhat out-of-date. And she happily shows off a collectible action figure—still in its display box—a colleague brought back from Belgium. It's a"cyberagent" with a gun in one hand and a laptop computer in the other. But if you let your eyes drift back to that red sticker and try to copy the bold, black words printed on it, Day will throw you out of her office.

Day belongs to the FBI's Boston Computer Crime Squad, one of 16 such units located throughout the United States. Each is composed of about 15 agents who investigate all manner of assaults on computers and networks—everything from lone-hacker to cyberterrorist attacks—with a dose of international espionage thrown in for good measure. Crimes range from Web site defacements and break-ins to so-called denial-of-service attacks, which prevent legitimate users from accessing targeted networks.

The Computer Crime Squads form the heart of the FBI's new Cyber Division. Created as part of the FBI's reorganization that followed September 11, the Cyber Division is the U.S. government's first line of defense against cybercrime and cyberterrorism. Its mission, said FBI Director Robert S. Mueller, when he appeared before the Senate Committee on the Judiciary last May, is "preventing and responding to high tech and computer crimes, which terrorists around the world are increasingly exploiting to attack America and its allies."

The emphasis on cybercrime is a big departure for the FBI. The bureau's agents traditionally got the most attention—and the biggest promotions—by pursuing bank robbers, kidnappers, and extortionists. J. Michael Gibbons worked on one of the FBI's very first computer-crime cases back in 1986; when he left the FBI in 1999, he was chief of computer investigations. "Frankly," says Gibbons, now a senior manager at KPMG Consulting in McLean, VA, "there was no great glory in the FBI on working computer investigation cases."

But that attitude is changing as Washington increasingly realizes that big damage can be inflicted on U.S. businesses through their computers and networks. Remember back in February 2000 when a massive denial-of-service attack shut down Web sites belonging to companies such as Yahoo!, eBay, and Amazon.com? It cost those companies literally millions of dollars in lost revenue. That attack, it turns out, was executed by a single high school student. Experts worry that a similar assault on the nation's electric utilities, financial sector, and news delivery infrastructure could dramatically exacerbate the resulting confusion and possibly even the death toll of a conventional terrorist attack, if the two attacks were coordinated.

Even without the specter of terrorism, cybercrime is bleeding millions of dollars from businesses. Earlier this year, the Computer Security Institute surveyed 503 organizations: together, they reported $456 million dollars in

Hall of Cyberinfamy

JOHN DRAPER, "CAPTAIN CRUNCH"

Crime: Draper discovered in 1972 that by blowing the whistle that came with Cap'n Crunch cereal, he could create the 2600-hertz tone necessary to seize control of telephone systems and place free long-distance phone calls.

Punishment: Draper was arrested in May 1972 for illegal use of telephone company property. He was put on probation, but in 1976 he was arrested again on wire fraud charges and spent four months in prison. While serving time, he started programming the Easy-Writer word processor for the Apple II computer

KEVIN MITNICK

Crime: While in high school, Mitnick broke into computer systems operated by Digital Equipment Corp. and downloaded the source code to the operating system. By 1994 Mitnick was considered the federal government's most wanted computer hacker.

Punishment: Following a nationwide manhunt, Mitnick was arrested in February 1995 and held for four years without trial. Specific allegations were never published on the grounds of "national security." Mitnick was released from prison in January 2000 under a plea bargain.

KEVIN POULSEN

Crime: A friend of Kevin Mitnick, Poulsen rigged Los Angeles radio call-in shows to guarantee that a pal would win a car giveaway. He also broke into the FBI's National Crime Information Center, downloading active case files and alerting suspects in undercover FBI investigations.

Punishment: Poulsen spent three years in prison for hacking and was forbidden to touch a computer for three additional years after his release. He is now a journalist, covering computer security for SecurityFocus, an online business service.

"MAFIABOY"

Crime: This Canadian juvenile was responsible for the February 2000 denial-of-service attacks on CNN, Yahoo!, E*Trade, and other major Web sites.

Punishment: Arrested in April 2000 by the Royal Canadian Mounted Police working in cooperation with the FBI, the youth, whose name was withheld because of his age, pled guilty to 56 counts of computer crime in January 2001. He was sentenced in September 2001 to eight months of "open custody" and one year probation, as well as restricted access to the internet.

ONEL DE GUZMAN

Crime: In May 2000 the ILOVEYOU computer worm spread throughout the world as an e-mail attachment. Worldwide damage in lost productivity and clogged networks was estimated at $10 billion.

Punishment: The FBI quickly traced the worm to the Philippines and identified computer science student De Guzman as the perpetrator. Philippine authorities brought charges against him but then dismissed the case in August 2000, saying that the country's laws did not cover computer crime.

---

damages due to attacks on their computers and networks over the past year, and more than $1 billion in damage over the previous six years. Those numbers—which are the closest thing that the computer establishment has to reliable figures for the incidence of computer crime—have climbed more than 20 percent since 2001.

AGENTS LIKE DAY SERVE AS A GROWING DETERRENT AGAINST CRIMINAL ATTACKS ON A MACHINE-DEPENDENT SOCIETY.

Day's activities show that although the FBI, the nation's premier law-enforcement agency, is starting to come to terms with cybercrime, it still has a long way to go. Agents such as Day receive special training and have access to specialized tools (many of which the FBI refuses to discuss). Their equipment, if not always at the James Bond cutting edge, is no longer embarrassingly outdated. On the other hand, the FBI's cybercrime squads are locked in a battle to keep current in the face of unrelenting

technological change, and they are so short-staffed that they can investigate only a tiny fraction of the computer crimes that occur. Agents such as Day have served as only a small deterrent to hackers and high tech criminals bent on attacking a society that has become hopelessly dependent on its machines. But the deterrent is growing.

How to Catch a Cybercrook

The phone rings at the FBI Crime Squad and a "complaint agent" answers. Most calls are short, not too sweet, and not terribly satisfying for the person seeking help. "We get a lot of phone calls from people who say that somebody has hacked their home computer," says Day. Others report death threats delivered in online chat rooms.

Unsettling as such events are for the victims, most callers are told that there's nothing the FBI can do for them. For one thing, federal computer-crime statutes don't even kick in unless there is at least $5,000 damage or an attack on a so-called "federal interest computer"—a broad category that includes computers owned by the federal government, as well as those involved in interstate banking, communications, or commerce. In places especially rife with computer crime, like New York City, the intervention bar is even higher.

Even cases whose damages reach the threshold often die for lack of evidence. Many victims don't call the FBI right away. Instead, they try to fix their computers themselves, erasing their hard drives and reinstalling the operating system. That's like wiping fingerprints off the handle of a murder weapon: "If you have no evidence, we can't work it," says Day. And, of course, an attack over the Internet can originate from practically anywhere—the other side of the street or the other side of the world. "We can't do a neighborhood sweep and ask, 'Did you see anybody suspicious walking around here?'" she explains.

For many computer offenses, the FBI lacks not only solid evidence but even the knowledge that an incident has occurred at all. According to this year's Computer Security Institute survey, only about one-third of computer intrusions are ever reported to law enforcement. "There is much more illegal and unauthorized activity going on in cyberspace than corporations admit to their clients, stockholders, and business partners, or report to law enforcement," says Computer Security Institute director Patrice Rapalus.

Every now and then, however, all the ingredients for a successful case come together: a caller who has suffered a significant loss, undisturbed evidence, and a perpetrator who is either known or easily findable.

Day remembers a case from October 2000. The call came from the vice president of Bricsnet US, a software company in Portsmouth, NH. Bricsnet had just suffered a massive attack over the Internet. Somebody had broken into its systems, erased customer files, modified financial records, and sent e-mail to Bricsnet's customers, announcing that the company was going out of business.

When Day arrived on the scene she went quickly for what she hoped would be the key source of evidence: the log files. These are the routine records—the digital diary—computers retain about their actions. Computers can keep highly detailed logs: an e-mail server, for example, might track the "To" and "From" addresses, as well as the date, of every message it processes. Some computers keep no log files at all. Getting lucky, Day found that Bricsnet's log file contained the time of the attack and the Internet Protocol, or IP, address of the attacker's computer.

Every address on the Internet is assigned to either an organization or an Internet service provider. In the Bricsnet case, the address belonged to a local service provider. Day issued a subpoena to that company, asking for the name of the customer "who had connected on this IP address" when the attack took place. This information came from the service provider's own log files.

It turned out that the offending address corresponded to a dial-up connection. Each time a subscriber dials in, the service provider's log files record the date, time, username, and the originating phone number. Within a week

of launching the investigation, Day had fingered a likely suspect: Patrick McKenna, a help desk worker whom Bricsnet had fired on the morning of the first attack. McKenna was arrested, charged, and convicted under the Computer Fraud and Abuse Act. He was sentenced in June 2001 to six months in federal prison, followed by a two-year parole. He was also ordered to pay restitution for the damage he had caused, which the court determined to be $13,614.11.

Masked Men and Dead Ends

Day's bust in the Bricsnet case was unusual for its speed and for the resulting conviction. That's because many crimes are perpetrated with stolen usernames and passwords. In the Bricsnet case, for instance, McKenna had broken into the company's computers using his former supervisor's username and password.

The key to cracking the Bricsnet case was caller ID and automatic number identification (ANI), two technologies more and more Internet service providers are using to automatically record the phone numbers of people dialing up their servers. When a crime is committed over a telephone line, this information is invaluable.

"I love ANI," says Day. "The last thing you want to do is show up at Joe Smith's house because some hacker has logged in using Smith's username and password." This tool, she says, "lets you know if you are on the right track. It has made a huge difference." Not all new telecommunications technologies are so helpful, though. Many recent computer attacks, for example, flow from the growing availability of always-on high-speed Internet connections. Attackers employ computer viruses and other programs to compromise users' home computers, and then they use the compromised computers as platforms for launching other attacks without the owners' knowledge. Even worse, an attacker can jump from system to system, forging a long chain that cannot be traced. Microsoft Windows typically does not keep logs of its activity. "A lot of our investigations have been stopped cold in their tracks because someone is trotting through one of those computers," Day says, referring to cable-modem-connected PCs that run vulnerable copies of Microsoft Windows 95.

Even caller ID and automatic number-identification information can be faked by a person who has control of a corporate telephone system with a certain kind of connection to the public telephone network. So far, faked caller ID hasn't been a problem—but that could change, too.

The Internet's cloak of anonymity has made fighting crime especially tough. It's almost as if there were booths outside banks distributing free ski masks and sunglasses to everybody walking inside. "Anonymity is one of the biggest problems for the FBI crime squads," former agent Gibbons says. He maintains that cybercriminals' ability to disguise their identities does more than just complicate investigations; it also makes attackers more aggressive and more willing to take chances and do damage.

"People act differently when they don't think that they are being held accountable for their actions," says Gibbons. For years, computer security experts have maintained that corrupt employees and former insiders—such as McKenna at Bricsnet—perpetrate the lion's share of computer crime. But Day's experience contradicts this prevailing wisdom. Today things are changing: according to Day, most cases she investigates involve outsiders who commit their crimes anonymously over the Internet, frequently from overseas. Day says she has traced some 70 percent of the attacks to foreign Internet addresses. Nevertheless, insiders still represent the bulk of her investigations as they represent the most damaging attacks.

In one case, Day says, she determined that a major break-in had originated at a cybercafe in a small town in Romania. Because computer hacking is not a crime in Romania, the local police offered no assistance. Seeking help elsewhere, she phoned the cafe itself and talked with its owner, who spoke fluent English. "The owner said he has a bunch of cyberhackers who come there, but this is Romania, and they pay cash," Day says.

The investigation was terminated.

Attack of the Grownups

The media frequently portray the typical computer criminal as a disaffected male youth, a computer wizard who lacks social skills. In the archetypal scene, FBI agents conduct a predawn raid: with their guns drawn, they arrest a teenager while his horrified parents look on. And in fact, Day says that as recently as five years ago, juveniles made up the majority of the perpetrators she encountered. They were teenagers who broke into Web sites that had little security, and their digital crowbars were tools that they downloaded freely from the Internet. These kids made no attempt to hide their success. Instead, they set up their own servers on the penetrated computers, bragged to their friends, and left behind lots of evidence of their misdeeds.

But such attacks are no longer the most important cases that Day's office investigates. Recent years have brought "an interesting shift," she says. Now she sees attackers breaking into computers that are supposedly protected by firewalls and security systems. These perpetrators—virtually all of them adults—mount extremely sophisticated attacks. They don't brag, and they don't leave obvious tracks. "It's economic espionage," Day concludes.

It's not surprising that these cases are the hardest to crack, she says. One incident involved a suspect who had used a stolen credit card to purchase dial-up accounts at Internet service providers, specifically smaller providers that did not use caller ID or automatic number identification. He then proceeded to quietly break into thousands of computers. Day monitored the attacker for four

months, trying to figure out who he was. "He was very good," she recounts. Then, in the middle of her investigation, the stolen credit card was canceled and the dial-up accounts were closed. "I was horrified," she says. The investigation fell apart, and the perpetrator is still at large.

Computer crime culprits defy stereotyping. One case that was successfully prosecuted—after a three-year investigation by the FBI—involved an assistant principal at a Long Island high school. The school administrator flooded the e-mail systems at Suffolk, James Madison, and Drexel universities with tens of thousands of messages, causing significant damage. In July 2001 the culprit, whose crimes carried punishments as high as a year in jail and $200,000 in fines, was sentenced to six months in a halfway house.

THE INTERNET'S CLOAK OF ANONYMITY MAKES ATTACKERS MORE WILLING TO TAKE CHANCES AND TO DO DAMAGE.

In the coming years the widespread adoption of wireless networking technology will probably pose the biggest problem for the FBI cybercrime squad. These networks, based on the 802.11(b), or Wi-Fi, standard, let people use laptops and handheld computers as they move freely about their homes and offices. But unless additional protective measures are taken, wireless signals invariably leak beyond buildings' walls: simply lurking within the 100- to 300-meter range of a typical base station, an attacker can break into a network without even picking up a telephone or stepping onto the victim's property. "Many people who are moving to wireless as a costsaving measure don't have any appreciation of the security measures they should employ," explains Special Agent Jim Hegarty, Day's supervisor.

And as the Boston cybercrime unit has discovered, wireless attacks are not just theoretical. The wireless network of one high tech company recently suffered a break-in. According to Hegarty, the attacker—an activist who was opposed to the company's product and management—literally stationed himself on a park bench outside the company's offices and over the course of several weeks, used the wireless network to "sniff" usernames and passwords of the company's president and other senior-level executives. The activist then used the information to break into the company's computers—again, making his entry through its wireless network. Armed with this illicit access, the attacker downloaded months of e-mail and posted it on the Web.

The e-mail contained confidential information about customers and their contracts. Once that became public, all hell broke loose. Some customers who discovered that they were paying higher rates than others demanded better deals; others canceled orders upon discovering that the vendor had been selling the same product to their competitors. Ultimately, the attacked company suffered more than $10 million in direct losses from the break-in. As wireless networks proliferate, attacks of this kind are likely to become more common, according to Hegarty. The advent of 802.11, he says, "is going to be a watershed event for us."

All in a Day's Work

When *Technology Review* first approached the FBI about interviewing an agent of the computer crime squad, the idea was to write about an agent's "average day." The public affairs manager at the FBI's Boston office nixed the idea: there are no average days for an FBI agent, she said. Indeed, Day says that one of the best things about her job is its endless variety.

"I might spend one day in trial preparation. I could spend an entire day milling through computer files doing evidence assessment. The next day I could be scheduled to testify in a trial. And last month I spent a couple weeks in Bangkok, Thailand, teaching police from 10 different Asian countries." She spends some days on the phone, perhaps overseeing a new case coming in from a financial institution or phoning FBI headquarters with information that needs to be relayed to other field offices. A few days later she might be off to the range for weapons training. Agent Day carries a .40-caliber Glock 23 and assists on the occasional drug raid. "It is very long work, and it's very hard," she says about her job, "but it gives you something that you would never see in the private sector."

The Glock doesn't get much use out there on the Internet, of course, but Day's FBI training in understanding criminal behavior does. She is, for example, involved in a project at the FBI's research center in Quantico, VA, developing a psychological profile of serial hackers—people who might become criminals or could be hired by a foreign government. A serial hacker could be a powerful tool for Al Qaeda or some other terrorist organization.

Moving forward, the biggest challenge, says Day, will be for society as a whole "to try to define and distinguish between what is basically online vandalism—when somebody is damaging a business or a computer—and cyberterrorism. All of those things are conflated in the discussion of the criminal prosecution of hackers. In my mind those are different kinds of contact with different social harm."

Today cybercrime is one of the FBI's top priorities—even above fraud, drugs, and gun running, says Day. But while scary talk of cyberterrorism captures the headlines, the most damaging cybercrime may actually be old-fashioned crimes being committed with new and virtually untraceable tools. Catching the new bad guys will require people like Nenette Day to stay on technology's leading edge, but it will also require an FBI able to build an organization that gives Day and her fellow agents adequate support. Furthermore, it will require the capability to bring superior computing firepower against the cyberattackers and beat them at their own high tech game.

Toward a Transvaluation of Criminal 'Justice:' On Vengeance, Peacemaking, and Punishment

Christopher R. Williams
State University of West Georgia

REFLEXIVE STATEMENT

As both teacher and scholar of criminal "justice," I am continually reminded of a profound absence in popular and academic discourse on crime and justice. What seems conspicuous to me by its absence seems to others assumed and expected in its absence. The reactions I receive from students and colleagues at the very mention of attitudes and practices such as compassion, forgiveness, and mercy when mentioned in the context of criminal justice are surprising if not discouraging. I continue to be troubled by the degree to which resentment and retribution seem "natural" and expected to students, scholars, and practitioners of criminal justice. I am equally troubled by the degree to which pro-social, life-affirming values such as compassion and forgiveness are absent in the same discursive spheres. This essay reflects my continuing effort to understand the dynamics of anger, hatred, and violence that permeate not only the system of criminal justice, but human relations on all levels.

INTRODUCTION

> For *that man be delivered from revenge*, that is for me the bridge to the highest hope, and a rainbow after long storms.
>
> Nietzsche, *Thus Spoke Zarathustra*, II, 7

Human civilization displays a storied history of vengeance, cruelty, and other manifestations of the passion for justice (e.g., Jacoby, 1983; Solomon, 1989). The passion for justice, however, does not often beget justice. History is replete with suggestions that it has been and is far more likely to perpetuate vicious cycles of injustice, inhumanity, and regressing human welfare (e.g., Fuller, 1998). In place of extirpating such a cycle, "civilized" society has merely institutionalized and, consequently, legitimated this passion. The perpetuity of "wars" on crime and drugs, for example, can be regarded as indicative of a broader and deeper cultural ethos—one characterized by anger, hatred, and a desire for vengeance and cathartic punishment of the identified "enemy." In manifest form, such sensibilities have contributed to increases in such criminal justice practices as mandatory minimum and determinate sentencing, justified or excused violations of human rights at the hands of police, court, and correctional officials, increased reliance on the death penalty, and a more general polarization of the rehabilitative sentiments prevalent in the 1950's and 1960's. As Bentham (1948) offered, such instances of institutionalized punitiveness are no less "evil" or violent than their non-legitimated counterparts; and, as Quinney (2000) reminds us, evil conceives only more and greater evil and violence conceives only more violence.

Understanding the problematic use of violence in the contemporary United States—particularly its appearance as an element of "justice"—requires acknowledging the permeation of the passion for vengeance at all levels of humanity and, further, the practice and perpetuation of such an ethos by the very institutions that are designed to remedy it. If criminal "justice" is to appear less as an instrument of cyclic maintenance and more as a means of promoting, affirming, and restoring social welfare, it should be conceptually reconstrued as and practically redirected toward *overcoming* its historically impassioned underpinnings. In the interest of fostering nonviolent, cooperative, and healthy human relationships at every level of humanity—from intrapersonal through global—what is necessary is a transvaluation of criminal justice. A transvaluation entails an identification and reconsideration of the existing values that inform understandings, policies, and practices of criminal justice. More accurately, such a reconstitution entails recognition of the absence of affirmative values in the logic upon which practices of criminal justice are premised. Transvaluation implies that such a reconsideration occur, not only, but especially in the face of accepted morality and ethical practice. It requires an appeal to the "human" when current practice, popular sensibilities and public desire demand the less-than-human.

A transvaluation of criminal justice, I will argue, requires acknowledging the primacy of *resentment* as the basis for much criminal justice policy and practice. Despite claims that the system of criminal justice operates in a reasoned, objective fashion, its underlying logic is the beneficiary of a tradition and culture that allows passion an integral role in the *concept* of justice itself. What becomes necessary is not mere embodiment of humanistic values in the agents of justice and the practices in which they engage but, rather, a corrective conceptualization of what criminal "justice" *is*.

Resentment is a multifaceted phenomenon, operating as a complex interplay of psychological (human emotion), cultural (social), and institutional (state policies and practices), which inform and are subsequently informed by human emotion and cultural reality. If resentment is acknowledged as a basis for harmful social attitudes and practices, what becomes more important is the displacement of such sentiments. Criminal "justice," in the interest of fostering a new ethos of affirmative social relations, requires a conceptual turn that overcomes resentment. As Jeffrie Murphy (1982) notes following Bishop Butler, overcoming resentment is, by definition, the basis of *forgiveness*. Forgiveness, in turn, serves as a psychological foundation for the institutional practice of *mercy*.

Forgiveness and mercy can be understood as keys to a reconstituted ideal of criminal "justice"—as humanistic alternatives to the institutionalization of anger and the desire for vengeance. Overcoming resentment, embodying forgiveness, and practicing mercy are certain to be met with staunch public disapproval. The tension existing on the political level is one of felt pressure from the public "to go to the upper limits of punishment" (Misner, 2000: 1306). Yet it is precisely when faced with such pressures and potential disapproval that the courage to do what is "just" is most necessary. In what follows, I offer a conceptual exploration of resentment, forgiveness, and mercy, attending in particular to distinctions necessary to insulate the latter from popular misconceptions as to their true character. While my primary focus is on criminal "justice," the importance of forgiveness and mercy should not be read as limited to that realm. Rather, overcoming resentment and a subsequent regard for forgiveness and mercy should be understood as essential concerns for the promotion of non-violent, compassionate, and benevolent relations in all spheres of human existence.

RESENTMENT AND THE PASSION FOR JUSTICE

The relationship between resentment and criminal justice lies in the latter's use of vengeance as philosophically justified retribution. Though scholarly debate concerning the philosophy of punishment has attempted to distinguish between a retributive philosophy of punishment and punishment as vengeance (e.g., Primoratz, 1989), the latter inevitably permeates our varied rationalizations of criminal punishment. Most forms of crime induce emotional reactions of anger and hatred in the experiencing and witnessing public. It is inevitable that public desire for emotional satisfaction or catharsis informs the political climate of the country (Misner, 2000: 1340). The logic applied in popular discourse concerning, for example, the death penalty and the desire for harsher punishment of criminal offenders is informed, not often by a rationally deduced logic of retribution, but by a "pre-philosophical intuition" (*ibid:* n139) or unreasoned desire to inflict harm upon those who have harmed "us."

To this degree, punishment is a political reality more than a philosophical one (e.g., Fairchild & Webb, 1985). The posture of the system of justice is in part a reflection of public desire and demand (e.g., Fuller, 1998). As a political reality, crime and justice cannot escape embodiment of popular sensibilities; and, in turn, as a social reality, popular sensibilities cannot escape embodiment of the political reality of crime and justice. As the social informs the political, so too does political rhetoric and corresponding institutional practice give force to the emotions, passions, and beliefs of the populous. Institutional practices effectively promote a broader cultural ethos that shapes not only public opinion, but human relationships on the level of community, family, and individual as well. The relationship between the social and the political with regard to "justice," then, is one of interdependence. As such, the relationship between resentment and criminal justice exists on several interrelated levels: anger as human emotion; the desire for vengeance as cultural ethos dictating appropriate experience and expression of such emotions; and cathartic retribution as an institutionalized characteristic of criminal "justice."

Resentment

"Resentment" refers to some negative feeling or feelings directed toward some person, persons, or organized collection of persons (e.g., social groups, cultures, institutions) that we perceive to have harmed us in some fashion. The negative feelings associated with resentment are often those of anger and hatred. What is significant is that the passion for vengeance is not equivalent to resentment; rather, the passion for vengeance is an incentive to action where resentment is the motivating psychological force. Aristotle suggested that what we think of as anger is doubly constituted: it entails both a belief that one has been wronged; as well as a subsequent belief that harming s/he or those responsible is desirable (i.e. wishing ill on the perpetrator) (Nussbaum, 1994: 90, 243). The two elements of what is commonly understood as anger are not one and the same. The initial experience of anger toward an offender and the subsequent desire to harm that offender in return (i.e. retaliation, vengeance) are distinct—though interrelated—aspects of the same psychological event. Anger does not necessarily entail a desire to retaliate, nor is anger sufficient to induce such a desire. To seek or wish harm upon an offending other requires either the absence of a moderating force of intervention, and/or the presence of an aggravating force of intervention.

Anger is often regarded as a problematic emotion in that it often involves a "desire to harm others ... and so may lead to all sorts of problems for individuals, their community, and our society at large" (Lazarus and Lazarus, 1994: 13). Yet this desire occurs subsequent to the experience of anger. Anger itself may be a natural, human response to a *demeaning offense against me or mine* (Lazarus & Lazarus, 1994: 20). The problematics of anger lie not in the emotional experience, but in the often corresponding retaliatory impulse. The desire for vengeance is not a visceral reaction; rather, anger is a visceral reaction and the desire for vengeance emerges only if the experience of anger is left unmoderated or unchecked. In such instances, anger—through desire—can find embodiment in individual and/or institutional behavior (i.e. decisions, policies, and practices). It is at this point where anger becomes troublesome—if not overtly harmful—to other persons, communities and society as a whole.

In addition to having an affective basis in individual psychology, resentment also entails a social psychological dynamic. The "me or mine" in the above quotation from Lazarus and Lazarus (1994) suggests that the harm arousing anger need not directly lead to our own suffering. It is reasonable to assume that when offended others are *not* perceived to be "like us" (i.e. as one of "mine"), the resentment felt and the desire for retaliatory action will not be similarly experienced. It is for this reason, perhaps, that many injustices or harms against other nations, races, ethnicities, species, etc. can be and are often trivialialized, while similar harms endured by those of our own nation, race, ethnicity, or species are magnified in terms of our emotional experience, the perceived degree of harm and suffering, and in our subsequent desire for action in the name of "justice." The most extreme scenario of this sort involves an offender who is "not like us" and a victim who is "like us." In this scenario, the experience of resentment and the passion for vengeance are likely experienced in excess. European-Americans, for example, have been shown to have more punitive attitudes toward criminals, especially when contrasted with attitudes of racial and ethnic minorities toward criminals. It has been suggested, for example, that such punitiveness reflects a broader prejudice harbored by European-Americans toward minorities more generally (Cohn, et al. 1991). European-Americans often understand or experience crime as a minority problem—i.e. a problem caused by minorities in that most criminals are perceived to be minorities (*ibid*). If crime can be understood as a problem caused by "them" which affects "us," it is likely that "we" will be less tolerant, understanding, forgiving and, consequently, more punitive. When such "us versus them" attitudes pervade a given culture, it is likely that resentment and the desire for vengeance against

"them" will be an integral component of a generalized cultural ethos.

Culture and Resentment

In reference to Marongiu and Newman's (1987) exposition of the Sardinian Code of Vengeance, Solomon (1990: 247) suggests that, "the idea that vengeance is a primitive emotion or even an instinct neglects the enormous amount of cultural stimulation, support, and structure, as well as some semblance of legitimacy vengeance receives from particular social rules and expectations." Sardinian "justice" is centered around the core belief that retaliation is a personal or family matter—not one of institutionalized punishment. Though affective anger is often regarded as a universal human experience, culture invariably plays a role in how we experience and express it. The desire for vengeance and the expression of such desires appears subsequent to the initial affective experience and, unlike anger, cannot be regarded as universal nor purely natural. Culture both informs shapes, and provides a cognitive framework for assessing which offenses are appropriately responded to in anger, as well as informing and shaping the ways in which emotions are to be expressed and controlled (Lazarus & Lazarus, 1994).

As an expression of the desire for vengeance, violence and punishment as a form of violence are choices involving a cognitive dimension—the thought and belief that the offending other should be harmed. In this way, "punishment can no more be identified with revenge 'than love can be identified with lust'" (Misner, 2000: 1339). To exemplify this point, we can point to the historical character of the U.S. as one that has condoned aggression, violence and, more generally, "accomplishment of desired ends over a concern for legitimate and humane means" (Fuller, 1998: 164). Americans are taught that violence has been and is necessary as a means to achieve (or maintain) a desired state of affairs. Interestingly, Americans do not often acknowledge violence and aggression as a socially and morally desirable component of our value system. As Brown (1990) notes, violence has become part of our "underground" value system. While we are formally objectionable to the use of violence, we are quick to condone the use of violence if it is regarded as necessary in a given context. Not coincidentally the context within which violence has historically garnered the most support as a means to an end is that of war. It is popularly believed that violence is necessary in times of war. Should we be surprised, then, to find increasing levels of violence being condoned if not demanded by the public in the context of the ongoing "war" on crime? In short, violence appears as an inherent feature of the national character of the United States and has created a culture of violence wherein individual thoughts, feelings, and behaviors concerning violence are shaped in a manner consistent with cultural values. Though we are all prone to feel anger, the ways in which we experience and express our anger is shaped by culture. If vengeance and violence are culturally valued as "just" expressions of anger, we are likely to find aggression and violence at all levels of human relationships, from intra- and interpersonal through institutional and global.

The "War On Crime" as Institutionalized Resentment

Resentment becomes institutionalized to the extent that it finds embodiment in the rhetoric, policies and practices of our social institutions (e.g., the criminal justice system). Equally, if not more, problematic is the mutuality of the relationship between culture and institution. We should not consider the impact of human emotion on the system of justice without lending some attention to the impact of the system of justice on human emotion and desires based on those emotions. The system of justice not only expresses popular sentiment, but serves to define and shape popular sensibilities concerning crime and justice. The prevailing "war on crime" exemplifies this bilaterality with regard to affect and desire.

The "war" perspective on crime and justice has increasingly evidenced itself in various criminal justice practices as well as professional and popular sensibilities. Despite the fact that the ongoing "war" on social problems (e.g., crime, drugs, poverty) is merely a metaphorical war, it is one that has had a profound effect on the way we conceive of social problems and their solutions. The way we understand and experience crime, criminals, and justice becomes more consistent with the way we understand and experience war. The issue, however, is not how the "war on crime" has been used as an instrument of distortion but, rather, the *effect* that such an instrument has had on public perception and criminal justice practices.

Fuller (1998: 22) suggests that war rhetoric is intended to "mobilize the population to attack social problems." I would add that it is intended to impassion the population with a desire for vengeance by appealing to fears, vulnerabilities, and universal (negative) human emotions. While the anger we experience in relation to crime is not outside the realm of human nature, political rhetoric maintains the force necessary to define and mold such emotions and, further, to lend impetus to desires stemming from them. In particular, the "war" on crime engenders a belief that vengeance is an acceptable solution to human problems—not only should we experience resentment toward crime and criminals, but we should succumb to the passion to express that resentment by "fighting fire with fire."

Throughout this process, several effects become notable. First, the war on crime encourages the public to experience persons who violate criminal law and other social norms as "enemies," thus perpetuating the circulation of an "us and them" mentality and actuating a process of dehumanization. "Oftentime I have heard you speak of one who commits a wrong," in Gibran's (1923) words, "as

though he were not one of you, but a stranger unto you and an intruder upon your world." To the degree that social reality is understood in terms of divisions of good and evil wherein "evil" is something other than ourselves, we lose our greater capacity to experience ourselves as part of the greater whole of humanity. In instances of criminal offense, any initial experience of compassion and understanding toward the suffering of the offender is easily negated by consideration for the suffering of the victim(s). The "us and them" mentality effectively establishes an ethic of sympathy for "us" at the expense of similar possibilities for "them." The latter sympathies, however, are essential to human welfare to the extent that they reflect an understanding of universal interconnectedness and a need for globalized compassion.

Failure to recognize and embody such a realization is demonstrably harmful on all levels. On a global level, for example, the "us versus them" mentality manifests as war between nations, races, religions, and even civil wars within nations, races, religions, etc. On a social level, it manifests as racism, ethnocentrism, and justifies exclusion, expulsion, and other forms of prejudice and overt discrimination. Most importantly, on the level of criminal justice, the "us versus them" mentality creates a social environment wherein policies of excess are practiced and condoned, if not demanded, by the public whose hypothetical "orderly community" is being threatened by "outsiders," "enemies," or simply "evil" people. As a result of the dissemination of these attitudes, we are further alienated from the experience of ourselves as part of the greater whole of humanity.

This has several significant consequences both within the criminal justice system and without. First, an "us and them" attitude toward others inhibits, if not destroys, our capacity to empathize and, thus, the possibility of compassion. Compassion is as much part of human nature as anger. As anger requires culture to shape its experience and expression, compassion requires culture to encourage its manifest existence as an integral component of human relationships. If our ability to identify with the "other" is destroyed, our ability to be compassionate toward the "other" is destroyed; if our capacity for compassion is destroyed, justice is destroyed. Secondly, the "us and them" mentality justifies treatment of persons who violate the criminal law as "enemies," "them," or something less-than-human. This, in turn, encourages or, at least, makes possible the condonation of excess in our treatment of such persons. Excess, in this context, manifests as ruthlessness, cruelty, and other injustices of the extreme. In addition, it encourages implementation of policies and practices that place less emphasis on fairness as opposed to desired ends (i.e. retribution). The last of these consequences implicates a problematic emphasis of the criminal justice system—namely, an emphasis on "doing" rather than "being." A transvaluation of criminal justice establishes the necessity of reversing this emphasis and, subsequently, a consideration of forgiveness and mercy as bases for the policies and practices of criminal justice.

OVERCOMING RESENTMENT: TOWARD A TRANSVALUATION OF CRIMINAL "JUSTICE"

Within resentment is embedded a near inevitable propensity for the creation of further harm. Consequently, *overcoming* resentment is more and more a "humanitarian imperative," embodiment of which seems one of the few means of "recaptur[ing] a sense of humaneness" (Misner, 2000: 1306) on every level and in every sphere of human existence. In many ways, this means going beyond or rising above the passion for "justice." In the remainder of this essay, I focus on two interrelated "humanitarian imperatives:" forgiveness and mercy. Both are exercises in overcoming that offer means of going beyond the passion for justice. While reclaiming the attitude of forgiveness and practices of mercy are essential concerns at every level of human relating, they carry special significance at the institutional level. Forgiveness and mercy, like resentment, are contagious. As "educator" (e.g., Fromm, 1930), the State is positioned to effect both cultural and individual practices by way of example. To the degree that resentment and vengeance inform legal and penal responses to crime, forgiveness and mercy become imperative considerations as affirmative antitheses: forgiveness in our attitudes toward the offenses of others; and mercy in our treatment of the offenses of others.

Forgiveness and Attitudes Toward the Offenses of Others

I have suggested, following Aristotle, that responses to the offenses of others are not often merely affective, but also entail a cognitive component. The emotional experience of anger is not inexorably entwined to the belief or desire that another should be harmed as a consequence of her or his offense. The initial experience of anger following the experience or witness of wrongdoing may well be justified; yet the subsequent experience of resentment and consequent desire to harm s/he who is responsible for such sufferings is not inevitable. Rather, it is largely a learned *expression* of anger that is perpetuated and justified by broader cultural and institutional dynamics. As such, it becomes important to recognize alternative possibilities with regard to attitudes toward the offenses of others.

On the ethical spectrum, forgiveness lies opposite resentment. Forgiveness warrants special attention in that it is too often and too easily misinterpreted and subject to dismissal as a desirable attitude and practice. Forgiveness does not entail erasing some wrong nor erasing some wrong from the memory of either the offender or the victim. To forgive does not necessarily mean to forget. What forgiveness requires is that we "cease to hate" (Comte-Sponville, 2001: 119), or, cease to resent. The attitude of forgiveness carries no implication that one who has been wronged is in some way unjustified in *initial* feelings of anger. Instead, it asks that one *overcome* such contextually justified human emotions. It does not ask that we not *feel* anger nor that, consequent to being harmed, we never *have* desires for punishment and revenge. Forgiveness asks that, from the intrapersonal to the institutional and global spheres of human relating, we overcome that which is all too human in the emotional realm.

The value of forgiveness, then, lies in its role as a mediator between emotion and action. Unlike anger, forgiveness is not purely affective. Forgiveness stands alongside the cognitive component of anger—that which entails thoughts and beliefs related to the experience and expression of anger. In this regard, forgiveness is that which overcomes the experience of resentment and prohibits the realization in action of the desire for vengeance. In other words, forgiveness does not *replace* anger, but "checks" it. We may experience anger and be justified in our experience of anger, yet "not revengeful … [but] … inclined to be forgiving" (Aristotle, 1976: 161 [1126al-3]). Ignoring, overlooking, or forgetting an offense is indicative of an absence of anger. Yet anger may itself be regarded as desirable in that the *experience of anger is necessary for forgiveness*. What is problematic is the character of the experienced anger.

Aristotle suggested that anger be felt "in the right manner" and "for the right length of time." "The right manner" of anger is a core obstacle in both human relationships as well as justice. Resentment is often inappropriate in that it is directed toward wrongs or harms that are objectively trivial, but subjectively experienced as wicked, sinister, or evil. In other cases, though harms may not be trivial, there is considerable discord between subjective and objective assessments of the degree of harm. As Baumeister (1997) suggests, the anger experienced by a victim is rarely if ever in agreement with either the experience of the offender or even an objective assessment of the harm. There is a "magnitude gap" between victim and offender in terms of the experience of a harmful incident (*ibid*). Such differences in perception and emotional experience can often lead to excessive anger, hatred, and set the stage for excess in expression of anger.

Experiencing the offender as an "enemy" or, perhaps, "evil," "possessed," or a psychopath is the easiest means to dehumanize, distance oneself from the offender and, consequently, condone if not demand excessive treatment. Nussbaum (1994: 404) alludes to such a state of alienation from fellow human beings in quoting General Schwartzkopf on the Gulf War: "Look, these Iraqis are no better that animals. They are not up to our standards of civilization, they don't really belong to the same species. So it was good that we killed as many of them as we did, wasn't it? And it will be fine at any time to kill a lot more." Schwartzkopf's reference implicates, not only anger, but the manifestation of anger in action—it is illustrative of how easy it can be to "slip" from appropriate and justified anger to the excessive and unjustified (*ibid*: 403-04). Anger often becomes problematic in cases wherein some wrong was done and anger is a legitimate and justified response, yet the anger is not proportionate to the degree of harm.

A deficiency in our attitude toward the offenses of others, then, would entail ignoring or forgetting the offense(s). Deficiency is an important consideration in discourse on forgiveness in light of the popular belief that forgiveness amounts to overlooking or forgetting the offense. Forgiveness asks no such impossibility. As a "golden mean" (Aristotle, 1976) between the two undesirable extremes of deficiency and excess, forgiveness does not require us to be deficient in our attitudes toward the offenses of others, nor does it allow for excess in those same attitudes. Yet excess is arguably embedded in the attitudes currently prevalent in the criminal justice system and society at large. Resentment and desires for revenge (alternately, vengeance, retribution, or "justice") are characteristic attitudes of excess when applied to offenses of others. The "golden mean" in such cases is that of forgiveness, understood as justifiable anger, yet overcoming the hatred and desire for revenge that are all-too-common when understanding and forgiveness are absent. Forgiveness should not be understood as a natural and universal emotion, but as that which overcomes the natural human emotion of anger and checks the desire for vengeance. Because the embodiment of forgiveness in all spheres of human existence—from self to society—is an integral component of an affirmative, humanistic cultural ethos, it is essential that forgiveness find embodiment on the institutional level. Overcoming resentment at the institutional level is a question of policy and practice, however, not human psychology. In the former, embodiment of forgiveness manifests as the practice of mercy.

Mercy and Treatment of the Offenses of Others

Mercy can be understood as institutionalized forgiveness. Mercy is, by definition, "the virtue that triumphs over rancor, over justified hatred … over resentment, over the desire for revenge or punishment" (Comte-Sponville, 2001: 119). Mercy is that which offsets, balances, or "checks" the vice of vengeance already embedded in public consciousness and legal and penal policy and practice. For this reason, as Comte-Sponville suggests, mercy goes *beyond* justice. It asks more than justice insofar as that which it overcomes is that which is *justified*. Like forgiveness, however, it is important to understand what mercy is not. While mercy is a desirable and essential practice for human welfare, it is as much prone to misinterpretation as forgiveness.

Mercy is, first, not forgiveness. Mercy is better defined as treating others less harshly than we have the right to do by law, rule, tradition, etc. (Murphy, 1982). Unlike forgiveness, mercy involves the *expression* of our experi-

enced emotions toward others who have offended. It is possible to forgive yet not express forgiveness and understanding through mercy. Likewise, it is possible—though not probable—to show mercy without having forgiven. Mercy implies or is preconditioned by the legal right to treat (i.e. punish) an offender in a way that is harsher or less forgiving than merciful treatment of the same offender. It is a decision to "check" both the passion for excess and the legal right to excess by tempering the type and/or extent of punishment with an air of understanding, compassion, and respect for the humanity of the offender. While forgiveness is the virtue that checks passion, keeping it within the bounds of justice, mercy is the expression in practice of that forgiveness and understanding. Without mercy—without discretion implied by mercy—justice can be "an intolerable engine of tyranny" (quoted in Misner, 2000: 1320).

Secondly, mercy is not clemency. Clemency can be understood as pardoning, excusing, or letting an offense pass without consequence and, in this regard, clemency is an occasional consideration for justice. Clemency, however, is fundamentally different from mercy. Comte-Sponville (2001: 119) defines clemency as the renunciation of punishment. To renounce punishment, for example, may entail an ethical opposition to punishment or one of its forms. One may stand opposed to capital punishment on ethical grounds, yet remain in hatred toward the offender who has taken innocent life. Thus, clemency is insufficient in that it does not negate the hatred that may follow the experience of harm. Such hatred is equally, if not more, problematic than punishment itself. It is, first and foremost, the hatred that forgiveness seeks to overcome and which allows for the possibility of mercy.

Further still, both forgiveness and mercy should not be confused with compassion or even the necessity of compassion in human attitude and action. While compassion is an essential—if not *the* essential—component of social justice, mercy pertains more specifically to criminal "justice." Compassion is understood as the experience of suffering at the sight, sound, or thought of another's suffering. The human capacity to empathize with others provides an emotional ground for the virtue of compassion. Yet compassion is one-dimensional in that it sympathizes with suffering only. The virtue of compassion requires us to identify with the past, present, or potential future suffering of others, putting ourselves "in another's shoes." Such empathic exercises are often limited to the degree that their effect varies in relation to the other's perceived likeness to oneself. In the example of the offender as "enemy," the monstrous murderer is turned into some*thing* less-than-human and, consequently, some*thing* different from oneself. Consequently, the capacity (or, perhaps, willingness) to empathize—even when great suffering is present—is limited if not altogether negated. In other cases, there may be no evidence of an offender's suffering at all or, if so, such evidence may be offset by the more pronounced and more readily understood suffering of the victim. A prime example of the latter is the introduction of victim impact evidence at the sentencing phase of criminal trials. Victim impact evidence relates, in written or spoken form, the suffering that the victim and/or victim's family has suffered as a consequence of the offender's actions. In such cases, juries and, perhaps, judges can more readily empathize with stories of victims suffering. Though offenders are offered opportunity to present evidence of their own suffering or other mitigating evidence, it is recognized that the weight of the latter may be little in light of evidence of victim suffering (e.g., Arrigo and Williams, 2004).

In many cases, then, compassion may not go far enough when confronted by criminal offenders. In cases involving no evidence of an offender's suffering or in which the offender's suffering seems insignificant in light of the victim's suffering, compassion may not be enough to allow us to overcome the anger, hatred, and desire for vengeance and punishment that is often experienced. For this reason, Comte-Sponville (2001: 120) suggests that mercy is the rarer and, certainly, more difficult virtue to embody. Faced with such difficulty, we must recognize that a virtue would not be a virtue if it were easy to embody. Mercy becomes all the more important when we consider that, if compassion is not available to open the door to forgiveness, then forgiveness may be necessary to open the door to compassion. Indeed, "it is easier to feel compassion once we have stopped hating" (ibid).

The difference between mercy and compassion is thus one of the subject toward which one's emotions or actions are directed. Both mercy and compassion are other-directed in that they are both concerned with one's attitude toward others. The distinguishing feature lies in the characteristics of the other toward whom our attitudes are directed. Compassion entails a certain attitude toward the *suffering* of others, while mercy entails a certain attitude toward the *offenses* of others. As suggested, one and the same "other" may be both a subject of compassion and mercy. It is not uncommon that an offender has both harmed and suffered in some meaningful ways. Most offenders are or have been victimized, and many victims are or have been offenders. The abused spouse who's suffering has crossed the threshold of endurance and, in turn, harms the offending spouse exemplifies this point. The "victim" in such a case is the harmed spouse, the suffering of whose family and friends we are to empathize with. Yet most would agree that it is as easy—if not moreso—to empathize with the suffering endured and currently experienced by the "offender." In such a case, the offending "victim" may be *both* a subject of compassion *and* a subject of our mercy.

As noted, however, other cases may provide no such suffering to empathize with. Such cases require movement beyond compassion and toward mercy. Much of the world's suffering may be perceived as innocent suffering and, thus, compassion is both a desirable response as well as a readily experienced response. What mercy offers is a virtuous and socially desirable response to situations in which we are confronted with wrongdoing—intentionally inflicted harm—wherein the offending party suffers in no significant or, at least, obvious way and, further, when the offending party may not be received as "like us" is any meaningful way. We may have less difficulty embodying mercy if we are able to identify with the offense(s) the subject has committed. It is easier to forgive the antisocial behaviors of rebellious juveniles—even in the absence of recognizable suffering—if we ourselves engaged in similar displays of antisocialism. Yet mercy offered because of an identification with the act committed still requires the process of identification. In this way it is only minimally different from mercy offered in light of compassion toward a suffering other. Embodiment of mercy requires that such virtuous attitudes and actions are offered, not only in easily forgivable cases or in cases that present the possibility of empathic identification, but even in—and especially in—the most disturbing of circumstances.

CRIMINAL 'JUSTICE' AND SOCIAL HEALTH: TOWARD AN AFFIRMATIVE CULTURAL ETHOS

Durkheim (1965; see also Wolff, 1960) argued that retribution is necessary as social practice because of its contribution to social solidarity. Retribution is functional in that it is useful for the moral well-being of society as a whole. I anomic times, when moral erosion seems the hallmark of the collective character and traditional values and moral norms appear in a state of anarchy, law must be the tie that binds society. Retribution becomes *value-affirming* and restores a sense of moral orderliness in affirming the seemingly eroding normative structure of the community. While law can serve as educator and offer a restorative function to the whole of society, retribution as expression of the collective desire for vengeance is questionable as a desirable value to affirm. By embodying in forgiveness in attitude and mercy in practice, the system of justice has some capacity to promote values that are more conducive to social cohesion and solidarity than those of resentment. If eroding values are a product of individualism and diversity without unity, the values restoring a cultural ethos of community, unity, and general concern for the welfare of others are those of understanding, compassion, forgiveness, and mercy that instill a more general climate of nonviolence. In this case, it is the latter are affirmative of socially desirable and socially healthy humanitarian values. Punishment, in turn, has precisely the opposite effect.

Punishment, as Gilligan notes (2000: 746), "is the most powerful stimulus of violence that we have yet discovered." Whether criminal or noncriminal, the practice of responding to violence with violence, evil with evil, pain with pain is the most effective means of creating violence, evil, and pain (e.g., Gilligan, 1996). Punishment is counterproductive and its irony lies in the reality that punishment, as an effort to prevent or deter further harm, leads simply to more harm. In part, this vicious cycle is reinforced precisely because teaching someone "a lesson" is, indeed, a lesson—one which latently functions to orchestrate the way we treat others. Both s/he who is punished, and we are witnesses are implicated in its effect. As Justice Brandeis once noted, "Our government is the potent, the omnipresent teacher. For good or ill, it teaches the whole people by its example" (quoted in Gilligan, 2000).

Justice Brandeis was referring to the inevitability of criminal justice values finding embodiment in the attitudes and practices of our everyday lives. I have described, as well, how the attitudes and practices of the populous can, in turn, impact the values of criminal justice. This in itself is a vicious cycle that serves to justify and perpetuate punitive sensibilities on an intrapersonal, interpersonal, socio-cultural, and global level (e.g., Fuller, 1998; Braswell, Fuller, and Lozoff, 2001). It stands to reason, however, that such a cycle can be broken and the dawn of a new cycle is not beyond our social horizon.

Working toward such a dawn requires a transvaluation of criminal "justice." While not to suggest that a similar transvaluation is unnecessary on intra- and interpersonal levels, social institutions have the unique ability to article values that will be received—directly or indirectly—by vast numbers of people. In a society where the public looks to law, politics, and media for information about crime and justice, such institutions have an obligation to model practices that are conducive to social health. What would such a model entail? Certainly, our institutional attitude toward the offenses of others would not be one of resentment and hatred; our incentives to act toward the offenses of others would not be based on desires for vengeance that issue from resentment; and our practices or actual treatment of the offenses of others would not entail punishment as a fulfillment of the desire for vengeance. Resentment fuels the vice of vengeance, and punishment is an instrument of that vice.

As Quinney (2000: 28) points out, responses to crime that are motivated by hate are a form of violence themselves. Three thousand years of recorded Western civilization have shown that violence is the most effective means of creating more violence. Nonviolence, in turn, is the most effective means of fostering an air of nonviolence at all levels of human relationships (e.g., Quinney, 1991). As Tolstoy once replied to Lombroso, "all punishment is criminal" (Troyat, 1967: 579). Responding to crime with punishment, in turn, is inevitably criminogenic. As Fuller (1998) suggests, the means used predetermine the ends that can be attained. Means that promote health are those of nonviolence—actions issuing from compassion, forgiveness, and mercy at all level of human relationships. As the values intrinsic to vengeful means are pathogenic, the values intrinsic to positive means can be equally "ethogenic."

REFERENCES

Aristotle (1976). *Nicomachean ethics.* J. Thomson (ed.). New York: Penguin.
Arrigo, B. & Williams, C. (forthcoming, 2003). Victim voices, victim vices, and restorative justice: Rethinking the use of victim impact evidence in capital sentencing. *Crime and Delinquency.*
Baumesiter, R. (1997). *Evil: Inside human violence and cruelty.* New York: W.H. Freeman and Company.
Bentham, J. (1948). *An introduction to the principles of morals and legislation.* New York: Hafner.
Braswell, M., Fuller, J., & Lozoff, B. (2001). *Corrections, peacemaking, and restorative justice: Transforming individuals and institutions.* Cincinnati: Anderson.
Brown, R. (1990). Historical patterns in American violence. In N. Weiner, M. Zahn, and R. Sagi (eds.), Violence: *Patterns, causes, and public policy in San Diego*: Harcourt Brace Jovanovich.
Cohn, S., Barkan, S., & Aveni, A. (1991). Punitive attitudes toward criminals: Racial consensus or racial conflict? *Social Problems*, 38, 287-296.
Comte-Sponville, A. (2001). A small treatise on the great virtues. C. Temersor trld. New York: Metropolitan Books.
Dhammapada. (1994). T. Cleary (trld.). New York: Bantam Books.
Durkheim, E. (1965). *The rules of the sociological method.* S. Solovay & J. Mueller (trlds.). G. Catlin (ed.). New York: The Free Press.
Fairchild. E. & Webb, V. (1985). *The politics of crime and criminal justice.* Beverly Hills: Sage.
Fromm, E. (1930). The state as educator: On the psychology of criminal justice. In K. Anderson and R. Quinney (eds.) *Erich Fromm and critical criminology: Beyond the punitive society.* Urbana: University of Illinois Press.
Fuller, J. (1998). *Criminal justice: A peacemaking perspective.* Boston: Allyn and Bacon.
Gibran, K. (1923). *The prophet.*
Gilligan, J. (1996). *Violence: Reflections on a national epidemic.* New York: Vintage Books.
Gilligan, J. (2000). Punishment and violence: Is the criminal law based on one huge mistake? *Social Research*, Fall.
Jacoby, S. (1983). Wild justice. New York: Harper and Row.
Lazarus, R. & Lazarus, B. (1994). *Passion and emotion: Making sense of our emotions.* New York: Oxford University Press.
Marongiu, P. & Newman, G. (1987). *Vengeance.* Roman and Littlefield, Publishers, Inc.
Misner, R. (2000). A strategy for mercy. *William and Mary Law Review*, 41, 1303.
Murphy, J. (1982). Forgiveness and resentment. *Midwest Studies in Philosphy*, 7, 503-516.
Nietzsche, F. (1995). *Thus spoke Zarathustra.* W. Kauffman, trld. New York: The Modern Library.
Nietzsche, F. (1967). *The genealogy of morals and Ecce Homo.* W. Kauffman, trld. New York: Vintage Books.
Nussbaum, M. (1994). *The therapy of desire: Theory and practice in Hellenistic ethics.* Princeton, NJ: Princeton University Press.
Primoratz, I. (1989). *Justifying legal punishment.* New Jeresey: Humanities Press.
Quinney, R. (1991). The way of peace: On crime, suffering, and service. In R. Quinney & H. Pepinsky (eds.), *Criminology as peacemaking.* Bloomington: Indiana University Press.
Quinney, R. (2000). Socialist humanism and the problem of crime: Thinking about Erich Fromm in the development of critical/peacemaking criminology. In K. Anderson and R. Quinney (eds.), *Erich Fromm and critical criminology: Beyond the punitive society.* Urbana, IL: University of Illinois Press.
Solomon, R. & Murphy, M. (1990). *What is justice: Classic and contemporary readings.* New York: Oxford University Press.

Solomon, R. (1989). *The passion for justice: Emotions and the origins of the social contract*. Reading, MA: Addison Wesley Co, Inc.

Tachibana, S. (1926). *The ethics of Buddhism*. Oxford: Clarendon Press.

Troyat, H. (1967). *Tolstoy*. Garden City: Doubleday.

Wolff, K. (1960). Emile Durkheim et al., Writings on sociology and philosophy. New York: Harper and Row.

ENOUGH IS ENOUGH

WHITE-COLLAR CRIMINALS: THEY LIE THEY CHEAT THEY STEAL AND THEY'VE BEEN GETTING AWAY WITH IT FOR TOO LONG

BY CLIFTON LEAF

Arthur Levitt, the tough-talking former chairman of the Securities and Exchange Commission, spoke of a "multitude of villains." Red-faced Congressmen hurled insults, going so far as to compare the figures at the center of the Enron debacle unfavorably to carnival hucksters. The Treasury Secretary presided over a high-level working group aimed at punishing negligent CEOs and directors. Legislators from all but a handful of states threatened to sue the firm that bollixed up the auditing, Arthur Andersen. There was as much handwringing, proselytizing, and bloviating in front of the witness stand as there was shredding behind it.

It took a late-night comedian, though, to zero in on the central mystery of this latest corporate shame. After a parade of executives from Enron and Arthur Andersen flashed on the television monitor, Jon Stewart, anchor of *The Daily Show*, turned to the camera and shouted, "Why aren't all of you in jail? And not like white-guy jail—*jail* jail. With people by the weight room going, 'Mmmmm.'"

It was a pitch-perfect question. And, sadly, one that was sure to get a laugh.

Not since the savings-and-loan scandal a decade ago have high crimes in the boardroom provided such rich television entertainment. But that's not for any lack of malfeasance. Before Enronitis inflamed the public, gigantic white-collar swindles were rolling through the business world and the legal system with their customary regularity. And though they displayed the full creative range of executive thievery, they had one thing in common: Hardly anyone ever went to prison.

Regulators alleged that divisional managers at investment firm Credit Suisse First Boston participated in a "pervasive" scheme to siphon tens of millions of dollars of their customers' trading profits during the Internet boom of 1999 and early 2000 by demanding excessive trading fees. (For one 1999 quarter the backdoor bonuses amounted to as much as a fifth of the firm's total commissions.) Those were the facts, as outlined by the SEC and the National Association of Securities Dealers in a high-profile news conference earlier this year. But the January news conference wasn't to announce an indictment. It was to herald a settlement, in which CSFB neither admitted nor denied wrongdoing. Sure, the SEC concluded that the investment bank had failed to observe "high standards of commercial honor," and the company paid $100 million in fines and "disgorgement," and CSFB itself punished 19 of its employees with fines ranging from $250,000 to $500,000. But whatever may or may not have happened, no one was charged with a crime. The U.S. Attorney's office in Manhattan dropped its investigation when the case was settled. Nobody, in other words, is headed for the hoosegow.

A month earlier drugmaker ICN Pharmaceuticals actually pleaded guilty to one count of criminal fraud for intentionally misleading investors—over many years, it now seems—about the FDA approval status of its flagship drug, ribavirin. The result of a five-year grand jury investigation? A $5.6 million fine and the company's accession to a three-year "probationary" period. Prosecutors said that not only had the company deceived investors, but its chairman, Milan Panic, had also made more than a million dollars off the fraud as he hurriedly sold shares. He was never charged with insider trading or any other criminal act. The SEC is taking a firm stand, though, "seeking to bar Mr. Panic from serving as a director or officer of any publicly traded company." Tough luck.

And who can forget those other powerhouse scandals, Sunbeam and Waste Management? The notorious Al "Chainsaw" Dunlap, accused of zealously fabricating Sunbeam's financial statements when he was chief executive, is facing only civil, not criminal, charges. The SEC charged that Dunlap and his minions made use of every accounting fraud in the book, from "channel stuffing" to "cookie jar reserves." The case is now in the discovery phase of trial and likely to be settled; he has denied wrongdoing. (Earlier Chainsaw rid himself of a class-

Schemers and scams: a brief history of bad business

It takes some pretty spectacular behavior to get busted in this country for a white-collar crime. But the business world has had a lot of overachievers willing to give it a shot.

by Ellen Florian

1920: The Ponzi scheme

Charles Ponzi planned to arbitrage postal coupons—buying them from Spain and selling them to the U.S. Postal Service at a profit. To raise capital, he outlandishly promised investors a 50% return in 90 days. They naturally swarmed in, and he paid the first with cash collected from those coming later. He was imprisoned for defrauding 40,000 people of $15 million.

1929: Albert Wiggin

In the summer of 1929, Wiggin, head of Chase National Bank, cashed in by shorting 42,000 shares of his company's stock. His trades, though legal, were counter to the interests of his shareholders and led to passage of a law prohibiting executives from shorting their own stock.

1930: Ivar Krueger, the Match King

Heading companies that made two-thirds of the world's matches, Krueger ruled—until the Depression. To keep going, he employed 400 off-the-books vehicles that only he understood, scammed his bankers, and forged signatures. His empire collapsed when he had a stroke.

1938: Richard Whitney

Ex-NYSE president Whitney propped up his liquor business by tapping a fund for widows and orphans of which he was trustee and stealing from the New York Yacht Club and a relative's estate. He did three years' time.

1961: The electrical cartel

Executives of GE, Westinghouse, and other big-name companies conspired to serially win bids on federal projects. Seven served time—among the first imprisonments in the 70-year history of the Sherman Antitrust Act.

1962: Billie Sol Estes

A wheeler-dealer out to corner the West Texas fertilizer market, Estes built up capital by mortgaging nonexistent farm gear. Jailed in 1965 and paroled in 1971, he did the mortgage bit again, this time with nonexistent oil equipment. He was re-jailed in 1979 for tax evasion and did five years.

1970: Cornfeld and Vesco

Bernie Cornfeld's Investors Overseas Service, a fund-of-funds outfit, tanked in 1970, and Cornfeld was jailed in Switzerland. Robert Vesco "rescued" IOS with $5 million and then absconded with an estimated $250 million, fleeing the U.S. He's said to be in Cuba serving time for unrelated crimes.

1983: Marc Rich

Fraudulent oil trades in 1980–1981 netted Rich and his partner, Pincus Green, $105 million, which they moved to offshore subsidiaries. Expecting to be indicted by U.S. Attorney Rudy Giuliani for evading taxes, they fled to Switzerland, where tax evasion is not an extraditable crime. Clinton pardoned Rich in 2001.

1986: Boesky and Milken and Drexel Burnham Lambert

The Feds got Wall Streeter Ivan Boesky for insider trading, and then Boesky's testimony helped them convict Drexel's Michael Milken for market manipulation. Milken did two years in prison, Boesky 22 months. Drexel died.

1989: Charles Keating and the collapse of Lincoln S&L

Keating was convicted of fraudulently marketing junk bonds and making sham deals to manufacture profits. Sentenced to 12½ years, he served less than five. Cost to taxpayers: $3.4 billion, a sum making this the most expensive S&L failure.

(continued)

Schemers and Scams (continued)

1991: BCCI	1991: Salomon Brothers	1995: Nick Leeson and Barings Bank	1995: Bankers Trust	1997: Walter Forbes
The Bank of Credit & Commerce International got tagged the "Bank for Crooks & Criminals International" after it came crashing down in a money-laundering scandal that disgraced, among others, Clark Clifford, advisor to four Presidents.	Trader Paul Mozer violated rules barring one firm from bidding for more than 35% of the securities offered at a Treasury auction. He did four months' time. Salomon came close to bankruptcy. Chairman John Gutfreund resigned.	A 28-year-old derivatives trader based in Singapore, Leeson brought down 233-year-old Barings by betting Japanese stocks would rise. He hid his losses—$1.4 billion—for a while but eventually served more than three years in jail.	Derivatives traders misled clients Gibson Greetings and Procter & Gamble about the risks of exotic contracts they entered into. P&G sustained about $200 million in losses but got most of it back from BT. The Federal Reserve sanctioned the bank.	Only months after Cendant was formed by the merger of CUC and HFS, cooked books that created more than $500 million in phony profits showed up at CUC. Walter Forbes, head of CUC, has been indicted on fraud charges and faces trial this year.

1997: Columbia/HCA	1998: Waste Management	1998: Al Dunlap	1999: Martin Frankel	2000: Sotheby's and Al Taubman
This Nashville company became the target of the largest-ever federal investigation into healthcare scams and agreed in 2000 to an $840 million Medicare-fraud settlement. Included was a criminal fine—rare in corporate America—of $95 million.	Fighting to keep its reputation as a fast grower, the company engaged in aggressive accounting for years and then tried straight-out books cooking. In 1998 it took a massive charge, restating years of earnings.	He became famous as "Chainsaw Al" by firing people. But he was then axed at Sunbeam for illicitly manufacturing earnings. He loved overstating revenues—booking sales, for example, on grills neither paid for nor shipped.	A financier who siphoned off at least $200 million from a series of insurance companies he controlled, Frankel was arrested in Germany four months after going on the lam. Now jailed in Rhode Island—no bail for this guy—he awaits trial on charges of fraud and conspiracy.	The world's elite were ripped off by years of price-fixing on the part of those supposed bitter competitors, auction houses Sotheby's and Christie's. Sotheby's chairman, Taubman, was found guilty of conspiracy last year. He is yet to be sentenced.

action shareholder suit for $15 million, without admitting culpability.) Whatever the current trial's outcome, Dunlap will still come out well ahead. Sunbeam, now under bankruptcy protection, gave him $12.7 million in stock and salary during 1998 alone. And if worse comes to worst, he can always tap the stash he got from the sale of the disemboweled Scott Paper to Kimberly-Clark, which by Dunlap's own estimate netted him a $100 million bonanza.

Sunbeam investors, naturally, didn't fare as well. When the fraud was discovered internally, the company was forced to restate its earnings, slashing half the reported profits from fiscal 1997. After that embarrassment, Sunbeam shares fell from $52 to $7 in just six months—a loss of $3.8 billion in market cap. Sound familiar?

The auditor in that case, you'll recall, was Arthur Andersen, which paid $110 million to settle a civil action. According to an SEC release in May, an Andersen partner authorized unqualified audit opinions even though "he was aware of many of the company's accounting improprieties and disclosure failures." The opinions were false and misleading. But nobody is going to jail.

At Waste Management, yet another Andersen client, income reported over six years was overstated by $1.4 billion. Andersen coughed up $220 million to shareholders to wipe its hands clean. The auditor, agreeing to the SEC's first antifraud injunction against a major firm in more than 20 years, also paid a $7 million fine to close the complaint. Three partners were assessed fines, ranging from $30,000 to $50,000, as well. (You guessed it. Not even home detention.) Concedes one former regulator familiar with the case: "Senior people at Andersen got off when we felt we had the goods." Andersen did not respond to a request for comment.

The list goes on—from phony bookkeeping at the former Bankers Trust (now part of Deutsche Bank) to allegations of insider trading by a former Citigroup vice president. One employee of California tech firm nVidia admitted that he cleared

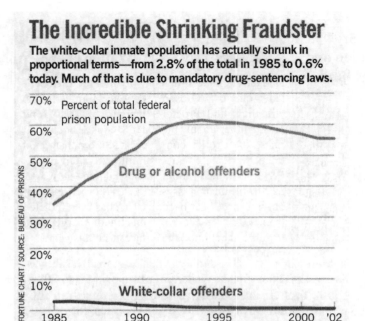

The Incredible Shrinking Fraudster

The white-collar inmate population has actually shrunk in proportional terms—from 2.8% of the total in 1985 to 0.6% today. Much of that is due to mandatory drug-sentencing laws.

nearly half a million dollars in a single day in March 2000 from an illegal insider tip. He pleaded guilty to criminal charges, paid fines, and got a 12-month grounding at home.

The problem will not go away until white-collar thieves face a consequence they're actually scared of: time in jail.

While none of those misbehaviors may rise to Enronian proportions, at least in terms of salacious detail, taken en masse they say something far more distressing. The double standard in criminal justice in this country is starker and more embedded than many realize. Bob Dylan was right: Steal a little, and they put you in jail. Steal a lot, and you're likely to walk away with a lecture and a court-ordered promise not to do it again.

Far beyond the pure social inequity—and that would be bad enough, we admit—is a very real dollar-and-cents cost, a doozy of a recurring charge that ripples through the financial markets. As the Enron case makes abundantly clear, white-collar fraud is not a victimless crime. In this age of the 401(k), when the retirement dreams of middle-class America are tied to the integrity of the stock market, crooks in the corner office are everybody's problem. And the problem will not go away until white-collar thieves face a consequence they're actually scared of: time in jail.

The U.S. regulatory and judiciary systems, however, do little if anything to deter the most damaging Wall Street crimes. Interviews with some six dozen current and former federal prosecutors, regulatory officials, defense lawyers, criminologists, and high-ranking corporate executives paint a disturbing pic-

ture. The already stretched "white-collar" task forces of the FBI focus on wide-ranging schemes like Internet, insurance, and Medicare fraud, abandoning traditional securities and accounting offenses to the SEC. Federal securities regulators, while determined and well trained, are so understaffed that they often have to let good cases slip away. Prosecutors leave scores of would-be criminal cases referred by the SEC in the dustbin, declining to prosecute more than half of what comes their way. State regulators, with a few notable exceptions, shy away from the complicated stuff. So-called self-regulatory organizations like the National Association of Securities Dealers are relatively toothless; trade groups like the American Institute of Certified Public Accountants stubbornly protect their own. And perhaps worst of all, corporate chiefs often wink at (or nod off to) overly aggressive tactics that speed along the margins of the law.

LET'S START WITH THE NUMBERS. WALL STREET, AFTER ALL, IS about numbers, about playing the percentages. And that may be the very heart of the problem. Though securities officials like to brag about their enforcement records, few in America's top-floor suites and corporate boardrooms fear the local sheriff. They know the odds of getting caught.

The U.S. Attorneys' Annual Statistical Report is the official reckoning of the Department of Justice. For the year 2000, the most recent statistics available, federal prosecutors say they charged 8,766 defendants with what they term white-collar crimes, convicting 6,876, or an impressive 78% of the cases brought. Not bad. Of that number, about 4,000 were sentenced to prison—nearly all of them for less than three years. (The average time served, experts say, is closer to 16 months.)

But that 4,000 number isn't what you probably think it is. The Justice Department uses the white-collar appellation for virtually every kind of fraud, says Henry Pontell, a leading criminologist at the University of California at Irvine, and co-author of *Big-Money Crime: Fraud and Politics in the Savings and Loan Crisis.* "I've seen welfare frauds labeled as white-collar crimes," he says. Digging deeper into the Justice Department's 2000 statistics, we find that only 226 of the cases involved securities or commodities fraud.

And guess what: Even those are rarely the highfliers, says Kip Schlegel, chairman of the department of criminal justice at Indiana University, who wrote a study on Wall Street lawbreaking for the Justice Department's research wing. Many of the government's largest sting operations come from busting up cross-state Ponzi schemes, "affinity" investment scams (which prey on the elderly or on particular ethnic or religious groups), and penny-stock boiler rooms, like the infamous Stratton Oakmont and Sterling Foster. They are bad seeds, certainly. But let's not kid ourselves: They are not corporate-officer types or high-level Wall Street traders and bankers—what we might call *starched*-collar criminals. "The criminal sanction is generally reserved for the losers," says Schlegel, "the scamsters, the low-rent crimes."

Statistics from the Federal Bureau of Prisons, up to date as of October 2001, make it even clearer how few white-collar criminals are behind bars. Of a total federal inmate population of

The SEC's Impressive Margins

Did someone say "resource problem"? The SEC is, in fact, a moneymaking machine. The U.S. Treasury keeps fees and penalties. Disgorgements go into a fund for fraud victims.

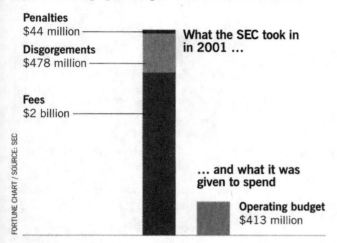

Penalties
$44 million

Disgorgements
$478 million

Fees
$2 billion

What the SEC took in in 2001 ...

... and what it was given to spend

Operating budget
$413 million

FORTUNE CHART / SOURCE: SEC

156,238, prison authorities say only 1,021 fit the description—which includes everyone from insurance schemers to bankruptcy fraudsters, counterfeiters to election-law tamperers to postal thieves. Out of those 1,000 or so, well more than half are held at minimum-security levels—often privately managed "Club Feds" that are about two steps down the comfort ladder from Motel 6.

And how many of them are the starched-collar crooks who commit securities fraud? The Bureau of Prisons can't say precisely. The Department of Justice won't say either—but the answer lies in its database.

Susan Long, a professor of quantitative methods at the school of management at Syracuse University, co-founded a Web data clearinghouse called TRAC, which has been tracking prosecutor referrals from virtually every federal agency for more than a decade. Using a barrage of Freedom of Information Act lawsuits, TRAC has been able to gather data buried in the Justice Department's own computer files (minus the individual case numbers that might be used to identify defendants). And the data, which follow each matter from referral to the prison steps, tell a story the Justice Department doesn't want you to know.

In the full ten years from 1992 to 2001, according to TRAC data, SEC enforcement attorneys referred 609 cases to the Justice Department for possible criminal charges. Of that number, U.S. Attorneys decided what to do on about 525 of the cases—declining to prosecute just over 64% of them. Of those they did press forward, the feds obtained guilty verdicts in a respectable 76%. But even then, some 40% of the convicted starched-collars didn't spend a day in jail. In case you're wondering, here's the magic number that did: 87.

FIVE-POINT TYPE IS SMALL PRINT, SO TINY THAT ALMOST everyone who remembers the Bay of Pigs or the fall of Saigon will need bifocals to read it. For those who love pulp fiction or

the crime blotters in their town weeklies, however, there is no better place to look than in the small print of the *Wall Street Journal*'s B section. Once a month, buried in the thick folds of newsprint, are bullet reports of the NASD's disciplinary actions. February's disclosures about alleged misbehavior, for example, range from the unseemly to the lurid—from an Ohio bond firm accused of systematically overcharging customers and fraudulently marking up trades to a California broker who deposited a client's $143,000 check in his own account. Two senior VPs of a Pittsburgh firm, say NASD officials, cashed out of stock, thanks to timely inside information they received about an upcoming loss; a Dallas broker reportedly converted someone's 401(k) rollover check to his personal use.

In all, the group's regulatory arm received 23,753 customer complaints against its registered reps between the years 1997 and 2000. After often extensive investigations, the NASD barred "for life" during this period 1,662 members and suspended another 1,000 or so for violations of its rules or of laws on the federal books. But despite its impressive 117-page *Sanction Guidelines*, the NASD can't do much of anything to its miscreant broker-dealers other than throw them out of the club. It has no statutory right to file civil actions against rule breakers, it has no subpoena power, and from the looks of things it can't even get the bums to return phone calls. Too often the disciplinary write-ups conclude with a boilerplate "failed to respond to NASD requests for information."

"That's a good thing when they default," says Barry Goldsmith, executive vice president for enforcement at NASD Regulation. "It gives us the ability to get the wrongdoers out quickly to prevent them from doing more harm."

Goldsmith won't say how many cases the NASD passes on to the SEC or to criminal prosecutors for further investigation. But he does acknowledge that the securities group refers a couple of hundred suspected insider-trading cases to its higher-ups in the regulatory chain.

Thus fails the first line of defense against white-collar crime: self-policing. The situation is worse, if anything, among accountants than it is among securities dealers, says John C. Coffee Jr., a Columbia Law School professor and a leading authority on securities enforcement issues. At the American Institute of Certified Public Accountants, he says, "no real effort is made to enforce the rules." Except one, apparently. "They have a rule that they do not take action against auditors until all civil litigation has been resolved," Coffee says, "because they don't want their actions to be used against their members in a civil suit." Lynn E. Turner, who until last summer was the SEC's chief accountant and is now a professor at Colorado State University, agrees. "The AICPA," he says, "often failed to discipline members in a timely fashion, if at all. And when it did, its most severe remedy was just to expel the member from the organization."

Al Anderson, senior VP of AICPA, says the criticism is unfounded. "We have been and always will be committed to enforcing the rules," he says. The next line of defense after the professional associations is the SEC. The central role of this independent regulatory agency is to protect investors in the financial markets by making sure that publicly traded companies

The Odds Against Doing Time

Regulators like to talk tough, but when it comes to actual punishment, all but a handful of Wall Street cheats get off with a slap on the wrist.

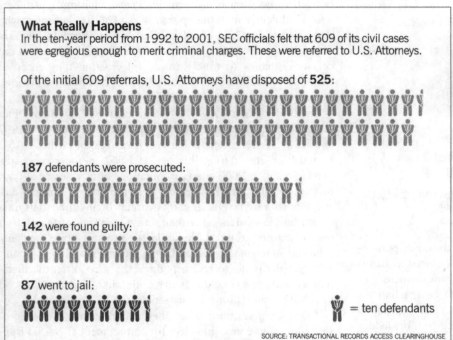

What Really Happens

In the ten-year period from 1992 to 2001, SEC officials felt that 609 of its civil cases were egregious enough to merit criminal charges. These were referred to U.S. Attorneys.

Of the initial 609 referrals, U.S. Attorneys have disposed of **525**:

187 defendants were prosecuted:

142 were found guilty:

87 went to jail:

= ten defendants

SOURCE: TRANSACTIONAL RECORDS ACCESS CLEARINGHOUSE

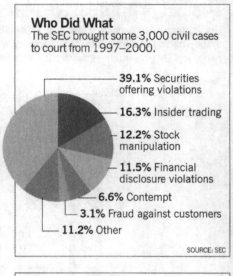

Who Did What

The SEC brought some 3,000 civil cases to court from 1997–2000.

- **39.1%** Securities offering violations
- **16.3%** Insider trading
- **12.2%** Stock manipulation
- **11.5%** Financial disclosure violations
- **6.6%** Contempt
- **3.1%** Fraud against customers
- **11.2%** Other

SOURCE: SEC

A Look at Self-Policing

Few complaints received last year by the NASD resulted in serious sanctions.

Registered reps	675,821
Customer complaints received	5,155
Individuals barred	466
Individuals suspended	346

SOURCE: NASD REGULATION

play by the rules. With jurisdiction over every constituent in the securities trade, from brokers to mutual funds to accountants to corporate filers, it would seem to be the voice of Oz. But the SEC's power, like that of the Wizard, lies more in persuasion than in punishment. The commission can force companies to comply with securities rules, it can fine them when they don't, it can even charge them in civil court with violating the law. But it can't drag anybody off to prison. To that end, the SEC's enforcement division must work with federal and state prosecutors—a game that often turns into weak cop/bad cop.

Nevertheless, the last commission chairman, Arthur Levitt, did manage to shake the ground with the power he had. For the 1997–2000 period, for instance, attorneys at the agency's enforcement division brought civil actions against 2,989 respondents. That figure includes 487 individual cases of alleged insider trading, 365 for stock manipulation, 343 for violations of laws and rules related to financial disclosure, 196 for contempt of the regulatory agency, and another 94 for fraud against customers. In other words, enough bad stuff to go around. What would make them civil crimes, vs. actual handcuff-and-fingerprint ones? Evidence, says one SEC regional director. "In a civil case you need only a preponderance of evidence that there was an intent to defraud," she says. "In a criminal case you have to prove that intent beyond a reasonable doubt."

When the SEC does find a case that smacks of criminal intent, the commission refers it to a U.S. Attorney. And that is where the second line of defense often breaks down. The SEC has the expertise to sniff out such wrongdoing but not the big stick of prison to wave in front of its targets. The U.S. Attorney's office has the power to order in the SWAT teams but often lacks the expertise—and, quite frankly, the inclination—to deconstruct a complex financial crime. After all, it is busy pursuing drug kingpins and terrorists.

And there is also the key issue of institutional kinship, say an overwhelming number of government authorities. U.S. Attorneys, for example, have kissing-cousin relationships with the agencies they work with most, the FBI and DEA. Prosecutors and investigators often work together from the start and know the elements required on each side to make a case stick. That is hardly true with the SEC and all but a handful of U.S. Attorneys around the country. In candid conversations, current and former regulators cited the lack of warm cooperation between the law-enforcement groups, saying one had no clue about how the other worked.

THIRTEEN BLOCKS FROM WALL STREET IS A DIFFERENT KIND of ground zero. Here, in the shadow of the imposing Federalist-style courthouses of lower Manhattan, is a nine-story stone fortress of indeterminate color, somewhere in the unhappy genus of waiting-room beige. As with every federal building these days, there are reminders of the threat of terrorism, but this particular outpost has taken those reminders to the status of a four-bell alarm. To get to the U.S. Attorney's office, a visitor must wind his way through a phalanx of blue police barricades, stop by a kiosk manned by a U.S. marshal, enter a giant white tent with police and metal detectors, and proceed to a bulletproof visitors desk, replete with armed guards. Even if you make it to the third floor, home of the Securities and Commodities Fraud Task Force, Southern District of New York, you'll need an electronic passkey to get in.

This, the office which Rudy Giuliani led to national prominence with his late-1980s busts of junk-bond king Michael Milken, Ivan Boesky, and the Drexel Burnham insider-trading ring, is one of the few outfits in the country that even know how to prosecute complex securities crimes. Or at least one of the few willing to take them on. Over the years it has become the favorite (and at times lone) repository for the SEC's enforcement hit list.

And how many attorneys are in this office to fight the nation's book cookers, insider traders, and other Wall Street thieves? Twenty-five—including three on loan from the SEC. The unit has a fraction of the paralegal and administrative help of even a small private law firm. Assistant U.S. Attorneys do their own copying, and in one recent sting it was Sandy—one of the unit's two secretaries—who did the records analysis that broke the case wide open.

Even this office declines to prosecute more than half the cases referred to it by the SEC. Richard Owens, the newly minted chief of the securities task force and a six-year veteran of the unit, insists that it is not for lack of resources. There are plenty of legitimate reasons, he says, why a prosecutor would choose not to pursue a case—starting with the possibility that there may not have been true criminal intent.

But many federal regulators scoff at such bravado. "We've got too many crooks and not enough cops," says one. "We could fill Riker's Island if we had the resources."

And Owens' office is as good as it gets in this country. In other cities, federal and state prosecutors shun securities cases for all kinds of understandable reasons. They're harder to pull off than almost any other type of case—and the payoff is rarely worth it from the standpoint of local political impact. "The typical state prosecution is for a standard common-law crime," explains Philip A. Feigin, an attorney with Rothgerber Johnson & Lyons in Denver and a former commissioner of the Colorado Securities Division. "An ordinary trial will probably last for five days, it'll have 12 witnesses, involve an act that occurred in one day, and was done by one person." Now hear the pitch coming from a securities regulator thousands of miles away. "Hi. We've never met, but I've got this case I'd like you to take on. The law that was broken is just 158 pages long. It involves only three years of conduct—and the trial should last no more than three months. What do you say?" The prosecutor has eight burglaries or drug cases he could bring in the time it takes to prosecute a single white-collar crime. "It's a completely easy choice," says Feigin.

That easy choice, sadly, has left a glaring logical—and moral—fallacy in the nation's justice system: Suite thugs don't go to jail because street thugs have to. And there's one more thing on which many crime experts are adamant. The double standard makes no sense whatsoever when you consider the damage done by the offense. Sociologist Pontell and his col-

leagues Kitty Calavita, at U.C. Irvine, and Robert Tillman, at New York's St. John's University, have demonstrated this in a number of compelling academic studies. In one the researchers compared the sentences received by major players (that is, those who stole $100,000 or more) in the savings-and-loan scandal a decade ago with the sentences handed to other types of nonviolent federal offenders. The starched-collar S&L crooks got an average of 36.4 months in the slammer. Those who committed burglary—generally swiping $300 or less—got 55.6 months; car thieves, 38 months; and first-time drug offenders, 64.9 months. Now compare the costs of the two kinds of crime: The losses from all bank robberies in the U.S. in 1992 *totaled* $35 million, according to the FBI's Uniform Crime Reports. That's about 1% of the estimated cost of Charles Keating's fraud at Lincoln Savings & Loan.

"Nobody writes an e-mail that says, 'Gee, I think I'll screw the public today.' There's never been a fraud of passion."

"OF ALL THE FACTORS THAT LEAD TO CORPORATE CRIME, NONE comes close in importance to the role top management plays in tolerating, even shaping, a culture that allows for it," says William Laufer, the director of the Zicklin Center for Business Ethics Research at the Wharton School. Laufer calls it "winking." And with each wink, nod, and nudge-nudge, instructions of a sort are passed down the management chain. Accounting fraud, for example, often starts in this way. "Nobody writes an e-mail that says, 'Gee, I think I'll screw the public today,'" says former regulator Feigin. "There's never been a fraud of passion. These things take years." They breed slowly over time.

So does the impetus to fight them. Enron, of course, has stirred an embarrassed Administration and Congress to action. But it isn't merely Enron that worries legislators and the public—it's *another* Enron. Every day brings news of one more accounting gas leak that for too long lay undetected. Wariness about Lucent, Rite Aid, Raytheon, Tyco, and a host of other big names has left investors not only rattled but also questioning the very integrity of the financial reporting system.

And with good reason. Two statistics in particular suggest that no small degree of executive misconduct has been brewing in the corporate petri dish. In 1999 and 2000 the SEC demanded 96 restatements of earnings or other financial statements—a figure that was more than in the previous nine years combined. Then, in January, the Federal Deposit Insurance Corp. announced more disturbing news. The number of publicly traded companies declaring bankruptcy shot up to a record 257, a stunning 46% over the prior year's total, which itself had been a record. These companies shunted $259 billion in assets into protective custody—that is, away from shareholders. And a record 45 of these losers were biggies, companies with assets greater than $1 billion. That might all seem normal in a time of burst bubbles and economic recession. But the number of nonpublic bankruptcies has barely risen. Regulators and plaintiffs lawyers say both restatements and sudden public bankruptcies often signal the presence of fraud.

The ultimate cost could be monumental. "Integrity of the markets, and the willingness of people to invest, are critical to us," says Harvey J. Goldschmid, a professor of law at Columbia since 1970 and soon to be an SEC commissioner. "Widespread false disclosure would be incredibly dangerous. People could lose trust in corporate filings altogether."

So will all this be enough to spark meaningful changes in the system? Professor Coffee thinks the Enron matter might move Congress to take action. "I call it the phenomenon of crash-then-law," he says. "You need three things to get a wave of legislation and litigation: a recession, a stock market crash, and a true villain." For instance, Albert Wiggin, head of Chase National Bank, cleaned up during the crash of 1929 by short-selling his own company stock. "From that came a new securities law, Section 16(b), that prohibits short sales by executives," Coffee says.

But the real issue isn't more laws on the books—it's enforcing the ones that are already there. And that, says criminologist Kip Schlegel, is where the government's action falls far short of the rhetoric. In his 1994 study on securities law-breaking for the Justice Department, Schlegel found that while officials were talking tough about locking up insider traders, there was little evidence to suggest that the punishments imposed—either the incarceration rates or the sentences themselves—were more severe. "In fact," he says, "the data suggest the opposite trend. The government lacks the will to bring these people to justice."

DENNY CRAWFORD SAYS THERE'S AN ALL-TOO-SIMPLE REASON for this. The longtime commissioner of the Texas Securities Board, who has probably put away more bad guys than any other state commissioner, says most prosecutors make the crimes too complicated. "You've got to boil it down to lying, cheating, and stealing," she says, in a warbly voice that sounds like pink lemonade. "That's all it is—the best way to end securities fraud is to put every one of these crooks in jail."

Trust and Confidence in Criminal Justice

by Lawrence W. Sherman

Criminal justice in America today is a paradox of progress: While the fairness and effectiveness of criminal justice have improved, public trust and confidence apparently have not.

Criminal justice is far less corrupt, brutal, and racially unfair than it has been in the past. It is arguably more effective at preventing crime. It has far greater diversity in its staffing. Yet these objectively defined improvements seem to have had little impact on American attitudes toward criminal justice.

Understanding this paradox—better work but low marks—is central to improving public trust and confidence in the criminal justice system.

How Low Is Public Confidence?

Gallup polls over the last few years have consistently found that Americans have less confidence in the criminal justice system than in other institutions, such as banking, the medical system, public schools, television news, newspapers, big business,and organized labor.[1]

The most striking finding in the Gallup poll is the difference between the low evaluation of "criminal justice" and the high evaluation given to the police and the Supreme Court. Other sources of data show similar attitudes: Confidence in local courts and prisons is far lower than it is for the police.[2] These large differences suggest that Americans may not think of police in the same way as they do the criminal justice system.

The Racial Divide

A 1998 Gallup poll reports little overall demographic difference among the respondents saying they had confidence in the criminal justice system. But what is most clear is the difference in opinion between whites and blacks about the individual components of the criminal justice system and especially the police. Whites express considerably more confidence in the police, local court

system, and State prison system than blacks (see exhibit 1).

Race, Victimization, and Punishment. Racial differences also appear in rates of victimization and punishment: Blacks are 31 percent more likely to be victimized by personal crime than whites and twice as likely as whites to suffer a completed violent crime.[3]

The personal opinions of the survey respondents are consistent with a major theory about the declining public confidence in all government— not just criminal justice—in all modern nations, not just the United States. The concerns arise from the decline of hierarchy and the rise of equality in all walks of life. The rise in egalitarian culture increases the demand for government officials to show more respect to citizens.

Young black males are historically 10 times more likely to be murdered than white males.[4]

Arrest rates for robbery are five times higher for blacks than for whites; four times higher for murder and rape; and three times higher for drug violations and weapons possession.[5]

Blacks are eight times more likely to be in a State or Federal prison than non-Hispanic whites (and three times more likely than Hispanic whites). Almost 2 percent of the black population, or 1 of every 63 blacks, was in prison in 1996.[6]

Race and Neighborhood. What these data fail to show, however, is the extent to which the racial differences in

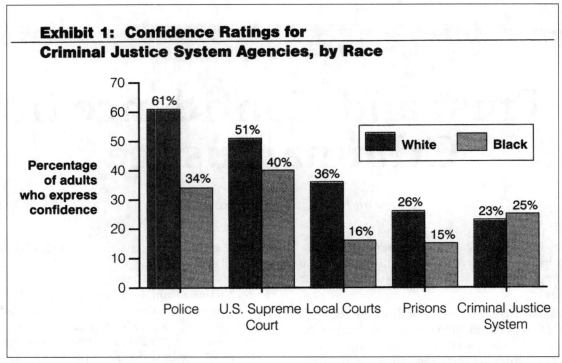

Exhibit 1: Confidence Ratings for Criminal Justice System Agencies, by Race

Source: The Gallup Organization, "Confidence In Institutions," Retrieved From The WORLD WIDE WEB SITE HTTP://WWW.GALLUP.COM, October 10, 2000.

attitudes, victimization, and punishment may be largely related to more blacks being the residents of a small number of high-crime, high-poverty areas concentrated in a small fraction of urban neighborhoods. This is the case even though Harvard University sociologist Orlando Patterson has estimated that only 1 in every 30 black adults resides in these high-crime, high-poverty areas; the proportion is higher for children.

What we may understand as a problem of race in America may largely reflect conditions in those neighborhoods that are generalized by both blacks and whites to conditions of the larger society.

Due to limited national data, it is difficult to determine what precisely drives the lower levels of confidence in criminal justice among blacks, but insights from city-by-city analysis suggest two conclusions:

- **There is no race-based subculture of violence.** Blacks and whites who live in neighborhoods with similar conditions have similar views on the legitimacy of law. To the extent that race is associated with attitudes toward law, it may be a reflection of the greater likelihood that blacks reside in poverty areas.
- **There is no race-based hostility to police in high-crime areas.** High levels of dissatisfaction with police are endemic to high-crime areas. Whites residing in such areas express attitudes just as hostile as blacks toward police.[7] The distrust of police in high-crime areas may be related to the prevalence of crime rather than to

police practice. If negative attitudes are driven by police practice, it may be because those practices fail to prevent crime rather than because police presence or behavior is excessive. Or it may be that the practice of policing in such areas offers less recognition and dignity to citizen consumers than is found in lower crime areas.

Strong Demands for Change

The findings and responses from a random digit-dialing telephone survey of 4,000 residents of 10 northeastern States in 1998 found that more than 80 percent—four out of five respondents—preferred the idea of "totally revamping the way the [criminal justice] system works" for violent crime; 75 percent said the same for all crime.[8] The responses varied little from State to State or from one demographic group to another. The majority of respondents believed that:

- Victims are not accorded sufficient rights in the criminal justice process.
- Victims are not informed enough about the status of their cases.
- Victims are not able to talk to prosecutors enough.
- Victims should be able to tell the court what impact the crime had on them, but most victims do not get that chance.

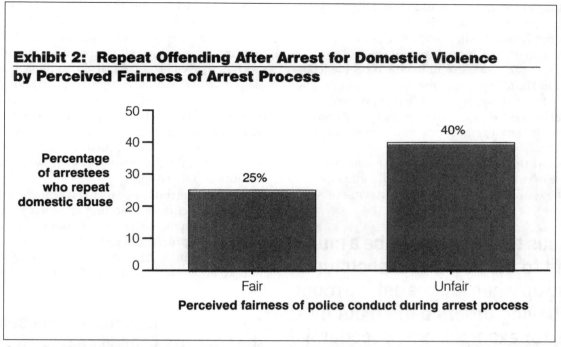

Exhibit 2: Repeat Offending After Arrest for Domestic Violence by Perceived Fairness of Arrest Process

Percentage of arrestees who repeat domestic abuse

25% (Fair)   40% (Unfair)

Perceived fairness of police conduct during arrest process

Source: Paternoster, R., R. Brame, R. Bachman, and L. W. Sherman, "Do Fair Procedures Matter? The Effect of Procedural Justice on Spousal Assault," *Law & Society Review*, 31(1997): 185.

- Offenders, even if jailed, should reimburse victims for the cost of the crime.
- Offenders should acknowledge their responsibility for the crime.
- Victims should have the opportunity to meet with the offender to find out why the crime occurred and to learn whether the offender accepted responsibility.
- Ordinary citizens, not courts, should set penalties for non-violent crimes.
- Drug treatment should be used more widely for drug-using offenders.

The personal opinions of the survey respondents are consistent with a major theory about the declining public confidence in all government—not just criminal justice—in all modern nations, not just the United States. The concerns arise from the decline of hierarchy and the rise of equality in all walks of life. The rise in egalitarian culture increases the demand for government officials to show more respect to citizens.[9]

Egalitarianism in Modern Culture: Raised Expectations, Reduced Trust

Americans' trust in government has declined sharply in the last quarter century.[10] A similar loss of trust has been found in 18 other democracies. Citizens now expect higher levels of recognition, respect, and status from the government. Criminal justice serves as a flash point for this change in citizen attitudes because so many

Americans have contact with the criminal justice system and because the hierarchical design of criminal justice institutions juxtaposes so starkly with the egalitarian demands of the public.

As the spread of equality has combined with growing freedom from want, political culture has shifted away from Puritan views of a *hierarchical* communal democracy to Quaker views of a more *egalitarian* individualistic democracy. Indeed, the consistently greater support for police than for courts may result from a perception of police as egalitarian individualists (the new cultural ideal) while judges are seen as bossy conformists (the outdated ideal).

The massive three-decade decline of public trust in liberal democratic governments suggests a deeper paradox of success: As democracies become more materially successful and better educated, the perceived need for governance declines and expectations of government for appropriate conduct increase.[11] The crisis of government legitimacy has thus been prompted less by declining quality of government conduct than by increasing public dissatisfaction with institutions in general, driven by what Ronald F. Inglehart, Professor, University of Michigan, calls "postmaterialist values."[12]

Social changes taking place around the globe appear to be resulting in challenges to the legitimacy of virtually all forms of social hierarchy of authority (although not hierarchy of wealth)—of husbands over wives, doctors over patients, schoolteachers over students and parents, parents over children, and government officials over citizens. This evolution may have led to widespread preference for the recognition of individual dignity over the recognition of communal authority.[13]

Thus, what Robert J. Sampson, Professor of Sociology, University of Chicago, and other scholars refer to as "legal cynicism"—the extent to which people feel that laws are not binding—is not the product of a criminal subculture.[14] It is a 400-year-old Christian political theology that has become globally accepted across people of all religions in a more egalitarian and individualistic modern culture.

In such a world, people are less likely to obey the law out of a sense of communal obligation, and more likely to obey laws they support through a personal sense of what is moral.

Consensus thus appears to be a much better fit to the new political culture. Standing up when judges enter a room and obeying orders barked out by police, for example, are procedural forms that may imply officials are more important than citizens. Such forms may do more to undermine legal trust than to build respect for the law.

Trust and Recognition

What changing culture may be creating is a world in which people trust *laws* but not *legal institutions*. This new world may be one in which trust in criminal justice is no longer automatic; it must be earned everyday, with each encounter between legal agents and citizens.

The research of Tom R. Tyler, Department of Psychology, New York University, shows that Americans—especially members of minority groups—are extremely sensitive to the respect they perceive and the procedures employed when they come into contact with criminal justice.[15] Tyler's evidence suggests that in building citizen trust in the legal system, it may matter less whether you receive the speeding ticket than whether the police officer addresses you politely or rudely during the traffic stop. Similarly, sentencing guidelines that punish possession of crack more harshly than possession of powdered cocaine may discriminate against blacks. But dissatisfaction may be greater with some police officers engaged in drug enforcement who treat suspects and arrestees like people who are enemies rather than like people who are equal fellow citizens.

Tyler concludes that the procedural justice perceived in treatment by legal officials affects the level of trust citizens have in government.[16] That level of trust, in turn, affects the pride we have in our government and the

degree to which we feel we are respected by other members of our democracy—including the government.

Tyler further concludes that the odds of citizens reaching the conclusion that the law is morally right are much higher when citizens feel that the law has given each of them adequate recognition and respect.

Rather than creating a willingness to *defer* to the power of the law, Tyler suggests that respectful treatment creates a stronger *consensus* about what is moral and what the law must be. The consensus model assumes more equality than the deference model on which our legal institutions were designed.[17]

Consensus thus appears to be a much better fit to the new political culture. Standing up when judges enter a room and obeying orders barked out by police, for example, are procedural forms that may imply officials are more important than citizens. Such forms may do more to undermine legal trust than to build respect for the law.

Fitting Legal Institutions to the Culture: The Canberra Experiments

For all Americans, regardless of race, the central cause of declining trust may be the misfit of hierarchical legal institutions in an egalitarian culture. In many ways, citizens may experience the conduct of judges, prosecutors, and police as being overly "bossy" and unnecessarily authoritarian.

Results of experiments in Canberra, Australia, suggest that an egalitarian, consensual procedure of stakeholder citizens deciding the sentence for a crime creates more legitimacy in the eyes of both offenders and victims than the hierarchical, deferential process of sentencing by a judge.[18]

The experiments compared traditional court sentencing of youthful violent and property offenders to an alternative community justice conference making the same decisions.

Offenders who were sent to conferences were far less likely than offenders who were sent to traditional court to say that they were pushed around; disadvantaged by their age, income, or education; treated as if they were untrustworthy; or not listened to. They also were more likely to report that their experience increased their respect for the justice system and the police, as well as their feeling that the crime they had committed was morally wrong.

Victims also were far more satisfied with community justice conferences than with court proceedings. Much of this difference may be because most victims of criminals sent to court were never informed of the offenders' court appearances, either before or after sentencing. The victims invited to community justice conferences with offenders, in sharp contrast, gained increased trust in police and justice, as well as decreased fear of and anger

Alternative Community Justice Conferences

In the Canberra experiments, the police invite victims, offenders, and their respective supporters to a meeting in which the offenders must not—for these purposes—dispute their guilt. At the meetings, everyone sits in a circle to discuss the harm the crime has caused, acknowledge the pain and emotional impact of that harm, and deliberate democratically as to how the offenders should repair that harm.

The egalitarian proceedings begin with the police officer moderating the proceedings, offering only questions, not answers. For example, what did the offender do? How did it hurt the victim? How does the victim feel about that hurt? How do the victim's friends and family feel? How do the offender's family and friends feel about what has been said? What would be the right way for the offender to repay the debt to the victim and to society? Does everyone agree? Is there anything the offender wants to say to the victim (sometimes the offender says "I'm sorry")? Is there anything the victim wants to say to the offender (possibly "I forgive you")?

One of the most important parts of the proceedings is that everyone is allowed to talk, just as in a Quaker meeting, but no one person dominates speech, as might happen in a Calvinist church or in an Anglo-American courtroom. Emotions can be intense at the conferences—unlike the restraint valued by Puritan cultures and Western courts.

No Lawyers. Lawyers are not allowed to attend the conferences as legal advocates for either an offender or the State, although they may attend as personal supporters. They are always on call, ready to act to protect anyone whose rights may seem abused. But as long as the victim-offender consensus is under discussion, everyone in the circle has equal authority, regardless of age or education.

Extra Time Required. A community justice conference takes, on average, about 70 minutes to resolve. A similar case in traditional court may take 10 minutes spread across several different appearances, which have no emotional significance for victim or offender, and thus leave citizens feeling like cogs in a wheel. A community justice conference is about the people present rather than the legal formalities. People come only once, prepared to stay until the case is resolved.

Trust in Justice. Research shows that sentences imposed in the community justice conferences and the traditional court process were fairly similar despite the major differences in the decision making procedures employed.[1] But the conferences produced far better results in terms of citizen respect for legal institutions.

[1]Sherman, L.W., H. Strang, and G.C. Barnes, "Stratification of Justice: Legitimacy of Hierarchical and Egalitarian Sentencing Procedures," unpublished manuscript, Fels Center of Government, University of Pennsylvania, 1999.

at the offender. (For more details, see "Alternative Community Justice Conferences.")

Building Trust One Case at a Time

The Canberra experiments suggest the highly personal nature of citizen trust in criminal justice. The *personal* legitimacy of legal agents may depend on a leveling of distinctions in rank between citizen and official.

As Albert J. Reiss, Jr., Professor Emeritus, Sociology Department, Yale University, observed, the legitimacy of police authority in the eyes of citizens varies widely from one situation to the next.[19] Thus, officials must earn the legitimacy of their authority one case at a time.

The most dramatic demonstration of this principle is the finding that *how* police make arrests for domestic violence affects the rate of repeat offending. Raymond Paternoster, Ph.D., University of Maryland, et al. demonstrated that offenders who were arrested for domestic violence and who perceived that the police officers' arresting procedures were fair were less likely to repeat

the offense than offenders who perceived the arresting procedures as unfair.[20] Actions that constituted "procedural justice" included the police taking the time to listen to both the offender and the victim, not handcuffing the offender in front of the victim, and not using physical force.

As exhibit 2 shows, the risk of repeat offending was 40 percent for offenders who had a low perception of police procedural fairness, but only 25 percent for those who perceived a high level of police fairness. The estimate of offending risk took prior levels of violence into account; hence the findings shown in exhibit 2 increase our confidence that *how* the police make an arrest may affect the crime rate (much of which comes from repeat offending)—through trust and confidence in the criminal justice system.

Reducing Complaints Against Police. Other tests of the hypothesis that trust in criminal justice comes from egalitarian procedures can be seen in actions that have been shown to reduce complaints against police.

In sum, a growing body of theory and evidence suggests that it is not the fairness or effectiveness of decisions criminal justice officials make that determines the public's level of trust. Changes in modern culture have made the *procedures* and manners of criminal justice officials far more important to public trust and left officials out of step with modern culture.

In the 42nd and 44th precincts in The Bronx, complaints reached a 10-year high in 1996. But after the precinct commanders instituted a program to promote respectful policing and improve police relations with community residents, complaints dropped dramatically. Among the elements of the new program was vigorous training for officers on how to treat citizens respectfully, zealous monitoring of complaints, and follow through with consequences for officers who received complaints.

In addition, the simple elimination of the precinct's high desk and bar in front of the desk in the reception area helped the precinct present a less hierarchical face to the community. Research on the effects of the strategy, conducted by the Vera Institute of Justice, found that citizens began to perceive the police as responsive to community concerns.[21]

The second test of the procedural equality theory comes from a community with a population of almost one million; 55 percent of the population is African American.

Complaints dropped in this department of 1,400 officers when a new procedure for traffic stops was initiated in 1997–99. The procedure, called "Take Away Guns" (TAG), was one part of a larger strategy to reduce gun violence. One of the first steps the department took was to increase traffic enforcement—a 400-some percent increase—so that police had an opportunity to explain the program at each traffic stop and distribute a letter from the district police captain explaining the program. The letter contained the captain's phone number and invited citizens to call the captain with complaints or questions. Officers were trained to be very polite in explaining the program to drivers and then asking permission to search the car for guns.

The program not only received a high rate of compliance with the requests, but also received praise from the drivers stopped who approved of the efforts to get guns off the street. Over the first 2 years of the program, both gun violence and citizen complaints of excessive force by police dropped substantially.

In sum, a growing body of theory and evidence suggests that it is not the fairness or effectiveness of decisions criminal justice officials make that determines the public's level of trust. Changes in modern culture have made the *procedures* and manners of criminal justice officials far more important to public trust and left officials out of step with modern culture.

This explanation gains further support from scholarship on the effect of television and other communications media on the nature of authority and trust in government. For despite Tyler's focus on personal contacts with criminal justice, most citizens have little if any personal contact with legal officials. For this majority of Americans, the level of trust in criminal justice may depend on what they hear about criminal justice encounters with other citizens, a little-studied area. But it also may depend on how legal agencies are portrayed in entertainment and news media.

Authority and Media Celebrity

The future authority of the criminal justice system may well depend on how the system appears not just to those directly involved in the system, but to all citizens. That, in turn, may depend heavily on how criminal justice manages its image in the electronic media. Legal historian Lawrence Friedman notes that modern culture has changed the very nature of authority from *vertical* (where people look up to leaders in high position) to *horizontal* (where people look in to the center of society to find leaders who are celebrities, defined by the number of people who recognize their names and faces). "Leaders are no longer distant, awesome, and unknown; they are familiar figures on TV…. The horizontal society is [one in which] the men and women who get and hold power become celebrities" and the public come to know them, or think they know them, through the media. "By contrast," Friedman writes, "traditional authority was vertical, and the higher up the authority, the more stern, distant, and remote it was."[22]

A celebrity culture creates still another paradox: Americans now feel more personal connections with celebrities living far away than they do with legal officials in their own hometown. Just as many people felt more emotional loss at the death of Princess Diana than at the death of a neighbor, the celebrity culture makes us feel personal connections to people we do not know.

Thus, for all the programs designed to foster community policing or community prosecution with legal officials in the neighborhood, Americans still are more likely to form their impressions of criminal justice from vicarious contact through friends or through television shows than from personal experience with their own legal system. The evidence is clear: On a Wednesday night when police convene a neighborhood meeting in a church basement, more local residents are home watching television than attending the meeting.

We may well ask if there are any celebrities of American criminal justice, and if so, who they are—The Chief Justice of the Supreme Court? The director of the FBI? Probably not. These positions appear to fit Friedman's characteristics of traditional authority: stern, distant, and remote. Television's Judge Judy, on the other hand, is an internationally recognized celebrity, with far greater name-face recognition than the traditional authority figures.

Unfortunately, the entertainment values of the television business conflict with the core values of legal institutions. What sells TV audiences is conflict and putdowns, tools Judge Judy uses to portray a rude, in-your-face (but perhaps egalitarian), power-control image of the bench. Audiences find this fun to watch, although Judge Judy may confirm their worst fears, leaving them reluctant to have anything to do with the legal system.

The difficulty in using celebrity power to send messages about the trustworthiness of criminal justice is the clash of cultures between law and entertainment. The reticence of the legal culture conflicts with the chattiness of celebrity culture.

One can imagine a legal official appearing weekly on a talk show with a huge audience, saying things that could help shore up public faith in criminal justice as an egalitarian and fair system. One can equally imagine such a strategy being condemned by leaders of the American Bar Association, conservative journalists, and other defenders of traditional remoteness of authority.

The kind of public education programs that legal culture would approve of—such as tasteful PBS specials or public service announcements on radio and television—would seem unlikely to reach much of the public, let alone those citizens most distrustful of the system.

Portraying Values in the Media

The media often portray criminal justice through a morality play that explores themes of what Elijah Anderson, Charles and William L. Day Professor, Sociology Department, University of Pennsylvania, calls "street" and "decent" values. Based on years of field research in high-crime areas of Philadelphia, Anderson has observed people who exhibit "decent" values as patient, hopeful, respectful of authority, and with a belief in the predictability of punishment. Those who exhibit "street" values take on a bitter, impatient, antisystem outlook that is disrespectful of authority and demanding of deference.[23]

Television dramas that portray a hero's impatience with red tape may glorify the "street" enforcement of vengeance and personal respect. TV interviewers who

ask officials provocative and insulting questions may reflect an effort to produce a "street" response.

The paradox of such media portrayals is that the more frequently legal officials are portrayed breaking the official rules out of distrust for "decent" government, the less reason the public has to believe the criminal justice system will treat citizens decently. By showing criminal justice agents pursuing street values, the media may create a self-fulfilling prophecy, defining conduct for legal officials and the public alike.

The research on respect for authority suggests that street sanctioning styles interact with different kinds of citizen personalities in ways that produce the following differences in repeat offending:

- Decent sanctioning of "decent" people produces the lowest repeat offending.
- Street sanctioning of "decent" people produces higher repeat offending.
- Decent sanctioning of "street" people may produce even higher repeat offending.
- Street sanctioning of "street" people produces the highest levels of repeat offending.[24]

The research on respect for authority consistently suggests that when people in positions of authority impose "street" attitudes or sanctions, the reaction is almost always negative. It is more productive for criminal justice officials to show more respect to, and take more time to listen to, citizens. To the extent that this message is portrayed in entertainment media and identified with celebrity authority, the criminal justice system might be able to increase its public trust and confidence. Yet to the extent that "decent" values are themselves communicated in an illegitimate way, it will be difficult to foster a more "decent" legal culture.

Half a century ago and half a world away, a French journalist observed during a 2-month tour of China in the early 1950's that police had become far more polite under Mao's early communism:

> In the olden days the Peking police were renowned for their brutality, and pedestrians frequently suffered at their hands, smacks in the face being the least form of violence offered them. Today they are formally forbidden to use any kind of force. Their instructions are to explain, to make people understand, to convince them.[25]

It may be easier to change official conduct in a dictatorship than in a democracy, but the power of electronic media may make the dynamics totally different today. Electronic communications comprise a highly democratized, free-market institution that cannot be manipulated easily for official purposes. But the media can be avenue in which celebrity power is built and put to use in fostering support for "decent" styles of criminal justice, both in the image and the reality of how criminal justice works.

The Domains of Public Trust

Three major domains appear to affect public trust and confidence in criminal justice:

- The conduct and practices of the criminal justice system.
- The changing values and expectations of the culture the system serves.
- The images of the system presented in electronic media.

Changes in each domain affect the others. Trust, as the product of all three combined, is likely to increase only when changes in all three domains can be aligned to create practices and values that are perceived to be fair, inclusive, and trustworthy.

Discovering how that can be made to happen is a daunting task. But the data suggest that fairness builds trust in criminal justice, and trust builds compliance with law. Thus what is fairer is more effective, and to be effective it is necessary to be fair.

Notes

1. Retrieved from the World Wide Web site http://www.gallup.com, October 10, 2000.
2. Maguire, K., and A. Pastore, eds., *Sourcebook of Criminal Justice Statistics, 1997*, Washington, DC: U.S. Department of Justice, Bureau of Justice Statistics, 1998 (NCJ 171147).
3. Maguire and Pastore, *Sourcebook*, 182, see note 2.
4. Reiss, A.J., Jr., and J. Roth, *Understanding and Preventing Violence*, Washington, DC: National Academy of Sciences, 1993: 64 (NCJ 140290).
5. Hacker, A., *Two Nations: Black and White, Separate, Hostile, and Unequal*, New York: Free Press, 1992: 181.
6. Maguire and Pastore, *Sourcebook*, 494, see note 2.
7. Sampson, R., and D. Bartusch, "Legal Cynicism and Subcultural Tolerance of Deviance: The Neighborhood Context of Racial Differences," *Law & Society Review*, 32 (4) (1999): 777–804.
8. Boyle, J.M., *Crime Issues in the Northeast: Statewide Surveys of the Public and Crime Victims in Connecticut, Delaware, Maine, Massachusetts, Vermont, New Hampshire, New Jersey, New York, and Rhode Island*, Silver Spring, MD: Schulman, Ronca, and Bucuvalas, Inc., 1999.
9. Fukuyama, F., *The End of History and the Last Man*, New York: Free Press, 1992.
10. Orren, G., "Fall From Grace: The Public's Loss of Faith in the Government," in *Why People Don't Trust Government*, eds. J.S. Nye, Jr.,

11. Fukuyama, *The End of History*, see note 9; Heclo, H., "The Sixties' False Dawn: Awakenings, Movements, and Postmodern Policymaking," *Journal of Policy History*, 8 (1996): 50–58; Balogh, B., "Introduction," *Journal of Policy History*, 8 (1996): 25.
12. Inglehart, R., "Postmaterialist Values and the Erosion of Institutional Authority," in *Why People Don't Trust Government*, eds. J.S. Nye, Jr., P.D. Zelikow, and D.C. King, Cambridge, MA: Harvard University Press, 1997.
13. Baltzell, E.D., *Puritan Boston and Quaker Philadelphia: Two Protestant Ethics and the Spirit of Class Authority and Leadership*, New York: Free Press, 1979.
14. Sampson and Bartusch, "Legal Cynicism and Subcultural Tolerance of Deviance," see note 7.
15. Tyler, T., *Why People Obey the Law*, New Haven, CT: Yale University Press, 1990; Tyler, T., "Trust and Democratic Governance," in *Trust and Governance*, eds. V. Braithwaite and M. Levi, New York: Russell Sage Foundation, 1998.
16. Tyler, "Trust and Democratic Governance," see note 15.
17. Baltzell, *Puritan Boston*, 369, see note 13.
18. See details of the Reintegrative Shaming Experiments project at http://www.aic.gov.au/rjustice/rise.
19. Reiss and Roth, *Understanding and Preventing Violence*, 2, 3, 59–65, see note 4.
20. Paternoster, R., R. Brame, R.Bachman, and L.W. Sherman, "Do Fair Procedures Matter? The Effect of Procedural Justice on Spouse Assault," *Law & Society Review*, 31 (1997): 185.
21. A more complete description of the Vera Institute of Justice study can be found in *NIJ Journal*, July 2000, p. 24, http://www.ncjrs.org/pdffiles1/jr000244f.pdf. The authors' presentation of findings also is available on videotape from NCJRS (NCJ 181106).
22. Friedman, L., *The Horizontal Society*, New Haven, CT: Yale University Press, 1999: 14–15.
23. Anderson, E., *Crime and Justice*, Chicago: Chicago University Press, 1999.
24. Just how much harmful impact "street" conduct by agents of criminal justice can have has been revealed by experimental and quasi-experimental research on diverse situations using different levels of analysis. See, for example, Nisbett, R.E., and D. Cohen, *Culture of Honor: The Psychology of Violence in the South*, Boulder, CO: Westview Press, 1996: 46–48; Raine, A., P. Brennan, and S.A. Mednick, "Birth Complications Combined With Early Maternal Rejection at Age 1 Year Predispose to Violent Crime at Age 18 Years," *Archives of General Psychiatry*, 51 (1994): 986; Greenberg, J., "Employee Theft as a Reaction to Underpayment Inequity: The Hidden Costs of Pay Cuts," *Journal of Applied Psychology*, 75 (1990): 561–568; Makkai, T., and J. Braithwaite, "Reintegrative Shaming and Compliance With Regulatory Standards," *Criminology*, 32 (1994): 361–385.
25. de Segonzac, A., *Visa for Peking*, London: Heinemann, 1956.

about the author

Lawrence W. Sherman is the Albert M. Greenfield Professor of Human Relations and Director of the Jerry Lee Center of Criminology at the University of Pennsylvania. Contact him at 3814 Walnut Street, Philadelphia, PA 19104, 215-898-9216, lws@pobox.upenn.edu.

From *National Institute of Justice Journal*, Number 248, 2002 pp. 22–31. Published by Office of Justice/U.S. Department of Justice.

Dirty bomber?
DIRTY JUSTICE

According to John Ashcroft's Justice Department, even U.S.
citizens are not entitled to their constitutional right to legal representation.

by Lewis Z. Koch

ON MAY 8, 2002, 31-YEAR-old Brooklyn-born Jose Padilla was arrested by FBI agents at Chicago's O'Hare International Airport and held as a witness in connection with the September 11, 2001, attacks.

Speaking at a special news conference in Moscow a month later, U.S. Attorney General John Ashcroft accused Padilla of being a new kind of terrorist bomber. Ashcroft professed no doubts and offered no equivocation—just a flat out accusation: "We have captured a known terrorist who was exploring a plan to build and explode a radiological dispersion device, or 'dirty bomb,' in the United States." Ashcroft said the arrest of Padilla "disrupted an unfolding terrorist plot," one that could have caused "mass death and injury." President George W. Bush accused Padilla of "conduct in preparation for acts of international terrorism" and declared him an "enemy combatant." Using the little understood USA Patriot Act, Padilla was denied access to an attorney.

In a matter of minutes, the 40-plus-year history of Miranda rights was swept away. At the time of this writing, Padilla is still sitting in a cell at the Consolidated Naval Brig in Charleston, South Carolina, subject to an unknown number of hours or days or months of questioning, ignorant of his legal rights and the charges against him, and without the advice of an attorney. The government contends Padilla falls under a special exception to the Constitution, but a host of legal scholars feel otherwise.

You have the right ...

Anyone with a television set is familiar with Miranda rights; they've been repeated on thousands of cop shows: "You have the right to remain silent. Anything you say can and will be used against you in a court of law. You have the right to speak to an attorney, and to have an attorney present during any questioning. If you cannot afford a lawyer, one will be provided for you at government expense." The Miranda warning stems from the 1960 case of Clarence Earl Gideon, a two-bit criminal charged and convicted of breaking and entering the Bay Harbor Poolroom in Panama City, Flor-

ida, and stealing some coins and wine. The Supreme Court decided that Gideon had been wrongly denied the right to a lawyer in his criminal trial.

Six years later, the Supreme Court applied similar principles to Ernesto Miranda, a man arrested and accused of kidnapping and raping a mildly retarded 18-year-old woman. The court ruled Miranda deserved to have an attorney present at his questioning.

Never before in the history of the Justice Department, or solely through an assertion by the attorney general, has an American citizen been deliberately deprived of his rights.

Thus, one would surely think that in 2002 a man publicly described by the attorney general of the United States as a "known terrorist," whose arrest disrupted an unfolding plot to attack the United States by exploding a dirty bomb, would be entitled to legal counsel.

As Pulitzer Prize-winning journalist Anthony Lewis asked in an April 20, 2003, *New York Times* magazine article, who but an advocate for Padilla could challenge Ashcroft's statement? Who but Padilla's lawyer could challenge the news media to test the truth of the accusation? By denying Padilla an attorney, Ashcroft's comments amounted to "conviction by government announcement," Lewis wrote.

In light of the threat from Al Qaeda, exactly how far should the government be allowed to go in denying its citizens constitutional guarantees and rights? How far is too far? Should Jose Padilla, an untried, unconvicted, alleged dirty bomber, be denied his constitutional rights and guarantees? As an enemy combatant, is Padilla in the same class as foreign soldiers captured in Afghanistan and now held for questioning and perhaps military tribunals at Guantanamo Bay?

The Sixth Amendment employs clear and precise language: "In all criminal prosecutions, the accused shall enjoy the right to a speedy and public trial, by an impartial jury of the state and district wherein the crime shall have been committed . . . and to be informed of the nature and cause of the accusation; to be confronted with the witnesses against him; to have compulsory process for obtaining witnesses in his favor, and to have the assistance of counsel for his defense."

Padilla has not had a speedy public trial nor is it known if he has been fairly confronted with the nature of the charges against him—nor has he had "the assistance of counsel for his defense." Never before in the history of the Justice Department, or solely through an assertion by the attorney general, has an American citizen been deliberately deprived of these rights.

A likely suspect?

Who is Jose Padilla? Does he possess the intellectual sophistication and the organizational skills to gather a half dozen capable thieves, including at least one person with enough knowledge in nuclear engineering, to successfully obtain enough radioactive material, fuse it with explosives, and detonate a dirty bomb?

Born October 18, 1970, in Brooklyn, New York, Padilla moved with his family to Chicago when he was four. His childhood nickname was *Pucho*—Spanish for "Pudgy." He enjoyed playing basketball and spent time studying, according to those who lived in his Logan Square neighborhood. But starting in the mid-1980s, Padilla built up a substantial police record and associated himself with the Latin Disciples street gang. In 1985, when he was 15, he was charged as a juvenile in connection with a murder. Padilla and a friend were convicted of robbing and stabbing a drunken man. Padilla kicked the unconscious, bleeding man in the head while he lay on the street, later telling police he did it because he "felt like it." Confined to an Illinois juvenile detention facility, he was released at 18 and started a string of menial jobs, all the while using a variety of aliases, including Hernandez and Rivera.[1]

In 1989, while working as a $420 a-month dishwasher, Padilla reportedly punched a police officer in a dispute over a doughnut. In 1990, he moved to southern Florida, where he shot at a motorist who offended him, an offense that cost him 303 days in the Broward County jail. After his release, Padilla began studying at the Masjid Al-Iman mosque in Fort Lauderdale and making contacts within the local Muslim population. He converted to Islam and in June 1994 filed for a name change with Broward County. Padilla wanted to be called Ibrahim, and later began referring to himself as Abdullah al Muhajir.[2] He allegedly interacted with Adham Hassoun, an outspoken and fanatical 40-year-old supporter of Palestinian causes, including two charities—the Benevolence International Foundation and the Global Relief Foundation—both of which have been shuttered for allegedly funneling money to Al Qaeda. (Hassoun denied having met Padilla.)

Padilla studied Arabic for a while at the Darul Uloom Institute in Pembroke Pines, Florida, then claimed he was going to study religion in Egypt and left the United States. According to government documents, in the late 1990s he traveled to Saudi Arabia and Pakistan. During this time, the U.S. government contends, he began associating with people who knew people in Al Qaeda. It is also likely that in his travels and meetings, Padilla unknowingly encountered one or more individuals who were on the payroll of the CIA.

On May 8, 2002, Padilla arrived back at O'Hare, with a reported $10,000 cash in his pocket, and was promptly arrested by FBI agents as Chicago police trailed behind, perhaps wondering why all the federal firepower for a punk gangbanger.

A day after the Ashcroft announcement, Deputy Defense Secretary Paul Wolfowitz told the CBS *Early Show*'s Jane Clayson that Padilla "came into this country with the intention, by various means [not just the dirty-bomb idea], of killing hundreds and maybe thousands of Americans." In other television appearances, Wolfowitz claimed Padilla "was working on plots to do the most horrendous things in this country," including exploding a bomb that would spread radioactive materials over a large area.[3]

At the same time that Ashcroft and Wolfowitz were offering their take on Padilla, unnamed U.S. intelligence officials, in not-for-attribution interviews with reporters, quietly began backing off the idea that Padilla was an Al Qaeda operative with the skills and knowledge to build and detonate a dirty bomb.

Could he have built a bomb?

The components of a radiological dispersion device, at first glance, may seem obvious and easy to obtain. Building a dirty bomb requires a source of radioactivity, explosives, and someone to put the two together.

Although some materials from hospitals, research universities, and other facilities are radioactive enough

Fear, uncertainty, and doubt

Physicist Gene Amdahl first identified the concept of motivation by fear, uncertainty, and doubt (FUD). Amdahl worked as the director of advanced computer systems at International Business Machines (IBM) before leaving to form the Amdahl Corporation and other companies based on his proprietary technological innovations.

While all his companies successfully competed with IBM, Amdahl recognized that it was difficult—sometimes nearly impossible—to outsell Big Blue because of IBM's FUD-based sales techniques. According to Amdahl, "FUD is the fear, uncertainty, and doubt IBM salespeople instill in the minds of potential customers who might be considering other [allegedly unsafe or unproven] products." As the IBM sales staff often said, "No one ever got fired for buying IBM products."

Generating FUD is now a nationally abused, manipulative technique, honed to perfection by those claiming to have specialized knowledge or insight, used to effectively promote a policy or an idea. FUD-based pronouncements emanate daily from government offices, including the White House, FBI, CIA, and Defense and Energy departments. FUD is heard in the halls and hearing rooms of Congress, uttered by witnesses and congressmen alike. The language is carefully crafted by speechwriters at the direction of political operatives, written and rewritten, rehearsed, and uttered with complete earnestness. The public, synapses at rest, awaken to the sounds of FUD-inspired phrases like "domino effect," "electronic Pearl Harbor," or "weapons of mass destruction."

FUD sells papers and yields higher Nielsen ratings. Often, newsgathering and information sources incestuously feed off one another's FUD. Take the Council on Foreign Relations's Web site, www.terrorismanswers.com. The site, in a white paper on dirty bombs, flatly states, with no attribution, "In January 2003, British officials found documents in the Afghan city of Herat that led them to conclude that Al Qaeda had successfully built a small dirty bomb."

I pressed the Council's Michael Glennon for the unnamed source of the story. He responded by citing a January 31, 2003 *BBC News* world edition story: "Al Qaeda had successfully built a small dirty bomb." The BBC, in turn, claimed it was given evidence of dirty bomb plans, which it then had evaluated by an "expert on Al Qaeda"—Mustafa Alani, an associate fellow at the Royal United Services Institute for Defense and Security Studies, a British think tank. Alani was quoted as saying of the "evidence," "I think this is genuine. It is credible. This is proof that Al Qaeda put a lot of effort into collecting information and educating other members of the organization. It is possible to produce this sort of weapon."

The BBC left the clear impression that Alani had some measure of expertise in physics or dirty bomb-making. But in fact, his so-called expertise is in "Islamic extremism."

L.Z.K.

---

to be lethal, it would be very difficult to deliver high doses to more than a few people. (On the other hand, an attack with such materials could create panic and might cause a great deal of economic damage.)

The richest source of radioactivity, is spent fuel rods. But spent nuclear rods are not exactly lying around like piles of abandoned automobiles. Terrorists looking to get the "dirt" for a dirty bomb from spent nuclear fuel rods would have to get them from a nuclear facility.

Putting aside the controversy surrounding security at U.S. nuclear power plants, a would-be dirty bomber faces a Herculean task. A spent fuel rod weighs about 28 kilograms, with 36 rods weighing more than a metric ton. Heavy shielding and remote controls are required in their handling, because each rod exposes anyone standing nearby (within a meter) to a lethal dose within seconds. To prevent a quick death from radiation, the thieves would need to encase the rods in a

40-plus-ton, lead-lined shipping cask (18 rods will fit in one cask) and use shielding and remote handling equipment to move the rods at every stage of the operation. After securing the rods in a protective cask, the thieves would need to move them to a location where they could be matched with explosives, then move them to the target site. All that shuttling means the gang would need a specialized truck built to handle the rods and cask. These trucks are, as one can imagine, large, cumbersome, slow-moving, and easily identifiable—not exactly stealthy.

Of course, one can chance the move without the cumbersome shipping cask. That would suggest a scenario of this sort: A group of six people approaches an area where spent-fuel rods are assembled. These rods are two and a half years old. From a distance of 300 meters, gamma rays are beginning to be distributed in enough quantity to become lethal. The group spends 20-30 minutes approaching and absorbs a

five-gray dose. The closer they get to the rods, the greater the amount of gamma rays absorbed. Even if they were to cease their operations and flee the scene at this point, they would die of radiation poisoning in a few weeks. If they carried on, they would absorb even more radiation as they gathered the spent rods and placed them in lead-lined concrete containers. To be generous, the group would spend at least another 20-30 minutes in close proximity to the rods, absorbing more lethal gamma rays. Now the bombers would have a week to live. Next, after moving the stolen rods to a safe house (let's estimate two hours' travel time) the rods would have to be uncrated (one hour) and united with the to-be-constructed explosive device. One can be charitable here, but using Oklahoma City bomber Timothy McVeigh's record as an example of bomb-construction time (without radioactive materials), it would take more than three hours.[4] Then there would be the time used in

Dirty laundry

What makes a more lasting, concept-changing impression: rational, moderated voices of thoughtful scientists, or "dirty bomb" scenarios based on fear, uncertainty, and doubt?

In a documentary on the dirty bomb, broadcast on February 25, 2003, the acclaimed television series *Nova* began with a hyped scenario that negated the serious content found in the presentation's more responsible interviews.

The program's narrator noted that in 2001 U.S. forces in Afghanistan discovered papers containing research on a new weapon of terror (never offered for evaluation by independent U.S. experts). This was followed by an interview with non-nuclear physicist Vince Cannistraro, ex-chief of counterterrorism for the CIA, who claimed, "One of these [captured] documents spells out in very great detail how to make a dirty bomb. The understanding was basically at a fairly advanced physics level. It is a pretty well thought-out scenario on how to make the most deadly kind of dirty bomb imaginable."

No evidence of what Cannistraro considers "very great detail" or "fairly advanced physics level" or "a pretty well thought-out scenario" was presented. His conclusion that the weapon was "the most deadly dirty bomb imaginable" seems fanciful in light of expert findings that dirty bombs aren't very deadly at all.

The documentary offers two misleading scenarios. In the first, 10 pounds of plastic explosives and 74,000 gigabequerels of cesium chloride, "the contents of just one Soviet seed-irradiating device—just a handful of powder, but highly concentrated," is exploded in Trafalgar Square in the heart of London. Only later does the narrator explain: "The good news is that there would be few immediate health problems. The radioactivity in this hypothetical dirty bomb would disperse so quickly that no one is likely to get a strong dose." A more honest account would have admitted at the beginning that there would likely be few if any health problems.

A second scenario starts with the small amount of cesium found inside a typical industrial gauge—1,000 times less powerful than the hypothetical Trafalgar Square bomb. In this scenario, the material is coupled with store-bought fireworks and set off in the Washington, D.C., Metrorail. What sort of threat would that pose?

The narrator says, "the typical consumer would receive twice the background dose [of radiation] they get in the course of an average year, but only for a short period—an average of 15 minutes." Physicist Charles Ferguson, who along with a few others on the program presents a voice of thoughtful moderation and sanity, remarks that in the Metro scenario, "You'd probably have more death due to traffic accidents than due to ionizing radiation." But Cannistraro believes panic would ensue: "The news media comes on [and] says a small device has been exploded in Washington. What is the reaction of the public? How do you control that? What do you say to them?"

Andrew Karam, an expert in radiation safety at the University of Rochester (and another of the saner voices on the program), puts the panic reaction in perspective. "I think, initially, people would get the hell out. Emergency workers would have to deal with the real peril from panic. And that's something that presumably, hopefully, city emergency planners are working on right now."

The key concept here is "presumably." But the Department of Homeland Security has failed in its obligation to educate Americans against panic. There is no reason to believe that overburdened, underfunded, cash-starved state and local emergency services departments can cope with panic in the case of such an event. And the Homeland Security Web page isn't much help with banalities like "Don't be afraid. Be ready," "Make a kit," "Make a plan," and "Be informed."

L.Z.K.

wedding the radioactive materials to the explosives. Another hour, perhaps. And finally the time necessary to transport the dirty bomb from point B to its destination, point C. (In McVeigh's case that took three hours.)

Our gang of thieves would have, at the very least, spent almost 10 hours within seven feet of unshielded spent nuclear rods, absorbing, conservatively, 5,000 grays, enough radiation to make them burnt toast.[5]

What would it deliver?

For the sake of argument, let's say Padilla's gang was able to gather the materials and construct the device without killing themselves. How powerful—how destructive—would such a bomb be? The answer depends on who is asked. There is wide disagreement when it comes to describing a dirty bomb's destructive capabilities.

For instance, Bruce G. Blair, president of the Center for Defense Information, told the *St. Louis Post-Dispatch* on October 21, 2001: "Detonation of a dynamite-laden casket of spent fuel from a power plant would not kill quite as many people as died on September 11.... But if it happened in Manhattan, you could expect 2,000 deaths and thousands more suffering from radiation poisoning."

No, not exactly.

What Blair failed to calculate is that the intensity of the dynamite explosive would scatter the radioactivity over a wide area, lessening by a significant degree its potential le-

thality. Furthermore, in an urban environment like New York City, many people in the blast area would be protected from radiation by the shielding of the buildings and the offices in which they live and work. They would receive a much lower dose of radioactivity than those walking down the street near the explosion. And people on the streets outside the immediate blast zone would be exposed to a very small dose of dissipating radiation, made even more diffuse by the explosion itself.

Richard Garwin, an expert on nuclear weapons and nuclear power, has been a member of the scientific advisory group to the Joint Chiefs' Joint Strategic Target Planning Staff and was a member of the Rumsfeld commission that assessed the ballis-

Dirty bomb No. 1

It may come as a surprise, but the first person to think up a "dirty bomb" was physicist Enrico Fermi in 1942 after he and his colleagues had developed the first controlled chain reaction in a uranium pile at the University of Chicago. Fermi and his colleagues had little doubt that Adolf Hitler had already done or would soon be able to do the same.

As Robert Jungk put it in one of the first histories of the bomb, his 1956 book *Brighter than a Thousand Suns*, "If a uranium reactor of this kind had now been produced in Chicago, after the American atomic project had got off to such a slow start, it might also have been constructed somewhere in Germany. Fermi and the physicists around him at Chicago began to believe it was possible since they assumed the Germans had already enough radioactive matter in their piles to poison all the large cities of their enemies."

In December 1942, some were convinced that Hitler, to head off Allied bomb efforts, would risk the first air raid on the United States, with Chicago, the center of U.S. atomic research, as the target. "The whisper around Chicago's Metallurgical Laboratory was that the Germans would probably drop not the usual explosive bombs, but great quantities of radioactive dust to poison the air and water of the city," wrote Jungk.

Of course, as it turned out, the Germans never came close to achieving a controlled nuclear reaction. Yet, 60 years later, millions of tons of radioactive materials are being used or stored throughout the world, all of which inherently poses a security risk because of their potential as "added value" in a radiological dispersal device—Fermi's dirty bomb.

L.Z.K.

---

tic missile threat to the United States. In his essay "The Many Threats of Terror," Garwin describes the estimated consequences of a hypothetical explosion of one kilogram of plutonium in Munich, Germany: "The average population density of Munich is about 4,300 people per square kilometer. The study estimated that 12 cancers would occur per milligram of inhaled plutonium. Under the pessimistic assumption that very still air would cause the radioactive cloud to hover over the city for 12 hours, about 120 deaths from cancer would eventually be anticipated. (This would be in addition to the 400,000 people in the city who would likely die of cancer from natural causes.)"

Garwin cites a 1983 report by Sandia National Laboratories' California branch (located at Lawrence Livermore National Laboratory) on the results of a hypothetical explosive attack on a shipping cask containing spent nuclear fuel. The Nuclear Regulatory Commission indicated that for the most densely populated area studied (as many as 200,000 persons per square mile), at evening rush hour on a business day there would be no immediate fatalities and fewer than three fatalities from latent cancer. The scenario projected a six-inch diameter hole releasing three grams of radioactive fuel as aerosol—fine particles wafted in the air. As with

the hypothetical example for Munich, more harmful consequences could be achieved by using conventional explosives in a sports stadium.

When it comes to the use of low-level radioactive sources, the Centers for Disease Control notes in "Radiation Emergencies," in the "Terrorism and Public Health" section of the agency's Web site: "If low-level radioactive sources were to be used, the primary danger from a dirty bomb would be the blast itself. Gauging how much radiation might be present is difficult when the source of the radiation is unknown. However, at the levels created by most probable sources, not enough radiation would be present in a dirty bomb to cause severe illness from exposure to radiation."

There are millions of commercial radioactive sources globally, but only a fraction, "perhaps several tens of thousands, pose inherently high security risks because of their portability, dispensability, and higher levels of radioactivity," say Charles Ferguson, Tahseen Kazi, and Judith Perera, in "Commercial Radioactive Sources: Surveying the Security Risks," a report for the Monterey Institute of International Studies' Center for Nonproliferation Studies. Those sources include americium 241, californium 252, cesium 137, cobalt 60, iridium 192, plutonium 238, and strontium 90. Some of the iso-

topes (americium 241, californium 252, and plutonium 238) would pose health hazards only if ingested or inhaled; others would present both internal and external health hazards because the ionizing radiation they emit penetrates the outer layer of human skin. Even with "perhaps several tens of thousands" of commercial, high-risk radioactive isotopes throughout the world as potential contaminants for a radioactive delivery device, those dirty bombs "will have so little radioactivity as to pose little, if any danger to the public," Ferguson, Kazi, and Perera write.

Thus, scientific evidence puts in doubt the suggestion that Padilla possessed the ability to pull off an attack with a dirty bomb and cause a public health crisis.

Where to now?

After being arrested in Chicago, Padilla was taken to the Metropolitan Correctional Center in New York. He appeared before Michael B. Mukasey, U.S. district judge of the Southern District of New York. Mukasey, regarded as a no-nonsense jurist, insisted that legal charges be leveled against Padilla. But Justice Department attorneys claimed Padilla was a witness who needed to give testimony before a federal grand jury and that they couldn't foresee how long that requirement would last, so there was no end in sight to Padilla's detention.

In response to objections from Mukasey, the FBI reluctantly managed to cough up a paper affidavit created by Special Agent Joseph Ennis that claimed (without proof or cross examination) that Padilla "appeared to have knowledge of facts relevant to a grand jury investigation into the September 11 attacks. That investigation includes an ongoing inquiry into the activities of Al Qaeda, an organization believed to be responsible for the September 11 attacks, among others, and to be committed to and involved in planning further attacks."

Neither Ashcroft nor Ennis appeared in court to support those claims.

Just as the Supreme Court reasoned in 1962 that Clarence Earl Gideon deserved to have his own attorney, Mukasey reasoned in 2002 that Padilla, charged with being a terrorist and dirty-bomber for Al Qaeda, certainly deserved an attorney, maybe even a gaggle of them. So Mukasey appointed Donna Newman to represent Padilla. Newman met with Padilla on at least two occasions, then asked the judge to vacate the warrant for Padilla because he had not been charged with a crime. (Newman was quickly joined by some legal heavy hitters from the American Civil Liberties Union, the New York Civil Liberties Union, the Center for National Security Studies, the New York State Association of Criminal Defense Lawyers, and the National Association of Criminal Defense Lawyers.)

Entering the Twilight Zone

The government insisted on an ex parte (private) meeting with Mukasey. The Justice attorneys told the judge something to the effect of, "Oops, sorry about that, Judge, but the witness subpoena for Padilla is being withdrawn." Mukasey promptly signed papers vacating the warrant. Then the Justice attorneys announced that President Bush had designated Padilla an "enemy com-

batant," and before you could say *Mr. Mxyztplk*, Padilla was whisked off to the Consolidated Naval Brig, 769 miles away from his attorney. Outraged, Newman conferred with government attorneys—she wanted to see and speak with her client. She was told that she would not be permitted to speak with Padilla. She could write to him, but he might not receive the correspondence.

The government argued that Padilla should not be allowed to see a lawyer because he might pass messages to his fellow terrorists through his attorney. Mukasey didn't buy it. The idea that Padilla would pass on secrets for Al Qaeda through his attorney was, in Mukasey's words, "gossamer speculation." Padilla had already met with Newman, so whatever damage might have been done by those conversations was already done. And finally, "there was no reason that military personnel cannot monitor [within limits] Padilla's contacts," Mukasey said.

When pressed in open court by the angry Mukasey, on August 27, 2002, three and a half months after Padilla's arrest and incarceration, the government finally produced its first "evidence" against Padilla. This was a finding or "declaration" by Michael Mobbs, an obscure Pentagon bureaucrat with the title "Special Adviser to the Under Secretary of Defense for Policy," who claimed that "Padilla and his associate conducted research in the construction of a 'uranium-enhanced' explosive device … in particular, they engaged in research on this topic at one of the Al Qaeda safe houses in Lahore, Pakistan … [a plan in which] Padilla and his associate [would] build and then detonate a 'radiological dispersal device' (also known as a dirty bomb) within the United States, possibly in Washington, D.C."

There are problems with this declaration. In a footnote, Mobbs reveals that the information about Padilla came from two confidential sources. "It is believed," the footnote reads, "that these confidential sources have not been completely candid about their associations with Al Qaeda and

their terrorist activities." It then goes on to explain: "Much of the information from these sources has, however, been corroborated and proven accurate and reliable." On the other hand, it went on, "some information by the sources remains uncorroborated and may even be part of an effort to mislead or confuse U.S. officials." But not to worry, or as *Mad Magazine's* Alfred E. Neuman puts it, "What, me worry?" The Mobbs footnote concludes, "One of the sources, for example, in a subsequent interview with a U.S. law enforcement official recanted some of the information he provided, but most of this information has been independently corroborated by other sources. In addition, at the time of being interviewed by U.S. officials, one of the sources was being treated with various types of drugs to treat medical conditions."

Padilla's attorneys as well as the judge were unable to cross-examine Mobbs. The government offered a written statement, unaccompanied by Mobbs himself, on the witness stand. June 2003 reports suggest that some of the translations of captured sources may have been deliberately mistranslated by American translators working as Syrian spies.

The government, in what many believe is a highly unusual legal move, also appealed Mukasey's decision to grant Padilla the right to an attorney, sending it on to the court of appeals. A group of 14 legal scholars, world-class attorneys, and former federal court appellate judges, many of whom served in high positions with the federal government, filed *amici curiae* briefs with the court of appeals, demanding Padilla be accorded constitutional protections. They noted that Padilla is an American citizen, arrested on American territory. Even John Walker Lindh, who was arrested in Afghanistan, armed and attempting to kill U.S. forces, had an attorney throughout his legal negotiations and public trial.

No case

The government's case rests on an unusual argument. The spokesman for the Justice Department's Criminal Division, Bryan Sierra, contends that U.S. Code 18, section 4001(a), which reads, "No citizen shall be imprisoned or otherwise detained by the United States except pursuant to an Act of Congress," provides no check on the president's powers as commander in chief. Instead, Sierra cites section 4001(b)(1), which reads, "The control and management of federal penal and correctional institutions, except military or naval institutions, shall be vested in the attorney general." And to whom does the attorney general report? The president. In other words, in the Justice Department's tortured logic, as commander in chief, the president is not bound by Congress's rules on imprisonment and detention.

But it gets even more tenuous. According to Sierra, "It is our [Justice's] position that Congress drafted the law not to restrict the president's power, and according to the record, that point was even noted by then-Rep. Abner Mikva during the debate."

But Mikva, an eminent jurist and now a visiting professor at the University of Chicago Law School, says the law was not about giving the president more power, but rather, taking it away." The "debate," Mikva told me, had to do with delegitimizing American internment camps, such as those authorized by the president and built at the outset of World War II to house American citizens of Japanese ancestry. It was passed during the heyday of Sen. Joseph McCarthy and the House Un-American Activities Committee, when rumors were rampant that the government was building camps to house Americans suspected of leftist leanings. Mikva's position then and now (as a signatory to the *amicus* brief in Padilla) was to restrict the president (or his chain of command) from exercising extralegal powers to detain or imprison without fulfilling the letter of the law.

Ashcroft's argument is based on a single Civil War case: In 1864, one man, Lambdin P. Milligan, a U.S. citizen from Indiana, was tried on charges of conspiracy before a military commission and sentenced to be hanged. The Supreme Court rejected the verdict, holding that "military courts could not function in states where federal courts were open and operating," as Louis Fisher writes in his book *Nazi Saboteurs on Trial: A Military Tribunal and American Law*.

Congress was not pleased with the Supreme Court decision, Fisher says, and "passed legislation to limit the court's jurisdiction to hear cases involving martial law and military trials." The statute reads: "No civil court of the United States, or of any state, or of the District of Columbia, shall have or take jurisdiction of, or in any manner reverse any of the proceedings had or acts done as aforesaid." But this was in 1867, and it's a slim legal reed for Ashcroft to rest his case against Padilla on.

Ron Sievert, a University of Texas at Austin law school professor and U.S. assistant attorney, in his comprehensive book *Cases and Materials on U.S. Laws and National Security*, questions the powers of so-called military commissions, especially when a military commander, including the president acting as commander in chief, substitutes "military force for and to the exclusion of the laws and punish[es] all persons, as he thinks right and proper, without fixed and certain rules."

If unchecked, such power would mean that republican government, and liberty regulated by law, would come to an end. With such powers, martial law could be used to destroy every guarantee of the Constitution, and effectually render the military independent of and superior to civil power. The idea was deemed such an offense by this country's founders that they cited it as one of the main reasons for declaring independence from England. "Civil liberty and this kind of martial law cannot endure together; the antagonism is irreconcilable; and, in the conflict, one or the other must perish," Sievert writes.

During the turbulent Civil War years, Abraham Lincoln declared an emergency, suspended the writ of habeas corpus, and declared martial law both in 1861 and 1862. Chief Justice of the Supreme Court Roger B. Taney ruled that Lincoln did not have that right. In 1866, after the end of the Civil War, the Supreme Court reinstated habeas corpus. Despite the reinstatement, the government now contends it can hold Padilla incommunicado and subject him to constant and endless questioning without allowing him an attorney, or presenting him in court.

With such powers, martial law could be used to destroy every guarantee of the Constitution and render the military independent of civil power.

Illegal, say other former federal appellate court judges and legal scholars, whose *amicus curiae* brief states, "The right to habeas corpus—that is, to have a *court* determine the legality of detention—was one of the few individual rights enshrined in the Constitution itself, even before the Bill of Rights." The brief notes that President Bush's declaration of Padilla as an enemy combatant "would also strip away the most basic due process rights of notice and an opportunity to be heard by forbidding Padilla from even learning about this case or communicating in any manner with his counsel—*or even with the court*."

Roosevelt's rules

The most important precedent for denying Padilla legal representation comes from a World War II example where the prisoners were in fact accorded legal representation, some of it outstanding. Eight ill-equipped "spies" were sent by Germany to work against the United States in 1942. They were far from rocket scientists. Most had previously worked in the United States for a short while as fry cooks, chauffeurs, or tool and die makers; one worked in the meat-packing industry. After four months of spy and saboteur training, they were put aboard submarines and shipped to the United States.

When four of the eight landed on Long Island, the first person they encountered on the beach was an unarmed U.S. Coast Guardsman, Frank Collins, whom they tried to bribe. When Collins returned to base that night, he told his superiors, who then hurried to the beach, where they found Nazi paraphernalia and explosive devices. Five days later, when the four spies were in New York City, one of them, George Dasch, phoned the FBI in an effort to turn himself and his co-spies in. The FBI didn't believe him. Dasch then phoned government information and was told to call the Adjunct General's Office, but the secretary said her boss wasn't in.

In desperation, Dasch called the FBI again, and while the agent really didn't believe him, he was nevertheless told to go to a specific office in the Justice Department. The FBI agents still thought they were wasting their time until Dasch opened a suitcase with $82,550 in cash.

A few days later, four other German spies landed in Florida, but by now the FBI was hot on the case, and they were all rounded up.

President Franklin D. Roosevelt did not want the eight spies tried in a civilian court; the most prison time they might serve would be two years. Roosevelt wanted them dead, period. He wanted a trial by a military commission, something akin to a military tribunal. Roosevelt issued Proclamation 2561, creating a military tribunal referencing what he called the "law of war"—not all that different from President Bush calling an American citizen arrested on American territory an "enemy combatant." If Roosevelt had cited the Articles of War, he would have had to conform to the laws established by Congress for court-martial. But this way, "acts of war" could mean whatever Roosevelt and Attorney Gen-

eral Francis Biddle meant them to be, and the trial could be run by their rules, including allowing a two-thirds vote of the commission/tribunal to approve the death penalty and closing all proceedings to the public, except for 15 minutes when a few photographers snapped pictures and a few reporters took notes. Roosevelt got his way, and six of the eight were sentenced to death.

What makes the Padilla case different from the Nazi spy case is that even with the formation of Roosevelt's ad hoc, make-the-rules-up-as-you-go-along plan, no one argued that the Nazi spies did not deserve to have defense attorneys. In fact, one defense attorney, Col. Kenneth Royall, acknowledged that he worked under the military chain of command and would cease his efforts if so ordered. But his orders were for him to do what he thought was right, and Royall was rigorous in his defense, contending that his commander in chief, Roosevelt, had acted illegally in forming the commission. Once the verdict was rendered, Royall pressed for the case to be heard by the Supreme Court. The public, too, began to tire of all the secrecy and demanded more openness. The hearings before the Supreme Court were open to all, though it would take almost three months before a full-blown decision could be handed down.

The Supreme Court found in favor of the commission—months after six of the spies were executed. Later, Justice Felix Frankfurter said the finding "was not a happy precedent. The American legal system would do well not to see its like again."[7]

A year after the spies were caught, Hans Haupt, the father of one of the men, was arrested and sentenced to death because he had hidden some of his son's cash. In reversing that conviction, the appellate court in the Seventh Circuit unanimously denounced the Supreme Court's decision in the Nazi spy case for its failure to protect the fundamental right of a jury trial:

"Of the many rights guaranteed to the people of this Republic, there is none more sacred than that of trial by jury. Such right comprehends a fair determination, free from passion or prejudice, of the issues involved. The right is all-inclusive; it embraces every class and type of person. Those for whom we have contempt or even hatred are equally entitled to its benefits. It will be a sad day for our system of government if the time should come when any person, whoever he may be, is deprived of this fundamental safeguard. No more important responsibility rests upon courts than its preservation unimpaired. How wasted is American blood now being spilled in all parts of the world if we at home are unwilling or unable to accord every person charged with a crime a trial in conformity with this constitutional requirement."

Ashcroft would have it otherwise. In remarks before the Senate Judiciary Committee on December 7, 2001, Ashcroft denounced those who had voiced opposition to the extrajudicial, extralegal steps the Bush administration was taking: "Your tactics only aid terrorists, for they erode our national unity and diminish our resolve. They give ammunition to America's enemies and pause to America's friends."

A day after the Judiciary Committee hearing, the Justice Department announced that Ashcroft had not intended to discourage public debate; what he found unhelpful to the country were "misstatements and the spread of misinformation about the actions of the Justice Department."

But, according to Fisher, "Ashcroft appeared to claim that tribunals are created under the exclusive authority of the president and that according to judicial precedents Congress may not limit that authority. The legal and historical record of military tribunals presents quite a different picture: The creation of tribunals is typically decided jointly by Congress and the president; Congress has not recognized a unilateral presidential authority to create those tribunals; and the Supreme Court has repeatedly held that Congress has the constitutional authority to create tribunals, decide their authorities and jurisdiction, and limit the president if he acts unilaterally by military order or proclamation to create those tribunals."

In the Padilla case and other "terrorist" cases, American justice is sailing into uncharted territory.

If the science of Jose Padilla's dirty bomb most closely resembles alchemy, the legality of Padilla's arrest and confinement is in an invisible legal dimension where, as Lewis Carroll noted, legal logic is turned on its head.

"'Let the jury consider their verdict,' the King said, for about the twentieth time that day. 'No, no!' said the Queen. 'Sentence first—verdict afterwards.'"

Notes

1. Lucio Guerrero, Carlos Sadovi, Frank Main, and Robert C. Herguth, "A Couple Years Back, I Knew He Entered a Cult," *Chicago Sun-Times*, June 11, 2002.
2. Lynn Sweet and Frank Main, "Terror Suspect Says He Came Here to Visit Son," *Chicago Sun-Times*, June 12, 2002.
3. Ibid.
4. Lou Michel and Dan Herbeck, *American Terrorist: Timothy McVeigh and the Tragedy at Oklahoma City* (New York: Regan Books/ HarperCollins), p. 219.
5. These calculations were made by Mike Rosing, PhD, a nuclear engineer with several years' experience at Argonne National Labs as an engineer and physicist. They are estimates: At one meter the gang would receive two grays per second, or about 50,000 grays in seven hours. At two meters they would receive 0.2 grays per second, which is still 5,000 grays in seven hours. Since a fuel rod is four meters long and the gang would average about two meters away from the rods, it is as if the fuel rods would "wrap around" them and radiate them from all sides. If they should accidentally touch the rods with their bare hands, they would be dead in seconds.
6. Interview with Abner Mikva, October 20, 2003.
7. Louis Fisher, *Nazi Saboteurs on Trial: A Military Tribunal & American Law* (Lawrence, Kansas: University of Kansas Press, 2003), p. 171.
8. Ibid, p. 81.

Lewis Z. Koch is an award-winning investigative reporter. His Web site is www.lzkoch.com.

From *Bulletin of the Atomic Scientists,* January/February 2004, pp. 59-60, 65-68. Copyright © 2004 by Educational Foundation for Nuclear Science. Reprinted by permission

EVIDENCE *of* FAILURE

BY ELLEN PERLMAN

Warning to viewers: The television series "*CSI*" does not mirror life at public crime laboratories. On TV, crime scene investigators bring evidence into forensic crime labs outfitted with the latest technology. Lab tools splice and dice evidence to come up quickly with findings that finger whoever dunnit. "Every time I see "CSI," I cringe," says Paul Ferrara, director of Virginia's Division of Forensic Science. "Everyone's waiting to work on this one case. In 44 minutes, all that work is done."

Not so at Ferrara's lab, where 100,000 pieces of evidence now await scrutiny from only about 45 examiners. The average testing turnaround, from the time a piece of DNA evidence comes into the lab to the release of results, is more than six months. DNA examiners average six to eight cases a month.

> ## Overwhelmed by a flood of DNA evidence, public crime labs are performing poorly.

Virginia is not alone. The backlog in most public crime labs is four to eight months or longer. There are staff shortages and only enough resources to work on the most egregious crimes, if those.

The working conditions and other problems in labs can lead to serious errors. At the city crime laboratory in Philadelphia, for example, there was a mix-up of DNA samples from the accused and the victim in a rape case. At a New York State police crime lab, the cocaine rocks tested as evidence were not the actual drugs

that prosecutors had alleged were sold to a police informant. Then there was the man who was convicted in Tulsa, Oklahoma, based in part on a DNA test, the results of which were misinterpreted by a lab worker.

The emergence of DNA as a key crime-solving tool has added to the problem. As investigators rely more and more on DNA for solving crimes, the crime labs are overloaded. "Laboratories like my own, whether federal, state or local, are all reeling under the onslaught of physical evidence hitting the labs," Ferrara says.

The overloading, in turn, leads to difficulties further down the line. If lab work doesn't get done on time, it slows down or even defeats efforts at moving cases forward. "Crime labs are equivalent to the pinch in the middle," says David Epstein, chief scientist at the National Forensic Science Technology Center.

Despite the errors and delays, Ferrara insists that the work done in labs today is better than it's ever been. There seem to be more problems, he suggests, because labs results are in the limelight more than ever, with many more experts scrutinizing the work that's done. "Whenever humans are involved, mistakes can and will occur," he says. "You try to minimize it."

THE HOUSTON DISASTER

When you hear about crime lab problems these days, the recurring refrain is, "We don't want to become another Houston." Problems got so bad at that crime lab, housed within

> ## A COLD CASE
> ### Public crime lab issues
>
> ### 34%
> report staff
> turnover is a problem
>
> ### 79%
> do not have a sufficient
> number of scientists
>
> Source: "Staffing Issues in the Crime Lab:
> National Survey of Forensic Science Lab
> Directors," November 2003

the police department, that at least one innocent person was wrongly convicted of a crime based on incorrect lab results. The lab voluntarily disconnected itself from the FBI's DNA database—before the FBI could terminate the connection.

According to a needs-analysis report released in July by the National Forensic Science Technology Center, top-level staff was not providing adequate supervision or support and scientists promoted to supervisory positions were not given formal training in management. Deficiencies showed up in personnel qualifications, proficiency testing and other key areas. As further proof of inadequacies, while the needs analysis was being conducted, water was dripping from a leaky roof onto scientists working on evidence.

After the report came out, the head of the crime lab and the police chief resigned, and the DNA crime lab was shut down. The Houston Police Department has had to outsource 1,500 of its cases in the past 12 months. But help may be in sight: Last month, the lab posted a want ad for an experienced supervisor who could get the lab back on its feet.

The Houston lab still faces potential liability for court verdicts that used its results. "Hundreds of past cases could well be subject to court challenges, and rightly so," says William C. Thompson, a lawyer and professor at the University of California, Irvine.

Thompson believes Houston didn't have an adequate oversight system to expose problems in the crime lab. If, for instance, lab workers embellish findings to achieve what they believe are appropriate results in a case—"Some people become white-coat vigilantes," Thompson says—there is no impartial official or agency whose task it is to look into allegations of scientific misconduct or crime lab problems. If any state or city finds out that someone in their labs mishandled findings in one case, it's important, he points out, to have a neutral person or agency in place to look into other cases that person has handled.

TRIAL AND ERROR

There are proposed solutions to crime-lab problems. Critics say crime labs should be independent entities within the criminal justice system. They should not, as they do now, operate within police and sheriffs' departments or the offices of attorneys general, prosecutors or medical examiners. There can be a perception that they are not able to analyze evidence objectively.

Virginia is often held up as a model because its crime lab is not part of a law enforcement agency. Instead, it reports to the state Department of Criminal Justice Services, whose director reports to the governor's secretary of public safety. The crime scene investigators are trained by the lab, not by a law enforcement agency. But that has not saved it

from many of the problems labs face. As with labs all over the country, understaffing is a huge issue. "It's pretty bad," Ferrara says. "And we're probably one of the best-funded laboratories around."

Chronic staff shortages and lack of training contribute to mistakes everywhere. As more cases are dumped on lab workers, the pressure to finish cases too quickly increases markedly, as does pressure to "extend opinions beyond the scientific method" and to get a particular result, according to a national survey of forensic science lab directors, performed by Wendy S. Becker, an assistant professor at the State University of New York at Albany. "Staffing problems are systemic and pervasive, and impact the quality of labs and outcomes and effectiveness," she says.

It doesn't help that the starting pay for public lab analysts is $37,000 a year, compared with $50,000 for similar private-sector positions. When divisions attached to law enforcement fight for scarce dollars within their departments, "we get lost in the shuffle," says Barry Fisher, the crime lab director for Los Angeles County sheriff's department. "Most crime labs are pretty small compared to a much larger police function. They're easily overwhelmed by needs such as patrol and investigations."

Last year, the problems at the Houston crime lab led the Texas legislature to mandate accreditation by 2005 of all crime labs handling evidence in felony cases. When the law passed, about half of the 42 crime labs in the state were not accredited. Crime lab problems in Oklahoma led to a similar law there. New York has required for many years that all forensic labs be accredited, but few other states are moving in that direction.

The American Society of Crime Lab Directors strongly promotes accreditation for crime labs but not necessarily via state mandate. In general, however, accreditation

makes managing easier, says Roger Kahn, president of the lab directors' association and deputy superintendent of the Ohio Bureau of Criminal Identification and Investigation. "No one wants non-compliance issues to explain," he says. "It's a powerful risk management technique for the entire criminal justice system."

The Ohio bureau was able to standardize operations and put in policies and procedures that gave lab workers a better handle on their jobs. Training is now a requirement despite budget swings. Equipment must be operating properly.

Accreditation may force improvements, but it is no guarantee that crime labs will be performing their work smoothly. The *Houston Chronicle* reviewed audits of crime labs that were conducted between 1999 and 2002 and found problems at Department of Public Safety labs in Austin, Corpus Christi, El Paso, Garland, Houston, Lubbock and McAllen. All of them were accredited.

Accreditation may be only the beginning of necessary reforms. The Innocence Project, an independent non-profit legal clinic and resource center, would like crime labs to have standards as good as, or better than, any professional organization. It would also like to see each jurisdiction put in place an oversight agency with the authority to regulate lab practices and set standards for the use of private labs when public labs need to outsource. Moreover, it calls for accreditation standards that include spot-checking of labs, rigorous quality control and periodic inspection by a regulatory body. Labs should go through proficiency testing and be rated on their performance. At trial, the Project suggests, labs should be required to present information on their controls and error rates for testing procedures.

Steps like these would help make crime lab results more reliable. They might also help correct an injustice in the American legal system.

UNIT 2
Victimology

Unit Selections

Key Points to Consider

- What is needed in order to switch from calling oneself a "victim" of crime to a "survivor" of crime?

- Why do we need good statistics to talk sensibly about social problems?

- Have the terrorist attacks of September 11, 2001, affected your sense of safety, security, and emotional well-being? If so, how? If not, why not?

 **Links: www.dushkin.com/online/**
These sites are annotated in the World Wide Web pages.

National Crime Victim's Research and Treatment Center (NCVC)
http://www.musc.edu/cvc/
Office for Victims of Crime (OVC)
http://www.ojp.usdoj.gov/ovc

For many years, crime victims were not considered an important topic for criminological study. Now, however, criminologists consider that focusing on victims and victimization is essential to understand the phenomenon of crime. The popularity of this area of study can be attributed to the early work of Hans Von Hentig and the later work of Stephen Schafer. These writers were the first to assert that crime victims play an integral role in the criminal event, that their actions may actually precipitate crime, and that unless the victim's role is considered, the study of crime is not complete.

In recent years, a growing number of criminologists have devoted increasing attention to the victim's role in the criminal justice process. Generally, areas of particular interest include establishing probabilities of victimization risks, studying victim precipitation of crime and culpability, and designing services expressly for victims of crime. As more criminologists focus their attention on the victim's role in the criminal process, victimology will take on even greater importance.

This unit provides a sharp focus on several key issues. The lead article, "Ordering Restitution to the Crime Victim," provides an overview of state laws addressing the rights of victims to receive court-ordered restitution from offenders in criminal cases. In the article that follows, "Pickpockets, Their Victims, and the Transit Police," David Young points out that law enforcement officers can help citizens reduce their chances of becoming victims of pickpockets. The need for good statistics in order to talk sensibly about social problems is the point of the next article, "Telling the Truth About Damned Lies and Statistics."

A rape victim's account of her traumatic experience follows next in "Violence and the Remaking of a Self." "Prosecutors, Kids, and Domestic Violence Cases" then outlines the special role that a prosecutor can play in helping to guarantee the safety of battered women and their children. The unit closes by focusing on the crime of intimidation known as stalking, in "Strengthening Antistalking Statutes." According to a U.S. Department of Justice report, work must be done in the future to better protect stalking victims.

ORDERING RESTITUTION TO THE CRIME VICTIM

Introduction

Victims suffer staggering economic costs as a result of crime. The tangible cost of crime, including medical expenses, lost earnings, and public victim assistance costs, is an estimated $105 billion a year.[1] Crime victim compensation programs reimburse victims for part of this loss. During fiscal year 1998, state compensation programs paid close to $250 million to victims of violent crime.[2] However, most of the costs of crime are absorbed by the victims and victim service providers.

Restitution laws are designed to shift the burden. As one legislature noted, "It is the purpose of [restitution law] to encourage the compensation of victims by the person most responsible for the loss incurred by the victim, the offender."[3]

Status of the Law

Right to Restitution

Every state gives courts the statutory authority to order restitution. In addition, 18 of the 32 state crime victims' rights constitutional amendments give victims a right to restitution.[4]

In more than one-third of all states, courts are required by statute to order restitution unless there are compelling or extraordinary circumstances. Florida's law is typical, providing that "[i]n addition to any punishment, the court shall order the defendant to make restitution to the victim for: 1) Damage or loss caused directly or indirectly by the defendant's offense; and 2) Damage or loss related to the defendant's criminal episode, unless it finds clear and compelling reasons not to order such restitution."[5] In many states, the law requires restitution but allows broad exceptions to that rule. For instance, Connecticut and Nevada both require restitution "if restitution is appropriate."[6] Oregon provides that restitution shall be ordered "whenever possible."[7] Regardless of whether restitution is mandatory, about one-quarter of all states require courts to state on the record the reasons for failing to order restitution or for ordering only partial restitution.[8] This requirement is thought to further encourage courts to consider restitution to the victim when sentencing convicted offenders.

Where victims have a clear statutory right to restitution, the right has been found to apply to cases that result in a plea agreement. The California Court of Appeals recently ruled that restitution must be a part of every sentence, regardless of a plea agreement to the contrary: "The Legislature left no discretion or authority with the trial court or the prosecution to bargain away the victim's constitutional and statutory right to restitution. As such, it cannot properly be the subject of plea negotiations."[9] Oklahoma's statute expressly requires that restitution to the victim be part of every plea agreement.[10] Florida requires that an "order of restitution entered as part of a plea agreement is as definitive and binding as any other order of restitution, and a statement to such effect must be made part of the plea agreement."[11]

Although most restitution laws apply to crime victims in general, many states have enacted specific directives to order restitution to victims of particular offenses, such as crimes against the elderly,[12] domestic violence,[13] sexual assault,[14] hate crimes,[15] child abuse,[16] child sexual abuse,[17] drunk driving,[18] and identity fraud.[19]

Eligibility for Restitution

Generally, restitution laws provide for restitution to the direct victim(s) of a crime, including surviving family members of homicide victims. Many states also authorize an order of restitution to third parties, including insurers,[20] victim compensation programs,[21] government entities,[22] and victim service agencies.[23] Several states authorize restitution to any entity that has provided recovery to the victim as a collateral source.[24] Alaska authorizes a court to order restitution "to a public, private, or private nonprofit organization that has provided ...counseling, medical, or shelter services to the victim or other person injured by the offense."[25] In a recent New York case, an appellate court ruled that a defendant could be required to make restitution to a victim's employer for the victim's sick leave.[26]

Restitution need not be limited to victims of crimes for which a defendant was convicted. When a defendant is charged with similar crimes against many individuals, as in the case of a serial rapist or a perpetrator of large-scale fraud, he or she may plead guilty to one or more counts in exchange for an agreement by the prosecutor to drop other charges. In such a case, as part of the plea agreement, the defendant may agree to pay restitution to all victims. Many states specifically allow this by statute.[27] For example, Idaho's restitution law states that the "court may, with the consent of the parties, order restitution to victims, and/or any other person or entity, for economic loss or injury for crimes which are not adjudicated or are not before the court."[28]

Losses for Which Restitution May Be Ordered

Restitution may be ordered to cover numerous crime-related expenses incurred by a victim. Typically, statutes specify that the following may be included in setting the restitution amount:

- Medical expenses.
- Lost wages.
- Counseling expenses.
- Lost or damaged property.
- Funeral expenses.
- Other direct out-of-pocket expenses.

Medical expenses are defined as medical services and devices (often including "nonmedical care and treatment rendered in accordance with a recognized method of healing"), physical therapy, and rehabilitation.[29]

Lost wages can include time lost from work because of participation in the court process.[30] Courts have even applied this to self-employed individuals who have had to close a business or forego employment while testifying.[31] California law specifies that parents can receive restitution for wages lost while caring for an injured minor victim.[32] Although Arizona's statute is not so specific, its Court of Appeals has interpreted that statute to reach the same conclusion: the "parents … stood in the shoes of the victim and were entitled to restitution for their lost wages incurred while taking [her] to medical appointments and juvenile court hearings on this case."[33]

Counseling expenses are generally recoverable. Many states extend restitution for counseling expenses to victims' family members. Some states limit family counseling expenses to cases of homicide,[34] whereas others allow such expenses whenever the counseling is related to the commission of the offense.[35]

In homicide cases, a family's funeral and travel expenses and the ordinary and reasonable attorney fees incurred in closing the victim's estate have been found to be proper restitution items.[36] Other funeral expenses that might be covered include a headstone, flowers, chapel music, minister's honorarium, and chapel fee.[37]

Restitution may also be ordered for other out-of-pocket expenses directly related to the crime. In cases of identity fraud, this may include expenses for correcting a victim's credit history and costs incurred in any civil or administrative proceeding needed to satisfy any debt or other obligation of the victim, including lost wages and attorney fees.[38]

Many states authorize courts to order defendants to pay interest on the restitution. For example, California's law provides that a restitution order shall include "interest, at the rate of 10 percent per annum, that accrues as of the date of sentencing or loss, as determined by the court."[39] In some states, attorney fees are also recoverable. In Oregon, attorney fees have been found by the courts

to be recoverable as "special damages" if incurred to ensure indictment and criminal prosecution; the victim may later file a civil suit.[40] California's restitution statute provides for recovery of attorney fees and costs incurred for collecting restitution.[41]

In some states, future damages can be awarded. Iowa law specifically provides for future damages, stating that where the full extent of the loss is not known at the time of sentencing, the court is to issue a temporary order for a reasonable amount of restitution identified at that time. The court is authorized to issue a permanent supplemental order at a later date, setting out the full amount of restitution.[42] Arizona's Court of Appeals ruled that future damages were a permissible restitution element, reasoning that disallowing future expenses would defeat the legislative purpose of restitution, which is to make the victim whole.[43]

Meanwhile, Wyoming has a detailed statutory scheme for ordering restitution for long-term medical expenses. Under its law, the court is to consider and include as a special finding "each victim's reasonably foreseeable actual pecuniary damage that will result in the future as a result of the defendant's criminal activity."[44] Thus, a restitution order for long-term physical health care must be entered for any such damages.

Not every state allows restitution for future expenses, however. Indiana courts have stated that only actual costs incurred by the victim before sentencing may be considered for a restitution order.[45]

Considerations in Ordering Restitution

Restitution laws generally set out the elements the court is to consider before it rules on restitution. Alaska law provides that "[i]n determining the amount and method of payment of restitution, the court shall take into account the: 1) public policy that favors requiring criminals to compensate for damages and injury to their victims; and 2) financial burden placed on the victim and those who provide services to the victim and other persons injured by the offense as a result of the criminal conduct of the defendant."[46]

Most states also require the court to consider the current financial resources of the defendant, the defendant's future ability to pay, and, in some states, the burden restitution will place on the defendant and his or her dependents. States are beginning to move away from consideration of the defendant's ability to pay when setting the restitution amount. However, the defendant's assets and earning potential are taken into account in setting the payment schedule. Arizona's law states that the court "shall not consider the economic circumstances of the defendant in determining the amount of restitution,"[47] but the court is required to consider the economic circumstances of the defendant in specifying the manner of payment.[48] Similarly, in Florida, the court is charged only with considering the loss sustained by the victim in determining whether to order restitution and the amount of restitution. At the time the restitution order is enforced, the court is to consider the defendant's financial resources, the present and potential future financial needs and earning ability of the defendant and his or her dependents, and other appropriate factors.[49]

Current Issues

Conflicting Directives

Many states have conflicting restitution statutes. A state may have one statute that mandates restitution in every criminal case and another that expressly leaves the ordering of restitution to the court's discretion. States may give every victim the right to restitution "as provided by law" but fail to mandate that courts order restitution. In some states, a single statute contains conflicting provisions. For example, a Minnesota law states that every crime victim has the right to receive restitution as part of the disposition of a criminal charge or juvenile delinquency proceeding if the offender is convicted or found delinquent. The statute further provides that the court "shall grant or deny restitution or partial restitution and shall state on the record its reasons for its decision on restitution if information relating to restitution has been presented."[50] Other states have similar contradictions within their statutes. The Colorado Legislature addressed this issue in 1999 when it created a task force to develop a report on restitution and specifically charged the task force with identifying conflicting provisions in the law.[51]

Other Barriers to Restitution Orders

Despite progressively stronger restitution statutes, studies and anecdotal information suggest that crime victims are frequently not awarded restitution. In a 1996 study, less than half of the 1,300 crime victims surveyed reported that they were awarded restitution.[52]

As part of the same study, local criminal justice and victim service professionals were surveyed about their experiences with crime victims' rights and asked to identify why courts often failed to order restitution. The most common reasons were a victim's failure to request restitution, a victim's failure to demonstrate loss, the inability to calculate a victim's loss, the opinion that restitution was inappropriate in light of other penalties imposed (especially in cases where the defendant receives jail time), and a defendant's inability to pay.[53] Most of these reasons can be addressed in whole or in part by statute.

A Victim's Failure To Request Restitution

One way to address a victim's failure to request restitution is to strengthen the laws that require a victim to be notified of the right to request restitution. Victims are commonly informed of the availability of restitution at the time they receive general information about crime victims' rights, either when the crime is reported or when the prosecutor files charges.[54] Early notification of a victim's right to request restitution gives the victim time to gather evidence to document losses. In some states, victims are informed of their right to request restitution again when they are notified of the sentencing hearing or asked to complete a victim impact statement.[55]

Other states simply place the burden of requesting restitution on the prosecutor.[56] Wisconsin law requires the court to prompt the prosecutor: "The court, before imposing sentence or ordering probation, shall inquire of the district attorney regarding the amount of restitution, if any, that the victim claims."[57] Fi-

nally, a few states have avoided the issue of victims failing to request restitution by eliminating the need for such a request. In Arizona, for example, restitution is mandatory in every criminal case:[58] "The fact that a victim does not request restitution does not change the court's obligation to order it."[59]

A Victim's Failure To Demonstrate and a Court's Inability To Calculate Loss

Unless they are given sufficient evidence regarding a victim's financial loss and the degree to which the victim was harmed, courts are reluctant to enter an order of restitution. As a result, many states have adopted statutory procedures to gather information about a victim's losses. Oregon requires the prosecutor to investigate and present evidence on the nature and amount of the victim's damages before or at the time of sentencing unless the presentence report contained such information.[60] Wisconsin, meanwhile, requires the prosecutor to request information about losses from the victim.[61]

Many states also require that detailed information about the victim's losses be included in the presentence report.[62] Georgia requires the victim impact statement to be attached to the file so that the judge or prosecutor can use it at any stage of the proceedings, including restitution consideration.[63] Delaware and Oklahoma require the victim to submit a particular form describing losses in detail.[64] Victims who seek restitution in South Carolina must submit an itemized list of all financial losses.[65] Several states provide assistance to the crime victim in preparing such documentation. Oklahoma law states that "[e]very crime victim receiving the restitution claim form shall be provided assistance and direction to properly complete the form."[66]

The Opinion That Restitution Was Inappropriate in Light of Other Penalties Imposed

Traditionally, laws provide for restitution as a condition of probation or suspended sentence. There was limited statutory authority to order both restitution and incarceration.[67] This may be why many judges believe it is inappropriate to order restitution in cases in which a defendant is imprisoned as well. New laws requiring courts to consider restitution in every case may be a response to this judicial reluctance to issue restitution orders.

A Defendant's Inability To Pay

One of the most common reasons for failing to order restitution has been a defendant's inability to pay. As noted earlier, many states have addressed this problem by providing that the defendant's financial circumstances are to be considered at the time the payment schedule is developed but not when the amount of restitution is set. The South Dakota statute states that even if the defendant is currently unable to pay restitution, a restitution plan must be presented that states the conditions under which the defendant will begin making restitution.[68] Similarly, Idaho's law states that the immediate inability of a defendant to pay is not a reason to not order restitution.[69]

Illinois courts have addressed this issue by ruling that restitution may be ordered regardless of the term of incarceration and a defendant's financial resources. "The fact that [restitution] may never be collectible is of no importance,"[70] according to one Illinois case. Meanwhile, proceedings in another Illinois case indicate that "[w]ith respect to defendants sentenced to lengthy prison terms, the fact of a term of imprisonment is simply one factor for a trial judge to consider when assessing a defendant's postincarceration ability to pay for purposes of fashioning terms of the restitution order."[71]

States have also acted to ensure that courts are presented with more complete information about a defendant's financial status. Oklahoma's law states that

> The court shall order the offender to submit … such information as the court may direct and finds necessary to be disclosed for the purpose of ascertaining the type and manner of restitution to be ordered…. The willful failure or refusal of the offender to provide all or part of the requisite information prior to the sentencing, unless disclosure is deferred by the court, shall not deprive the court of the authority to set restitution or set the schedule of payment. The willful failure or refusal … shall constitute a waiver of any grounds to appeal or seek future amendment or alteration of the restitution order predicated on the undisclosed information.[72]

Such failure or refusal is also an act of contempt.[73]

In California, the defendant is required to file a disclosure identifying all assets, income, and liabilities. Failure to disclose this information may be considered an aggravating circumstance in sentencing and "a factor indicating that the interests of justice would not be served by admitting the defendant to probation … conditionally sentencing the defendant … [or] imposing less than the maximum fine and sentence."[74]

New Mexico requires defendants to prepare a plan of restitution with the probation or parole officer, "and the court, before approving, disapproving or modifying the plan of restitution, shall consider the physical and mental health and condition of the defendant, his age, his education, his employment circumstances, his potential for employment and vocational training, his family circumstances, [and] his financial condition," among other factors.[75]

Providing information about a defendant's ability to pay restitution can give courts more confidence in ordering restitution. Perhaps more important, it helps to fashion a workable payment plan.

Conclusion

Restitution to crime victims is an important criminal law objective. The act of ordering restitution serves as an acknowledgment by the criminal justice system that the victim sustained harm. Payment of restitution can help rectify that harm. Legislatures nationwide are reexamining their statutes regarding this issue and continuing to refine and expand this area of the law. Not only are legislatures acting to encourage more restitution orders, the increasing attention paid to quantifying a victim's

losses and investigating a defendant's assets before entering restitution orders will help improve the quality and workability of such orders. Victim service providers should continue to follow developments regarding this issue and be prepared to assist crime victims who seek restitution.

Notes

1. Miller, Ted, Mark Cohen, and Brian Wiersema (1996). *Victim Costs and Consequences: A New Look,* Washington, DC: National Institute of Justice, U.S. Department of Justice, p. 1.
2. National Association of Crime Victim Compensation Boards (1999). *Program Directory*, Alexandria, VA: National Association of Crime Victim Compensation Boards, p. 1.
3. ME. REV. STAT. ANN. tit. 17-A, § 1321 (West 2000).
4. ALASKA CONST. art. I, § 24; ARIZ. CONST. art. II, § 2.1; CAL. CONST. art. I, § 28; CONN. CONST. amend. 17(b); IDAHO CONST. art. I, § 22; ILL. CONST. art. I, § 8.1; LA. CONST. art. I, § 25; MICH. CONST. art. I, § 24; MO. CONST. art. I, § 32; N.M. CONST. art. II, § 24; N.C. art. I, § 37; OKLA. CONST. art. II, § 34; OR. CONST. art. I, § 42; R.I. CONST. art. I, § 23; S.C. CONST. art. I, § 24; TENN. CONST. art. I, § 35; TEX. CONST. art. I, § 30; WIS. CONST. art. I, § 9(m). Additionally, Montana recently adopted a constitutional amendment broadening the principles on which laws for the punishment of crime are based to include restitution to crime victims. MONT. CONST. art. II, § 28.
5. FLA. STAT. ANN. § 775.089 (West 2000).
6. CONN. GEN. STAT. § 53a-28 (2000); NEV. REV. STAT. § 176.033 (2001).
7. OR. REV. STAT. § 137.106 (1999).
8. As examples, see IDAHO CODE § 19-5304 (Michie 2000); MD. ANN. Code art. 27, § 807 (2001); N.C. GEN. STAT. § 15A-1340.36 (2000).
9. *People v. Valdez*, 24 Cal. App. 4th 1194, 30 Cal. Rptr. 2d 4. (1994, 5th Dist.). See also *State v. Barrs*, 172 Ariz. 42, 43, 833 P.2d 713 (Ariz. Ct. App. 1992): "The right of restitution belongs to the victim. We know of no authority that would grant the state or the court the option of not pursuing a restitution order in the absence of a waiver by the victim." However, in an Indiana case, the court found that the trial court was prohibited from ordering restitution where restitution had not been part of the plea agreement. In that state, the ordering of restitution is not required but is in the court's discretion. Indiana law also clearly states that once the court accepts a plea agreement, it is bound by the terms of the agreement. *Sinn v. State*, 693 N.E.2d 78 (Ind. App. 1998).
10. OKLA. STAT. tit. 22, § 991f (2000).
11. FLA. STAT. ANN. § 775.089 (West 2000).
12. FLA. STAT. Ann. § 784.08 (West 2000).
13. MINN. STAT. § 518B.01 (2000); UTAH CODE ANN. § 77-36-5.1 (2000).
14. MONT. CODE ANN. § 45-5-503 (2000); TEX. CODE CRIM. PROC. ANN. art. 42.12 (Vernon 2000).

15. CAL. PENAL CODE § 422.95 (Deering 2001).

16. COLO. REV. STAT. § 18-6-401.4 (2000).

17. COLO. REV. STAT. § 18-3-414 (2000).

18. KAN. STAT. ANN. § 8-1019 (2000).

19. MASS. GEN. LAWS ch. 266, § 37E (2001).

20. 18 PA. CONS. STAT. § 1106 (2000).

21. *Id.*

22. MONT. CODE ANN. § 46-18-243 (2000).

23. IND. CODE ANN. § 35-50-5-3 (Michie 2000); MICH. STAT. ANN. § 27.3178(598.30) (Law. Co-op. 2000).

24. For example, ME. REV. STAT. Ann. tit. 17-A, § 1324 (West 2000); WIS. STAT. § 973.20 (2000).

25. ALASKA STAT. § 12.55.045 (Michie 2001). See also MICH. STAT. Ann. § 28.1073 (Law. Co-op. 2000).

26. *People v. McDaniel*, 219 A.D. 2d 861, 631 N.Y.S.2d 957 (4th Dept. 1995), *appeal denied*, 88 N.Y.2d 850, 644 N.Y.S.2d 697, 667 N.E.2d 347 (1996).

27. For example, see FLA. STAT. ANN. § 775.089 (West 2000); 730 ILL. COMP. STAT. 5/5-5, -6 (2001); WASH. REV. CODE § 9.94A.140 (2001).

28. IDAHO Code § 19-5304 (Michie 2000).

29. FLA. STAT. ANN. § 775.089 (West 2000).

30. ALA. CODE § 15-18-66 (2001); *People v. Nguyen*, 23 Cal. App. 4th 32, 28 Cal. Rptr. 2d 140, *modified on other grounds, reh'g denied*, 23 Cal. App. 4th 1306e (6th Dist. 1994).

31. *State v. Russell*, 126 Idaho 38, 878 P.2d 212 (Ct. App. 1994).

32. CAL. PENAL CODE § 1202.4 (Deering 2001).

33. *In re Erika V.*, 983 P.2d 768; 297 Adv. Rep. 55 (1999).

34. N.H. REV. STAT. ANN. § 651:62 (2000).

35. MICH. STAT. ANN. § 28.1073 (Law. Co-op. 2000).

36. *State v. Spears*, 184 Ariz. 277, 292, 908 P.2d 1062 (1996).

37. *State v. Blanton*, 173 Ariz. 517, 520, 844 P.2d 1167 (Ct. App. 1993).

38. MASS. GEN. LAWS ch. 266, § 37E (2001).

39. CAL. PENAL CODE § 1202.4 (Deering 2001). See also IDAHO CODE § 19-5304 (Michie 2000); KY. REV. STAT. ANN. § 532.164 (Michie 2001); UTAH CODE ANN. § 76-3-201 (2000).

40. *State v. Mahoney*, 115 Or. App. 440, 838 P.2d 1100 (1992), Sup. Ct. *review denied, as modified by* 118 Or. App. 1, 846 P.2d 413 (1993).

41. CAL. PENAL CODE § 1202.4 (Deering 2001).

42. IOWA CODE § 910.3 (2001).

43. *State v. Howard*, 168 Ariz. 458, 459-60, 815 P.2d 5 (Ct. App. 1991).

44. WYO. STAT. ANN. § 7-9-103 (Michie 2001).

45. *Ault v. State*, 705 N.E.2d 1078 (Ind. App. 1999).

46. ALASKA STAT. § 12.55.045 (Michie 2001).

47. ARIZ. REV. STAT. § 13-804(C) (2000).

48. ARIZ. REV. STAT. § 13-804(E) (2000).

49. FLA. STAT. ANN. § 775.089(6) (West 2000). See also *Martinez v. State*, 974 P.2d 133 (Nev. 1999) (no requirement that court consider defendant's ability to pay in determining amount of restitution).

50. MINN. STAT. § 611A.04 (2000).

51. COLO. REV. STAT. § 16-11-101.5(6)(a) (2000).

52. Beatty, David, Susan Howley, and Dean Kilpatrick (1996). *Statutory and Constitutional Protections for Victims Rights*, Arlington, VA: National Center for Victims of Crime, table C-8, p. 39.

53. *Id.*, table D-28, p. 95.

54. For example, see ALA. CODE § 15-23-62 (2001); FLA. STAT. ANN. § 960.001 (West 2000); MISS. CODE ANN. § 99-43-7 (2001); OHIO REV. CODE ANN. § 109.42 (Anderson 2001).

55. MINN. STAT. § 611A.037; N.Y. CRIM. PROC. LAW § 390.30 (McKinney 2001).

56. For example, 725 ILL. COMP. STAT. 120/4.5 (2001).

57. WIS. STAT. § 973.20(13) (2000).

58. ARIZ. REV. STAT. § 13-603(c) (2000).

59. *State v. Steffy*, 173 Ariz. 90, 93, 839 P.2d 1135 (Ct. App. 1992).

60. OR. REV. STAT. § 137.106 (1999).

61. WIS. STAT. § 973.20(13) (2000).

62. For example, ALASKA STAT. § 12.55.025 (Michie 2001); KAN. STAT. ANN. § 21-4604 (2000); N.Y. CRIM. PROC. LAW § 390.30 (McKinney 2001).

63. GA. CODE ANN. § 17-10-1.1 (2000).

64. DEL. FAM. CT. R. CRIM. PROC. 32; OKLA. STAT. tit. 22, § 991f (2000).

65. S.C. CODE ANN. § 16-3-1515 (Law. Co-op. 2000).

66. OKLA. STAT. tit. 22, § 991f (2000). See also R.I. GEN. LAWS § 12-28-9 (2001).

67. See Alan T. Harland, *Monetary Remedies for the Victims of Crime: Assessing the Role of the Criminal Courts*, 30 UCLA L. Rev. 52-128, at 75-76 (1982).

68. S.D. CODIFIED LAWS § 23A-28-3 (Michie 2001).

69. IDAHO CODE § 19-5304 (Michie 2000).

70. *People v. Mitchell*, 241 Ill. App. 3d 1094, 182 Ill. Dec. 925, 610 N.E.2d 794 (4th Dist. 1993), *appeal denied*, 152 Ill. 2d 572, 190 Ill. Dec. 903, 622 N.E.2d 1220 (1993).

71. *People v. Brooks*, 158 Ill. 2d 260, 198 Ill. Dec. 851, 633 N.E.2d 692 (1994).

72. OKLA. STAT. tit. 22, § 991f (2000).

73. *Id.*

74. CAL. PENAL CODE § 1202.4 (Deering 2001).

75. N.M. STAT. ANN. § 31-17-1 (Michie 2000).

From *OVC Legal Series*, November 2002, pp. 1–7. Published by Office for Victims of Crimes/U.S. Dept. of Justice.

Pickpockets, Their Victims, and the Transit Police

By DAVID YOUNG

Pickpockets have pursued their trade almost as long as people have carried money. Many pickpockets begin their careers at a young age and, after many years of experience, acquire the patience, dexterity, and knowledge of human behavior to become successful criminals.

Pocket-picking is most common in places where large groups of people gather. Transportation facilities, such as bus terminals and railroad stations, are favorite hunting grounds for pickpockets, but a department store, public arena, or city street also can supply enough potential victims.[1] Several factors inherent in public areas increase opportunities for a pickpocket to commit a theft, while other variables reduce the risk that the pickpocket will be caught, prosecuted,

and penalized in a manner consistent with the seriousness of the crime.

Victim Profile

The author's research revealed that females became pickpocket victims more often than males. Most victims were approximately 30 years old and used the railroad as a means of transportation. The most likely places for a theft to occur were on station escalators and platforms and on trains near the doors of the car. Because a transportation facility is a public accommodation, everyone has almost unrestricted access to the common areas of the terminal. Thousands of people pass through these areas each day, and holiday travel dramatically increases customer vol-

ume. Pickpockets spend hours in terminals watching the crowds and searching for potential targets. Research did not find significant correlation between a victim's race and victimization.

Pickpocket incidents occurred most often during peak shopping times, which usually occurred outside the station, or during evening rush hours. These victims often reported the theft to railroad police officers because of a highly visible substation in the main concourse of the terminal. After people reported a pickpocket crime, preliminary interviews revealed that most victims had their wallets exposed during the 30 minutes prior to the theft. Then, they put their wallets back in their bags, purses, or knapsacks on top of other items, making the wallets easily accessible once the pickpocket opened the bag. Closing devices, such as snaps, buckles, zippers, or velcro, proved minor obstacles for the professional pickpocket.

Victims often unintentionally placed bags in an exposed position on their person, and most victims carried the bag over one shoulder. The pickpocket surveilled the victims and waited for their bags to slip into a vulnerable position to the rear of the victims, instead of at a more secure place under their arms or toward the front of their bodies. A wallet placed in an outer compartment of a knapsack and worn over the shoulders presents an easy target for even the novice pickpocket.

Incidents increased during cold weather and around holidays. In cold weather, both the pickpocket and the victim wear more clothing, which may facilitate the pickpocket s ability to commit the crime. The extra layers reduce the victim s sense of bodily awareness and provide pickpockets with added cover by shielding movements during the commission of the crime or providing a place to hide the stolen property if they get caught. Additionally, pickpockets simply may shed an outer layer of clothing for one of a different color that they are wearing underneath, thereby confusing identification by the victims and in broadcasts to other patrol officers. Pickpockets also use this tactic in warm weather; the outer garment either can be discarded or hidden in a plastic bag carried by the offender.

The most significant factor in the victim profile possibly may be psychological. A crowded terminal creates a distracting environment. People are packed together in cramped waiting areas listening for public announcements, watching a departure, carrying packages, or talking on a cellular telephone. The station s environment creates a

sensory overload. Further, the victims, conditioned by the rush hour atmosphere of the station, are accustomed to the close physical proximity of other people. Those who use mass transit expect to be bumped and jostled. The victim also expects to have even less personal space when descending the escalators and riding the train, focusing more on boarding the train and finding a seat than being concerned with others.

Pickpocket Profile

Research revealed that most pickpockets' are male. The pickpockets patterns of behavior quickly became evident during rush hours, which started around 4:30 p.m. and ended at approximately 8 p.m. The first victims usually began making their reports after 6 p.m. Typically, pickpockets bumped into their victims just as the victim stepped onto a crowded train. This usually happened a few seconds before the scheduled departure time for the train so that the pickpocket who bumped the victim simply could step off the train and let the doors close. Victims frequently realized that their wallets were stolen, but they were unable to exit the train. Instead, they had to travel to the next station before they could get off to make a report.

Most of the train rides lasted only about 18 minutes, but, during this period, the pickpocket had time to charge hundreds of dollars worth of unauthorized purchases using the victim's credit cards. Frequently, suspects used the cards within the first 5 minutes, most often to make purchases either in the station or at nearby department stores. Automatic teller machine cards regularly were compromised because victims either had the personal identification number (PIN) code in their wallets or had a PIN

that the pickpocket easily could determine.

Consequences of the Crime

Connecting the pickpocket suspects to the crime may present problems with the prosecution of these cases. Victims may have been unaware that someone had stolen their wallets; therefore, they could not identify the pickpocket. Alternatively, pickpockets apprehended by police already may have passed the victim's property to an accomplice and not have possession of it anymore. Further, when confronted, pickpockets often tried to convince the victims that they were making false accusations.

> "The most significant factor in the victim's profile possibly may be psychological."

Prosecution sometimes is not feasible because the victim lives too far away and the loss is relatively minor. Many years ago, crimes committed by pickpockets involved a pecuniary motive that came and went with the initial act of theft. Once the money was spent and the credit cards were maxed out, the pickpocket moved to a new victim. Now, however, many businesses and other institutions use personal information to identify clients, customers, and students; the information itself has real value. The profits realized by the pickpocket and the potential for harm to the victim increases exponentially if the victim's personal identifying information is used to commit identity theft.[2] The New York City Police Department's grand larceny task force has worked with the district attorneys offices in New York to familiarize prosecutors with the most active pickpockets and to coordinate prosecution resources. They hope to obtain longer sentences for recidivist offenders to keep them out of circulation for as long as possible. Permitting a pickpocket to plead to a reduced charge or to receive the minimum term on a felony conviction decreases the punishment to merely a cost of doing business.

Law Enforcement Response

Officers should learn how to recognize regular pickpocket suspects and observe actions indicative of pickpocket activity by unknown offenders. For example, has the suspect loitered in the station long enough to have missed several trains? Has the suspect moved to various platforms or trains without an apparent intent to travel? Officers should note times and locations when tracking a suspect's movements. Some offenders will arrive in groups, separate, and pretend not to know one another. Officers should note the suspects attire (e.g., layers of different colors of clothing) and if they are carrying items that they can use to conceal their hands, such as garment bags, portfolio cases, or rain coats. Officers should watch people who repeatedly bump up against others or those who use a ruse, such as assisting a passenger with luggage, to get close to a potential victim s wallet or purse. Some states have laws that make it an offense for people to put their hands in unnecessarily close proximity to a person s wallet or purse while in public areas.

Plainclothes officers assigned to pickpocket details will develop the investigative expertise needed to make an arrest and recover the victim's property. Detectives should share the results of long-term in-

vestigations through the dissemination of intelligence information to patrol and plainclothes officers. Officers who encounter known offenders should try to effect an immediate arrest if the offenders are subject to a supervisory order that prevents them from entering the station (e.g., restraining order, condition of parole, or open arrest warrant). Further, officers should take notes during their surveillance; their written observations can prove helpful when prosecuting pickpockets.

Crime analysis also plays an important role by revealing current trends and providing statistical justification for an antipickpocket program. Transit and railroad police agencies working in the same geographical area but for different authorities should communicate with one another on a regular basis to share information and coordinate their enforcement efforts. To protect customers, transit and railroad systems should allow their police departments wide latitude in developing programs to address pocket-picking problems.

Finally, people themselves must remain aware of their environment to avoid becoming a pickpocket victim. Officers can help prevent individuals from becoming a victim by observing and pointing out certain victim behaviors. For example, officers should alert those who do not safeguard their wallets and other valuables. All transit employees should assist people who appear lost or in a vulnerable position that would attract pickpockets. Officers should detail characteristics of pickpocket behavior and techniques to all transit employees, ensuring that they feel comfortable reporting suspicious behavior to the police. Further, law enforcement agencies should provide pamphlets that include tips on personal safety and security at ticket counters, customer service

areas, and on trains. When a passenger is victimized, officers should make every effort to quickly mitigate the damage. An officer should stay with the victim until the crisis is contained, giving the victim access to a telephone in a quiet area to make calls to credit card companies. Subsequently, officers should offer to take victims back to their station of origin.

Conclusion

Railroads have been an integral part of America's infrastructure since the 19th century. The environmental, social, and political concerns of the 20th century created an increased demand for new, light-rail, transit, and long-distance trains. Increased demand results in the construction of more terminals, the development of new rail systems, and, therefore, a growing number of customers.

Law enforcement officers must remain aware of pickpocket behaviors and techniques. Many passengers will become victims because they are careless or unaware that people will try to steal their wallets and other valuables. Officers should alert transit employees and passengers to profiles of victims, as well as offenders. Transportation authorities and their police departments assume the responsibility to protect these customers from victimization; they must ensure that they are prepared to face this challenge.

Endnotes

1. The author gained experience as a criminal investigator with the Amtrak Police Department in Penn Station, New York. He culled information for this article from the careful recording and analysis of data relating to station larcenies and onboard train larcenies, as well as from facts learned during

subsequent investigation from May 1999 through May 2000.

2. For more information on identity theft, see John Pollock and James May, "Authentication Technology: New Levels in the Fight Against

Identity Theft and Account Take-over," *FBI Law Enforcement Bulletin*, June 2002, 1-4; and Matthew L. Lease and Tod W. Burke, "Identity Theft: A Fast-Growing Crime," *FBI*

Law Enforcement Bulletin, August 2000, 8-13.

The author dedicates this article to the memory of Lieutenant James McHugh and Lieutenant John Delougherty, Amtrak Police.

From *FBI Law Enforcement Bulletin*, December 2003, pp. 1-5, by David Young. Published in 2003 by the Federal Bureau of Investigation.

Telling the Truth About Damned Lies and Statistics

By JOEL BEST

The dissertation prospectus began by quoting a statistic—a "grabber" meant to capture the reader's attention. The graduate student who wrote this prospectus undoubtedly wanted to seem scholarly to the professors who would read it; they would be supervising the proposed research. And what could be more scholarly than a nice, authoritative statistic, quoted from a professional journal in the student's field?

So the prospectus began with this (carefully footnoted) quotation: "Every year since 1950, the number of American children gunned down has doubled." I had been invited to serve on the student's dissertation committee. When I read the quotation, I assumed the student had made an error in copying it. I went to the library and looked up the article the student had cited. There, in the journal's 1995 volume, was exactly the same sentence: "Every year since 1950, the number of American children gunned down has doubled."

This quotation is my nomination for a dubious distinction: I think it may be the worst—that is, the most inaccurate—social statistic ever.

What makes this statistic so bad? Just for the sake of argument, let's assume that "the number of American children gunned down" in 1950 was one. If the number doubled each year, there must have been two children gunned down in 1951, four in 1952, eight in 1953, and so on. By 1960, the number would have been 1,024. By 1965, it would have been 32,768 (in 1965, the F.B.I. identified only 9,960 criminal homicides in the entire country, including adult as well as child victims). By 1970, the number would have passed one million; by 1980, one billion (more than four

times the total U.S. population in that year). Only three years later, in 1983, the number of American children gunned down would have been 8.6 billion (nearly twice the earth's population at the time). Another milestone would have been passed in 1987, when the number of gunned-down American children (137 billion) would have surpassed the best estimates for the total human population throughout history (110 billion). By 1995, when the article was published, the annual number of victims would have been over 35 trillion—a really big number, of a magnitude you rarely encounter outside economics or astronomy.

Thus my nomination: estimating the number of American child gunshot victims in 1995 at 35 trillion must be as far off—as hilariously, wildly wrong—as a social statistic can be. (If anyone spots a more inaccurate social statistic, I'd love to hear about it.)

Where did the article's author get this statistic? I wrote the author, who responded that the statistic came from the Children's Defense Fund, a well-known advocacy group for children. The C.D.F.'s *The State of America's Children Yearbook 1994* does state: "The number of American children killed each year by guns has doubled since 1950." Note the difference in the wording—the C.D.F. claimed there were twice as many deaths in 1994 as in 1950; the article's author reworded that claim and created a very different meaning.

It is worth examining the history of this statistic. It began with the C.D.F. noting that child gunshot deaths had doubled from 1950 to 1994. This is not quite as dramatic an increase as it might seem. Remember that the U.S. population also rose through-

out this period; in fact, it grew about 73 percent—or nearly double. Therefore, we might expect all sorts of things—including the number of child gunshot deaths—to increase, to nearly double, just because the population grew. Before we can decide whether twice as many deaths indicates that things are getting worse, we'd have to know more. The C.D.F. statistic raises other issues as well: Where did the statistic come from? Who counts child gunshot deaths, and how? What is meant by a "child" (some C.D.F. statistics about violence include everyone under age 25)? What is meant by "killed by guns" (gunshot-death statistics often include suicides and accidents, as well as homicides)? But people rarely ask questions of this sort when they encounter statistics. Most of the time, most people simply accept statistics without question.

Certainly, the article's author didn't ask many probing, critical questions about the C.D.F.'s claim. Impressed by the statistic, the author repeated it—well, meant to repeat it. Instead, by rewording the C.D.F.'s claim, the author created a mutant statistic, one garbled almost beyond recognition.

But people treat mutant statistics just as they do other statistics—that is, they usually accept even the most implausible claims without question. For example, the journal editor who accepted the author's article for publication did not bother to consider the implications of child victims doubling each year. And people repeat bad statistics: The graduate student copied the garbled statistic and inserted it into the dissertation prospectus. Who knows whether still other readers were impressed by the author's statistic and remembered it or repeated it? The article remains on the shelf in hundreds of libraries, available to anyone who needs a dramatic quote. The lesson should be clear: Bad statistics live on; they take on lives of their own.

Some statistics are born bad—they aren't much good from the start, because they are based on nothing more than guesses or dubious data. Other statistics mutate; they become bad after being mangled (as in the case of the author's creative rewording). Either way, bad statistics are potentially important: They can be used to stir up public outrage or fear; they can distort our understanding of our world; and they can lead us to make poor policy choices.

THE NOTION that we need to watch out for bad statistics isn't new. We've all heard people say, "You can prove anything with statistics." The title of my book, *Damned Lies and Statistics*, comes from a famous aphorism (usually attributed to Mark Twain or Benjamin Disraeli): "There are three kinds of lies: lies, damned lies, and statistics." There is even a useful little book, still in print after more than 40 years, called *How to Lie With Statistics*.

> We shouldn't ignore all statistics, or assume that every number is false. Some statistics are bad, but others are pretty good. And we need good statistics to talk sensibly about social problems.

Statistics, then, have a bad reputation. We suspect that statistics may be wrong, that people who use statistics may be "lying"—trying to manipulate us by using numbers to somehow distort the truth. Yet, at the same time, we need statistics; we depend upon them to summarize and clarify the nature of our complex society. This is particularly true when we talk about social problems. Debates about social problems routinely raise questions that demand statistical answers: Is the problem widespread? How many people—and which people—does it affect? Is it getting worse? What does it cost society? What will it cost to deal with it? Convincing answers to

such questions demand evidence, and that usually means numbers, measurements, statistics.

But can't you prove anything with statistics? It depends on what "prove" means. If we want to know, say, how many children are "gunned down" each year, we can't simply guess—pluck a number from thin air: 100, 1,000, 10,000, 35 trillion, whatever. Obviously, there's no reason to consider an arbitrary guess "proof" of anything. However, it might be possible for someone—using records kept by police departments or hospital emergency rooms or coroners—to keep track of children who have been shot; compiling careful, complete records might give us a fairly accurate idea of the number of gunned-down children. If that number seems accurate enough, we might consider it very strong evidence—or proof.

The solution to the problem of bad statistics is not to ignore all statistics, or to assume that every number is false. Some statistics are bad, but others are pretty good, and we need statistics—good statistics—to talk sensibly about social problems. The solution, then, is not to give up on statistics, but to become better judges of the numbers we encounter. We need to think critically about statistics—at least critically enough to suspect that the number of children gunned down hasn't been doubling each year since 1950.

A few years ago, the mathematician John Allen Paulos wrote *Innumeracy*, a short, readable book about "mathematical illiteracy." Too few people, he argued, are comfortable with basic mathematical principles, and this makes them poor judges of the numbers they encounter. No doubt this is one reason we have so many bad statistics. But there are other reasons, as well.

Social statistics describe society, but they are also products of our social arrangements. The people who bring social statistics to our attention have reasons for doing so; they inevitably want something, just as reporters and the other media figures who repeat and publicize statistics have their own goals. Statistics are tools, used for particular purposes. Thinking critically about statistics requires understanding their place in society.

While we may be more suspicious of statistics presented by people with whom we disagree—people who favor different political parties or have different beliefs—bad statistics are used to promote all sorts of causes. Bad statistics come from conservatives on the political right and liberals on the left, from wealthy corporations and

powerful government agencies, and from advocates of the poor and the powerless.

In order to interpret statistics, we need more than a checklist of common errors. We need a general approach, an orientation, a mind-set that we can use to think about new statistics that we encounter. We ought to approach statistics thoughtfully. This can be hard to do, precisely because so many people in our society treat statistics as fetishes. We might call this the mind-set of the Awestruck—the people who don't think critically, who act as though statistics have magical powers. The awestruck know they don't always understand the statistics they hear, but this doesn't bother them. After all, who can expect to understand magical numbers? The reverential fatalism of the awestruck is not thoughtful—it is a way of avoiding thought. We need a different approach.

One choice is to approach statistics critically. Being critical does not mean being negative or hostile—it is not cynicism. The critical approach statistics thoughtfully; they avoid the extremes of both naive acceptance and cynical rejection of the numbers they encounter. Instead, the critical attempt to evaluate numbers, to distinguish between good statistics and bad statistics.

The critical understand that, while some social statistics may be pretty good, they are never perfect. Every statistic is a way of summarizing complex information into relatively simple numbers. Inevitably, some information, some of the complexity, is lost whenever we use statistics. The critical recognize that this is an inevitable limitation of statistics. Moreover, they realize that every statistic is the product of choices—the choice between defining a category broadly or narrowly, the choice of one measurement over another, the choice of a sample. People choose definitions, measurements, and samples for all sorts of reasons: Perhaps they want to emphasize some aspect of a problem; perhaps it is easier or cheaper to gather data in a particular way—many considerations can come into play. Every statistic is a compromise among choices. This means that every definition—and every measurement and every sample—probably has limitations and can be criticized.

Being critical means more than simply pointing to the flaws in a statistic. Again, every statistic has flaws. The issue is whether a particular statistic's flaws are severe enough to damage its usefulness. Is the definition so broad that it encompasses too many false positives (or so narrow that it excludes too many false negatives)?

How would changing the definition alter the statistic? Similarly, how do the choices of measurements and samples affect the statistic? What would happen if different measures or samples were chosen? And how is the statistic used? Is it being interpreted appropriately, or has its meaning been mangled to create a mutant statistic? Are the comparisons that are being made appropriate, or are apples being confused with oranges? How do different choices produce the conflicting numbers found in stat wars? These are the sorts of questions the critical ask.

As a practical matter, it is virtually impossible for citizens in contemporary society to avoid statistics about social problems. Statistics arise in all sorts of ways, and in almost every case the people promoting statistics want to persuade us. Activists use statistics to convince us that social problems are serious and deserve our attention and concern. Charities use statistics to encourage donations. Politicians use statistics to persuade us that they understand society's problems and that they deserve our support. The media use statistics to make their reporting more dramatic, more convincing, more compelling. Corporations use statistics to promote and improve their products. Researchers use statistics to document their findings and support their conclusions. Those with whom we agree use statistics to reassure us that we're on the right side, while our opponents use statistics to try and convince us that we are wrong. Statistics are one of the standard types of evidence used by people in our society.

It is not possible simply to ignore statistics, to pretend they don't exist. That sort of head-in-the-sand approach would be too costly. Without statistics, we limit our ability to think thoughtfully about our society; without statistics, we have no accurate ways of judging how big a problem may be, whether it is getting worse, or how well the policies designed to address that problem actually work. And awestruck or naive attitudes toward statistics are no better than ignoring statistics; statistics have no magical properties, and it is foolish to assume that all statistics are equally valid. Nor is a cynical approach the answer; statistics are too widespread and too useful to be automatically discounted.

It would be nice to have a checklist, a set of items we could consider in evaluating any statistic. The list might detail potential problems with definitions, measurements, sampling, mutation, and so on. These are, in fact, common sorts of flaws found in many statistics, but they should not be considered a formal, complete checklist. It is probably impossible to produce a complete list of statistical flaws—no matter how long the list, there will be other possible problems that could affect statistics.

The goal is not to memorize a list, but to develop a thoughtful approach. Becoming critical about statistics requires being prepared to ask questions about numbers. When encountering a new statistic in, say, a news report, the critical try to assess it. What might be the sources for this number? How could one go about producing the figure? Who produced the number, and what interests might they have? What are the different ways key terms might have been defined, and which definitions have been chosen? How might the phenomena be measured, and which measurement choices have been made? What sort of sample was gathered, and how might that sample affect the result? Is the statistic being properly interpreted? Are comparisons being made, and if so, are the comparisons appropriate? Are there competing statistics? If so, what stakes do the opponents have in the issue, and how are those stakes likely to affect their use of statistics? And is it possible to figure out why the statistics seem to disagree, what the differences are in the ways the competing sides are using figures?

At first, this list of questions may seem overwhelming. How can an ordinary person—someone who reads a statistic in a magazine article or hears it on a news broadcast—determine the answers to such questions? Certainly news reports rarely give detailed information on the processes by which statistics are created. And few of us have time to drop everything and investigate the background of some new number we encounter. Being critical, it seems, involves an impossible amount of work.

In practice, however, the critical need not investigate the origin of every statistic. Rather, being critical means appreciating the inevitable limitations that affect all statistics, rather than being awestruck in the presence of numbers. It means not being too credulous, not accepting every statistic at face value. But it also means appreciating that statistics, while always imperfect, can be useful. Instead of automatically discounting every statistic, the critical reserve judgment. When confronted with an interesting number, they may try to learn more, to evaluate, to weigh the figure's strengths and weaknesses.

Of course, this critical approach need not—and should not—be limited to statistics. It ought to apply to all the evidence we encounter when we scan a news report, or listen to a speech—whenever we learn about social problems. Claims about social problems often feature dramatic, compelling examples; the critical might ask whether an example is likely to be a typical case or an extreme, exceptional instance. Claims about social problems often include quotations from different sources, and the critical might wonder why those sources have spoken and why they have been quoted: Do they have particular expertise? Do they stand to benefit if they influence others? Claims about social problems usually involve arguments about the problem's causes and potential solutions. The critical might ask whether these arguments are convincing. Are they logical? Does the proposed solution seem feasible and appropriate? And so on. Being critical—adopting a skeptical, analytical stance when confronted with claims—is an approach that goes far beyond simply dealing with statistics.

Statistics are not magical. Nor are they always true—or always false. Nor need they be incomprehensible. Adopting a critical approach offers an effective way of responding to the numbers we are sure to encounter. Being critical requires more thought, but failing to adopt a critical mind-set makes us powerless to evaluate what others tell us. When we fail to think critically, the statistics we hear might just as well be magical.

Joel Best is a professor of sociology and criminal justice at the University of Delaware. This essay is excerpted from Damned Lies and Statistics: Untangling Numbers From the Media, Politicians, and Activists, *published by the University of California Press and reprinted by permission. Copyright © 2001 by the Regents of the University of California.*

Violence and the Remaking of a Self

BY SUSAN J. BRISON

ON JULY 4, 1990, at 10:30 in the morning, I went for a walk along a country road in a village outside Grenoble, France. It was a gorgeous day, and I didn't envy my husband, Tom, who had to stay inside and work on a manuscript with a French colleague. I sang to myself as I set out, stopping along the way to pet a goat and pick a few wild strawberries. About an hour and a half later, I was lying face down in a muddy creek bed at the bottom of a dark ravine, struggling to stay alive.

I had been grabbed from behind, pulled into the bushes, beaten, and sexually assaulted. Helpless and entirely at my assailant's mercy, I talked to him, trying to appeal to his humanity, and, when that failed, addressing myself to his self-interest. He called me a whore and told me to shut up. Although I had said I'd do whatever he wanted, as the sexual assault began I instinctively fought back, which so enraged my attacker that he strangled me until I lost consciousness.

When I came to, I was being dragged by my feet down into the ravine. I had often thought I was awake while dreaming, but now I was awake and convinced I was having a nightmare. But it was no dream. After ordering me to get on my hands and knees, the man strangled me again. This time I was sure I was dying. But I revived, just in time to see him lunging toward me with a rock. He smashed it into my forehead, knocking me out. Eventually, after another strangulation attempt, he left me for dead.

After I was rescued and taken to the Grenoble hospital, where I spent the next 11 days, I was told repeatedly how "lucky" I was to be alive, and for a short while I even believed this myself. At the time, I did not yet know how trauma not only haunts the conscious and unconscious mind but also remains in the body, in each of the senses, in the heart that races and the skin that crawls whenever something resurrects the buried terror. I didn't know that the worst—the unimaginably painful aftermath of violence—was yet to come.

For the first several months after my attack, I led a spectral existence, not quite sure whether I had died and the world was going on without me, or whether I was alive but in a totally alien world. The line between life and death, once so clear and sustaining, now seemed carelessly drawn and easily erased. I felt as though I'd outlived myself, as if I'd stayed on a train one stop past my destination.

After I was rescued and taken to the hospital, I was told repeatedly how 'lucky' I was to be alive. For a short while I even believed this myself.

My sense of unreality was fed by the massive denial of those around me—a reaction that is an almost universal response to rape, I learned. Where the facts would appear to be incontrovertible, denial takes the shape of attempts to explain the assault in ways that leave the observers' worldview unscathed. Even those who are able to acknowledge the existence of violence try to protect themselves from the realization that the world in which it occurs is their world. They cannot allow themselves to imagine the victim's shattered life, or else their illusions about their own safety and control over their lives might begin to crumble.

The most well-meaning individuals, caught up in the myth of their own immunity, can inadvertently add to the victim's suffering by suggesting that the attack was avoidable or somehow her fault. One victims'-assistance coordinator, whom I had phoned for legal advice, stressed that she herself had never been a victim and said I would benefit from the experience by learning not to be so trusting of people and to take basic safety precautions, like not going out alone late at night. She didn't pause long enough for me to point out that I had been attacked suddenly, from behind, in broad daylight.

I was initially reluctant to tell people (other than medical and legal personnel) that I had been raped. I still wonder why I wanted the sexual aspect of the assault—so salient to me—kept secret. I was motivated in part by shame, I suppose, and I wanted to avoid being stereotyped as a victim. I did not want the academic work I had already done on pornography and violence against women to be dismissed as the ravings of a "hysterical rape victim." And I felt that I had very little control over the meaning of the word "rape." Using the term denied the particularity of what I had experienced and invoked in other people whatever rape scenario they had already constructed. I later identified myself publicly as a rape survivor, having decided that it was ethically and politically imperative for me to do so.

But my initial wariness about the use of the term was understandable and, at times, reinforced by others' responses—especially by the dismissive characterization of the rape by some in the criminal-justice system. Before my assailant's trial, I heard my lawyer conferring with another lawyer on the question of victim's compensation from the state (to cover legal expenses and unreimbursed medical bills). He said, without irony, that a certain amount was typically awarded for "*un viol gentil*" ("a nice rape") and somewhat more (which they would request on my behalf) for "*un viol méchant*" ("a nasty rape").

Not surprisingly, I felt that I was taken more seriously as a victim of a near-fatal murder attempt. But that description of the assault provided others with no explanation of what had happened. Later, when people asked why this man had tried to kill me, I revealed that the attack had begun as a sexual assault, and most people were satisfied with that as an explanation. It made some kind of sense to them. But it made no sense to me.

A FEW MONTHS AFTER THE ASSAULT, I sat down at my computer to write about it for the first time, and all I could come up with was a list of paradoxes. Just about everything had stopped making sense. I thought it was quite possible that I was brain-damaged as a result of the head injuries I had sustained. Or perhaps the heightened lucidity I had experienced during the assault remained, giving me a clearer, though profoundly disorienting, picture of the world. I turned to philosophy for meaning and consolation and could find neither. Had my reasoning broken down? Or was it the breakdown of Reason? I couldn't explain what had happened to me. I was attacked for no reason. I had ventured outside the human community, landed beyond the moral universe, beyond the realm of predictable events and comprehensible actions, and I didn't know how to get back.

As a philosopher, I was used to taking something apparently obvious and familiar—the nature of time, say, or the relation between words and things—and making it into something quite puzzling. But now, when I was confronted with the utterly strange and paradoxical, philosophy was, at least initially, of no use in helping me to make sense of it. And it was hard for me, given my philosophical background, to accept that knowledge isn't always desirable, that the truth doesn't always set you free. Sometimes, it fills you with incapacitating terror, and then uncontrollable rage.

I was surprised, perhaps naively, to find that there was virtually nothing in the philosophical literature about sexual violence; obviously, it raised numerous philosophical issues. The disintegration of the self experienced by victims of violence challenges our notions of personal identity over time, a major preoccupation of metaphysics. A victim's seemingly justified skepticism about everyone and everything is pertinent to epistemology, especially if the goal of epistemology is, as Wilfrid Sellars put it, that of feeling at home in the world. In aesthetics, as well as in the philosophy of law, the discussion of sexual violence in—or as—art could use the illumination provided by a victim's perspective. Perhaps the most important questions that sexual violence poses are in social, political, and legal philosophy. Insight into those areas, as well, requires an understanding of what it's like to be a victim of such violence.

It occurred to me that the fact that rape has not been considered a properly philosophical subject—unlike war, for example—resulted not only from the paucity of women in the profession but also from the disciplinary biases against thinking about the "personal" or the particular, and against writing in the form of narrative. (Of course, the avowedly personal experiences of *men* have been neglected in philosophical analysis as well. The study of the ethics of war, for example, has dealt with questions of strategy and justice as viewed from the outside, not with the wartime experiences of soldiers or with the aftermath of their trauma.) But first-person narratives, especially ones written by those with perspectives previously excluded from the discipline, are essential to philosophy. They are necessary for exposing previously hidden biases in the discipline's subject matter and methodology, for facilitating understanding of (or empathy with) those different from ourselves, and for laying on the table our own biases as scholars.

W HEN I RESUMED TEACHING at Dartmouth, the first student who came to my office told me that she had been raped. Since I had spoken out publicly several months earlier about my assault, I knew that I would be in contact with other survivors. I just didn't realize that there would be so many—not only students, but also female colleagues and friends, who had never before told me that they had been raped. I continued to teach my usual philosophy courses, but, in some ways philosophy struck me as a luxury when I knew, in a more visceral way than before, that people were being brutally attacked and killed—all the time. So I integrated my work on trauma with my academic interests by teaching a course on global violence against women. I was still somewhat afraid of what would happen if I wrote about my assault, but I was much more afraid of what would continue to happen if I, and others with similar experiences, didn't make them public.

It was one thing to have decided to speak and write about my rape, but another to find the voice with which to do it. Even after my fractured trachea had healed, I frequently had trouble speaking. I lost my voice, literally, when I lost my ability to continue my life's narrative, when things stopped making sense. I was never entirely mute, but I often had bouts of what a friend labeled "fractured speech," during which I stuttered and stammered, unable to string together a simple sentence without the words scattering like a broken necklace. During the assault itself, my heightened lucidity had seemed to be accompanied by an unusual linguistic fluency—in French, no less. But being able to speak quickly and (so it seemed to me) precisely in a foreign language when I felt I had to in order to survive was followed by episodes, spread over several years, when I couldn't, for the life of me, speak intelligibly even in my mother tongue.

The fact that rape has not been considered a properly philosophical subject results in part from disciplinary biases against thinking about the 'personal.'

For about a year after the assault, I rarely, if ever, spoke in smoothly flowing sentences. I could sing, though, after about six months, and, like aphasics who cannot say a word but can sing verse after verse, I never stumbled over the lyrics. I recall spending the hour's drive home from the weekly meetings of my support group of rape survivors singing every spiritual I'd ever heard. It was a comfort and a release. Mainly, it was something I could do, loudly, openly (by myself in a closed car), and easily, accompanied by unstoppable tears.

Even after I regained my ability to speak, more or less reliably, in English, I was unable to speak, without debilitating difficulty, in French. Before my ill-fated trip in the summer of 1990, I'd never have passed for a native speaker, but I'd visited France many times and spent several summers there. I came of age there, intellectually, immersing myself in the late 1970s in research on French feminism, which had led to my interviewing Simone de Beauvoir (in Rome) one summer. Now, more than 10 years after the assault, I still almost never speak French, even in Francophone company, in which I often find myself, given my husband's interests.

After regaining my voice, I sometimes lost it again—once for an entire week after my brother committed suicide on Christmas Eve, 1995. Although I'd managed to keep my speech impairment hidden from my colleagues and students for five and a half years, I found that I had to ask a colleague to take over a class I'd been scheduled to teach the day after the funeral. I feared that I'd suffer a linguistic breakdown in front of a lecture hall full of students.

I lost my voice again, intermittently, during my tenure review, about a year after my brother's death. And, although I could still write (and type) during this time, I can see now that my writing about violence had become increasingly hesitant and guarded, as I hid behind academic jargon and excessive citations of others' work. Not only had my brother's suicide caused me to doubt whether I, who had, after all, survived, was entitled to talk about the trauma I'd endured, but now I could not silence the internalized voices of those who had warned me not to publish my work on sexual violence before getting tenure. In spite of the warm reception my writing on the subject was receiving in the larger academic community—from feminist philosophers and legal theorists, people in women's studies, and scholars from various disciplines who were interested in trauma—I stopped writing in the personal voice and slipped back into the universal mode, thinking that only writing about trauma in general was important enough to justify the academic risks I was taking. And I took fewer and fewer risks.

After getting tenure, I was given sanctuary, for nearly two years, at the Institute for Advanced Study, in Princeton. There I gradually came to feel safe enough to write, once again, in my own voice, about what I considered to be philosophically important. It helped to be surrounded by a diverse group of scholars who, to my initial amazement and eternal gratitude, simply assumed that whatever I was working on must be of sufficient intellectual interest to be worth bothering about.

My linguistic disability never resurfaced in my many conversations at the institute, although it returned later, after a particularly stressful incident at Dartmouth. That episode, more than eight and a half years after the assault, forced me to accept that I have what may well be a permanent neurological glitch resulting from my brain's having been stunned into unconsciousness four times during the attack. Although I had spoken out as a rape survivor at a Take Back the Night rally nine months after the event, it took me nearly nine years to acknowledge, even to myself, that the assault had left me neurologically disabled—very minimally, to be sure, in a way that I could easily compensate for, by avoiding extremely stressful situations, but disabled nonetheless.

PEOPLE ASK ME if I'm recovered now, and I reply that it depends on what that means. If they mean, Am I back to where I was before the attack? I have to say no, and I never will be. I am not the same person who set off, singing, on that sunny Fourth of July in the French countryside. I left her in a rocky creek bed at the bottom of a ravine. I had to in order to survive. The trauma has changed me forever, and if I insist too often that my friends and family acknowledge it, that's because I'm afraid they don't know who I am.

But if recovery means being able to incorporate this awful knowledge of trauma and its aftermath into my life and carry on, then, yes, I'm recovered. I don't wake each day with a start, thinking: "This can't have happened to me!" It happened. I have no guarantee that it won't happen again. I don't expect to be able to transcend or redeem the trauma, or to solve the dilemmas of survival. I think the goal of recovery is simply to endure. That is hard enough, especially when sometimes it seems as if the only way to regain control over one's life is to end it.

A FEW MONTHS after my assault, I drove by myself for several hours to visit my friend Margot. Though driving felt like a much safer mode of transportation than walking, I worried throughout the journey, not only about the trajectory of every oncoming vehicle but also about my car breaking down, leaving me at the mercy of potentially murderous passersby. I wished I'd had a gun so that I could shoot myself rather than be forced to live through another assault. Later in my recovery, as depression gave way to rage, such suicidal thoughts were quickly quelled by a stubborn refusal to finish my assailant's job for him. I also learned, after martial-arts training, that I was capable, morally as well as physically, of killing in self-defense—an option that made the possibility of another life-threatening attack one I could live with.

Some rape survivors have remarked on the sense of moral loss they experienced when they realized that they could kill their assailants, but I think that this thought can be seen as a salutary character change in those whom society does not encourage to value their own lives enough. And, far from jeopardizing their connections with a community, this new-found ability to defend themselves—and to consider themselves worth fighting for—enables rape survivors to move once more among others, free of debilitating fears. It gave me the courage to bring a child into the world, in spite of the realization that doing so would, far from making me immortal, make me twice as mortal, doubling my chances of having my life destroyed by a speeding truck.

But many trauma survivors who endured much worse than I did, and for much longer, found, often years later, that it was impossible to go on. It is not a moral failing to leave a world that has become morally unacceptable. I wonder how some people can ask of battered women, Why didn't they leave? while saying of those driven to suicide by the brutal and inescapable aftermath of trauma, Why didn't they stay? Jean Améry wrote,

"Whoever was tortured, stays tortured," and that may explain why he, Primo Levi, Paul Celan, and other Holocaust survivors took their own lives decades after their physical torture ended, as if such an explanation were needed.

THOSE who have survived trauma understand the pull of that solution to their daily Beckettian dilemma—"I can't go on, I must go on"—for on some days the conclusion "I'll go on" can be reached by neither faith nor reason. How does one go on with a shattered self, with no guarantee of recovery, believing that one will always stay tortured and never feel at home in the world? One hopes for a bearable future, in spite of all the inductive evidence to the contrary. After all, the loss of faith in induction following an unpredictable trauma has a reassuring side: Since inferences from the past can no longer be relied upon to predict the future, there's no more reason to think that tomorrow will bring agony than to think that it won't. So one makes a wager, in which nothing is certain and the odds change daily, and sets about willing to believe that life, for all its unfathomable horror, still holds some undiscovered pleasures. And one re-makes oneself by finding meaning in a life of caring for and being sustained by others.

While I used to have to will myself out of bed each day, I now wake gladly to feed my son, whose birth gave me reason not to have died. Having him has forced me to rebuild my trust in the world, to try to believe that the world is a good enough place in which to raise him. He is so trusting that, before he learned to walk, he would stand with outstretched arms, wobbling, until he fell, stiff-limbed, forward, backward, certain the universe would catch him. So far it has, and when I tell myself it always will, the part of me that he's become believes it.

Susan J. Brison is an associate professor of philosophy at Dartmouth College and a visiting associate professor of philosophy at Princeton University. She is the author of Aftermath: Violence and the Remaking of a Self, *published by Princeton University Press.*

Prosecutors, Kids, and Domestic Violence Cases

by Debra Whitcomb

Police and prosecutors say they sometimes feel like they are walking a tightrope when they intervene in domestic violence cases. Each step into a heated domestic situation requires careful balance. On the one hand, the justice system must hold batterers accountable for their violent behavior; on the other hand, a woman needs to control her life and find safety and security for herself and her children as best she can.

As research reveals more about the effects of domestic violence on children, prosecutors are finding that both the law and public opinion have raised expectations for what criminal justice professionals should do and actually can do.

Some States have enacted legislation to better protect children exposed to violence, but the new laws are raising concern about the impact on mothers. Critics hypothesize that battered women will be increasingly charged with criminal child abuse or failure to protect their children if they do not take action against their batterer and could eventually lose custody. Others fear that children who are exposed to domestic violence will increasingly be forced to testify and therefore to "choose sides" in the cases against their mother or father.

This article describes some of the issues prosecutors should be aware of when they handle domestic violence cases involving children, especially in light of recent legislation aimed to protect children. It is the product of an NIJ-funded exploratory study that relied on two sources of data: a national telephone survey of prosecutors and field research in five jurisdictions. (See "The Survey and Its Findings.")

The exploratory study sought answers to the following questions:

- How are new laws, now in effect in a small number of States, affecting practice?
- What challenges do prosecutors face when children are exposed to domestic violence?
- What can prosecutors do to help battered women and their children?

Why the New Laws?

Children who witness domestic violence often manifest behavioral and emotional problems, poor academic performance, and delinquency.[1] Sadly, violence against women and violence against children often coexist in families—the frequency of child abuse doubles in families experiencing intimate partner violence, compared to families with nonviolent partners, and the rate of child abuse escalates with the severity and frequency of the abuse against the mother.[2]

Domestic violence is also a known risk factor for recurring child abuse reports[3] and for child fatalities.[4] In addition, domestic violence frequently coexists with substance abuse, so that children are exposed to the effects of dangerous substances and the parental neglect that usually comes with addiction.[5] One large study involving 9,500 HMO members revealed that the 1,010 people who reported that their mothers had been treated violently also reported being exposed to other adverse childhood experiences, such as substance abuse (59 percent reported exposure), mental illness (38 percent), sexual abuse (41 percent), psychological abuse (34 percent), and physical abuse (31 percent).[6]

It is generally recognized that the well-being of children who witness domestic violence is tied closely to that of their mothers,[7] but the mother's interests and the child's may not always be identical or even compatible. A mother may face serious concerns about their financial and physical well-being if she separates from her violent partner. She may lack resources or social networks to extricate herself from dangerous relationships, and the community's support system may be inadequate. Her efforts to seek help may be thwarted by waiting lists, lack of insurance, or high fees for services. She may believe that she and her children are better off staying with the violent partner despite the consequences.[8]

Meanwhile, the children remain in perilous environments. Child protection agencies may feel compelled to intervene to forestall the escalating risk of harm to children. Unfortunately, in many jurisdictions, a referral to the child protection agency is perceived as a mixed blessing. Many child protection agencies do not have adequate resources to respond to the volume of domestic violence reports they receive when exposure to violence is defined as a form of child maltreatment by law or policy. Elsewhere, critics charge, protective services workers are too quick to remove children from violent homes, inappropriately blaming women for the actions of their abusive partners.

> # Police officers are being encouraged to note the presence of children when they respond to domestic violence incidents and to collaborate with mental health professionals to address the children's trauma and anxiety.

How Are New Laws Affecting Practice?

The words of San Diego City Attorney Casey Gwinn capture the climate of growing concerns related to children and violence in the home:

> … children must be a central focus of all we do in the civil and criminal justice system… from the initial police investigation through the probationary period, we must prioritize children's issues.[9]

Police officers are being encouraged to note the presence of children when they respond to domestic violence incidents and to collaborate with mental health professionals to address the children's trauma and anxiety.[10] Battered women's shelters are hiring staff to work with children and developing policy for alerting child protection agencies when needed.[11] Juvenile and family courts are sponsoring programs to meet the needs of battered women whose children are at risk for maltreatment.[12] Child protection agencies are instituting training and protocols to better identify domestic violence; some are hiring domestic violence specialists to help develop appropriate case plans.[13] Legislators, too, are taking action by enhancing penalties when domestic violence occurs in front of children and creating new criminal child abuse offenses for cases involving children who are exposed to domestic violence.

The new laws are affecting prosecutors in different ways. For example, district attorneys in Multnomah County, Oregon, where a new law recently upgraded do-

mestic violence offenses to felonies when children are present,[14] issued nearly 150 percent more felony domestic violence cases in the year that the new law was passed.

In both Salt Lake County, Utah, and Houston County, Georgia, where committing domestic violence in the presence of a child is a new crime of child abuse,[15] prosecutors tend to use these charges as "bargaining chips" to exert leverage toward guilty pleas on domestic violence charges.

In these jurisdictions, the new State laws remind law enforcement investigators to document children as witnesses and to take statements from them whenever possible, which may strengthen prosecutors' domestic violence cases even if the children cannot testify.

To understand how prosecutors are responding to the changing attitudes, researchers asked them to explain how they would respond to three different scenarios involving children and domestic violence:

1. An abused mother is alleged to have abused her children.
2. Both mother and children are abused by the same male perpetrator.
3. Children are exposed to domestic violence, but not abused themselves.

For each scenario, respondents answered these questions:

- Would your office *report* the mother to the child protection agency?
- Would your office *prosecute* the mother in the first scenario for the abuse of her children?
- Would your office report or prosecute the mother in scenarios 2 and 3 for failure to protect her children from abuse or exposure to domestic violence?

Many respondents noted the lack of statutory authority in their States to prosecute mothers for failure to protect their children, especially from exposure to domestic violence. Some explained that they consider mothers' experience of victimization in their decisions to report or prosecute battered mothers for their children's exposure to abuse or domestic violence.

Factors in these decisions commonly include the severity of injury to the child, chronicity of the domestic violence, the degree to which the mother actively participated in the abuse of her child, and prior history of failure to comply with services or treatment plans.

Prosecutors in States with laws either creating or enhancing penalties for domestic violence in the presence of children were significantly more likely to report battered mothers for failure to protect their children from abuse or from exposure to domestic violence, but there is no significant difference in the likelihood of prosecution. (See table 1.)

The Survey and Its Findings

The study involved a telephone survey of prosecutors and in-depth site visits to five jurisdictions to collect information about current practice and to identify "promising practices" in response to cases involving domestic violence and child victims or witnesses.

The final report, *Children and Domestic Violence: Challenges for Prosecutors*, NCJ 185355; grant 99–WT–VX–0001) is available from NCJRS for $15. To order a copy, call 1-800-851-3420.

Findings from the Telephone Survey

The 128 prosecutors who completed the telephone survey worked in 93 office in 49 States. The offices had jurisdiction over both felony and misdemeanor cases at either the county or district level. Nearly half (48 percent) of the jurisdictions had units or prosecutors responsible for all family violence cases, 38 percent had separate domestic violence and child abuse prosecutors or units. The other respondents represented the singular perspectives of domestic violence (10 percent) or child abuse (4 percent).

Specific findings include the following:

Most respondents (78 percent) agreed that the presence of children provides added incentive to prosecute domestic violence cases. A few individuals pointed to the children's capacity to testify as an important factor in their decisions.

A majority of prosecutors' offices (59 percent) are aggressively pursuing enhanced sanctions for domestic violence offenders when incidents involve children as victims or witnesses. Most commonly, prosecutors argue for harsher sentencing or file separate charges of child endangerment. Responding offices in which prosecu-

tors had received at least some training on the co-occurrence of domestic violence and child maltreatment (65 percent) were significantly more likely to report employing these avenues in applicable cases.

Most jurisdictions lack a policy for prosecutors and investigators to identify co-occurring cases of domestic violence and child maltreatment. None of the 35 responding offices with separate domestic violence and child abuse units had protocols directing prosecutors in these units to inquire about co-occurrence or to communicate with one another when relevant cases arise. About half were aware of protocols directing law enforcement officers to ask about child victims or witnesses when investigating domestic violence reports. About one-fourth knew of protocols directing investigators to inquire about domestic violence when responding to child abuse reports.

Findings From the In-Depth Site Visits

Dallas, Texas. Prosecutors in Dallas pursue a fairly strict "no-drop" policy for domestic violence cases, and the presence of children only strengthens their resolve to move cases forward. However, with reluctant women, the officials can offer the option of filing an "affidavit of non-prosecution." This document helps women who fear retribution from their abusive partners because it allows the women to demonstrate their efforts to terminate law enforcement's intervention. However, it has no effect on the prosecutor's decision making or the court's proceedings.

Where there are concurrent charges of domestic violence and child abuse, prosecutors try to coordinate the cases to optimize the sanctions against the offender and the safety of the mother and children. For example, the family violence prose-

cutor can use child abuse cases to support the domestic violence charge. Even if the child abuse is a felony and the domestic violence is a misdemeanor, prosecutors may accept a plea to jail time on the domestic violence charge and a 10-year deferred adjudication on the child abuse charge, which typically carries with it numerous conditions (e.g., no contact, participation in substance abuse treatment, and so on). This avenue ensures a domestic violence conviction while imposing strict court oversight on the child abuse charge.

Respondents observed that deferred adjudication or a probation sentence is, in some ways, more severe and more effective than jail time, precisely because of the conditions that can be imposed, the length of time that the offender can remain under the court's supervision, and the threat of revocation and incarceration.

San Diego, California. Prosecutors in San Diego are both aggressive and creative in finding ways to enhance sanctions for perpetrators of domestic violence and child abuse. For example, domestic violence offenders can be charged with child endangerment when a child:

- Calls 911 to report domestic violence.
- Appears fearful, upset, or hysterical at the scene.
- Is an eyewitness to the incident.
- Is present in a room where objects are being thrown.
- Is in a car during a domestic violence incident.
- Is in the arms of the victim or suspect during an incident.[1]

Anyone convicted of child endangerment and sentenced to probation will be required to complete a yearlong child abuser's treatment program.

(continued on next page)

Several programs support the prosecutors. For example, the Child Advocacy Project (CAP) provides services to children and families in reported incidents of abuse, neglect, exploitation, or domestic violence that are *not* investigated for criminal justice system intervention. Through a collaboration with the San Diego Police Department and Children's Hospital Center for Child Protection, the San Diego City Attorney's Office reviews these reports with an eye toward any angle that might support a misdemeanor prosecution with the goal of creating an avenue for service delivery. Most defendants plead guilty and receive informal probation with referrals to parenting and counseling programs.

Salt Lake County, Utah. In May 1997, Utah became the first State to enact legislation specifically addressing the issue of children who witness domestic violence. Notable elements of this statute include the following:

- It creates a crime of child abuse, not domestic violence.
- It does not require the child to be physically present during the incident of domestic violence. The perpetrator simply must be aware that a child may see or hear it.
- Unless the precipitating domestic violence incident is quite severe, it requires at least one previous violation or act of domestic violence in the presence of a child. A police incident report documenting an earlier act in the presence of a child will suffice for this purpose.

Although criminal justice agencies in Salt Lake County were not able to provide statistical data, anecdotal evidence suggests that:

- The law is infrequently applied to mothers. But it could be applied if the women were arrested in the underlying incident of domestic violence.

- The law is largely symbolic. It adds minimal time to the offender's sentence—perhaps 6 months if the sentences for the domestic violence and child abuse charges run consecutively.
- The crime is relatively easy to prove, requiring either (a) testimony from the responding officer, (b) testimony or excited utterances from the victim parent, or (c) a 911 tape that records children's voices.

Concurrent with the enactment of the new criminal statute, Utah's Department of Child and Family Services created a new category of child abuse and neglect: "Domestic Violence-Related Child Abuse," or DVRCA, defined as "violent physical or verbal interaction between cohabitants in a household in the presence of a child."

In adopting the new category, the department hired domestic violence advocates and developed a protocol to guide child protection workers in their determinations.

Houston County, Georgia. Prosecutors in Houston County, Georgia, actively use new provisions of Georgia's "cruelty to children" statute that pertain to domestic violence committed in the presence of children. Because cruelty to children is almost always a misdemeanor offense, it makes little difference in the penalties imposed on a batterer; indeed, the sentence typically runs by concurrently with the underlying domestic violence charge. However, the law does give prosecutors a stronger argument for no contact as a condition of bond. Violations of no-contact orders are charged as aggravated stalking, a felony offense in Georgia.

Prosecutors perceive the severe consequences of violating no-contact orders as perhaps the most effective response to domestic violence among the sanctions available to them.

Also, by identifying children as victims of the family violence battery, the new law accomplishes at least three things:

- It helps to counter batterers' threats to gain custody of a child.
- It makes the children eligible for crime victims compensation.
- It enables the court to impose no-contact orders on the children's behalf.

Multnomah County, Oregon. The study team selected Multnomah County (Portland), Oregon, because Oregon enacted legislation upgrading certain assault offenses from misdemeanors to felonies when a child witnesses the crime. The felony upgrade applies only to assault in the fourth degree, a misdemeanor offense that applies to many incidents of domestic violence. Assaults in the first, second, or third degree are felonies that require more serious injuries or the use of weapons.

Even though the felony upgrade applies to defendants with prior convictions (either one against the same victim or three against any victims) regardless of the presence of children, prosecutors observe that the large majority of elevated cases are those involving child witnesses.

The felony upgrade law has had a noteworthy impact on the District Attorney's Office: The number of felonies reviewed more than tripled in 1998 (the year in which the law became effective), while the number of misdemeanors reviewed remained nearly constant. Also, the number of felonies issued exceeded the number of misdemeanors for the first time.

In that same year, the proportion of issued domestic violence cases declined. This pattern held true for misdemeanors as well as felonies. Prosecutors may have imposed higher standards as they began to interpret and apply the new law.

Note

1. Gwinn, C., "Domestic Violence and Children: Difficult Issues," Presentation for the National College of District Attorneys, 1998.

Table 1: Prosecutors' Responses to Scenarios Involving Children and Abuse

Scenario	Would *Report* At Least Sometimes	Would *Prosecute* At Least Sometimes
Mom Abuses Children	94% (n = 90)	100% (n = 82)
Mom Fails to Protect from Abuse	63% (n = 87)	77.5% (n = 80)
Mom Fails to Protect from Exposure	40% (n = 86)	25% (n = 73)

The more tangible benefits of the new laws—particularly those in Utah and Georgia—may accrue to the children. By identifying children as victims, these statutes:

- Allow children access to crime victims compensation funds to address health or mental health needs resulting from their exposure to domestic violence.
- Enable the courts to issue protective orders on the children's behalf (potentially affording prosecutors another tool for monitoring offenders' behavior).
- Signal a need to file a report with the child protection agency, even in the absence of laws naming domestic violence as a condition of mandatory reporting.

No other institution in the community has the capacity and power to force offenders to confront and change their behavior…. Prosecutors can bring together people with disparate views and hammer out ways to overcome distrust and conflict toward a common goal: protection of battered women and their children.

What Can Prosecutors Do?

Research suggests a number of steps prosecutors can take to help children who are exposed to domestic violence:

- Employ every available avenue to enforce the terms of no-contact orders and probationary sentences. Field research suggests that these measures may offer the most powerful means of holding domestic violence offenders accountable for their behavior.
- Establish protocols within prosecutors' offices to encourage information sharing among prosecutors with responsibility for domestic violence and child abuse caseloads.
- Identify avenues for early intervention (e.g., by placing greater emphasis on misdemeanor prosecution).
- Train law enforcement investigators to note the presence of children in domestic violence incidents and to take statements from them whenever appropriate to do so.
- Encourage law enforcement agencies to adopt a model of law enforcement–mental health partnership that was pioneered in New Haven, Connecticut, as a means of ensuring that children who are exposed to violence receive timely and appropriate therapeutic intervention.[16] Be prepared, however, to develop policies or protocols to guide law enforcement officers' decisions to report these incidents to the child protection agency.
- Wherever possible, prosecute domestic violence offenders on concurrent charges of child endangerment, emotional abuse, or other available charges reflecting the danger to children who witness violence. These additional charges can be used to argue for stricter conditions of pretrial release or probation, or perhaps for upward deviation from sentencing guidelines.
- Provide training on domestic violence, child abuse, and the impact of domestic violence on children for all prosecutors, victim advocates, and other court personnel whose job responsibilities include responding to allegations of family violence.
- Promote increased attention to services for battered women. Women cannot reasonably be expected to extricate themselves from dangerous relationships if the financial and social supports are not available in their communities. Particular attention should be paid to substance abuse

treatment; one recent study suggests that substance abuse predicts noncooperation with prosecution among battered women.[17]

- Ensure that social service agencies will connect with families that have been reported for domestic violence, both to offer referrals for needed services and to monitor future incidents. Some avenues need to be available for offering needed services to children in troubled families before they suffer serious harm.

No other institution in the community has the capacity and power to force offenders to confront and change their behavior. As political leaders in their communities, prosecutors have the status and opportunity to advocate for needed change, whether legislative, fiscal, or programmatic in nature. Prosecutors can bring together people with disparate views and hammer out ways to overcome distrust and conflict toward a common goal: protection of battered women and their children.

Notes

1. For a comprehensive review, see Edleson, J., "Children's Witnessing of Adult Domestic Violence," *Journal of Interpersonal Violence*, 14 (1999): 839–870.
2. Strauss, M., R. J. Gelles, and S. Steinmetz, *Behind Closed Doors: Violence in the American Family*, New York: Doubleday/Anchor, 1980.
3. English, D. J., D. B. Marshall, S. Brummel, and M. Orme, "Characteristics of Repeated Referrals to Child Protective Services in Washington State," *Child Maltreatment*, 4 (1999): 297–307.
4. U.S. Advisory Board on Child Abuse and Neglect, *A Nation's Shame: Fatal Child Abuse and Neglect in the United States*, Washington, DC: U.S. Department of Health and Human Services, Administration for Children and Families, 1995.
5. U.S. Department of Health and Human Services, *Blending Perspectives and Building Common Ground: A Report to Congress on Substance Abuse and Child Protection*, Washington, DC: Administration for Children and Families, Substance Abuse and Mental Health Services Administration, Assistant Secretary for Planning and Evaluation, 1999.
6. Felitti, V. J., R. F. Anda, D. Nordenberg, et al., "Relationship of Childhood Abuse and Household Dysfunction to Many of the Leading Causes of Death in Adults," *American Journal of Preventive Medicine*, 14 (1998): 250.
7. Osofsky, J. D., "The Impact of Violence on Children," *The Future of Children: Domestic Violence and Children*, 9(1999): 33–49.
8. Hilton, N. Z., "Battered Women's Concerns About Their Children Witnessing Wife Assault," *Journal of Interpersonal Violence*, 7(1992): 77–86.
9. Personal communication, January 2000.
10. Marans, S., S. J. Berkowitz, and D. J. Cohen, "Police and Mental Health Professionals: Collaborative Responses to the Impact of Violence on Children and Families," *Child and Adolescent Psychiatric Clinics of North America*, 7(1998): 635–651.
11. Saathoff, A. J., and E. A. Stoffel, "Community-Based Domestic Violence Services," *The Future of Children: Domestic Violence and Children*, 9(1999): 97–110.
12. See, e.g., Lecklitner, G. L., N. M. Malik, S. M. Aaron, and C. S. Lederman, "Promoting Safety for Abused Children and Battered Mothers: Miami-Dade County's Model Dependency Court Intervention Program," *Child Maltreatment*, 4(1999): 175–182.
13. Whitney, P., and L. Davis, "Child Abuse and Domestic Violence in Massachusetts: Can Practice Be Integrated in a Public Child Welfare Setting?" *Child Maltreatment*, 4(1999): 158–166.
14. Oregon's legislation can be found at ORS 163.160(3)(b).
15. Utah: U.C.A. §76–5–109.1; Georgia: O.C.G.A. §16–5–70.
16. Marans, Berkowitz, and Cohen, "Police and Mental Health Professionals," see note 10.
17. Goodman, L., L. Bennett, and M. A. Bennett, "Obstacles to Victims' Cooperation with the Criminal Prosecution of Their Abusers: The Role of Social Support," *Violence and Victims*, 14(1999): 427–444.

about the author
Debra Whitcomb conducted this research while she was an NIJ Research Fellow. Whitcomb is Director, Grant Programs and Development, American Prosecutors Research Institute, 99 Canal Center Plaza, Suite 510, Alexandria, Virginia 22314, 703-519-1675, debra.whitcomb@ndaa-apri.org.

From *National Institute of Justice Journal*, Number 248, 2002 pp. 2–9. Published by the Office of Justice/U.S. Department of Justice.

STRENGTHENING ANTISTALKING STATUTES

Introduction

Stalking is a crime of intimidation. Stalkers harass and even terrorize through conduct that causes fear or substantial emotional distress in their victims. A recent study sponsored by the National Institute of Justice (NIJ) (U.S. Department of Justice) and the Centers for Disease Control and Prevention estimates that 1 in 12 women and 1 in 45 men have been stalked during their lifetime.[1] Although stalking behavior has been around for many years, it has been identified as a crime only within the past decade. Most laws a the state level were passed between 1991 and 1992. As more is learned about stalking and stalkers, legislatures are attempting to improve their laws.[2]

In 1993, under a grant from NIJ, a working group of experts was assembled to develop a model state stalking law.[3] Many of its recommendations have been followed as states have amended their laws.[4]

Status of the Law

Generally, stalking is defined as the willful or intentional commission of a series of acts that would cause a reasonable person to fear death or serious bodily injury and that, in fact, does place the victim in fear of death or serious bodily injury. Stalking is a crime in every state. Every state has a stalking law, although the harassment laws of some states also encompass stalking behaviors. In most states, stalking is a Class A or first degree misdemeanor except under certain circumstances, which include stalking in violation of a protective order, stalking while armed, or repeat offenses. In addition, states typically have harassment statutes, and one state's

harassment law might encompass behaviors that would be considered stalking in another state.

Significant variation exists among state stalking laws. These differences relate primarily to the type of repeated behavior that is prohibited, whether a threat is required as part of stalking, the reaction of the victim to the stalking, and the intent of the stalker.

Prohibited Behavior

Most states have broad definitions of the type of repeated behavior that is prohibited, using terms such as "harassing," "communicating," and "nonconsensual contact." In some states, specific descriptions of stalking behavior are included in the statute. For example, Michigan's stalking law provides that unconsented contact includes, but is not limited to, any of the following:

1. Following or appearing within sight of that individual.
2. Approaching or confronting that individual in a public place or on private property.
3. Appearing at that individual's workplace or residence.
4. Entering onto or remaining on property owned, leased, or occupied by that individual.
5. Contacting that individual by telephone.
6. Sending mail or electronic communications to that individual.
7. Placing an object on or delivering an object to property owned, leased, or occupied by that individual.[5]

A handful of states have narrow definitions of stalking. Illinois, for example, limits stalking to cases involving following or keeping a person under surveillance.[6]

Message From THE DIRECTOR

Over the past three decades, the criminal justice field has witnessed an astounding proliferation of statutory enhancements benefiting people who are most directly and intimately affected by crime. To date, all states have passed some form of legislation to benefit victims. In addition, 32 states have recognized the supreme importance of fundamental and express rights for crime victims by raising those protections to the constitutional level.

Of course, the nature, scope, and enforcement of victims' rights vary from state to state, and it is a complex and often frustrating matter for victims to determine what those rights mean for them. To help victims, victim advocates, and victim services providers understand the relevance of the myriad laws and constitutional guarantees, the Office for Victims of Crime awarded funding to the National Center for Victims of Crime to produce a series of bulletins addressing salient legal issues affecting crime victims.

Strengthening Antistalking Statutes, the first in the series, provides an overview of state legislation and current issues related to stalking. Although stalking is a crime in all 50 states, significant variation exists among statutes as to the type of behavior prohibited, the intent of the stalker, whether a threat is required, and the others in the Legal Series highlight various circumstances in which relevant laws are applied, emphasizing their successful implementation.

We hope that victims, victim advocates, victim service providers, criminal justice professionals, and policymakers in states across the Nation will find the bulletins in this series helpful in making sense of the criminal justice process and in identifying areas in which rights could be strengthened or more clearly defined. We encourage you to use these bulletins not simply as informational resources but as tools to support victims in their involvement with the criminal justice system.

John W. Gillis
Director

ability to carry out the threat. As understanding of stalking has grown, however, most states have modified or eliminated the credible-threat requirement. Stalkers often present an implied threat to their victims. For example, repeatedly following a person is generally perceived as threatening. The threat may not be expressed but be implicit in the context of the case.

Only two states—Arkansas and Massachusetts—require the making of a threat to be part of stalking,[11] although a few other states require an express threat as an element of aggravated stalking. Most states currently define stalking to include implied threats or specify that threats can be, but are not required to be, part of the pattern of harassing behavior.

Reactions of the Victim

Stalking is defined in part by a victim's reaction. Typically, stalking is conduct that "would cause a reasonable person to fear bodily injury to himself or a member of his immediate family or to fear the death of himself or a member of his immediate family"[12] or "would cause a reasonable person to suffer substantial emotional distress"[13] and does cause the victim to have such a reaction. Some states refer to conduct that seriously "alarms," "annoys," "torments," or "terrorizes" the victim, although many of those states also require that the conduct result in substantial emotional distress.[14] Others refer to the victim's fear for his or her "personal safety";[15] feeling "frightened, intimidated, or threatened";[16] or fear "that the stalker intends to injure the person, another person, or property of the person."[17] In general, however, stalking statutes provide that the conduct must be of a nature that would cause a specified reaction on the part of the victim and in fact does cause the victim to have that reaction.[18]

Intentions of the Stalker

Originally, most stalking statutes were "specific intent" crimes; they required proof that the stalker intended to cause the victim to fear death or personal injury or to have some other particular reaction to the stalker's actions. The subjective intent of a person, however, can be difficult to prove. Therefore, many states have revised their statutes to make stalking a "general intent" crime; rather than requiring proof that the defendant intended to cause a reaction on the part of the victim, many states simply require that the stalker intentionally committed prohibited acts. Other states require that in committing the acts, the defendant must know, or reasonably should know, that the acts would cause the victim to be placed in fear. The latter approach was recommended in the NIJ Model Antistalking Code project. At least two courts have discussed the model's language in finding that general intent is sufficient.[19]

Maryland requires that the pattern of conduct include approaching or pursuing another person.[7] Hawaii is similar, limiting stalking to cases in which the stalker pursues the victim or conducts surveillance of the victim.[8] Connecticut limits stalking to following or lying in wait.[9] Wisconsin requires "maintaining a visual or physical proximity to a person."[10]

Threat

When stalking laws were first adopted in states across the country, many laws required the making of a "credible threat" as an element of the offense. Generally, this was defined as a threat made with the intent and apparent

Exceptions

Most states have explicit exceptions under their stalking laws for certain behaviors, commonly described simply as "constitutionally protected activity." Many also specifically exempt licensed investigators or other professionals operating within the scope of their duties;[20] however, it may not be necessary to provide such exceptions within the statute itself. The Supreme Court of Illinois interpreted that state's stalking laws to prohibit only conduct performed "without lawful authority," even though the laws do not contain that phrase. The court reasoned that "[t]his construction... accords with the legislature's intent in enacting the statutes to prevent violent attacks by allowing the police to act before the victim was actually injured and to prevent the terror produced by harassing actions."[21]

Aggravating Circumstances

Many state codes include an offense of aggravated stalking or define stalking offenses in the first and second degrees. Often, the higher level offense is defined as stalking in violation of a protective order,[22] stalking while armed with a deadly weapon,[23] a second or subsequent conviction of stalking,[24] or stalking a minor.[25] Many states without a separately defined higher offense provide for enhanced punishment for stalking under such conditions.

Challenges to Stalking Laws

Most of the cases challenging the constitutionality of stalking laws focus on one of two questions: whether the statute is overbroad or whether it is unconstitutionally vague. A statute is unconstitutionally overbroad when it inadvertently criminalizes legitimate behavior. In a Pennsylvania case, the defendant claimed the stalking statute was unconstitutional because it criminalized a substantial amount of constitutionally protected conduct. In that case, the defendant engaged in a campaign of intimidating behavior against a judge who had ruled against him in a landlord-tenant case. For nearly a year, the defendant made regular phone calls and distributed leaflets calling the judge "Judge Bimbo," "a cockroach," "a gangster," and "a mobster." During one of his many calls to the judge's chambers, her secretary asked him if his intentions were "to alarm and disturb" the judge. The defendant replied, "I would hope that my calls alarm her. I am working very hard at it. If my calls are disturbing, wait until she sees what happens next." He also called and spoke about the bodyguard hired for the judge and the judge carrying a gun "to let [her] know that he's watching and knows what is going on."

The court in that case found that the statute was not overbroad and did not criminalize constitutionally protected behavior. The court noted that "[t]he appellant cites us no cases, nor are we able to locate any,

announcing a constitutional right to 'engage in a course of conduct or repeatedly committed acts toward another person [with the] intent to cause substantial emotional distress to the person.'"[26]

Defendants have also argued that stalking laws are unconstitutionally vague. The essential test for vagueness was set out by the U.S. Supreme Court in 1926. A Government restriction is vague if it "either forbids or requires the doing of an act in terms so vague that men of common intelligence must necessarily guess at its meaning and differ as to its application."[27] Whether a given term is unconstitutionally vague is left to the interpretation of each state's courts.

In a New Jersey stalking case, the court rejected the defendant's claim that the statute was unconstitutionally vague, finding the defendant's conduct "unquestionably proscribed by the statute." In that case, the defendant had maintained physical proximity to the victim on numerous occasions, late at night, that the court found to be threatening, purposeful, and directed at the victim. He repeatedly asked for sexual contact that he knew was unwanted, and he implied that she had better agree. "To suggest, as the defendant does, that his activity could be seen as the pursuit of 'normal social interaction' is absurd. On the contrary, his conduct was a patent violation of the statute."[28]

In a Michigan case, the defendant also argued that the stalking statutes were unconstitutionally vague and violated his first amendment right to free speech. The court disagreed. "Defendant's repeated telephone calls to the victim, sometimes 50 to 60 times a day whether the victim was at home or at work, and his verbal threats to kill her and her family do not constitute protected speech or conduct serving a legitimate purpose, even if that purpose is 'to attempt to reconcile,' as defendant asserts."[29]

Claims that stalking laws were unconstitutionally vague have focused on the wide range of terms commonly used in such laws. For example, courts have ruled that the following terms were not unconstitutionally vague: "repeatedly,"[30] "pattern of conduct,"[31] "series,"[32] "closely related in time,"[33] "follows,"[34] "lingering outside,"[35] "harassing,"[36] "intimidating,"[37] "maliciously,"[38] "emotional distress"[39] "reasonable apprehension,"[40] "in connection with,"[41] and "contacting another person without the consent of the other person."[42]

Courts have also determined that terms such as "without lawful authority"[43] and "serves no legitimate purpose"[44] were not unconstitutionally vague. The Oregon Court of Appeals, however, did invalidate that state's stalking law on the grounds that the term "legitimate purpose" was unconstitutionally vague.[45] The court found that the statute did not tell a person of ordinary intelligence what was meant by the term "legitimate purpose"; therefore, the statute gave no warning as to what conduct must be avoided. The Oregon legislature later revised the statute to remove the phrase.

The Supreme Court of Kansas found that state's stalking statute unconstitutionally vague because it used the terms "alarms," "annoys," and "harasses" without defining them or using an objective standard to measure the prohibited conduct. "In the absence of an objective standard, the terms... subject the defendant to the particular sensibilities of the individual.... [C]onduct that annoys or alarms one person may not annoy or alarm another.... [A] victim may be of such a state of mind that conduct that would never annoy, alarm, or harass a reasonable person would seriously annoy, alarm, or harass this victim."[46] Kansas has since amended its statute, and the amended statute has been ruled constitutional. The court specifically found that the revised law included an objective standard, that is, the standard of a "reasonable person," and defined the key terms "course of conduct," "harassment," and "credible threat."[47]

Similarly, the Texas Court of Criminal Appeals found that state's original antistalking law unconstitutionally vague. Although there were several factors in this ruling, the expansive nature of the prohibited conduct was a key point in the decision. That conduct included actions that would "annoy" or "alarm" the victim. The court observed that "the First Amendment does not permit the outlawing of conduct merely because the speaker intends to annoy the listener and a reasonable person would in fact be annoyed."[48] The Texas Legislature subsequently revised the law to correct the problem.

Massachusetts's stalking law was also declared unconstitutionally vague because it provided that a person could be guilty of stalking if that person repeatedly harassed the victim. "Harass" was defined as a pattern of conduct or series of acts. Thus, the court found that the statutory requirement of repeated harassment meant that a person "must engage repeatedly (certainly at least twice) in a pattern of conduct or series of acts over a period of time.... One pattern or one series would not be enough." The court noted that the legislature presumably intended a single pattern of conduct or a single series of acts to constitute the crime but did not state this with sufficient clarity to meet the constitutional challenges.[49] The Commonwealth has since revised its stalking law to address the issue.

Other courts have disagreed with the reasoning of the Massachusetts decision. The Rhode Island Supreme Court declared that the Massachusetts court's "metaplasmic[†] approach... has attracted little, if any, following." The court found that the statute, as drafted, met the constitutional test by giving adequate warning to potential offenders of the prohibited conduct. "It indeed defies logic to conclude that a defendant would have to commit more than one series of harassing acts in order to be found guilty of stalking."[50] The D.C. Court of Appeals reached a similar conclusion.[51]

Attempted Stalking

At least one state has grappled with the question of whether a person can be charged with attempted stalking. In Georgia, a defendant made harassing and bizarre phone calls to his ex-wife. The defendant was arrested and released under the condition that he was to have "[a]bsolutely no contact with the victim or the victim's family." A few weeks later, he called his ex-wife's office, claiming to be the district attorney, and asked personal questions about his ex-wife. He later attempted to call his ex-wife at the office, but she was out of town. He told a coworker to tell his ex-wife that "when she gets home she can't get in." The Georgia Supreme Court found that it was not absurd or impractical to criminalize attempting to stalk, which under the terms of the statute meant attempting to follow, place under surveillance, or contact another, when it was done with the requisite specific intent to cause emotional distress by inducing a reasonable fear of death or bodily injury. A concurring Justice noted that to hold otherwise would be to permit a stalker "to intimidate and harass his intended victim simply by communicating his threats to third parties who (the stalker knows and expects) will inform the victim."[52]

Current Issues

Cyberstalking

As the use of computers for communication has increased, so have cases of "cyberstalking." A 1999 report by the U.S. Attorney General called cyberstalking a growing problem. After noting the number of people with access to the Internet, the report states, "Assuming the proportion of cyberstalking victims is even a fraction of the proportion of persons who have been the victims of offline stalking within the preceding 2 months, there may be potentially tens or even hundreds of thousands of victims of recent cyberstalking incidents in the United States."[53]

Many stalking laws are broad enough to encompass stalking via e-mail or other electronic communication, defining the prohibited conduct in terms of "communication," "harassment," or "threats" without specifying the means of such behavior. Others have specifically defined stalking via e-mail within their stalking or harassment statute.

For example, California recently amended its stalking law to expressly include stalking via the Internet.[54] Under California law, a person commits stalking if he or she "willfully, maliciously, and repeatedly follows or harasses another person and... makes a credible threat with the intent to place that person in reasonable fear for his or her safety, or the safety of his or her immediate family." The term "credible threat" includes "that performed through the use of an

89

electronic communication device, or a threat implied by a pattern of conduct or a combination of verbal, written, or electronically communicated statements." "Electronic communication device" includes "telephones, cellular phones, computers, video recorders, fax machines, or pagers."

Bail Restrictions

States are grappling with the matter of pretrial release of people charged with stalking. Because stalkers often remain dangerous after being charged with a crime, states have sought means to protect victims at the pretrial stage. Many states permit the court to enter a no-contact order as a condition of pretrial release.[55] A few give the court discretion to deny bail. For example, Illinois allows a court to deny bail when the court, after a hearing, "determines that the release of the defendant would pose a real and present threat to the physical safety of the alleged victim of the offense and denial of... bail... is necessary to prevent fulfillment of the threat upon which the charge is based.[56]

Lifetime Protection Orders

Stalkers frequently remain obsessed with their targets for years. Requiring victims to file for a new protective order every few years can be unduly burdensome. Because victims may have attempted to conceal their whereabouts from the stalkers, reapplying for a protective order may inadvertently reconnect stalkers with their victims. In New Jersey, this problem has been alleviated. A conviction for stalking in that state operates as an application for a permanent restraining order. The order may be dissolved on application of the victim.[57]

Conclusion

Stalking is a serious and pervasive criminal offense. The Nation is increasingly aware of the danger stalkers pose and of the need for effective intervention. Research into the nature and extent of stalking is ongoing. As more is learned about effective responses to stalkers, laws will continue to evolve. Victim advocates and victim service providers must work closely with law enforcement and prosecutors to identify what additional legislative changes are needed to better protect stalking victims.

---

†*Metaplasmia*: alteration of regular verbal, grammatical, or rhetorical structure usually by transposition of the letters or syllables of a word or of the words in a sentence. *Metaplasmic*, adj. (*Webster's Third New International Dictionary*, 1971).

Notes

1. Tjaden, Patricia, and Nancy Thoennes (1998). *Stalking in America: Findings From the National Violence Against Women Survey*. Washington, DC: U.S. Department of Justice, National Institute of Justice and the Centers for Disease Control and Prevention.
2. This bulletin focuses on state stalking laws. For the federal interstate stalking law, see 18 U.S.C. § 2261A (2001).
3. National Criminal Justice Association (1993). *Project To Develop a Model Anti-Stalking Code for States*. Washington, DC: National Institute of Justice. To receive a copy of the final report of this project, contact the National Criminal Justice Reference Service at 1–800–851–3420 and ask for publication NCJ 144477.
4. For more indepth information on the problem of stalking, see *Stalking and Domestic Violence: The Third Annual Report to Congress Under the Violence Against Women Act*, Washington, DC: U.S. Department of Justice, Violence Against Women Grants Office, 1998.
5. MICH. STAT. ANN. § 28.643(8) (2000).
6. 720 ILL. COMP. STAT. 5/12-7.3 (2001).
7. MD. ANN. CODE art. 27, § 124 (2001).
8. HAW. REV. STAT. §§ 711-1106.4, -1106.5 (2000).
9. CONN. GEN. STAT. §§ 53a-181d, -181e (2001).
10. WIS. STAT. ANN. § 940.32 (2000).
11. ARK. STAT. ANN. § 5-71-229 (2001); MASS. GEN. LAWS ANN. ch. 265, § 43 (2001).
12. N.J. STAT. ANN. § 2C:12-10 (2001).
13. For example, CAL. PENAL CODE § 646.9 (Deering 2001); KAN. STAT. ANN. § 21-3438 (2000).
14. KAN. STAT. ANN. § 21-3438 (2000). See also KY. REV. STAT. § 508.150 (2001); ME. REV. STAT. ANN. tit. 17-A, § 210-A (2000); MISS. CODE ANN. § 97-3-107 (2001).
15. N.H. REV. STAT. ANN. § 633:3-a (2000).
16. N.M. STAT. ANN. § 30-3A-3 (2000).
17. WASH. REV. CODE ANN. § 9A.46.110 (2001).
18. The specific terms are subject to the interpretation of each state's courts.
19. *State v. Neuzil*, 589 N.W.2d 708 (Iowa 1999); *State v. Cardell*, 318 N.J. Super. 175, 723 A.2d 111 (N.J. Super. Ct. App. Div. 1999).
20. For example, ARK. STAT. ANN. § 5-71-229 (2001).
21. *People v. Bailey*, 167 Ill. 2d 210, 657 N.E.2d 953 (1995).
22. For example, ALA. CODE § 13A-6-91 (2001); N.M. STAT. ANN. § 30-3A-3.1 (2000).
23. For example, ARK. STAT. ANN. § 5-71-229 (2001) (stalking in the first degree).
24. For example, VT. STAT. ANN. § 13-1063 (2001).
25. For example, FLA. STAT. § 784.048 (2000).
26. *Commonwealth v. Schierscher*, 447 Pa. Super. 61, 668 A.2d 164 (Pa. Super. Ct. 1995).
27. *Connally v. General Construction Co.*, 269 U.S. 385, 391, 46 S. Ct. 126, 70 L. Ed. 322 (1926).
28. *State v. Cardell*, 318 N.J. Super. 175, 723 A.2d 111 (N.J. Super. Ct. App. Div. 1999).
29. *People v. White*, 212 Mich. App. 298, 536 N.W.2d 876 (Mich. Ct. App. 1995).
30. *State v. Martel*, 273 Mont. 143, 902 P.2d 14 (1995); *State v. McGill*, 536 N.W.2d 89 (S.D. 1995).
31. *State v. Dario*, 106 Ohio App. 3d 232, 665 N.E.2d 759 (Ohio Ct. App. 1995).
32. *State v. Randall*, 669 So.2d 223 (Ala. Crim. App. 1995).
33. *State v. Dario*, 106 Ohio App. 3d 232, 665 N.E.2d 759 (Ohio Ct. App. 1995).
34. *State v. Lee*, 135 Wash. 2d 369, 957 P.2d 741 (1998); *People v. Zamudio*, 293 Ill. App. 3d 976, 689 N.E.2d 254 (Ill. App. Ct. 1997).
35. *State v. Schleiermacher*, 924 S.W.2d 269 (Mo. 1996).
36. *State v. Martel*, 273 Mont. 143, 902 P.2d 14 (1995).
37. Id.
38. *State v. McGill*, 536 N.W.2d 89 (S.D. 1995).
39. *Woolfolk v. Commonwealth*, 18 Va. App. 840, 447 S.E.2d 530 (Va. Ct. App. 1994); *Salt Lake City v. Lopez*, 313 Utah Adv. Rep. 26, 935 P.2d 1259 (Utah Ct. App. 1997).
40. *State v. Martel*, 273 Mont. 143, 902 P.2d 14 (1995).
41. *People v. Baer*, 973 P.2d 1225 (Colo. 1999).

42. *Johnson v. State*, 264 Ga. 590, 449 S.E.2d 94 (1994).

43. *State v. Lee*, 135 Wash. 2d 369, 957 P.2d 741 (1998).

44. *People v. Tran*, 47 Cal. App. 4th 253, 54 Cal. Rptr. 2d 650 (Cal. Ct. App. 1996).

45. *State v. Norris-Romine*, 134 Or. App. 204, 894 P.2d 1221 (Or. Ct. App. 1995).

46. *State v. Bryan*, 259 Kan. 143, 910 P.2d 212 (1996).

47. *State v. Rucker*, 1999 Kan. LEXIS 410 (1999).

48. *Long v. State*, 931 S.W.2d 285, 290 n. 4 (Tex. Crim. App. 1996).

49. *Commonwealth v. Kwiatkowski*, 418 Mass. 543, 637 N.E.2d 854 (1994).

50. *State v. Fonseca*, 670 A.2d 1237 (R.I. 1996).

51. *United States v. Smith*, 685 A.2d 380 (App. D.C. 1996).

52. *State v. Rooks*, 266 Ga. 528, 468 S.E.2d 354 (1996).

53. *Cyberstalking: A New Challenge for Law Enforcement and Industry*, A Report From the Attorney General to the Vice President, August 1999, p. 6.

54. CAL. PENAL CODE § 646.9 (Deering 2001).

55. For example, ALASKA STAT. § 12.30.025 (2001); MD. ANN. CODE art. 27, § 616 1/2 (2001).

56. 725 ILL. COMP. STAT. 5/110-4, -6.3 (2001).

57. N.J. STAT. § 2C:12-10.1 (2001).

From *OVC Legal Series*, January 2002. Published by the Office for Victims of Crimes/U.S. Department of Justice.

UNIT 3
The Police

Unit Selections

Key Points to Consider

• Can racial profiling ever be a legitimate police tactic? Explain.

• Is police work the cause of suicides among officers, or does the availability of a gun just make it easier?

• Do local police departments have a role to play in combating international terrorism? Why or why not?

 **Links: www.dushkin.com/online/**
These sites are annotated in the World Wide Web pages.

ACLU Criminal Justice Home Page
http://www.aclu.org/CriminalJustice/CriminalJusticeMain.cfm

Law Enforcement Guide to the World Wide Web
http://leolinks.com/

Violent Criminal Apprehension Program (VICAP)
http://www.state.ma.us/msp/unitpage/vicap.htm

Police officers are the guardians of our freedoms under the Constitution and the law, and as such they have an awesome task. They are asked to prevent crime, protect citizens, arrest wrongdoers, preserve the peace, aid the sick, control juveniles, control traffic, and provide emergency services on a moment's notice. They are also asked to be ready to lay down their lives, if necessary.

In recent years, the job of the police officer has become even more complex and dangerous. Illegal drug use and trafficking are still major problems; racial tensions are explosive; and terrorism is now an alarming reality. As our population grows more numerous and diverse, the role of the police in America becomes ever more challenging, requiring skills that can only be obtained by greater training and professionalism.

In the lead article in the section, "The NYPD's War on Terror," Craig Horowitz describes the frustration with Washington's lack of response to terrorism felt by NYPD's police commissioner, and the steps he has taken to try to make New York safe. The typical offender in violent crime categories is white, as pointed out by Tim Wise in "Racial Profiling and its Apologists."

Police departments must be prepared to handle crisis situations when they involve one of their own, according to Officer Terhune-Bickler in "Too Close for Comfort, Negotiating with Fellow Officers."

The next article, "Ethics and Criminal Justice: Some Observations on Police Misconduct", deals with police misconduct in terms of ethical violations. In "Community Policing: Exploring the Philosophy," David M. Allender argues that the concept of community policing has been misunderstood, but that it can provide real benefit to law enforcement agencies. Next, is a treatment of the tragedy of police suicide in "The Blue Plague of American Policing." This section concludes with the article, "Educating and Training the Future Police Officer," in which Michael Buerger discusses the link between education, training, and improved services.

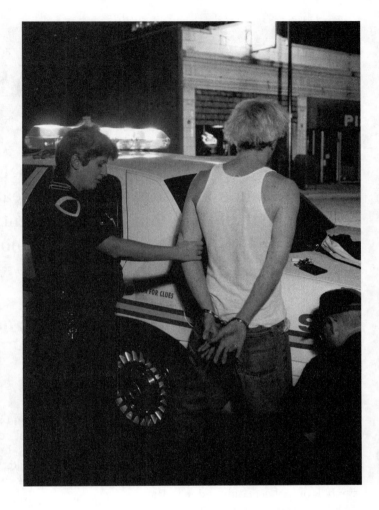

The NYPD's War On Terror

Frustrated by the lack of help from Washington, police commissioner Ray Kelly has created his own versions of the CIA and the FBI within the department. So how will we know if he has succeeded? If nothing happens.

BY CRAIG HOROWITZ

Buried deep in the heart of one of New York's outer boroughs, in an area inhabited by junkyards and auto-body shops, is an unmarked redbrick building that stands as an extraordinary symbol of police commissioner Ray Kelly's obsessive commitment to the fight against terrorism. Here, miles from Manhattan, is the headquarters of the NYPD's one-year-old counterterrorism bureau.

When you step through the plain metal door at the side of the building, it is like falling down the rabbit hole—you're transported from a mostly desolate, semi-industrial area in the shadow of an elevated highway into the new, high-tech, post-9/11 world of the New York City Police Department.

The place is so gleaming and futuristic—so unlike the average police precinct, with furniture and equipment circa 1950—that you half expect to see Q come charging out with his latest super-weapon for 007. Headlines race across LED news tickers. There are electronic maps and international-time walls with digital readouts for cities such as Moscow, London, Tel Aviv, Riyadh, Islamabad, Manila, Sydney, Baghdad, and Tokyo.

In what is called the Global Intelligence Room, twelve large flat-screen TVs that hang from ceiling mounts broadcast Al-Jazeera and a variety of other foreign programming received via satellite. The Police Department's newly identified language specialists—who speak, among other tongues, Arabic, Pashto, Urdu, and Fujianese—sit with headphones on, monitoring the broadcasts.

There are racks of high-end audio equipment for listening, taping, and dubbing; computer access to a host of superdatabases; stacks of intelligence reports and briefing books on all the world's known terrorist organizations; and a big bulletin board featuring a grid with the names and phone numbers of key people in other police departments in this country and around the world.

The security area just inside the door is encased not only in bulletproof glass but in ballistic Sheetrock as well. The building has its own backup generator (everyone learned the importance of redundancy on September 11); and the center is staffed 24 hours a day, seven days a week.

Even the 125 cops in the bureau (hand-picked from nearly 900 applicants) look a little sharper. Some are in dark-navy polo shirts that bear the counterterrorism-bureau logo, and others are in suits that seem to be a cut above the usual discount-warehouse version of cop fashion.

Though the counterterrorism bureau is still in its infancy, law-enforcement officials from around the U.S. and overseas regularly come to see it and learn. And it was all put together practically overnight—it opened in February of last year, little more than a month after Ray Kelly was sworn in as police commissioner.

The bureau, along with the NYPD's totally revamped intelligence division, and the high-level hires from Washington—a lieutenant general from the Pentagon and a spymaster from the CIA—is part of Kelly's vision to remake the NYPD into a force that can effectively respond to the world's dangerous new realities.

There are now New York City police officers stationed in London working with New Scotland Yard; in Lyons at the headquarters of Interpol; and in Hamburg, Tel Aviv, and Toronto. There are also two cops on assignment at FBI headquarters in Washington, and New York detectives have traveled to Afghanistan, Egypt, Yemen, Pakistan, and the military's prison at Guantánamo Bay in Cuba to conduct interrogations. Members of the department's command staff have also attended sessions at the Naval War College in Newport, Rhode Island.

And there are the Hercules Teams, elite, heavily armed, Special Forces-type police units that pop up daily around the city. It can be at the Empire State Building, the Brooklyn Bridge, Times Square, or the stock exchange, wherever the day's intelligence reports suggest they could be needed. These small teams arrive in black Suburbans, sheathed in armor-plated vests and carrying 9-mm. submachine guns—sometimes with air or sea support. Their purpose is to intimidate and to very publicly mount a show of force. Kelly knows that terrorists do a lot of reconnaissance, and the Hercules Teams were designed to disrupt their planning. Like an ADT warning sign in front of a house, they're also intended to send a message that this is not an easy target.

The police commissioner now has what's called an STU (Secured Telephone Unit) on his desk. It is a phone line that enables him to talk to someone in the White House or the Pentagon without fear of being monitored. When a key on the phone is turned, the conversation is electronically encrypted.

"We are doing all these things," Kelly says over coffee in his fourteenth-floor office at police headquarters, "because New York is still the No. 1 target. We have been targeted four times, twice successfully, and the

city remains the most symbolic, substantive target for the terrorists. These are cunning, patient, deliberate people who want to kill us and kill us in big numbers."

ON A BRIGHT OCTOBER DAY SEVERAL weeks after September 11, Kelly and his wife, Veronica, were finally allowed to return to their Battery Park City apartment—not to move back in, but to pick up a few personal items. Before they left the building, one block from the World Trade Center, they went up to the roof. There, Kelly consoled his weeping wife as they looked in stunned disbelief at the devastation of their neighborhood.

Eight years earlier, back in 1993 when the Trade Center was attacked the first time, Kelly was police commissioner. Mayor David Dinkins was in Japan when the buildings were bombed, so Kelly essentially took charge. It was Kelly who went on television to calm the city, to let everyone know in his powerful Marine kind of way that everything was under control.

Now Kelly is staking his reputation and his legacy on the fight against terrorism. "Four months after 9/11, when Kelly was about to be sworn in, you just didn't get a sense of confidence at the federal, state, or local level that changes were being made," says former NYPD first deputy commissioner John Timoney, who was recently named police chief of Miami. "Ray could easily have said, 'What do I know about this stuff? It's the Feds' job.' It takes a lot of courage to do what he's doing. He's leaving himself open to be second-guessed and criticized if things don't go well. So he's making decisions that may benefit the city but be detrimental to him personally."

Kelly is familiar with being second-guessed and criticized. He served as NYPD commissioner during the final eighteen months of the Dinkins administration, in 1992 and '93. Though he was essentially finishing Commissioner Lee Brown's term, he did manage several significant accomplishments. He cleaned up and

restructured Internal Affairs, which was a serious mess. And it was Kelly, not Bratton or Giuliani, who took care of the squeegee guys.

Not that anyone knows it. "When Bratton came in with his arrogance and swagger, he showed Ray up nine ways from Sunday," says a former high-level member of Bratton's own team. "Giuliani and Bratton lumped him in with Dinkins as one big ineffective management disaster."

"I knew we couldn't rely on the federal government. We're doing all the things we're doing because the federal government isn't doing them. It's not enough to say it's their job if the job isn't being done."

So Kelly has plenty of reasons to want to make his mark this time. Even so, isn't combating terrorism primarily a federal responsibility?

When I ask Kelly this question, he looks at me long and hard. He is a man who knows his way around Washington. In addition to his time in the mid-nineties as undersecretary of the Treasury, he was head of the Customs Service. He also worked for Interpol and was a special State Department envoy in Haiti where he was sent to establish and train a police force.

"I knew we couldn't rely on the federal government," Kelly says finally. "I know it from my own experience. We're doing all the things we're doing because the federal government isn't doing them. It's not enough to say it's their job if the job isn't being done. Since 9/11, the federal government hasn't taken any additional resources and put them here."

Has any kind of an increased federal presence been asked for? Soldiers? Fighter planes? More FBI agents? "Asked for?" he says, repeating my question incredulously. "Would you think it would have to be asked for? Look," he says, shifting in his chair and crossing his legs so the .38 in his ankle holster is visible. "It's a different world. We've redeployed. We've got 1,000 people on this. All seven subway tunnels under the river are covered, and it's the same with all the other sensitive locations. It's taken constant attention. It's extremely difficult. But make no mistake: It's something we have to do ourselves."

EVERY MORNING AT EIGHT, IN THE commissioner's conference room on the top floor of police headquarters (another NYPD venue where, by the way, you can watch Al-Jazeera), Kelly is briefed by his two key players in the counterterrorism battle: Lieutenant General Frank Libutti, who runs the department's counterterrorism bureau, and David Cohen, formerly No. 4 at the CIA, who is now in charge of the NYPD's intelligence division.

The two men couldn't play more to type if they were actors hired to fill these roles. Libutti, a fit, silver-haired 35-year veteran who was in charge of all Marine forces in the Pacific and the Persian Gulf, is, in a word, crisp. His navy pinstripe suit looks perfectly tailored, his shirt is starched, and he has an open, forthright manner. He is friendly in a lieutenant-general-determined-to-stay-on-message sort of way. He calls terrorists "the bad guys."

Cohen is a much grayer, more recessive presence. He has been described as "bookish," but that's not quite right. His look is much closer to that of, say, a software designer, someone who appears both geeky and cunning.

Cohen rarely gives interviews, and in the days following his appointment, he seemed to be amusing himself and perhaps trying to create a mysterious aura by playing with the reporters who questioned him. He was very sketchy on the details of his background. When asked his age, he'd respond only that he was "somewhere between 28 and 70." (For the record, he's 61.)

"I knew we had to do business differently," Kelly says of his marquee hires. "I thought we had to get some people with a fresh outlook and with federal experience to help us."

With Libutti, Kelly gets someone who has command presence, a man who has known pressure and conflict—he was injured three times in Vietnam. Libutti also has a record of accomplishment as someone who can, as they like to say in the military, organize and marshal forces and execute an objective. And in fact, he was able to "stand up" the counterterrorism bureau (Marine-speak for get it up and running) within weeks.

Job one for the new bureau is threat assessment on landmarks, public and private properties, and the city's infrastructure. The bureau has nine five-man teams, whose members were schooled at the federal law-enforcement training center in Georgia.

These teams could, for example, look at the Brooklyn Bridge, a Con Ed plant, or the offices of *New York* Magazine. Once an inspection is complete, the team produces a written report that includes detailed security suggestions. Though most of the sites are chosen by the bureau based on risk level, some are done by request. This process has helped the department establish closer ties to the business community.

The counterterrorism bureau also does independent intelligence analysis. The focus is on techniques. If two suicide bombers in a row in Israel are wearing Columbia ski jackets, for example, they'll identify the marker and issue an alert so cops here are aware of this.

Cohen's challenge, on the other hand, was to re-create and give new relevance to a division in the Police Department that already existed. "Our intelligence division was in essence an escort service," says Kelly. "They handled dignitaries and bigwigs when they came into town. It was an intelligence service in name only. We simply had to get better information. We didn't know what was going on in our own city, let alone the rest of the world."

On paper, Cohen is exactly what Kelly needed to execute his vision: a high-level guy from inside the intelligence community who has knowledge and access. Someone who can get the right people on the phone and find out what they know. Libutti is plugged in as well. Just before joining the NYPD, he was a special assistant to Homeland Security secretary Tom Ridge. He served as a liaison between Ridge and the Pentagon.

One morning in Libutti's ninth-floor office at police headquarters, he and Cohen talked about their roles. They are kind of like the Rumsfeld and Tenet of the Police Department. Cohen, who is fairly expansive considering his reputation, admits that when they signed on, their roles were not all that well defined.

"When we got here, there was no counterterrorism doctrine for a city like New York," he says in a faint Boston accent. "There was no playbook, no manual you could turn to and say, 'We should do two of these and a couple of the things in that chapter, and we have now built our counterterrorism program.' The process for us has been to write and implement the playbook simultaneously. And it's like trying to change the tires on a speeding car."

What comes through most clearly from the two men is that the lifeblood of their efforts is information. Cohen makes this point when he discusses the recent incident in London when authorities arrested three men suspected in a plot to unleash cyanide in the Underground: "When something like that happens, we need to know in real time everything we can find out about it. Obviously, the subway is a real hot spot for us given that three and a half million people a day use it. So we need to understand what kind of operation they tried to roll up, was it pre-surveillance-stage, planning-stage, was it really cyanide, was the subway the real target? The more times things get rolled up overseas, the smarter we get. And the smarter we get, the stronger we get."

The flow of quality information is also critical in helping Kelly decide how to respond to threats. Most threats that come in, according to Cohen, don't name a place, so it is often difficult even to be sure New York is the target. "You have to understand the nuances of the threat," Cohen says. "Where it's coming from, how to define it, what it really means. Frank and I help interpret the information, and that enables the commissioner to make an informed decision about responding. This war is going to go on a long time, and you've got to calibrate your response. You don't want to burn everyone out."

WHAT KELLY HAS DONE WITH Libutti and Cohen, essentially, is to create his own FBI and CIA within the New York City Police Department. "This is all about Ray Kelly's contempt for the Feds and how they blew it, over and over again," says a former member of the NYPD who knows the commissioner well.

"The Feds kept getting information they didn't act on," he continues. "So what Kelly's trying to do is say, 'Hey, just in case they don't fix all that stuff at the FBI and the CIA, we gotta find out the things they're finding out. And we gotta act on them.' Let's face it: A lot of this isn't rocket science. It's cultivating sources, talking to informants, running down leads, getting search warrants, and following up on every piece of information you get. In other words, it's good, solid investigative police work. The kind of thing New York cops do every day."

It's not every day, however, that a major figure in law enforcement like Kelly does something so contemptuous of the system. Yet there has been no outrage, no intramural rock-throwing over what he's done. Even the FBI, which has traditionally looked down on local cops, has barely raised an eyebrow over Kelly's moves.

One possible explanation for the FBI's passivity is that the agency has been under such relentless critical fire from Congress and the media that it is in no position to take on new battles. Another possibility is assistant FBI director Kevin Donovan, who was recently put in charge of the FBI's New York office. Donovan gets high marks for competence and as a team player. By all accounts, he is someone who looks to eliminate problems rather than create them.

But the most significant factor may be the most obvious. Given everything that has happened, the FBI may simply be happy to have the help. When I interviewed both Donovan and Joseph Billy, the agent in charge of counterterrorism in New York, they praised Kelly and his cops with alacrity.

"This is a very big city," says Donovan, "and we just don't have the resources to collect all the information. We don't have 40,000 eyes and ears on patrol like the NYPD. We have 1,100 agents in this office. And no one knows the streets here like the local officers. They know what to look for at two in the morning. They know what's out of place, what doesn't seem right. What Ray Kelly is doing makes perfect sense and is complementary to what we do. No city is better prepared right now than New York."

Tom Reppetto, who heads the Citizens Crime Commission and has written a history of the department called *NYPD: A City and Its Police*, more or less agrees with Donovan. In addition, he says, the FBI is not an immediate-response agency in any event. You wouldn't call the FBI, for example, if you found a bomb in Union Square Park.

"Remember, too, that the police can do a lot of the counterterrorism work as part of their regular duties," Reppetto says. "You'll notice there's been a surge in arrests of homeless people recently, and they seem to be getting arrested under bridges and in tunnels. Know why? Because police are spending a lot of time under bridges and in tunnels."

The relationship between the FBI and the NYPD has probably never been more critical than it is right now. The FBI-NYPD Joint Terrorism Task Force is one of the key instruments in the effort to protect the city. The task force was a relatively sleepy backwater run by the FBI but made up of both agents and detectives. One of Kelly's earliest moves was to pump up the number of detectives from 17 to 125, a huge commitment that the FBI matched. Kelly's intensity and his willingness to push the envelope were demonstrated early on when he tried to muscle control of the JTTF away from the FBI. According to sources, Kelly and Libutti sent a two-star police chief named Phil Pulaski over to the JTTF, which is housed at the FBI's New York headquarters.

Pulaski is generally viewed within the NYPD as brilliant—he designed and set up the police lab. However, as one cop put it to me, he also has a "Ph.D. in pissing people off." So he trooped over to the JTTF and told

them, after the FBI had been in charge for over twenty years, that he was now the boss. Though you can imagine the reaction by the Feds, Donovan managed to maintain his cool and prevent a truly damaging explosion.

He simply told Libutti it was not going to work. "You can't send a guy to my house," the director reportedly said, "and have him say he's in charge. Especially without even calling me." Libutti said he was sorry and reeled Pulaski back in.

"Our intelligence service was in essence an escort service," says Commissioner Kelly. "They handled dignitaries and bigwigs when they came into town. We simply had to get better information."

But the response from the two sides when this episode is brought up is perhaps more revealing than the incident itself. "Pulaski had a job to do," says the FBI's Joseph Billy. "He had to integrate a large number of detectives into the task force, and he's a very results-oriented individual. There was some tension, but it all worked out. The FBI is still the lead agency for the JTTF."

Libutti is not quite as conciliatory: "Without criticizing their efforts, part of our responsibility is to reach out to the federal side and demand excellence in support of what we're doing. I got a guy over there—Pulaski—who's hard-charging. His job is to keep me posted, and he's going to press, press, press, to turn over every rock to find out everything that's happening on the federal side. I think I know what's going on. What worries me is what I don't know."

PART OF WHAT KELLY LEARNED DURING his first term as commissioner—and its aftermath—is the importance of perception. It may not be fair and it may not be right, but sometimes it is not enough just to do a good job.

Self-promotion is not Kelly's natural mode, but it seems he has learned a few things from watching eight years of Giuliani. Kelly has become the face of the NYPD in the same way that Giuliani was always the face of New York. If there's a bodega robbed in the Bronx on a Sunday afternoon, it is most likely Ray Kelly who will be on the six- and eleven-o'clock news.

He also must have recognized, coming back to the NYPD, that no matter what he did on the crime front, he would not get any credit. When the FBI crime stats were released last month, New York's numbers were terrific. That week, in an editorial celebrating the continuing crime decline, the New York *Post* congratulated Kelly this way: "The local crime rate continues to drop—even as crime nationwide is on the rise—because Kelly and Mayor Bloomberg continue to employ the previous administration's anti-crime tactics."

Terrorism, by contrast, is Kelly's fight. But for all of the risk and the additional headaches, Kelly may, ironically, end up getting very little credit on this front even if he succeeds. When you're battling street crime, success and failure are easy to measure. Murder goes up or goes down. Rapes increase or they decrease. But how do you measure the terrorist acts that didn't happen? The ones all the painstaking work may have prevented? In fact, some of the successes may never even be made public when they do occur.

In November, the *Times* ran a full-page story with the headline DEEPENING SHADOWS that stated in its lead, "Once again, it's not uncommon to feel a vague sense of dread when walking down a shadowy street." And "New Yorkers are more fearful these days."

"You don't want this kind of perception to fester," Kelly says with a hint of frustration in his voice. "I'm aware it's out there. But it is a little difficult to deal with when it's not based on some reality."

With the crime numbers way down from four years ago, why do average people say they feel less safe? What has changed for them? "The elephant in the corner of the room," Kelly says, "is 9/11. That's why people feel less safe."

So Kelly's job is to end the fear. Not the fear of conventional street crime, which continues to be under control, but fear of a menace that can be very hard to see. "Kelly's a very methodical guy who does things step-by-step, by the numbers," says Reppetto. "And he is clearly determined that if something does happen, nobody is going to be able to say they didn't do everything possible to stop it. There won't be some report issued afterward saying the NYPD fell short."

THE MOST OBVIOUS TESTS OF KELLY'S new counterterrorism strategy are large public events. And two months ago, with several hundred thousand people gathered in Times Square for New Year's Eve, the pressure was really on the commissioner and the NYPD. They had executed what Kelly calls their "counterterrorism overlay package." Undercovers were everywhere. Intelligence officers mingled in the crowd. Sharpshooters were on the rooftops. Police boats were on the water, choppers were overhead, and Hercules Teams were ready to move.

Kelly also had the department's Archangel package in place, which includes ESU teams equipped to detect a chemical or biological attack and to respond if one does in fact occur.

Is New York less safe than it was? "You don't want this kind of perception to fester. I'm aware that it's out there. The elephant in the corner of the room is 9/11. That's why people feel less safe."

The five days leading up to the celebration had been especially difficult. There were intelligence reports detailing serious harbor threats, including information about a possible plan to stage eight separate diversionary acts culminating with a major terrorist attack. All the locations were covered. The water

had an eerie, blacker-than-usual look to it because it was mostly empty. No pleasure boats were allowed out.

Police had also been looking for the five men who might have come across the border from Canada using illegal documents. Michael John Hamdani, the Pakistani document forger under arrest in Toronto, told the NYPD detective who interrogated him about the men. This prompted the FBI to instigate and then call off a nationwide manhunt. Hamdani, however, didn't say they were terrorists, just that they were trying to sneak into the U.S. For Kelly, this highlighted what he believes is an ongoing alien-smuggling problem. Cops hit various locations around the city during the day, and several arrests were made.

Kelly also had credible intelligence that something might happen between Christmas and New Year's Day at the stock exchange. All week, Hercules Teams had been flooding the financial district. And then, of course, there was the gathering in Times Square itself.

"We were covering a lot of bases," says Kelly. "But we were addressing all these things appropriately. We all felt we'd done everything we could've reasonably done to make the night a safe one. You can really see the force and the power of the Police Department manifestly displayed on a night like New Year's Eve."

Finally, at around 1:30 in the morning, when most of the crowd had drifted away, Kelly had a momentary flash of relief, and satisfaction. The night had been so well handled that there were only three arrests—for disorderly conduct—in a crowd of hundreds of thousands of people. But Kelly's pleasure was short-lived. "When you get past a particular event now, there's the next event you have to address. And we were concerned about New Year's Day."

KELLY HAS TAKEN ON THIS BURDEN at an extraordinarily difficult moment for the Police Department. With the city facing its most serious deficits in 30 years, budget cuts have hit the department hard. By July, Kelly will be down 3,000 officers from the roughly 40,000-man force he took over last January. In addition, he has 1,000 cops assigned full-time to his fight against the terrorists.

In an attempt to fill in the gaps, Kelly has energetically tried to convince the federal government that the cost of protecting New York is no longer just a municipal responsibility. Though a half-billion dollars of need has been identified, Kelly and his staff have whittled it down to a $261 million list that includes money for training and equipment. Despite several trips to Washington, Kelly has so far made no progress.

He has also been a good soldier and not publicly fought with the mayor over budget issues. When the mayor was booed last week at the graduation ceremony for 2,108 new cops—largely because his budget-cutting included talk of police layoffs—Kelly enthusiastically came to his defense. However, the police commissioner was not always so sanguine about the cuts. When Bloomberg made his first statement last July calling for 7.5 percent cuts across all city departments, sources say, Kelly balked.

According to one source, Kelly initially told the mayor he couldn't play ball on the budget cuts. He was not going to be the police commissioner on whose watch crime began to go up because the department was underfunded and undermanned. Though everything was worked out amicably, Bloomberg's people actually contacted several former commissioners—including Bratton and Timoney—to see what they were up to. "The conversations were to put out friendly feelers that were one stop short of 'Are you still available?,' says the source.

The potential downside for Kelly of this focus on counterterrorism is enormous. "I know there's a universe out there just waiting to say, 'Aha, I told you so,'" he says. "But let me tell you something. We're taking care of business. There is this notion that this administration cannot do it all, something's gotta give. Well, the city is safer than it's ever been in modern history."

BEFORE SEPTEMBER 11, THE NIGHTMARE that haunted New York's police commissioners—and commissioners in other big cities as well—tended to revolve around police brutality and race—Amadou Diallo, say, or Rodney King. One commissioner who left his job not all that long ago while riding a wave of popularity in his city reportedly told a confidant that he believed he was "one 3 a.m. phone call away from having it all fall apart." Since 9/11, of course, "having it all fall apart" means something entirely different—and much scarier. "We don't know the time and we don't know the place," says Libutti, "but we do know the bad guys are coming back."

Sitting in his office one recent evening as a cold wind whipped across the plaza in front of police headquarters, Kelly showed no signs of the pressure he is under.

"I enjoy this job and I'm living in the moment," he said while eating a cookie. "The world has changed, but I believe I'm doing the right thing. We're the biggest, most important city in the world, and this is the biggest, most talented police force. And we have done everything we can reasonably do to prevent another attack."

From *Newyorkmetro.com*, February 3, 2003, pp. 36–39, 63. Copyright © 2003 by New York Magazine. Reprinted by permission.

Racial Profiling and its Apologists

Racist law enforcement is rooted in deceptive statistics, slippery logic, and telling indifference

By Tim Wise

It's just good police work." So comes the insistence by many—usually whites—that concentrating law enforcement efforts on blacks and Latinos is a perfectly legitimate idea. To listen to some folks tell it, the fact that people of color commit a disproportionate amount of crime (a claim that is true for some but not all offenses) is enough to warrant heightened suspicion of such persons. As for the humiliation experienced by those innocents unfairly singled out, stopped, and searched? Well, they should understand that such mistreatment is the price they'll have to pay, as long as others who look like them are heavily represented in various categories of criminal mischief.

Of course, the attempt to rationalize racism and discriminatory treatment has a long pedigree. Segregationists offer up many "rational" arguments for separation and even slave-owners found high-minded justifications for their control over persons of African descent. In the modern day, excuses for unequal treatment may be more nuanced and couched in calm, dispassionate, even academic jargon; but they remain fundamentally no more legitimate than the claims of racists past. From overt white supremacists to respected social scientists and political commentators, the soft-pedaling of racist law enforcement is a growing cottage industry: one rooted in deceptive statistics, slippery logic, and telling indifference to the victims of such practices.

As demonstrated convincingly in David Harris's new book *Profiles in Injustice: Why Racial Profiling Cannot Work* (New Press, 2002), racial profiling is neither ethically acceptable nor logical as a law enforcement tool. But try telling that to the practice's apologists.

According to racial separatist Jared Taylor of American Renaissance—a relatively highbrow white supremacist organization—black crime rates are so disproportionate relative to those of whites that it is perfectly acceptable for police to profile African Americans in the hopes of uncovering criminal activity. His group's report "The Color of Crime"— which has been touted by mainstream conservatives like Walter Williams—purports to demonstrate just how dangerous blacks are, what with murder, robbery, and assault rates that are considerably higher than the rates for whites. That these higher crime rates are the result of economic conditions disproportionately faced by people of color Taylor does not dispute in the report. But he insists that the reasons for the disparities hardly matter. All that need be known is that one group is statistically more dangerous than the other and avoiding those persons or stopping them for searches is not evidence of racism, but rather the result of rational calculations by citizens and police.

Although in simple numerical terms, whites commit three times more violent crimes each year than blacks, and whites are five to six times more likely to be attacked by another white person than by a black person, to Taylor, this is irrelevant. As he has explained about these white criminals: "They may be boobs, but they're our boobs."

Likewise, Heather MacDonald of the conservative Manhattan Institute has written that racial profiling is a "myth." Police, according to MacDonald—whose treatment of the subject was trumpeted in a column by George Will last year—merely play the odds, knowing "from experience" that blacks are likely to be the ones carrying drugs.

Michael Levin, a professor of philosophy at the City College of New York, argues it is rational for whites to fear young black men since one in four are either in prison, on probation, or on parole on any given day. According to Levin, the assumption that one in four black males encountered are therefore likely to be dangerous is logical and hardly indicates racism. Levin has also said that blacks should be treated as adults earlier by the justice system because they mature faster and trials should be shorter for blacks because they have a "shorter time horizon."

Conservative commentator Dinesh D'Souza says that "rational discrimination against young black men can be fully eradicated only by getting rid of destructive conduct by the group that forms the basis for statistically valid group distinctions. It is difficult to compel people to admire groups many of whose members do not act admirably."

Even when the profiling turns deadly, conservatives show little concern. Writing about Amadou Diallo, recipient of 19 bullets (out of 41 fired) from the NYPD Street Crimes Unit, columnist Mona Charen explained that he died for the sins of his black brethren, whose criminal proclivities gave the officers good reason to suspect that he was up to no good.

Putting aside the obvious racial hostility that forms the core of many if not all of these statements, racial profiling cannot be justified on the basis of general crime rate data showing that blacks commit a disproportionate amount of certain crimes, relative to their numbers in the population. Before making this point clear, it is worth clarifying what is meant by racial profiling.

Racial profiling means one of two things. First, the over-application of an incident-specific criminal description in a way that results in the stopping, searching, and harassment of people based solely or mostly on skin color alone. An example would be the decision by police in one upstate New York college town a few years ago to question every black male in the local university after an elderly white woman claimed to have been raped by a black man (turns out he was white).

So while there is nothing wrong with stopping black men who are 6′2″, 200 pounds, driving Ford Escorts, if the perp in a particular local crime is known to be 6′2″, 200 pounds, and driving a Ford Escort, but when that description is used to randomly stop black men, even who aren't 6′2″, aren't close to 200 pounds, and who are driving totally different cars, then that becomes a problem.

The second and more common form of racial profiling is the disproportionate stopping, searching, frisking, and harassment of people of color in the hopes of uncovering a crime, even when there is no crime already in evidence for which a particular description might be available. In other words: stopping black folks or Latinos and searching for drugs.

This is why general crime rates are irrelevant to the profiling issue. Police generally don't randomly stop and search people in the hopes of turning up last night's convenience store hold-up man. They tend to have more specific information to go on in those cases. As such, the fact that blacks commit a higher share of some crimes (robbery, murder, assault) than their population numbers is of no consequence to the issue of whether profiling them is legitimate. The "crime" for which people of color are being profiled mostly is drug possession. In that case, people of color are not a disproportionate number of violators and police do not find such contraband disproportionately on people of color.

All available evidence indicates that whites are equally or more likely to use (and thus possess at any given time) illegal narcotics. This is especially true for young adults and teenagers, in which categories whites are disproportionate among users.

Although black youth and young adults are more likely than white youth to have been approached by someone offering to give them or sell them drugs during the past month, they are less likely to have actually used drugs in the last 30 days. Among adults, data from California is instructive: although whites over the age of 30 are only 36 percent of the state's population, they comprise 60 percent of all heavy drug users in the state.

Although blacks and Latinos often control large drug sale networks, roughly eight in ten drug busts are not for dealing, but for possession. Drug busts for narcotics trafficking rarely stem from random searches of persons or vehicles—the kind of practice rightly labeled profiling—but rather, tend to take place after a carefully devised sting operation and intelligence gathering, leading to focused law enforcement efforts. As such, the usage numbers are the more pertinent when discussing the kinds of police stops and searches covered by the pejorative label of "profiling."

A Department of Justice study released in 2001 notes that although blacks are twice as likely as whites to have their cars stopped and searched, police are actually twice as likely to find evidence of illegal activity in cars driven by whites.

In New Jersey, for 2000, although blacks and Latinos were 78 percent of persons stopped and searched on the southern portion of the Jersey Turnpike, police were twice as likely to discover evidence of illegal activity in cars driven by whites, relative to blacks, and whites were five times more likely to be in possession of drugs, guns, or other illegal items relative to Latinos. In North Carolina, black drivers are two-thirds more likely than whites to be stopped and searched by the State Highway Patrol, but contraband is discovered in cars driven by whites 27 percent more often.

In New York City, even after controlling for the higher crime rates by blacks and Latinos and local demographics (after all, people of color will be the ones stopped and searched most often in communities where they make up most of the residents), police are still two to three times more likely to search them than whites. Yet, police hunches about who is in possession of drugs, guns, other illegal contraband, or who is wanted for commission of a violent crime turn out to be horribly inaccurate. Despite being stopped and searched more often, blacks and Latinos are less likely to be arrested because they are less likely to be found with evidence of criminal wrongdoing.

So much for MacDonald's "rational" police officers, operating from their personal experiences. Despite police claims that they only stop and search people of color more often because such folks engage in suspicious behavior more often, if the "hit rates" for such persons are no higher than, and even lower than the rates for whites, this calls into question the validity of the suspicious action criteria. If blacks seem suspicious more often, but are actually hiding something less often, then by definition the actions deemed suspicious should be reexamined, as they are not proving to be logical at all, let alone the result of good police work. Indeed, they appear to be proxies for racial stops and searches.

Nor can the disproportionate stopping of black vehicles be justified by differential driving behavior. Every study done on the subject has been clear: there are no significant differences between people of color and whites when it comes to the commission of moving or other violations. Police acknowledge that virtually every driver violates any number of minor laws every time they take to the road. But these violations are not enforced equally and that is the problem.

In one New Jersey study, for example, despite no observed differences in driving behavior, African Americans were 73 percent of all drivers stopped on the Jersey Turnpike, despite being less than 14 percent of the drivers on the road: a rate that is 27 times greater than what would be expected by random chance. Similar results were found in a study of stops in Maryland. On a particular stretch of Interstate 95 in Florida, known for being a drug trafficking route, blacks and Latinos comprise only 5 percent of drivers, but 70 percent of those stopped by members of the Highway Patrol. These stops were hardly justified, as only nine drivers, out of 1,100 stopped during the study, were ever ticketed for any violation, let alone arrested for possession of illegal contraband.

As for Levin's claim that whites should properly consider one in four black males encountered to be a threat to their personal safety, because of their involvement with the criminal justice system, it should be remembered that most of these have been arrested for non-violent offenses like drug possession. Blacks comprise 35 percent of all possession arrests and 75 percent of those sent to prison for a drug offense, despite being only 14 percent of users.

When it comes to truly dangerous violent crime, only a miniscule share of African Americans will commit such offenses in a given year and less than half of these will choose a white victim.

With about 1.5 million violent crimes committed by blacks each year (about 90 percent of these by males) and 70 percent of the crimes committed by just 7 percent of the offenders—a commonly accepted figure by criminologists—this means that less than 2 percent of blacks over age 12 (the cutoff for collecting crime data) and less than 3.5 percent of black males over 12 could even theoretically be considered dangerous. Less than 1.5 percent of black males will attack a white person in a given year, hardly lending credence to Levin's claim about the rationality of white panic.

The fact remains that the typical offender in violent crime categories is white. So even if black rates are disproportionate to their population percentages, any "profile" that tends to involve a black or Latino face is likely to be wrong more than half the time. Whites commit roughly 60 percent of violent crimes, for example. So if 6 in 10 violent criminals are white, how logical could it be to deploy a profile—either for purposes of law enforcement or merely personal purposes of avoiding certain people—that is only going to be correct 40 percent of the time? So too with drugs, where any profile that involves a person of color will be wrong three out of four times?

Additionally, the apologists for profiling are typically selective in terms of the kinds of profiling they support. Although whites are a disproportionate percentage of all drunk drivers, for example, and although drunk driving contributes to the deaths of more than 10,000 people each year, none of the defenders of anti-black or brown profiling suggests that drunk driving roadblocks be set up in white suburbs where the "hit rates" for catching violators would be highest.

Likewise, though white college students are considerably more likely to binge drink (often underage) and use narcotics than college students of color, no one suggests that police or campus cops should regularly stage raids on white fraternity houses or dorm rooms occupied by whites, even though the raw data would suggest such actions might be statistically justified.

Whites are also nearly twice as likely to engage in child sexual molestation, relative to blacks. Yet how would the Heather MacDonalds and Dinesh D'Souzas of the world react to an announcement that adoption agencies were going to begin screening out white couples seeking to adopt, or subjecting them to extra scrutiny, as a result of such factual information?

Similarly, those seeking to now justify intensified profiling of Arabs or Muslims since September 11 were hardly clamoring for the same treatment of white males in the wake of Oklahoma City. Even now, in the wake of anthrax incidents that the FBI says have almost certainly been domestic, possibly white supremacist in origin, no one is calling for heightened suspicion of whites as a result.

The absurdity of anti-Arab profiling is particularly obvious in the case of trying to catch members of al-Qaeda. The group, after all, operates in 64 countries, many of them non-Arab, and from which group members would not look anything like the image of a terrorist currently locked in the minds of so many. Likewise, Richard Reid, the would-be shoe bomber recently captured was able to get on the plane he sought to bring down precisely because he had a "proper English name," likely spoke with a proper English accent, and thus, didn't fit the description.

The bottom line is that racial profiling doesn't happen because data justifies the practice, but rather because those with power are able to get away with it, and find it functional to do so as a mechanism of social control over those who are less powerful. By typifying certain "others" as dangerous or undesirable, those seeking to maintain divisions between people whose economic and social interests are actually quite similar can successfully maintain those cleavages.

No conspiracy here, mind you: just the system working as intended, keeping people afraid of one another and committed to the maintenance of the system, by convincing us that certain folks are a danger to our well-being, which then must be safeguarded by a growing prison-industrial complex and draconian legal sanctions; or in the case of terrorist "profiles," by the imposition of unconstitutional detentions, beefed-up military and intelligence spending, and the creation of a paranoiac wartime footing.

Until and unless the stereotypes that underlie racial profiling are attacked and exposed as a fraud, the practice will likely continue: not because it makes good sense, but because racist assumptions about danger—reinforced by media and politicians looking for votes—lead us to think that it does.

Tim Wise is a Nashville-based writer, lecturer and antiracist activist. Footnotes for this article can be obtained at tjwise@mindspring.com.

Too Close for Comfort

Negotiating with Fellow Officers

By SANDRA D. TERHUNE-BICKLER, M.S.

While driving home, your cell phone rings. You answer and hear a woman crying. You recognize her as the estranged wife of your friend and fellow officer Rob. The woman asks you to come over because Rob has been drinking and has locked himself in the bathroom with his off-duty pistol and their 3-year-old son. She said he keeps yelling that he "can't take it anymore…can't take it anymore…."

Though not a circumstance any member of law enforcement wants to face, personnel of all ranks need to prepare for how to handle, supervise, or delegate this type of situation. Incidents requiring crisis negotiations often are difficult, highly emotional,

embarrassing, and dangerous. When the subject in crisis is a colleague, the emotions of everyone involved are deeply affected. Though most law enforcement agencies have specialized crisis/hostage negotiation teams, members of law enforcement may attempt to resolve the issue on their own because the subject in crisis serves with their agency. Both the officer placed in the position of the sniper who deploys lethal force when the barricaded suspect is a fellow member of the agency's special weapons and tactical (SWAT) team and the commander who placed the officer in that sniper position face difficult predicaments.

RESEARCH

Although limited published research is available on officers negotiating with fellow officers, crisis negotiations involving law enforcement personnel do occur. According to the FBI's Hostage and Barricaded Database System (HOBAS), 22 incidents involving either a barricaded or suicidal officer were reported in the United States between 1995 and 2002.[1] Of these 22 reported incidents, 3 resulted in suicides. However, law enforcement suicide incidents may occur more frequently than the number actually reported. Some of the most common reasons given for suicides among law enforcement include relationship problems, legal trouble, psychological problems, and work-related stress.[2]

Recently, the author interviewed several crisis negotiators from the FBI and the police and sheriff's departments in both Los Angeles and San Diego, California, regarding their experiences with officer-involved incidents.[3] These negotiators reported that they had experienced or knew of an incident at their agency involving a suicidal or barricaded officer. Some of those interviewed negotiated with an in-crisis member of other departments and others negotiated with members of their own agency. One of the interviewees reported negotiating with a relative, although the officer in crisis did not know the negotiator's identity. Interview results have shown that negotiating with another police officer does not constitute a phenomenon but, rather, an issue that agencies must confront and handle.

> "...agencies should have a well-respected peer support program that encourages employees to call a coworker for mental health referrals and resources."

In an attempt to protect fellow officers from embarrassment or potential disciplinary action, some members of law enforcement try to resolve the situation privately, even covertly. Law enforcement suicide, like law enforcement domestic violence, is not a topic comfortably discussed.[4] For officers to admit that they feel suicidal or have domestic problems is close to admitting that they have lost control. In a profession

that expects its members to always be in control, law enforcement can be unforgiving or ill-prepared to handle an officer's admission of personal or interpersonal problems. This does not mean that officer-involved crisis incidents could be prevented if law enforcement culture became more accepting of vulnerabilities among its own personnel. Rather, it is important to acknowledge that these situations do occur and law enforcement agency personnel must remain mindful of how best to respond to that unexpected, dreaded phone call.

THE APPROPRIATE RESPONSE

When responding to an incident, most law enforcement personnel probably would say that they act tactically, logically, and compassionately. However, would their response be the same if the subject was a fellow officer? Perhaps, the responder would consider using the lowest level of intervention with a colleague, trying to engage him in conversation.[5] This may prove a viable option when a low level of intervention can resolve a particular situation. For this reason, agencies should have a well-respected peer support program that encourages employees to call a coworker for mental health referrals and resources. However, when the officer in distress needs more immediate crisis intervention, well-intentioned colleagues may find themselves in an overwhelming circumstance.

When dealing with an in-crisis law enforcement officer, the responding officer should determine which agency to call first, the employing agency or the agency nearest the in-crisis officer's location. Although the right answer may seem obvious, the employing agency may respond, even if the incident did not occur in its jurisdiction. In an attempt to subdue the crisis, decision makers

may place themselves in situations for which they are dangerously unprepared. Should officer safety be disregarded because the suicidal subject is a fellow member of law enforcement? Suicide-by-cop does not only apply to civilian personnel. Is protecting a fellow officer from potential embarrassment an adequate reason for not notifying the jurisdictional agency when a tactical intervention is necessary?

> "...problems sometimes occur when the in-crisis officer's agency responds."

If the officer in distress lives in the city where he is employed, the ethical response should occur as it would in any standard critical incident. It is easy to speculate about the right way to respond, but harder to assume what actually would occur. Officers may find it difficult to respond to a crisis situation if they have a personal stake in it (i.e., a family member, friend, or colleague is the one in crisis). Commanders from both the employing and the jurisdictional agencies should share in the decision-making process and take responsibility if lethal force is required. In this circumstance, mutual aid reinforces objectivity in tactical response and procedure. Agencies should have contingency plans, such as mutual aid agreements, in the event a tactical intervention seems likely; asking for assistance is not admitting an inability to handle a situation. For example, FBI agents are regular members on the San Diego, California, Police Department's crisis negotiation team. Though no officer ever should have to use lethal force against another, it remains an unfortunate possibility.

NEGOTIATING WITH FELLOW OFFICERS

Dynamics Supporting Negotiations

- Rapport already may be established; in-crisis officers are known and know the negotiator
- Easy to obtain information about in-crisis officers
- Negotiator may be able to relate common problems/themes with in-crisis officers
- Third-party intermediaries are known and easily controlled
- Keeping the problem in-house may give in-crisis officers the illusion that it is "not a big thing"

Dynamics Harming Negotiations

- In-crisis officers may see the department as the source of the problem
- In-crisis officers perceive the negotiator as "one of them"
- In-crisis officers are too embarrassed to talk to someone they know
- Negotiator may be too emotionally attached to be objective/effective
- In-crisis officers know what the department will deliver
- Suicide is a high possibility
- In-crisis officers may be armed
- Negotiator is a secondary victim if the resolution ends in death

For additional information, contact Officer Terhune-Bickler at sandy-terhune@santa-monica.org.

NEGOTIATION DECISIONS

If the officer in distress will speak only to a particular person, should agencies put that person on the phone? Should the crisis negotiator be someone the officer in crisis knows? Some law enforcement agencies have no other choice. One of the benefits of allowing a colleague to speak to the in-crisis officer is the rapport already established between them, which may help the distressed officer feel more comfortable and understood. If handling the negotiation in-house, information on the officer is easily accessible. Additionally, when the distressed officer's agency handles the negotiations, it may have easy access to third-party intermediaries who could communicate with that officer.[6]

However, problems sometimes occur when the in-crisis officer's agency responds. Even though many agencies have crisis negotiation teams, upper-level administrators may neglect to use them—they may attempt to solve the situation by themselves. Similar to citizens who encounter a distressed or suicidal relative, well-intentioned members of law enforcement sometimes inadvertently allow their emotions to interfere with their judgment, which can result in mistakes and tragedies. For example, if the officer in crisis sees the department as the source of the problem, he may perceive the negotiator as "one of them." Also, the officer in crisis may be too embarrassed to speak to someone he knows. Because he understands departmental procedures, he may not trust supervisors' promises. Realistically, when negotiating with a member of law enforcement, responders must assume that the in-crisis officer is armed, making suicide or suicide-by-cop possible.

CONCLUSION

Determining and conducting an appropriate response to situations involving in-crisis law enforcement personnel can prove overwhelming even to seasoned managers. Team leaders and department commanders should ensure that they are prepared to deal with the secondary victimization of their officers when handling a suicidal or barricaded situation involving one of their own employees.

Because crisis negotiations can prove a difficult and emotionally draining process, negotiation teams should consult with mental health professionals. When the subject in crisis is a police officer, the rules remain the same, but the losses can be more tragic, as well as everlasting. Further, agencies should take advantage of mutual aid relationships. In addition to the combined resources of both agencies, this alliance eliminates negotiators from having to negotiate with a fellow officer from their own department.[7] By establishing certain protocol for these tragic incidents, agencies will be better prepared if, unfortunately, negotiating with one of their own becomes necessary.

Endnotes

1. Based on statistics from the FBI's HOBAS database, 2002.
2. Michael G. Aadmodt and Nicole A. Stalnaker, "Police Officer Suicide: Frequency and Officer Profiles," in Donald C. Sheehan and Janet I. Warren, eds., U.S. Department of Justice, Federal Bureau of Investigation, *Suicide and Law Enforcement* (Washington, DC, 2001), 383-398.
3. The author interviewed several law enforcement officers from these agencies. Due to liability issues, interviewees agreed to share their experiences but requested that their names and identifying information of the in-crisis officers remain anonymous.
4. For additional information, see Donald C. Sheehan, ed., U.S. Department of Justice, Federal Bureau of Investigation, *Domestic Violence by Police Officers* (Washington, DC, 2000); Lonald D. Lott, "Deadly Secrets: Violence in the Police Family," *FBI Law Enforcement Bulletin*, November 1995, 12-16; Thomas E. Baker and Jane P. Baker, "Preventing Police Suicide," *FBI Law Enforcement Bulletin*, October 1996, 24-27; and Paul Quinnett, "QPR: Police Suicide Prevention," *FBI Law Enforcement Bulletin*, July 1998, 19-24.
5. For clarity and illustrative purposes, the author refers to all in-crisis officers as males.
6. M. J. McMains and W.C. Mullins, *Crisis Negotiations: Managing Crit-*

ical Incidents and Hostage Situations in Law Enforcement and Corrections, 2d ed., (Cincinnati, OH: Anderson Publishing Co., 2001). For more information on third-party in-

termediaries, see Steven J. Romano, "Third-Party Intermediaries and Crisis Negotiations," *FBI Law Enforcement Bulletin,* October 1998, 20-24.

7. Lieutenant Jim Barker, San Diego, California, Police Department, interview by author on December 4, 2002.

From *FBI Law Enforcement Bulletin*, April 2004, pp. 1-5, by Sandra D. Terhune-Bickler, M.S. Published in 2004 by the Federal Bureau of Investigation.

Ethics and Criminal Justice: Some Observations on Police Misconduct

by Bryan Byers
Ball State University

One need not look far to see evidence of the societal importance placed on ethics in criminal justice. Ethics has been a hot topic in the 1990s and promises to be equally important as we venture into the new millennium. Often, the issue of ethics in criminal justice is considered synonymous with police ethics. However, ethics touches all of the main branches of criminal justice practice as well as the academic realm. Due to the high profile nature of policing in our society, however, ethics is commonly connected with policing. Therefore, particular focus is given to this dimension in the following discussion. Within this essay the topic of ethics is addressed by first examining a general understanding of this concept. Second, a brief discussion of our societal concern over ethics and criminal justice practice is examined. Third, the discussion centers on selected scholarship in criminal justice ethics. Finally, some concluding remarks are offered.

ETHICS AND ETHICAL ISSUES: A PRIMER

According to the Merriam-Webster Dictionary, "ethics" is defined as (1) "a discipline dealing with good and evil and with moral duty" or (2) "moral principles or practice." The first definition suggests that ethics is a discipline or area of study. This certainly has been the case when we examine the academic field of Philosophy. Criminal justice is, admittedly, a hybrid discipline drawing from many academic fields—one being Philosophy. Interestingly, a good portion of the published academic scholarship in criminal justice ethics is philosophical in nature and can be found in the journal *Criminal Justice Ethics*. The other part of the definition sug-

gests that ethics is a combination of cognition ('moral principles') and behavior ('practice'). Therefore, we might conclude that ethics is the study of the principle and practice of good, evil, and moral duty.

As we consider the nature of criminal justice, and in particular policing, within contemporary society, the behavior of law enforcement officers is continually the target of ethical evaluation. The field of law enforcement has been under scrutiny during various historical epochs for behavior that has been called into question on ethical grounds. Whether it be search and seizure "fishing expeditions" prior to *Mapp v. Ohio*, the fallout from the Knapp Commission report (*à la Serpico*) or the latest instance of police misconduct to flood the media, essentially the concern is over conduct or behavior. Cognitive processes and the socialization that reinforces unprofessional and unethical conduct influence the onset and proliferation of undesirable behavior. Thus, while one must be concerned with psychological and sociological forces that help to produce police unprofessionalism and unethical behavior, we should not lose sight of the role choice has in police misconduct.

One would be hard pressed to produce credible evidence to suggest that policing has not become more professional over the past several decades. It seems equally unreasonable to suggest that the entire field of policing is corrupt and permeated with graft. However, and as most readers will know, such an explanation has been offered. The venerable "rotten barrel theory"[1] of police corruption suggests such permeation within a police department. As most readers know, the rotten barrel theory of police corruption suggests that unethical and illegal behavior not only occurs at the individual officer level but is pervasive

enough within a police department that unethical conduct may be traced to top administrative officials.

Another interpretation of police corruption is the "rotten apple theory."[2] This approach does not suggest that corruption and unethical conduct is so pervasive that it spreads to the highest ranks and throughout the organization. This approach, rather, suggests that there are a few "rotten apples" in a police department and inappropriate behavior is isolated to a few individuals. Police administrators have been keen on this explanation in the wake of police corruption because it avoids suggestion of wholesale departmental corruption, allows for a tidy response (e.g., fire the offending officer), and does not necessarily have to result in a tarnished image of an entire department.

An additional form of police misconduct has also been identified. In addition to the rotten apple and the rotten barrel, there may also be a "rotten group theory" of police corruption. According to a 1998 report by the General Accounting Office on police corruption in the United States, "The most commonly identified pattern of drug-related police corruption involved small groups of officers who protected and assisted each other in criminal activities, rather than the traditional patterns of non-drug-related police corruption that involved just a few isolated individuals or systemic corruption pervading an entire police department or precinct."[3]

Whether unethical behavior is systematic, small group, or individual, one cannot deny the importance placed on the intellectual process that allows for such conduct to take place. One might still be left wondering what it is about policing that produces opportunities to engage in unethical behavior. That is, what is it about the policing profession that affords officers the opportunity to engage in unethical conduct? The answer might be found in the concepts of "authority" and "power." Police wield a tremendous amount of power and authority within society. The powers to arrest, question and detain are entrusted with the police. The authority given to the police to protect our belongings and persons is unmatched by any other profession. Unethical or illegal behavior results when a law enforcement officer makes a conscious decision to abuse authority or wield power that is not appropriate to the situation. What is fundamental to unethical behavior by police is the conscious decision to abuse authority or power and circumstances, peer pressure, socialization, loyalty, and individual psychology are secondary in their ability to explain the behavior.

It might be best to interpret the role played by factors such as circumstances, peer pressure, socialization, loyalty, and individual psychology as a means of excusing or justifying the unethical or illegal act committed by an officer. That is, while the individual officer makes a decision to violate the public's trust and engage in unethical behavior, one might suggest that the officer's loyalty to his peers was a justification for the conduct. Let us examine this dynamic by way of an ethical dilemma. Assume that Officer X has just pulled over a drunk driver and realizes that the suspect is a fellow officer and friend. In fact, the driver has helped Officer X out of a few "tight spots" over the years. Instead of placing the colleague through a field sobriety test, Officer X helps his buddy park the car and then drives him home with the understanding from his friend that he will "sleep it off." What was the ethical dilemma? The choice between doing what was appropriate (the field sobriety test and subsequent arrest if appropriate) and being loyal to his friend. This situation, at the very least, describes a scenario ripe for abuse of discretion. Since discretion is a power that police have, it can be abused. Thus, many might examine this situation and suggest that the officer abused his discretionary authority. The officer made a decision to abuse his power but did so out of loyalty to the friend that is promoted through socialization behind the "blue curtain."

CONCERN OVER ETHICS: CAN WE CALL IT A TREND?

Media reports of police misconduct pepper us whenever there is an incident of alleged misbehavior or corruption. It might

be the nightly newscaster reporting on the Rodney King incident at the start of the 1990s. It could be the recent case of the Philadelphia Police Department officers viewed on tape kicking a downed felony crime suspect at the birth of the twenty-first century. Whatever the instance, the topic of ethics and ethical behavior within the criminal justice profession grabs headlines. The media likes to report on such "ethical misadventures" because it sells. Some of the public, and powerful leaders, use such instances to legitimize their negative attitudes toward police. The police loathe the "bad press" in the wake of their self-perception of "doing good" for the community.

The media might be the only winner in the wake of police misconduct. However, the public loses and so do the fields of policing and criminal justice, in general. Even the academic field of criminal justice loses because policing is so closely linked in the public mind to it. I am reminded of this reality when recalling my flight back from the 1991 Academy of Criminal Justice Sciences meeting in Nashville. As plane passengers do, I began a conversation with the person seated next to me. We engaged in the typical small talk of "where are you from" and "where are you going." When my fellow passenger heard that I was returning from a "criminal justice" meeting, his response was immediate and unequivocal. He said, "why are cops such jerks?" The conversation occurred in the wake of the Rodney King incident and he was referring to the behavior of the L.A. police officers captured on tape. Admittedly taken aback, I was speechless. Part of the reason was personal, given my experiences in the field as a practitioner and those of close family members and friends. The other part of my speechlessness was professional and social scientific in nature, given how astounding it was to me to find a person willing to generalize so broadly from one highly celebrated incident. This seemingly innocuous exchange had an indelible impression on me. It made me think about the impact the field of criminal justice might have in the topic of ethics.

There is little doubt that real world events and their impact on the collective conscience influence the academic field. In fact, one could reasonably argue that societal events drive research agendas and define, to some degree, what is popular to investigate criminologically and what is not. Ethics may be no exception. For instance, the Rodney King incident, one might argue, had a tremendous impact not

only on the practical dimensions of policing and police-community relations but also on the academic field of criminal justice. For instance, the book jacket for *Above the Law: Police and the Excessive Use of Force* by Jerome Skolnick and James Fyfe has a frame from the Rodney King video just below the title. The impact goes beyond one book, however.

Using 1991 as a pivotal year, given that the Rodney King beating occurred then, the author decided to conduct a computer search for articles on ethics in criminal justice. The findings, albeit not scientific, are interesting nonetheless. Using Periodical Abstracts, an on-line search method at my institution and offered through the university library, a search was conducted for "criminal justice" + "ethics" comparing the years 1986–1990 to 1991–1999. What I wanted to find out is this: were there more publications in criminal justice ethics prior to Rodney King or after? Since the incident occurred relatively early in 1991, that year was placed in the "post-Rodney King" group of years. From 1986 (the first year the index covers) through 1990, there were 28 "hits" or publications on criminal justice ethics. From 1991 through 1999 there were 152 publications. Admittedly, the "post" period encompassed nine years and the "pre" period only contained five years. However, it is still rather telling that such a difference exists.

Only time will tell if the aforementioned suggests a trend for the discipline. However, there is certainly every indication that criminal justice scholarship and practice will continue with an emphasis on ethics. A key reason why ethics promises to have a strong future presence has less to do with the lasting impact of Rodney King and more to do with constant reminders that ethical misadventures keep occurring. For example, during the past ten years, the cities of New Orleans, Chicago, New York, Miami, and Los Angeles, to name a few, have all reeled in the aftermath of ethical transgressions among their sworn law enforcement officers.

ETHICS AND CRIMINAL JUSTICE PRACTICE

In addition to the Rodney King case, there have been many other instances in which law enforcement officers have been found in ethically compromising or illegal positions. Every major city police force in the United States has experienced some form of unethical or illegal behavior within its ranks. Some of the situations in recent history have involved drugs and drug units. A few examples are listed below:

- A 1998 report by the General Accounting Office cites examples of publicly disclosed drug-related police corruption in the following cities: Atlanta, Chicago, Cleveland, Detroit, Los Angeles, Miami, New Orleans, New York, Philadelphia, Savannah, and Washington, DC. [4]

- On average, half of all police officers convicted as a result of FBI-led corruption cases between 1993 and 1997 were convicted for drug-related offenses. [5]

- A 1998 report by the General Accounting Office notes, "… several studies and investigations of drug-related police corruption found on-duty police officers engaged in serious criminal activities, such as (1) conducting unconstitutional searches and seizures; (2) stealing money and/or drugs from drug dealers; (3) selling stolen drugs; (4) protecting drug operations; (5) providing false testimony; and (6) submitting false crime reports." [6]

- A 1998 report by the General Accounting Office notes, "Although profit was found to be a motive common to traditional and drug-related police corruption, New York City's Mollen Commission identified power and vigilante justice as two additional motives for drug-related police corruption." [7]

- As an example of police corruption, the GAO cites Philadelphia, where "Since 1995, 10 police officers from Philadelphia's 39th District have been charged with planting drugs on suspects, shaking down drug dealers for hundreds of thousands of dollars, and breaking into homes to steal drugs and cash." [8]

- In New Orleans, 11 police officers were convicted of accepting nearly $100,000 from undercover agents to protect a cocaine supply warehouse containing 286 pounds of cocaine. The undercover portion of the investigation was terminated when a witness was killed under orders from a New Orleans police officer. [9]

Part of the fallout from a major finding of unethical or illegal behavior within a police department is a call to "clean up" the agency. As a result, departments in the aftermath of such an embarrassing situation might become more open to citizen review panels, pledge to re-examine their internal affairs division, require officers to participate in "ethics training," or reinforce the importance of "ethics codes."

The concept of citizen review panels has been in existence for several decades; the first panel may have been formed in Philadelphia around 1958. Citizen review panels, sometimes also called civilian review boards, are in place in some jurisdictions for the purpose of assisting with the investigation of citizen complaints that police officers within the jurisdiction engaged in the unfair treatment of civilians. Review panels can help to build or repair strained police-community relations. However, officers sometimes respond to such efforts with a defensive posture and resentment over "civilians trying to tell them how to do their job."

A department might also pledge to examine its own internal affairs division, the policy and procedure for investigating complaints and cases against officers, and typical responses to officers who have violated departmental policy and/or who have violated the law. It is important to note from the onset that a police department internal affairs division runs the risk of being considered "suspect" from officers and a community's citizenry alike. Officers can view internal affair or "I.A." as the "enemy" and a division that is bent on punishing officers who are risking their lives on the streets every day. From the community, there might be the perception that the police department cannot possibly take on the task of investigating itself. At the very least, this cannot be done "ethically." Thus, I.A. can find itself in a no-win situation. Whether a division in a large department or an officer charged with this responsibility in a smaller department, the I.A. role is critical. However, internal remedies are effective only if they are meted out in a fair and just fashion. I.A. recommendations that are carried out by police administration must bolster the respect of line officers. If perceptions exist that an officer has been treated unfairly, the department will lose any deterrent effect I.A. recommendations might produce.

Yet another response is the concept of "ethics training" for police officers and recruits. The notion of "ethics *training*" (with an emphasis on 'training') is an interesting one given that the concept of 'training' assumes that what a person is being "trained in" can be taught. In this case, the term 'ethics training' suggests, either correctly or incorrectly, that ethics can somehow be taught to people. I prefer the term "Ethics Awareness Training" in lieu of the aforementioned. Why? The reason is rather elementary. Is it possible to teach someone to be ethical as "ethics training" might suggest? This seems far-fetched, at best. If a department has an officer who has a propensity toward unethical behavior, and this person was not weeded out during the hiring process, the best one might hope for is a heightened awareness and sensitivity for ethical issues and dilemmas. Emphasizing codes of ethics, common today in most disciplines and professions, [10] is another avenue for police departments in the wake of ethical scandal. However, if a code of ethics [11] is printed in the departmental policy and procedure manual, never to be referred to again, it will have very little impact. A code of ethics for any department or organization must be a "living document" that is referenced often and held in high esteem. The code should be a document that officers have pride in and believe to be relevant to their lives as law enforcement officers. Otherwise, the code will have little, if any, impact on officer decision making and conduct.

THE SCHOLARS WEIGH IN

As mentioned above, a large portion of the academic scholarship in criminal justice ethics is philosophical in nature. However, a few academicians have attempted to examine ethics in criminal justice empirically and quantitatively. When discussing scholarship in criminal justice ethics, a few names immediately come to mind, including James Fyfe, Herman Goldstein, Victor Keppeler, Carl Klockars, Joycelyn Pollock, Lawrence Sherman, Jerome Skolnick and Sam Souryal. This is certainly not an exhaustive list, and we cannot possibly survey all of the literature in this field here. However, I would like to spend a few moments discussing two major studies funded by NIJ. The studies are *The Measurement of Police Integrity* by Klockars, Ivkovitch, Harver, and Haberfeld [12] and *Police Attitudes Toward Abuse of Authority: Findings from a National Study* by Weisburd and Greenspan. [13] Both studies were published in May of 2000. While the two studies do not represent the entire literature on police ethics, both studies are national in scope, recent and empirical.

The Klockars et al. study used 3,235 police officer respondents from 30 police agencies within the United States. The respondents were given 11 vignettes describing various types of possible police misconduct. In response to each vignette, officers were asked to answer six questions intended to measure "… the normative inclination of police to resist temptations to abuse the rights and privileges of their occupation." While the results indicate vast differences from agency to agency regarding the "environment of integrity," one finding is consistent with the protections afforded members of the police subculture. The survey revealed that most officers would not report a fellow officer who was engaged in "less serious" types of misconduct (e.g., running a security business on the side, receiving free meals and gifts, or even leaving a minor traffic accident while under the influence). What this suggests, even though the survey revealed little tolerance for what was defined as "serious" police misconduct, is that there is a culture of acceptance within police ranks for some forms of misconduct. While such conduct is typically referred to as "grass eating" (less serious forms of police misconduct) as opposed to "meat eating" (more serious forms of police misconduct), many members of society would find the behavior unacceptable. James W. Birch in *Reflections on Police Corruption*[14] makes an interesting observation regarding such behavior. He states that the public creates an environment for "grass eating" that makes it difficult to not accept the "discount" or the free meal. It would appear that there may be a different definition of what constitutes "misconduct" depending on whether a person is a member of the police subculture or an outsider looking in.

The second NIJ study, by Weisburd and Greenspan, entitled "*Police Attitudes Toward Abuse of Authority: Findings From a National Study*" is the result of the Police Foundation's national telephone survey of over 900 officers from various agencies across the country and addresses police attitudes concerning excessive force. The results indicate that the majority of respondents believed it was not acceptable to use more force than was legally permissible to effect control over a person who had assaulted an officer. However, respondents reported that "… it is not unusual for officers to ignore improper

conduct by their fellow officers." Other findings suggest that the majority of officers/respondents believed that serious instances of abuse were rare and that their department maintained a 'tough stand' on police abuse of citizenry. What about possible solutions to the problem of police abuse? Officers report two fruitful avenues for addressing police abuse. First, it was reported police administrators could have an impact on the occurrence of police abuse by "taking a stand" against abuse and through better supervision. Second, officers believed that training in ethics, interpersonal skills and cultural diversity would be effective in preventing abuse. What about turning fellow officers in for abuse? This was perceived as risky. While the majority of officers maintained that the "code of silence" was not essential to good policing, the majority also maintained that whistle blowing was not worth the consequences within the police subculture.

TOWARD A CONCLUSION

It is difficult to conclude this discussion because there is so much more to say about the topic of ethics in criminal justice. However, I will attempt to make a few concluding observations to make closure on this discussion. First, ethics is an important area within criminal justice practice and scholarship since criminal justice practitioners, especially the police, are continually under scrutiny. Therefore, the discipline has an obligation to remain interested in this topic and to promote the study of ethics. Second, scholars can be of assistance to practitioners by studying the sociological and psychological forces that impact ethical and unethical behavior. There is much the academy can offer criminal justice agencies in the form of research within organizations and training pertinent to ethics. Third, unethical behavior is the result of a conscious decision-making process to abuse one's authority while in a position of public trust. However, one must still take into account social forces that help to perpetuate, excuse, and justify unethical behavior. Fourth, there has been a proliferation of ethics scholarship in criminal justice since the Rodney King case but there is a need for more research of an empirical nature

much like the two studies profiled in this essay. While qualitative and philosophical literature is important to our understanding of ethics in criminal justice there is a need for additional research of a quantitative nature. With more study of ethics and ethical dilemmas faced by police, we might better understand the dynamics that propel officers into the dark side of policing and the factors that serve to justify misbehavior.

ENDNOTES

1. Police Deviance and Ethics. http://faculty.ncwc.edu/toconnor/205/205lec11.htm.

2. Knapp Commission Report. (1973). New York: George Braziller.

3. Government Accounting Office. Report to the Honorable Charles B. Rangel, House of Representatives, Law Enforcement: Information on Drug-Related Police Corruption. Washington, DC: USGPO (1998 May), p. 3.

4. Ibid. p. 36–37.

5. Ibid. p. 35.

6. Ibid. p. 8.

7. Ibid. p. 3.

8. Ibid. p. 37.

9. Ibid. p. 36.

10. The Academy of Criminal Justice Sciences (ACJS) recently adopted a code of ethics modeled after the American Sociological Association's (ASA) code.

11. The International Association of Chiefs of Police (IACP) has a model code of ethics and also publishes a training key on ethics and policing.

12. Klockars, C.B., S.K. Ivkovich, W.E. Harver, and M.R. Haberfeld. (2000, May). "The Measurement of Police Integrity." National Institute of Justice, Research in Brief. U.S. Government Printing Office: Washington, DC.

13. Weisburd, D. and R. Greenspan. (2000, May). "Police Attitudes Toward Abuse of Authority: Findings from a National Study." National Institute of Justice, Research in Brief. U.S. Government Printing Office: Washington, DC.

14. Birch, James W. (1983). "Reflections on Police Corruption." *Criminal Justice Ethics*, Volume 2.

From *Academy of Criminal Justice Sciences (ACJS) Today*, September/October 2000, pp. 1, 4-7. Reprinted with permission of the Academy of Criminal Justice Sciences.

Community Policing
Exploring the Philosophy

By DAVID M. ALLENDER

A discussion concerning the definition of community policing can include vastly different connotations, depending upon the views held by those involved. Street level officers might conjure up a scenario that requires the transfer of officers from traditional enforcement duties to an assignment that requires little "police action" but, instead, concentrates on helping citizens confront "order maintenance" issues. Community groups may envision a police force that responds exclusively to the demands voiced by them. Researchers usually define the model by their particular orientation. Politicians typically support the concept, but often remain unsure of what the theory means. Law enforcement administrators tend to view the idea as another federally supported initiative that they must implement to receive grant funds. Finally, officers and citizens working in a successful project often reach a consensus interpretation entirely dissimilar to any of these. With such a wide range of viewpoints, formulating a definition of community policing becomes a daunting task. However, one explanation highlights nine words that can provide the key to better understanding the concept.

Community policing is a *philosophy* of full-service, *personalized policing* where the same officer *patrols* and works in the same area on a *permanent* basis, from a decentralized *place*, working in a *proactive partnership* with citizens to identify and solve *problems*.[1]

Based on this definition, the first indication that this form of policing differs from other approaches is its label as a philosophy. Three other critical aspects include personalized, partnership, and problem-solving ingredients. Other identified factors, while important, are not as essential to understanding the concept of community policing.

Changing the Approach

Over the years, American society has embraced a number of policing methodologies. Many scholars have defined the type of work done by officers in the 1950s through the early 1970s as "traditional" policing. This terminology, in fact, can prove misleading. Several factors, including the massive shift of many police forces into vehicles equipped with radios, reform initiatives designed to remove politics from the police agencies, and early steps toward professionalism, already had altered the methods and tactics employed by law enforcement. Moreover, not everyone in the profession accepted the traditional policing approach.

To this end, several law enforcement agencies attempted to implement "team policing" in the 1980s. Poorly defined and improperly marketed to law enforcement and the public, this model had little chance of success. Rising crime rates, especially in the categories of violent crime, dictated the need to develop a more successful model for police to follow. Community policing, which attempts to form a partnership between the police and residents in the neighborhoods the officers serve, developed primarily because many people desired an improved American police force.

Early advocates of community policing identified order maintenance issues as important factors in the overall control of crime.[2] Reports identifying the amount of crime in the country indicated that most Americans were much more likely to encounter problems associated with uncivil behavior than to become a victim of crime. Fear on the part of residents, however, often caused community groups to equate disorderly persons with criminal activity. Academic information supported the feeling that resident fear represented an important factor in determining police effectiveness. Thus, reducing civil disorder became a main ingredient of the emerging community policing philosophy.

> "Public support for community policing can vary depending on how an agency plans and implements the effort."

Law enforcement professionals, equipped with lessons learned during the problem-laden traditional policing period and the failed team policing initiative, realized the need to work with the various communities they served to identify issues viewed by each neighborhood as significant. Traditional policing "is centered on serious crime, as opposed to maintenance of community social order or general service delivery."[3] Those designing community policing projects were determined to go in a different direction, but they faced many challenges. The first obstacle to overcome was formulating a definition for the concept.

Defining the Concept

Confusion about what constituted community policing arose from the beginning. Everyone from citizens to politicians, academics, and even law enforcement managers espoused conflicting ideas of what comprised community policing. Community advocates latched onto the name and decided that it signaled a new value system in which police would become more involved with the social problems within their neighborhoods. Grant programs encouraged community policing measures that satisfied written grant requirements and attempted to meet the needs of the target area receiving funds. Grant writers, however, often failed to define what those measures entailed. Law enforcement managers began holding meetings for their rank and file sworn personnel informing them that with the advent of community policing, officers would be "empowered" to take care of problems on their beats. These managers, however, sometimes failed to explain adequately all of the responsibilities that would accompany this policy. Uncertainty about what the program entailed hindered its implementation in the law enforcement community. Some veteran officers began to feel that community policing was just another federal program that would disappear as soon as the grant money dried up.

> "Confusion about what constituted community policing arose from the beginning."

How, then, could the proponents of community policing identify the expected outcomes of the program? The common theme running through all of the definitions of community policing remains the desire to improve the quality of life for local residents. To accomplish the goals and objectives of the program, most community policing theories state that an order maintenance component must exist that targets problems specific to each community or environment.

However, coupled with order maintenance, police also must engage in problem solving designed to deal with both the immediate situation and with the underlying causes for the problems. The general public and law enforcement must partner to identify problems and formulate solutions. The local law enforcement agency and its citizens must arrive at a consensus definition for community policing *before* they attempt its implementation. The definition needs to be flexible and subject to change as problems in the neighborhood evolve.

Implementing the Strategy

Besides law enforcement officers, other components of the criminal justice system can be impacted by the implementation of a community policing strategy. Prosecutors or district attorneys need to be part of the planning process before officers bring them arrests for order maintenance concerns that otherwise might have been overlooked. Judges need to understand that cases brought before them from these areas are part of a systematic approach to alleviate problems in a targeted area. Aggressive enforcement that results in increased arrests might impact the jail because of an increased inmate population. Probation and parole officers may benefit from working with community policing officers, who could offer them a better understanding of problematic persons living in the area. Public defenders may encounter an increased caseload and possibly find prosecutors more resistant to plea bargaining. Officials charged with enforcing city ordinances involving zoning and housing will be asked to assist police with a variety of projects. To achieve maximum success, each component of the criminal justice system must mesh with the others and keep in mind certain influential factors, including constitutional issues, cost considerations, and the level of public support.

Constitutional Issues

Constitutional issues may arise from community policing efforts. Changes in the way police enforce the law or institute new programs may give rise to challenges or complaints. Community police are encouraged to try new concepts. Whenever police enter an uncharted area, legal challenges generally result. Some issues will be decided in the favor of law enforcement, whereas others will be decided in favor of the defendants. For example, if the target area is located in a part of the city populated mostly by minorities, charges of racial profiling may result from aggressive enforcement. The law enforcement administrator charged with planning a community policing program must make every effort to plan for and avoid legal complications, such as in the previous example wherein it may be necessary to gather statistical information on both victims and suspects. Planning will help legal advisors defend controversial efforts.

Cost Considerations

Costs associated with community policing need not be high. After all, law enforcement's single largest expenditure is officer salaries. The officers assigned to a given area can work either in the traditional mode or in a more directed manner under established community policing guidelines. Regardless of the approach, salaries will remain the same.

As a philosophy, community policing can make use of existing resources. Integration of law enforcement assets with other components of the community actually can make for a more efficient and cost-effective police agency. It is true that in the start-up phase of the effort, the use of overtime and other grant funds can be an important way to get personnel to support the program. To continue the effort after grant funds run out, a department can tap into money that it ordinarily would budget for public relations activities, normal overtime expenditures, and officers already assigned to the neighborhood. With increased interaction with the community, officers, at the very least, will gain intelligence information that can enable them to better deal with neighborhood problems.

Public Support

Public support for community policing can vary depending on how an agency plans and implements the effort. If officers work with the community to establish a mutual goal, the program probably will be accepted. In locations where officers make little or no effort to achieve a consensus of opinion, problems will arise.[4] Political support will come only if the residents support the concept. Civil liberties groups will monitor the effort closely to see if constitutional problems or other irregularities occur.

Conclusion

The philosophy of community policing states that successful programs require the formation of a partnership between the police and area residents. Problem solving represents an important component of the effort. Flexibility remains a necessity in dealing with evolving problems in the target area.

Regular interaction between residents and the police builds trust and an increased flow of information. Intelligence gained from the public is an invaluable tool for police. Information gained as a result of community policing can lead police to criminal activity that otherwise would have gone undetected. Although criminal activity may mutate and continue, a successful community policing program will help formulate new solutions for new problems.

Endnotes

1. Robert C. Trojanowicz, U.S. Department of Justice, Federal Bureau of Inves-

tigation, Behavioral Science Unit, and Michigan State University, National Center for Community Policing, *Community Policing: A Survey of Police Departments in the United States,* (1994), 6.
2. James Q. Wilson and George L. Kelling, "Broken Windows," *Atlantic Monthly* 249 (March 1982): 29-38.
3. Jack R. Greene, "Community Policing in America: Changing the Nature, Structure, and Function of the Police," in *Policies, Processes, and Decisions of the Criminal Justice System* vol. 3 (Washington, DC: U.S. Department of Justice, National Institute of Justice, 2000), 299-370.
4. The author based this statement on his observations during a 6-month detail

working in the Executive Office for Weed and Seed as a part of the FBI's Executive Fellowship Program. He visited several cities that had instituted community policing as part of Weed and Seed, which strategically links concentrated and enhanced law enforcement efforts (weeding) with health and human services (seeding) to prevent and deter further crime. One city had three sites that varied greatly in police commitment and resident participation. The most successful had high levels of both. The least successful site had low police involvement, little resident support, and even some evidence of resident opposition to the program.

From *FBI Law Enforcement Bulletin,* March 2004, pp. 18-22, by David M. Allender. Published in 2004 by the Federal Bureau of Investigation.

THE BLUE PLAGUE OF AMERICAN POLICING

By Robert A. Fox

Cops kill themselves three times more often than other Americans. They suffer more depression, divorce more, and drink more—as many as one in four police officers have alcohol abuse problems. Cops are unhappy. They feel estranged from their departments and from a public eager to find a scapegoat for their own social, economic and political woes. This problem should give pause to everyone, to supporters and critics of the police department alike. Society needs police officers, and we need them to be happy and healthy.

The numbers are staggering. Lt. Peter J. Pranzo of the New York City Police Department estimates that America's cops kill themselves at a rate roughly triple the national average. Researchers at the University of Buffalo have found that police officers are eight times more likely to commit suicide than to be killed in a homicide. The most recent U.S. Census estimates that police officers divorce twice as often the national average. The respected researchers J.J. Hurrell and W.H. Kroes say that as many as 25 percent of police officers have alcohol abuse problems. This evidence cannot be ignored. Police officers are suffering from anomie; they believe that society is turning its back on them.

The irony is that police perceive society to be shunning them even as society believes them to be doing their jobs better than ever. A recent Harris poll found that over the past decade police improved their ratings in all of the following categories: "helpful and friendly," "not using excessive force," and "treating people fairly." The poll also reported dramatic improvements in the ratings Americans gave police in preventing crime and solving crime and, most impressively, significant improvement in the fair treatment of minorities and a decline in the fear of being arrested when completely innocent.

So what's going wrong? Why do cops feel unappreciated even as their performance improves? The convenient conclusion is to attribute officer stress to increased violent crime, budget cuts, and low pay, matters beyond the control of the agency and public. The truth, though, is that the most common and debilitating source of stress in law enforcement comes from within the agency itself. Cops don't complain about the added complexity of their jobs nearly as much as they do about the agency for which they work. Cops feel estranged, caught between a public that is both distrustful and unappreciative of them and an agency that marginalizes them. Ask cops what they don't like about their jobs and they cite internal politics, favoritism and impersonal treatment as their most common criticisms of their work environment. Internal surveys reveal that cops rate personal stress management as the most pressing need. Working in a paramilitary structure depersonalizes and marginalizes people from top to bottom. Decision-making structures that deprive them of input embitter officers and breeds cynicism. They resent supervisors who treat them as numbers, who have no consideration for their personal or family lives, who play favorites in terms of choice assignments, shifts, and recognition. They doubt whether or not they will be backed up by their superiors in times of trouble.

No cop ever joined the force to drink or get divorced. They became cops to make a difference. But the ideal is difficult to maintain as the chasm of distrust and alienation between police officers and the public widens. Police officers have an incredible capacity to deal with incidental stress. What police cannot deal with is the chronic stress of a system that marginalizes them. Psychologist William James said it well: "The deepest principle in human nature is the craving to be appreciated."

STRESS REDUCTION KIT

Bang Head Here

Directions:
1. Place kit on FIRM surface.
2. Follow directions in circle of kit.
3. Repeat step 2 as necessary, or until unconscious.
4. If unconscious, cease stress reduction activity.

Many police officers suffer from Post Traumatic Stress Syndrome. PTSD is commonly associated with war survivors, but isn't just experienced by veterans. We know now that it can be experienced by anyone working in an environment where individuals feel marginalized and dehumanized. Up until the 1980's, victims of PTSD were often seen as "weak" or in a transient state of recovery. We understand now that PTSD sufferers often have alcohol and drug problems, and experience depression, feelings of isolation, and confusion. They have sleep problems and coping difficulties, and often feel irritable, hyper-alert and angry. It is not uncommon for PTSD sufferers to contemplate and attempt suicide to escape their anxiety. Sound familiar?

So what do we do?

We need to create a non-toxic work environment for the men and women that protect us. The training and education a police officer receives address the criminal justice system, race relations, constitutional law, self-defense and ethics, among other subjects. It offers little or nothing to prepare the future police officer to successfully adjust to the new and very different working environment of law enforcement. It's time for officials at the highest policy-making levels to take responsibility for the fact that stress is killing and incapacitating more police officers than bullets. Along with body armor, every man and woman entering this profession deserves a "stress vest" that provides them with the knowledge, skills and on-going services to combat the deadly consequences of stress.

Like any problem, the solution begins with awareness and education. Before young people are exposed to the realities of life as a police officer in a paramilitary environment, they deserve to be properly trained and educated in their profession. Beginning with the police academy experience, future police officers (cadets) need to learn about working in a complex bureaucracy. They need to learn how to deal with human tragedy and separate it from the way they interact with their own families and loved ones. Police officers need ongoing services in stress management to maintain their identities as human beings first and understand that law enforcement is a job and career, not who they are. Police officers who lose their humanity become cynical and are at risk of losing their connections to their families and society. Police administrators, often perceived by their subordinates as uncaring and disrespectful, need to learn more effective management skills.

(Robert A. Fox, Ph.D., is a professor at John Jay College of Criminal Justice, where he developed the Stress Management in Law Enforcement course. He is also a review board panelist for the National Institute of Justice in the area of stress management in law enforcement.)

Educating and Training the Future Police Officer

By Michael Buerger, Ph.D.

The vision of a college-educated police profession is a dream almost a century old and, moreover, a dream still unrealized. Both policing and higher education are tradition-bound institutions with divergent interests. The internal concerns of each occupation has had greater immediacy than a discussion of how to build an educational curriculum with common purpose and benefit. Though advancements have been made since the 1960s, the old issues remain salient, even as current events and rapidly evolving technology add new ones.

As new challenges present themselves, policing still is struggling to realize the benefits of older commitments and reforms. It is time for a new dialogue between the law enforcement and academic communities to better integrate education with the training and service needs of agencies. By cooperatively identifying current and future needs, police professionals and academicians may develop tools to address both lingering promises and emerging challenges. To this end, a look at the existing system of criminal justice education, the history of the uneasy alliance of policing and education, the differences between education and training, and the future needs of the law enforcement profession can offer some guidance for creating a stronger link between education, training, and an end result of improved police services.[1]

A Three-tiered System

Over the years, criminal justice education has developed three distinct types of programs, linked in many ways to the entry-level qualifications of policing. The first step on the ladder remains the high school diploma or general equivalency degree (GED), which seems to depict the "industry standard" despite considerable change elsewhere. An improvement over the previous era's lack of educational standards, it, nonetheless, remains a relatively modest criterion. Once hired, the recruit attends a police training academy (ranging from about 400 hours to almost a year, depending upon jurisdiction) to study a wide range of topics, most of which the state Police Officer Standards and Training (POST) Board or equivalent body has mandated. Topics covered include domestic violence, defensive driving, multiculturalism, interpersonal communications, firearms retention, the criminal code, basics of forensics, introduction to weapons of mass destruction, and many others compressed into as short a program as possible.

The associate degree, a 2-year program, constitutes the middle rung on the higher education ladder. Some programs offer purely academic courses; others incorporate basic law enforcement certification into their 2-year curricula. Many states have integrated their mandate-based police training into their 2-year programs on a preservice basis. Students

who complete criminal justice programs in those settings often earn both an associate degree and certification necessary for employment.

> "The future will create new training needs not currently standard in either college programs or police training academies."

At the third level, an increasing number of police agencies now require the 4-year bachelor's degree as a hiring credential. Generally regarded as part of the social sciences, 4-year criminal justice programs focus more on research than on skills training, in accordance with longstanding dictates of the disciplines. Students learn criminal justice from a systems perspective and generally are taught skills in research methods and statistics, rather than interviewing or managing problem individuals. Bachelor of arts and bachelor of science degrees are awarded either by an independent criminal justice department or from programs within another discipline, typically sociology, public affairs, or political science. The 4-year programs continue to follow the social science model, offering knowledge about the system and developing skills to study the system. Training academies instill the skills to function adequately within the field as currently constituted (and hopefully lay the groundwork for successfully coping with changes in the social and legal environments).

Speaking broadly, the law enforcement profession apparently has not known what to do with a college education. Although college-educated persons have succeeded in policing, "education" seems to remain tied in an abstract way to professionalization and more optional than necessary. For example, the degree from the substandard institution can carry as much weight as that from a flagship university; professional development through additional training can count as much or more in promotional processes than mere education; and training itself still begins at the level of the least skilled, rather than the more educated. In addition, the assertion that the credential indicates a more rounded person, of broader vision, who can be molded into a superior police officer remains difficult to prove in more than anecdotal terms. Nor has the criminal justice degree necessarily proven itself valuable as a preparation credential; after all, many of today's college-educated officers hold degrees from other disciplines, ranging from English literature to chemical engineering.

On the other hand, higher education has taken great pains to distinguish itself from "training," even though a portion of police academy training already falls under the guise of the liberal arts discipline in some states. Many programs rightfully boast of widening their students' perceptions and ability to think critically about topics, but most criminal justice curricula focus on understanding criminal justice theory and practice through the lens of social science research. In turn, the best students possibly may leave educational institutions with well-honed skills of analysis more suited for academia than for their chosen occupation. If they present themselves for employment with abilities that their employers will never ask them to use but without those with direct application to their professional lives, then the net result is the "educated individual" whose professional development begins only after being hired.

> **"...both training and education compete with a cultural view that experiential learning constitutes the only real preparation for police work."**

In the end, though, both training and education compete with a cultural view that experiential learning constitutes the only real preparation for police work. The platitude of "Listen, kid, forget all that stuff you learned in college or at the academy" still can be heard in some quarters. Experience even has a toehold in the hiring queue, as many agencies accept 2 years of military service in lieu of 2 years of college, apparently on the grounds that the experience is somehow equivalent to a formal education.[2]

A Short History

The awkward marriage of policing and education is a legacy of the 1967 *Report of the President's Commission on Law Enforcement and the Administration of Justice*, which forced a formerly insular profession to confront the weaknesses in its structure. In the wake of widespread dissatisfaction over crime rates, police relations with minority citizens, and police handling of civil rights and antiwar protests, the report proffered "better-educated police officers" as a vehicle for change.

Criminal justice education grew out of the handful of police science programs that existed at the time. It expanded rapidly with the availability of Law Enforcement Education Program (LEEP) funds from the Omnibus Crime Control and Safe Streets Act of 1968. The creation and rapid expansion of those programs proved erratic, as practitioners often were thrust into faculty roles to meet demand. This led to criticisms that the educational component was weak, with credit given for training (or, worse, for "war stories") containing

no thinking component comparable to the established collegiate majors.

As a result, the criminal justice discipline continues to fight a battle for legitimacy within the educational community, seeking to shed the early stigma of "Handcuffing 101." The antidote within higher education has involved replicating the methods and standards of criminal justice's parent disciplines—sociology, psychology, and political science—emphasizing research methods and statistical analysis as a way of understanding system outcomes. Except in rare cases, the 4-year programs have not developed personal skills components comparable to the clinical portion of medical training. Overall, graduates may appear better prepared to become social scientists, rather than police officers, although exceptions to such a sweeping statement certainly could exist.[3] Since the 1970s, economic forces have altered the framework. As legislative mandates have added to the skills core of traditional training curricula, employer-sponsored training has become more expensive. To compensate, mechanisms for preservice certification, which places the financial burden for training on the prospective employee, have created training programs in academic settings. As a result, despite misgivings, 4-year programs end up giving academic credit for completing police academy training in some systems under the transfer rules that carry 2-year students into the 4-year institutions (even though the actual number of credit hours tends to be limited).

Different Goals

Education and training are fundamentally different tasks, though in an ideal world they should complement each other. Education should prepare students to succeed in any training regimen or philosophy or in any occupation, regardless of their academic major. The process of education is less a transfer of fact or philosophy than that of obtaining the skills of learning how to learn. A college education is designed to build within each student the ability to critically assess new situations, undertake new learning as needed, and even to question the "facts" and underlying assumptions of existing canons of knowledge, when necessary. Educated individuals who graduate from college or university possess abilities that transcend even the most specific vocational aspirations (e.g., singular areas of study, such as pre-med and prelaw), as well as multiple changes in career trajectory.

By comparison, training systematically builds particular skills to achieve certain ends. The oft-expressed idea that a person "falls back on training" in high-stress situations embodies one aspect of training goals, the repeated achievement of a desired action (and result) in a variety of contexts. Although the "Handcuffing 101" pejorative of higher education implied that skills training is physical (and education, therefore, mental), police academy training curricula also contain a growing number of topics that embody a learning component quite different from the strictly tactical mastery of wrist locks and Weaver stances, such as the nuances of domestic violence and child abuse, multicultural issues, and legal rights of the accused. Moreover, several dimensions distinguish criminal justice education from police academy training, including the amount of time spent on material, the different educational and experiential credentials of the instructors, the nature of testing and grading, and the scope of application beyond a particular vocational setting.

While the course title "Criminal Law" may appear the same, a university may feel that the "cookbook" approach of some police academy training courses—learning the material elements of each category of offenses in the criminal code—does not compare to the broader approach that examines the underlying philosophy of law, the nature of legal reasoning that informs U.S. Supreme Court opinions, and other similar issues. By the same token, though, law enforcement agencies need someone who can write a report that materially supports an affidavit and court complaint for robbery or burglary. Therefore, in a well-developed system, the collegiate process would feed well-prepared individuals into a police training process that capitalizes on their education, thus creating a complementary approach to improving police services.

Different Strengths, Different Weaknesses

The future will create new training needs not currently standard in either college programs or police training academies. New developments in technology will create a need for investigators who can cope with the criminal uses of those technologies. The sheer volume of financial crimes perpetrated via computer hacking and identity theft will exceed the capacity of federal agencies to investigate. If local police do not adapt to the need, private resources likely will fill the gap or leave local jurisdictions and their constituents without legal recourse.

Most police training curricula and most traditional social science-based criminal justice programs lack the ability to prepare students to deal with technology-based crime or with financial crime. Those skills are taught in business and computer science programs in universities and elsewhere. Originally promoted as an interdisciplinary field of study, criminal justice has narrowed. The struggle of criminal justice programs for legitimacy within the higher education sphere has forced them to hew close to the doctrinal requirements of the parent disciplines: sociology, psychology, and public administration. Doctoral-level faculty come from those disciplines and may model their programs on their own courses of study.

> "Education and training are fundamentally different tasks, though in an ideal world they should complement each other."

The social scientists who teach how to draw valid conclusions by analyzing databases do not have the skills to teach students to deal with distraught, intoxicated, scared and aggressive, or deceitful individuals. Nor are they necessarily the best persons to teach students how to recognize behavioral manifestations of mental illness or emotional disturbance; those clinical skills are taught by nursing or social work programs.

It also may be that police instructors do not have those skills either, preferring norm-driven instruction that focuses on officer safety. Historically, few practitioner instructors met (or even understood) the levels of scholarship demanded by colleges and universities, though that has changed dramatically in recent years. Practitioners able to integrate macro-level social science knowledge with street-level experiential learning remain a scarce commodity.

That said, there should be no reason that a preferred college education cannot be an interdisciplinary course of study that encompasses both understanding and a usable skill set that undergirds subsequent training. A variety of baccalaureate programs have a clinical component that involves developing skills with direct application to the job market under the tutelage of seasoned practitioners. The medical and psychological sciences have such a mix, as do accredited programs in social work. Many criminal justice programs allow or require internship or practicum experiences, providing a framework to develop a comparable "clinical" aspect to criminal justice education.

With all of these factors in mind, what can the law enforcement and academic communities do to improve the balance between educating and training future police officers? Three main models—creating a new model of interdisciplinary criminal justice degree; modifying the existing social science curricula to similar effect; and placing greater emphasis at the point of hiring upon the course of study, rather than on mere possession of a degree—demonstrate some possible approaches.

Model 1: A New Interdisciplinary Approach

The faculty of the top academic criminal justice programs came from a wide range of fields, such as sociology, psychology, urban planning, political science, and public affairs. They applied the tools of those disciplines to the study of the criminal justice system, offering different perspectives and raising different questions. In the more than 30 years since that time, the field has become homogenized, with a fairly standard set of curricular offerings common to most programs, built upon an ever-expanding body of research findings.

In a newly multidisciplinary approach, criminal justice programs might require a specified number of hours in accounting, computer science, and ethnic studies, in addition to the social science core of criminal justice. If the old concern that "the new kids don't know how to talk with people" remains, then the programs might consider including drama classes, public speaking, or even courses in the great antithesis of policing, social work, that require students to interact in person with people. The whole idea is to use the academic environment to teach the thornier social lessons so difficult to approach in police training settings. The academic atmosphere is different, less politically or emotionally charged, and the venue allows for a more pluralistic (i.e., not "all cops") exploration of the issues raised.

Teaching "multiculturalism" or "cultural sensitivity" in a police training environment often results in an awkward experience for instructor and attendees alike. Exposure to different cultures through educational study may be a better, more results-oriented approach. The exploration of new ideas occurs over a longer time and requires a different level of engagement than an 8-hour in-service training session. Using literature and a variety of media, educators can present and discuss related issues in a manner that police training typically does not accommodate. Understanding of other cultures becomes a foundation—even if a fairly narrow one—upon which police training can build, as opposed to a bolt-on module that flies in the face of police cultural norms and becomes something to be endured, rather than adopted.

Model 2:
Adapting Existing Programs

Creating new programs represents a visionary approach that may be possible in institutions that do not have a crimi-

nal justice program. The larger reality is that the institutions with existing criminal justice programs are unlikely to make radical changes without cause. Issues of academic tenure and contractual matters are as real as their counterparts in policing. The study of criminal justice will continue as a social science pursuit, with the programs serving those who aspire to the professoriat, as well as those with ambitions toward becoming police officers, detectives, or federal agents.

Change in academia will not come about without a strong signal from the receiving professions, those who ultimately will hire the products of academic endeavors. If the field speaks with a concerted voice about the need for certain skills and emphasizes hiring individuals with those skills, then academia will move to provide them. For example, it is gratifying—if a bit surprising—to have police agencies complain about the lack of writing skills of some college graduates and interns. Given the competitive marketplace of higher education, "employability of graduates" remains a selling point for many institutions.

Model 3:
Course of Study, Not Major

The third option does not require institutional change on the part of academia. Instead, it places the onus on the aspiring police professional. If the field signals that it considers proof of certain skills, acquired in an academic setting, as a bona fide occupational qualification, the existing programs will make the recommendation, and the students will seek the courses themselves. Academia already gives such direction concerning second languages and accounting skills (for those who aspire to be federal investigators); it easily could do the same for clinical skills. Students will have to surmount institutional barriers, such as the unavailability of prerequisite courses and those requiring academic major status. Nevertheless, if the field provides the signal, an impetus exists for institutional adaptation, and it well may be that this third model might ultimately turn into the first, a third-generation criminal justice major that is multidimensional.

Conclusion

During a coffee-break conversation at a training session, a police officer said to the author, "No offense, Doc, but I could teach the useful parts of your 4-year program in a day." His point was essentially correct if the only things that counted were the factoids students could recall 3 years after graduation. The author countered with the observation that he could fill the 4-year curriculum with war stories and the students would leave the program as ignorant as the day they arrived.

> **"By cooperatively identifying current and future needs, police professionals and academicians may develop tools to address both lingering promises and emerging challenges."**

Both points were equally valid and equally off the mark. Without integration, neither formal study nor secondhand experience is an adequate preparation for the demanding tasks of police work. Experience is an important teacher, to be sure, but the old adage remains that fools can learn from their own mistakes. Wise individuals minimize their mistakes by learning from the mistakes and successes of others. Both training and education share the mandate to make such learning possible. A future in which the two endeavors complement each other can occur, but appears unlikely to happen of its own accord. A dialogue that explores the needs of the law enforcement profession and the capacities and possibilities of the academic field is needed to fuel such change; the challenges of the future should create the spark.

Endnotes

1. The author based this article on his experiences as a police officer and academician, as well as his close association

with numerous law enforcement professionals.

2. Such a view is anathema in academic circles. Instead, the value of military service is recognized as a complementary process and as a maturing influence, but not as comparable to formal education.

3. The author acknowledges the probability of local exceptions. It is not possible, however, to know the offerings of every program in the United States without an extensive research effort far beyond the scope of this article.

Dr. Buerger, a former police officer, is an associate professor of criminal justice at Bowling Green State University in Ohio.

From *FBI Law Enforcement Bulletin*, January 2004, pp. 26-32, by Michael Buerger, Ph.D. Published in 2004 by the Federal Bureau of Investigation.

UNIT 4
The Judicial System

Unit Selections

Key Points to Consider

- Are experts truly unbiased, or do they shade their testimony to favor the side that is paying them?

- Can a defendant pick a favorable jury simply by hiring a jury consultant?

- Do you think prosecutors should recieve some sort of discipline when they cause an innocent person to be convicted of a crime?

 **Links: www.dushkin.com/online/**
These sites are annotated in the World Wide Web pages.

Center for Rational Correctional Policy
http://www.correctionalpolicy.com
Justice Information Center (JIC)
http://www.ncjrs.org
National Center for Policy Analysis (NCPA)
http://www.public-policy.org/~ncpa/pd/law/index3.html
U.S. Department of Justice (DOJ)
http://www.usdoj.gov

The courts are an equal partner in the American justice system. Just as the police have the responsibility of guarding our liberties by enforcing the law, the courts play an important role in defending these liberties by applying and interpreting the law. The courts are the battlegrounds where civilized "wars" are fought without bloodshed to protect individual rights and to settle disputes.

The articles in this unit discuss several issues concerning the judicial process. Ours is an adversary system of justice, and the protagonists—the state and the defendant—are usually represented by counsel.

In the opening article in this section, "Jury Consulting on Trial," D. W. Miller discusses the notion of "scientific jury selection." Following is "You As An Expert Witness: Are You Ready?" in which Frank MacHovec addresses the role of expert witnesses at trials.

In "Looking Askance at Eyewitness Testimony," the problem of unreliable eyewitness evidence is examined by D. W. Miller. In his article "Courts Asked to Consider Culture," Richard Willing asks whether the justice system should take an offender's culture into consideration.

This unit concludes with "When Prosecutors Err, Others Pay the Price," where Elliot and Weiser write about the problem of misconduct and errors by prosecutors and the price paid by innocent people.

Jury Consulting on Trial

Scholars doubt claims that jurors' votes can be predicted

BY D.W. MILLER

"**B**eware of the Lutherans, especially the Scandinavians; they are almost always sure to convict," Clarence Darrow advised fellow defense lawyers in a 1936 *Esquire* article called "How to Pick a Jury." By contrast, the "religious emotions" of Methodists "can be transmuted into love and charity." Irishmen, he added, are "emotional, kindly, and sympathetic." But the Presbyterian juror "believes in John Calvin and eternal punishment. Get rid of him with the fewest possible words before he contaminates the others."

Judges instruct jurors to render verdicts based on evidence and law, not prejudice and sympathy. But few lawyers believe that fallible humans simply leave their backgrounds, opinions, and attitudes outside the courtroom. So they still aspire to predict how jurors' biases will affect their deliberations.

Of course, in assembling a jury or shaping an argument, lawyers no longer credit the quaint stereotypes expressed — perhaps tongue in cheek — by Darrow. Many lawyers are content to rely on experience and intuition to identify people unfriendly to their side and strike them from a jury. Those who can afford it, however, are turning to trial consultants to conduct mock trials, design community surveys, and probe the attitudes and experiences of potential jurors.

Many of the nearly 400 members of the American Society of Trial Consultants are trained social scientists. But scholars question how much trial consultants have really improved upon Darrow.

"The plausibility of being able to predict is very low," says Shari Seidman Diamond, a professor of law at Northwestern University and a leading researcher of jury behavior. "Who makes the decision is less important than how the evidence is presented," says Saul Kassin, a professor of psychology at Williams College.

"The best conclusion is that there are cases where jury-selection consultants can make a difference but that such cases are few and far between," write Neil J. Kressel and Dorit F. Kressel in *Stack and Sway: The New Science of Jury Consulting* (just out from Westview Press). "Like the fanciful stereotypes about jurors that lawyers trusted in the past, scientific jury selection can help attorneys manage their stress far more often than it helps them capture a verdict."

NO CRYSTAL BALL

The notion of "scientific jury selection" took hold in the early 1970s, when the late Jay Schulman, a sociologist at Columbia University, and a team of colleagues helped defend antiwar activists accused of plotting to kidnap Henry Kissinger. After conducting surveys and interviewing a cross section of the community, the defense used its peremptory challenges to eliminate members of the jury pool considered likely to vote for conviction. The jury ultimately hung, on a 10–2 vote for acquittal.

Since then, however, scholars have found little evidence that social science makes a big difference in jury selection. "For most cases, most of the time, people decide on the basis of evidence," says Mr. Kressel, a psychologist at William Paterson University. "We know from mock-jury research that personality variables don't matter that much."

In a study of 461 mock jurors in Ohio, Michael Saks, a professor of law and psychology at Arizona State University, measured 27 attitudes and background characteristics and then asked the jurors to render a verdict in a fictitious burglary case. The best predictor of their decisions was their answer to the question "Do you believe crime is mainly the product of 'bad people' or 'bad social conditions'?" But that explained only 9 percent of the variation among verdicts. Together, those personal attributes accounted for very little.

IT'S AN ART

Steven D. Penrod, a psychologist at the University of Nebraska at Lincoln, got similar results in a study of Massachusetts jurors. He tested the salience of 21 personal characteristics in four kinds of cases. He found that the single best predictor of an inclination to vote guilty in a rape case was whether jurors agreed that evidence of physical resistance was necessary to convict. But that predictor alone explained only 7 percent of the variation in outcomes, and the best predictors in each case were not helpful in any others.

Mr. Kressel and his wife, a lawyer, concluded that scientific jury selection matters mainly when a case is very public, the facts are inflammatory, and the evidence favors neither side.

That scholars' insight into juries is hazy should not be surprising. Courts hardly ever allow researchers to watch deliberations firsthand, so they have to rely on cruder methods to divine how personality affects jury deliberations: post-trial interviews, case studies, and mock juries among them. Furthermore, scholars have found that observations rarely apply in all situations.

"Who makes the decisions is less important than how the evidence is presented."

"It's not really a science — it's more of an art," says Neil Vidmar, a professor of psychology and law at Duke University who has himself been a consultant on pre-trial publicity. "Almost every case is unique. It's got different facts, it's got a different context." Even so, the data that the nation's trial consultants collect in hundreds of cases each year might still be valuable to scholars — except that the information is all proprietary and closely held.

In their book, the Kressels argue that the value of scientific jury selection rests on a chain of unproven assumptions: that potential jurors give honest answers to personal questions, that jurors' pretrial verdict preferences will determine their final votes, and that jurors stricken from a jury pool will be replaced by ones that lawyers find more favorable. But that hasn't deterred scholars like Linda Foley.

A trial consultant and professor of psychology at the University of North Florida, Ms. Foley also conducts academic research on decision making by jurors that may prove useful in court. She has studied, for instance, why some jurors are less sympathetic than others to rape victims who sue their assailants. She found that college-age men are much less likely to sympathize with victims the same age than with those who are older. She speculates that young men can imagine themselves being falsely accused of rape by a peer, and so defensively attribute a plaintiff's fate to her own behavior.

In theory, lawyers armed with such insights could refine their efforts to choose favorable jurors and craft effective arguments. Since the 1970s, for example, researchers have believed that people who score high on a scale of "authoritarian" attitudes seem to be more likely to convict. Even that trait, however, has counterintuitive implications. Authoritarian types, says Ms. Foley, tend to make

snap judgments, but they also tend to conform to the majority. In general, researchers have failed to connect attitudes with verdicts in predictable ways.

Ms. Foley's experiments this semester exemplify both the promise and perils of efforts to put jurors' motivations under a microscope. Several times a week, she assembles a new group of North Florida students in Jacksonville to play jury in a fictitious medical-malpractice lawsuit.

On a recent Wednesday morning, seven women and three men filed into a conference room near Ms. Foley's office, in the psychology department. First they filled out a lengthy questionnaire exploring their personality traits. Then they watched a videotape of dueling experts.

"Martin Madison," a 53-year-old accountant, had died of a brain aneurysm after complaining of headaches and dizziness. Were the hospital and its emergency-room doctor negligent? In that day's version of the experiment, the expert hired by Mr. Madison's widow boasted of his years of clinical experience, while the defense expert brandished his tenured professorship at the Johns Hopkins University and a long list of publications on aneurysms.

As usual, a handful of jurors dominated the discussion that followed. The forewoman, a ponytailed student in a sweatshirt and baseball cap who said she had worked in a hospital, criticized "Dr. Hector" for failing to order timely tests once he had diagnosed the aneurysm. "People die, that's all I gotta say," said Juror 105, a young man with a brush cut, but he went along with the majority, which laid most of the blame for the patient's death on the doctor.

Courts hardly ever allow researchers to watch deliberations firsthand, so scholars have to rely on cruder methods to divine how personality affects jury deliberations.

Only Juror 98, a woman in khaki pants and a jean jacket, remained dubious. "How do we know it would have made a difference?" she said. "The aneurysm was so big, he might have died on the MRI table."

Later, Juror 98 stood alone in her reluctance to compensate the Madison family beyond lost income. Despite her misgivings, the group awarded hefty damages and apportioned fault between the doctor and the hospital in a ratio of 70:30. Before leaving, the jurors filled out another survey, to assess how influential they had found each of their peers.

After observing 32 of those mock juries, Ms. Foley will investigate whether jurors in such cases are more easily persuaded by expert witnesses with impressive credentials or by those with more clinical experience. But she

Flies on the Wall of the Jury Room

HARRY KALVEN JR. and Hans Zeisel, who pioneered academic research on juries in the 1950s, were among the first American scholars to observe real jurors deliberating. For decades, it seemed they would also be the last.

When they revealed that they had taped the deliberations of five civil juries in a federal court in Wichita, Kan., without the jurors' consent, they were unprepared for the uproar that followed. The U.S. attorney general censured the project, Congress held hearings, and dozens of jurisdictions moved to ban "jury-tapping." With few exceptions, outsiders have been unwelcome in the jury room ever since—-until now.

NOT SO PASSIVE

Shari Seidman Diamond, a law professor at Northwestern University, and Neil Vidmar, a professor of law and psychology at Duke University, noticed in the mid-1990s that courts in Arizona had begun experimenting with giving jurors more latitude to participate in court, such as taking notes, asking questions of witnesses, and discussing testimony before the lawyers had rested their cases. To investigate the effects of such reforms, they won permission from courts, juries, and litigants to videotape 50 civil cases.

> In many ways, the American legal system treats jurors like empty repositories for information, holding their opinions and experiences in check.

The first findings from their Arizona Jury Project, in a paper to be published soon in the *Virginia Law Review,* seem to confirm that jurors often confound the courts' expectations of their passive role. In many ways, the American legal system treats jurors like empty repositories for information, holding their opinions and experiences in check until a judge dispatches them to the jury room. That is the premise for the legal practice of "blindfolding"—excluding certain facts, such as defendants' past criminal acts, that might unfairly influence jury verdicts.

In their paper, Ms. Diamond and Mr. Vidmar investigate two such matters thought to influence jurors'

decisions in lawsuits: whether defendants and plaintiffs are covered by insurance, and how much the parties will owe in lawyers' fees. They found some evidence that those factors might affect juries' verdicts on defendants' liability, and even more evidence that they count when juries consider damages: At that stage, the researchers found, juries frequently overlook or misunderstand judges' instructions not to speculate about those issues, and take into account testimony about insurance revealed inadvertently or through an exception to courtroom rules.

Of the 40 cases in which insurance was relevant, the scholars found that jurors raised the issue in 34. Comments like the following were typical:

"His insurance paid all his bills, so he's not really out anything."

"This is what we have insurance for…. [O]ne of the plaintiff's doctor's said she sent the claims to plaintiff's insurers so the plaintiff is probably not paying for most of this."

"Insurance usually covers chiropractic care. Why should we give her above and beyond what she is probably going to get on her insurance?"

In 16 of those cases, or 40 percent, the authors write, "the discussion was substantial enough that an effect [on the verdict] could not be ruled out." In three cases, "a juror's verdict preference can be directly linked" to the juror's expressed beliefs about a litigant's insurance coverage.

In 24 of 33 applicable cases, juries discussed lawyers' fees in their deliberations. In four cases, the fees actually affected their decisions on damages: Three juries raised their damages award to cover their estimate of the plaintiff's legal bill, and the fourth reduced its award because jurors thought the plaintiff's lawyers did not deserve the full one-third contingency that they were likely to charge.

Ms. Diamond and Mr. Vidmar believe that the problem is exacerbated by judges who respond to juries' queries about taboo subjects with terse answers. "The traditional approach of merely forbidding evidence on certain topics is of limited value when jurors draw on life experiences and peek through blindfolds," they conclude. So the authors recommend that courts confront the problem squarely. A more comprehensive instruction to juries, they write, would acknowledge their temptation to consider forbidden topics, explain why the courts have deemed them irrelevant, and remind them that any such speculation would have [to] rely on guesswork. In mock-trial studies, they say, that approach has worked.

—D.W.M.

also hopes to learn more about the effects of personality on juries' decisions: Do jurors' views of guilt and liability in particular cases correspond predictably to measurable attitudes and personality traits, such as a belief in a just world, a predilection for manipulating others, or a tendency to see issues in absolute terms? And does a juror's influence during deliberations correspond predictably to measurable leadership traits and an ease with public speaking?

MUDDY WATERS

That kind of experiment has limits. For one thing, the psychology students she relies on are hardly representative of eligible jurors in Jacksonville, much less the nation. Furthermore, with such a small pool to draw from, some of the subjects are bound to be acquainted, a fact that may muddy her analysis of how members of the group influence one another. Jurors 100 and 101 had walked in holding hands, while Jurors 103 and 104 appeared to be identical twin sisters.

As a check on those flaws, Ms. Foley is collaborating with a trial consultant in Pompano Beach who will eventually conduct similar experiments with a cross section of "real people." But that research is at least a year away.

Even if research offered lawyers a wealth of predictive information, they would often have trouble using it. For instance, they don't have utter discretion over the number and kind of questions asked during jury selection. Researchers have established, for instance, that people who support capital punishment are generally more likely to vote to convict. But lawyers aren't allowed to probe jurors' attitudes toward the death penalty unless they are trying a capital case. "Depending on the judge, the lawyers don't have a lot of leeway about what kinds of questions they can ask," says Ms. Foley. "So they try to get at the essence in one or two questions."

Those caveats hardly mean that trial consultants have no influence. Even the Kressels agree that consultants appear to be effective at post-selection tasks, such as helping lawyers hone their arguments and understand how ordinary people will see the issues. "In most instances, it's the techniques and practices of social science that are helpful, rather than any particular body of knowledge," says Duke's Mr. Vidmar.

"This is an opportunity to test the clarity and plausibility of an argument in a more systematic way," says Northwestern's Ms. Diamond. "That's a valuable thing, because there's nothing sadder than seeing an unnecessarily unintelligible presentation of evidence. That makes it harder to make a decision based on the evidence."

YOU
as an
EXPERT WITNESS
ARE YOU READY?

By Frank J. MacHovec Ph.D.

Before you brush aside the possibility of being called to court as an expert witness, know that anyone with specialized knowledge or experience can be considered as an expert witness. Black's Law Dictionary defines expert witnesses as "persons qualified to speak authoritatively by reason of their special training, skill, or familiarity with a subject." "Fact witnesses" testify only about what they saw, heard, and did. They are not permitted to interpret or give an opinion about a case. Expert witnesses, however, are permitted to analyze, compare, and interpret facts to provide information (opinion testimony) important to the court. The legal basis for expert witnesses dates back to 1923 in "the Frye test." In *Frye v. United States* 293 F. 1013 (D.C. Cir. 1923), Judge Baselon ruled expert testimony must be based on "generally accepted scientific theory and practice." While rules of evidence vary state to state, most follow Rule 702 of *Federal Rules of Evidence*, that "those with knowledge, skill, experience, training or education" are qualified to testify to provide needed information.

The process begins when an attorney contacts a prospective expert and inquires about willingness and availability to testify. In most jurisdictions, the expert's name is submitted to the court. Attorneys on both sides and the judge must agree. This doesn't mean the expert adopts an adversarial role since the expectation is that testimony is to be unbiased and based on professional standards. Still, experts have been called "hired guns" or vulgarly as "whores" who are "bought and paid for."

You are the profession.

Professional investigators are called upon to serve courts as expert witnesses in cases involving standards of proficiency and conduct, confidentiality and privilege, compliance with state and federal regulations, and civil and criminal law. They work to minimize property loss or damage and reduce risk of harm to workers and the public. Those are areas especially sensitive to litigation when there is loss or injury. As an expert witness, you can help by providing information to the attorney on current standards and ethics in the investigation profession, and recognizing possible problems in presenting the case. When serving as an expert witness, an investigator represents the profession as well as reflecting personal training, knowledge and experience. In the Frye case the court referred to "a twilight zone" between fact and fiction, and the need to separate them: "While courts will go a long way in admitting expert testimony deduced from a well-recognized scientific principle of discovery, the thing from which the deduction is made must be sufficiently established to have gained general acceptance in the particular field in which it belongs." Keep in mind:

- You should look and behave professionally.
- Your testimony should reflect competence and personal integrity.
- You belong to a distinguished profession with very high credentials. As an expert witness, you can continue, or tarnish, that tradition. To be accepted as someone whose expertise is recog-

nized by a court is a special distinction and an honor.

- There is a duty to testify to the best of your ability. State truth and reality regardless of an attorney's verbal attack or effort to "put a spin" on your opinion or its basis.

Cicero, more than 2000 years ago in ancient Rome gave good advice, as timely today as it was then: "The first law is never to dare utter an untruth. The second is to suppress nothing that is true. Moreover, there should be no partiality or malice" (*De Oratore II*).

The Process

Being an expert witness begins long before a scheduled trial or hearing:

- The attorney who retained you, or one of the associates, should meet with you.
- You will likely be asked to review data, and to submit a written report.
- Since your name will have been submitted to the court (not true in all jurisdictions),the opposing attorney may mail you interrogatories, questions requiring written answers, or reasons why any are not answered.
- You may be asked to appear at the opposing attorney's office to give a deposition, a pretrial hearing where you will be asked questions, your answers transcribed, and may be entered in evidence. The attorney for whom you testify will be sitting next to you. At trial, anything you say that contradicts your deposition will be used to try to discredit (impeach) you. One classical attack is: "Were you lying then or are you lying now?"
- You will be served with a *subpoena* commanding you to appear in court on a certain date and time. A *subpoena duces tecum* requires you to bring your written records.
- At the trial, you may be *sequestered*. The opposing attorney may not want you in court to hear the proceedings that might influence your testimony.
- After being called and sworn in you will be presented to the court as an expert witness. The opposing attorney can either stipulate, which means without question, or grill you about your qualifications.

If your testimony is key to the success or failure of a case, you will be targeted for verbal attack by the opposing attorney.

- Your testimony begins with *direct examination* led by the attorney who retained you. Use this time to orient yourself to the room and adjust your voice volume to be heard, neither too loud nor too low. Sit erect, back against the chair, both feet on the floor, hands folded in your lap or on your records.
- It's important to sound professional in your direct testimony for the next step, *cross*-examination by the opposing attorney. It is then you may be asked what you have in front of you (copy of report, other data). Some attorneys do that to stress you but it also ensures you don't have anything not previously submitted to both sides or admitted as evidence. If it's an attack, it will continue: "Is that because you're not sure of your opinion?" A good response could be: "No, I want to be sure what I testify is valid and based on fact."
- The attorney who engaged you may clarify your testimony by *redirect examination* followed by *recross examination* by the opposing attorney.
- Always pause before answering questions by opposing attorneys at trial or deposition. This gives a few seconds for "your" attorney to object.
- A male attorney with a baritone voice may bellow at a woman witness who can only respond in the softer higher pitch of the female voice. Women should not match him in a raised voice that may sound shrill, crack, seem a weakly defensive or suggest uncertainty. Women can cope with direct eye contact that signals: "I'm on to you, man," at a moderate volume, measured rate, projecting competence.

Tactics

Law is a word world and attorneys are skilled in the use of words. As officers of the court, they have a sworn duty to champion their side of a case. Without pretrial settlement in civil cases or plea bargaining in criminal cases, the trial process is adversarial. Only one side wins. If your testimony is key to the success or failure of a case, you will be targeted for verbal attack by the opposing attorney. Prepare for the worst. You will never be taken unaware. Here are some tips:

- Before your testimony, develop a stress reduction strategy by ensuring breathing is normal and regular. That will prevent hyperventilation and increasing anxiety.
- Maintain a stable, relaxed sitting position. Be prepared for any loud, emotional, or sarcastic comments and pointed questions from the opposing attorney.

- Rehearse your testimony with the attorney or a member of the team and ask that it be as stressful as anything that could happen at trial.
- Rehearse your testimony in your mind as often as possible.

Some tactics that have been used *against* expert witnesses:

- *Isolation:* "Would other expert witnesses agree with you?" To answer you don't know weakens your testimony even though it may be correct and well-founded. A better answer: "Based on the same evidence I would expect others to arrive at the same conclusion." Notice the answer is fact-based and bolsters credibility for any questions that follow. It helps if you can refer to professional investigation literature (books, articles), consultations with other experts about similar cases, and your training and experience. This adds other resources to your testimony making it more difficult to be discredited. Referring to books, articles, and authorities in the field always strengthens your testimony and weakens opposing tactics.
- *Hypotheticals:* "What if" questions are a favorite of trial lawyers. The object is to put a spin on your opinion—a little at first—then with subsequent hypotheticals, draw you into the attorney's version of truth. A good defense is to begin with "that's hypothetical and did not happen in this case." To the next: "That also is a hypothetical that in my opinion further departs from what happened." Your hidden message is that you're aware of the attorney's tactic and usually stops it.
- *Leading questions:* These usually begin with "Isn't it true that" and like hypotheticals lead you toward answers to question or contradict your testimony. The answer the attorney hopes for is in the question. Beware of each step that leads away from your opinion. It may help to add to your answer: "Based on facts, evidence, and standards of practice, that does not appear to be what happened." Be prepared for the stinger: "Just answer the question." Point out your opinion is based solely on the case and not on non-existent possibilities.

Testifying as an expert witness is a way of strengthening the public's image of investigators.

- *Learned treatise:* "Dr. Shlock disagrees with you, on page 76 of his book" which the opposing attorney may then read aloud. While you can't

know or remember everything published you should be familiar with professional investigation literature and current issues to explain relevant concepts. That's why expert witnesses are needed. Possible answer: "Yes, I'm aware of Dr. Shlock's opinion which has been questioned by others" and "in my opinion it does not completely describe all aspects." Making reference to a book or article that you have written enhances your credibility. An attorney may try to discredit your testimony of the quoted publication. A defense could be: "I have not read it, but I will be happy to do so then give you my opinion of it." If pressed to react to the quoted statement, avoid giving an opinion: "I'd have to read the entire piece to place what you have read in the total context." Few attorneys will continue this tactic and the judge may well interrupt and suggest moving on.

- *Machine gunning:* This is rapidly asking complicated or many-faceted questions or many simple questions. It's like: "If A is B and C is like D could M be N, and what effect would that have on Y or even Z?" Here a *Columbo* tactic" helps: "I'm sorry, I can't follow you. Would you repeat the question?" This not only gives you more time to reflect on where the lawyer's headed and what's behind the question but the rewording may differ from the original, usually more simple. It may signal the lawyer the tactic isn't working. Looking at the judge when asking for a repeat involves him or her—lawyers hate that!
- *The bear trap:* Lawyers like to word questions requiring simple "yes" or "no" answers. Each question leads to a planned end point, the "bear trap" to discredit your testimony. Track the direction of the question. Often the answer is not so simple: "I can't answer 'yes' or 'no' to that question." If the lawyer insists, try: "The only answer I can give is maybe." If the tactic continues and your attorney hasn't objected, you have two options. You can turn to the judge and say: "Your Honor, I can't answer 'yes' or 'no' to that question." If the judge agrees, the attorney has lost ground and will probably switch to another tactic. You can emit a smoke screen: "It could be A or B, and L and M are possible, even Y or Z." The attorney will have to follow you onto those tangents, try to return the original question (which you've blocked) or move on.
- *You perfect?* How would you answer the question: "Do you ever make mistakes?" The only correct answer is "Yes." The next question is the killer shot: "Could you have made a mistake in your report (or opinion)?" Answering "Yes" discredits you. Answering "Everyone makes mistakes" just delays the killer question. "I did

the best I could" invites the attorney's stinging rebuke: "Yes, and that wasn't enough. No further questions." Better to answer: "Not in this case" or "my testimony is based on my knowledge and experience. I carefully plan what I'm doing and build in checks and balances to prevent mistakes." Usually attorneys will avoid such an answer by insisting on a 'yes' or 'no' response. If so, keep it general and not personal: "Everybody makes mistakes but in this case I do not think I made any."

- *You judge.* Only the judge or jury are "triers of fact." Expert witnesses give carefully considered professional opinions about evidence and current theory and practice. They do not legally decide cases. This tactic can be disguised in questions only the court answers such as: "What do you think this court should decide? Do you think she/he was insane at the time? Do you think Company X was negligent as charged? Do you think this case should have been nol prossed? This tactic aims to discredit your testimony by showing you have prejudged the case and are biased. The best defense is a candid statement: "This court will decide the case. I am here only to provide an expert opinion as needed."

- *You've been bought!* This tactic begins with: "Weren't you paid for writing this report?" Don't answer "Yes." Better: "I was paid for my time and work." This word game is used sometimes to test how vulnerable you are to being manipulated. It's like a boxer in the ring being thrown punches to test defenses.

Testifying as an expert witness can be satisfying, helpful in developing your knowledge of law, and your skills in communicating clearly and effectively. It is also a way of strengthening the public's image of investigators, and continuing the heritage of a noble profession.

©Frank MacHovec
Frank MacHovec, Ph.D., retired in 1995 after 30 years as a clinical psychologist, certified forensics examiner, and private investigator. Charles C. Thomas Publishers has published two of his books. Contact: fmachov@inna.net

Jury Duty:
When History and Life Coincide

By Elisabeth I. Perry

NOT LONG AGO, I served on a jury for the first time. Most people groan when a jury summons arrives, but I was thrilled. I hadn't received one since 1964, and I had avoided serving then on grounds that I only later realized were discriminatory.

When the first summons came, I was a history graduate student in Southern California, busy teaching sections of "Western Civilization" and preparing for a trip to France for my dissertation research. I panicked. I didn't have time for jury duty! I read the summons through, hoping for a way to escape its imperative. At last I got down to the list of exempted categories. Surely "student" or "teacher" would be on it. No, but "woman" was.

I had no idea why. My graduate-student friends were equally ignorant. One suggested that it was because women menstruate. "You know how they get emotionally unstable every month," he said. I had never suffered from such instability, but getting out of jury duty on any grounds looked good to me. With barely a moment's hesitation, I checked the "woman" box.

Years later, I regretted that act of youthful insouciance. In the mid-1970s, I began to do research in a field new to me, American women's history. I wanted to write a biography of my paternal grandmother, Belle Moskowitz, the social reformer and suffragist who served as New York Gov. Alfred E. Smith's political strategist in the 1920s. After the book came out in 1987, I started a new, still continuing, project that, to myself, I call "From Belle to Bella," on the New York Women active in politics from Moskowitz to Bella Abzug, the colorful New York congresswoman of the 1970s.

Early on in the project, I learned why I had been able to get out of jury duty. When women's suffrage was ratified in 1920, more than half the states had not yet legalized woman jurors. Over the next two decades, a number changed their laws to allow women to serve—but only on an elective basis.

In New York, opposition to women on juries rested on two widely held stereotypes. The first was that women were not "fit" to serve: They were incapable of rational judgment and too "delicate" to tolerate the gory details of criminal behavior. The second was that their domestic roles—watching over children and preparing meals—made it hard for them to be away from home. It is interesting that the strongest opposition came from rural women, who argued that jury service would place an extraordinary burden on their already difficult lives.

We think too little about the role that gender and race play in the jury room.

By 1937, several national and local developments—including the U.S. Department of Justice's approving women as jurors for all federal courts, and a case in which an all-male jury convicted a woman of infanticide—finally persuaded New York legislators to allow women on juries. With a bow to the state's rural women, they made service nonmandatory.

Convinced that women would always be treated as second-class citizens unless they had an equal obligation to civic duties

like jury service, a small cadre of New York women persisted in a campaign for mandatory service. Although they made little progress, and gave up their campaign in the 1950s, their cause was making its way through the federal judicial system. In 1975, the U.S. Supreme Court ruled in *Taylor v. Louisiana* that all juries must represent a "fair cross section" of the community. The issue of voluntary versus mandatory service was henceforth moot.

AS I REPORTED for jury service, I was thus pleased to have the opportunity. Friends warned me that I might have a long and boring wait before being called. "Take a lunch and a book," they advised. They also predicted that I probably wouldn't make it onto a jury. "Attorneys never pick women academics," they said. Not true. By that afternoon, I was empaneled on a jury for a murder trial and told to count on being there all week.

In his memoir of jury duty last year, *A Trial by Jury*, the historian D. Graham Burnett notes that we expect much, but think too little, about what happens in the jury room. That, I found, is also true about the role gender plays on a jury.

The case before us was complicated. Late one night, two armed men in their 20s, members of the same gang, confronted a third man at the front door of his home. By their own admission, they intended to "get back at him" for an insult. When the man saw their guns, he fled upstairs, out a back porch, and jumped to the alley below. The two would-be assailants followed. A few moments later, the man who fled lay dead in a cellar stairwell. He had seven bullets in his body.

His pursuers had been seen. Knowing that, they threw their shirts into a dumpster and ran. The police found the shirts and picked up one man quickly. He denied having been the shooter, plea-bargained on the lesser charge of burglary (armed breaking and entering), and had begun serving five years. The police did not find his partner for six months. A bruiser of a man, that was our defendant. He had been called in only as "backup," he said, and denied shooting the fatal bullets. Neither man's weapon was ever found.

The testimony was confusingly presented and strikingly incomplete. The prosecutor seemed ill prepared. The public defender was brand-new at her job. The jailed assailant testified, but was so terrified by the presence of the defendant's buddies in the courtroom that he was barely audible. We did, however, grasp his central point: His partner had fired the fatal shots. There was much "expert" testimony about DNA tests on the discarded shirts and the locations of spent shells and bullets; there were photographs of the crime scene and the deceased's body, which we passed among us. We noted that his genitals had been pierced by a bullet. No one flinched, but it was a gruesome sight.

The defendant testified, with his lawyer concentrating more on establishing his good character—despite prior convictions on drug and weapons charges, he was about to be married and to become a father—rather than his innocence, which she could not prove.

The testimony took a day a half to be heard. None of it illuminated the key question in the case. Someone had fired seven bullets into an unarmed man fleeing for his life. Which assailant had been the shooter?

*H*ad the one person I failed to convince dug in his heels because he wasn't willing to accept a woman's suggestion?

We, the jury, retired to deliberate. It turned out that we all agreed that the evidence had been poorly presented, but we were nowhere near unanimity. Two jurors favored a finding of first-degree murder. Eight favored second-degree, and two were undecided. We read and reread the judge's instructions about being sure "beyond a reasonable doubt." Endlessly, we

rehearsed the definitions of "murder in the first" (planned), "murder in the second" (unplanned), "manslaughter" (recklessly endangering another's life), and "burglary," with which our defendant was also charged. But no matter how many hours we talked and recast our votes, we could reach unanimity only on "burglary." At 5 p.m. on a Friday evening, the judge declared a mistrial on the murder charge. We never found out if the state would try the case again.

MONTHS HAVE PASSED since my jury service, and I still think about what happened, both in the courtroom and the jury room, to bring about such an unsatisfactory ending. In part, the answer has to do with the way the rules that regulate juries hindered our ability to make well-informed judgments. In our court (although not, I have since learned, in all courts), we were not allowed to take notes. When an elderly juror snoozed, well, that was just too bad. Nor could we question witnesses or lawyers; in our system, the lawyers are in control of presenting the evidence.

Further, our judge refused to let us see the transcript. After the trial was over, she came to the jury room to answer questions. Her tone was consoling. Mistrials are common in murder trials, she said, because the burden of proof is so high. "Why couldn't we consult the transcript?" I asked. Because, she answered, you might focus too closely on one part of the testimony. "We want you to weigh all of the evidence, and we trust that 12 jurors from different walks of life will remember enough correctly to make a sound judgment."

Although probably based on experience, her position disturbed me. Why deny jurors the chance to refresh their memories? Until we had begun to deliberate, we had no idea which part of the testimony was going to be crucial. By the time we knew, it was too late.

More than the limitations on what jurors could see, ask, or hear, however, the gender and racial politics of the jury's deliberations—and the way gender and race overlapped with each other—proved determinative to the trial's outcome. And that is where my scholarship and experience came together for me.

Gender issues were only indirectly at stake in the trial, but it still made a difference that four of us on the jury were women. And it mattered that only *four* of us were. The two jurors who initially wanted first degree murder were both men.

During a break, one of them, a middle-aged white man, made hostile remarks about the judge. She's "me-e-e-an," he drawled. He liked "my women" to be "ladylike," "on a pedestal."

The other man, a retired African-American, had a deep bass voice. When he kept raising its volume to assert his points, I had to ask him to stop shouting. Later, a soft-spoken young African-American woman, who must have found the man intimidating, took me aside and thanked me.

Five of the jurors were white, and seven were African-American, as were all the major players in the trial except the judge and the public defender. Our deliberations reached a climax when, on Friday, the soft-spoken young woman, undecided until then, suddenly blurted out that nothing had convinced her that the bullets in the dead man's body came from a gun our defendant had carried. With intense feeling, she warned that, should we convict the man, we would be "lynching him just because he was a big black nigger."

A shocked silence fell over the room. Her language threw us. What's more, many of us felt guilty. Maybe we had rushed to judgment because our defendant was "big" and "black." By then, the two men who originally voted for a first-degree verdict had already "come down" to second degree. But the young woman remained unconvinced that the evidence was persuasive enough for even that.

We took a short break. When we sat down again, I suggested that, perhaps we should consider manslaughter. No matter which assailant was lying, I argued, we knew "beyond a reasonable doubt" that our defendant had arrived on the scene armed, and that his "reckless" behavior had endangered the victim's life. At the very least, our defendant was partially responsible for the death.

We took a new vote. This time, everyone, including the young woman, agreed on manslaughter—except for the deep-voiced, African-American man. He had already compromised enough by accepting second-degree murder, he said.

It took us barely a minute to agree on the burglary charge. We all sensed that the defendant, despite his lawyer's efforts to convince us otherwise, was dangerous. On the other charges, we were "hung."

Clearly, the interplay of race and gender were complex. The young African-American woman's reference to "lynching," and her use of the inflammatory "N" word, was the group's only overt reference to race. Two of the men had originally voted for the harshest sentence; yet one of them, surely the most "sexist" of the men on the jury, had allowed himself to be swayed by a woman's impassioned plea. All but one man had accepted my proposal for manslaughter. Had the one person I failed to convince dug in his heels because I had asked him to compromise? Was he unwilling to accept a suggestion from a woman? Was he just a stubborn person? I'll never know.

Perhaps that's the point. As the historian Linda K. Kerber showed in her 1998 book *No Constitutional Right to Be Ladies: Women and the Obligations of Citizenship*, until quite recently our laws—because of either ban or exemption—often meant that no women served on juries. And the lack of diversity had an impact, in different ways in different cases.

My experience was undeniably frustrating. I cannot pin down just how race and gender affected each of us on my panel. Indeed, the influence of diversity on a jury cannot be foretold along stereotypical lines—just as it cannot be foretold in the classroom or in society at large. Disqualifying jurors along racial or ethnic or gender grounds is a strategy that cannot have predictable results.

Defending diversity on college campuses, in the work force, or in society, is not a matter of saying that X, or Y, or Z will happen if you include more women, more members of minority or ethnic groups. But my experience showed me that my feminist forebears did make a difference by working so hard to include women on juries. The interplay among factors on a jury will always be complex, messy, and unpredictable. To deny any group participation would skew our system of justice. To allow, indeed to require, women to serve on juries is crucial to creating a true panel of peers. It is crucial to keeping our system of justice as fair and as honest as we can make it.

Elisabeth I. Perry is a professor of history at Saint Louis University. Her books include Belle Moskowitz: Feminine Politics and the Exercise of Power in the Age of Alfred E. Smith *(Oxford University Press, 1987; reprinted by Northeastern University Press, 2000). Her article "Culture, Strategy, and Politics in the New York Campaign for Women's Jury Service, 1917-1975" appeared in* New York History *(Winter, 2001).*

Looking Askance at Eyewitness Testimony

Psychologists, showing how errors reach the courts, offer advice on handling such evidence

BY D. W. MILLER

RONNIE BULLOCK was sentenced to 60 years in jail for kidnapping and raping a young Illinois girl. Edward Honaker spent a decade in a Virginia prison for sexually assaulting a woman at gunpoint. Kirk Bloodsworth was shipped off to Maryland's death row for raping and strangling a 9-year-old girl.

All three of those men were convicted in part because eyewitnesses or victims firmly placed them at the scene of the crime. But not one of them was guilty. They were among the first convicts to be exonerated by DNA tests proving that someone else was responsible.

Some psychologists believe that such mistakes happen in thousands of courtrooms every year. But most crimes leave no DNA traces to rule out the innocent. For more than two decades, psychological researchers have asked, How could so many witnesses be wrong, and what can be done about it? Only recently have they seen their findings influence the way the criminal-justice system handles eyewitness testimony.

Psychologists have conducted hundreds of studies on errors in eyewitness identification. In some cases, of course, witnesses simply lie. But research has shown that flawed police procedures and the vagaries of memory often lead witnesses to identify the wrong person, and that credulous jurors too easily credit their testimony.

To those familiar with the mountain of evidence about the way the human mind works, that comes as no surprise. "Why should people make good eyewitnesses?" asks Gary L. Wells, a psychologist at Iowa State University who is widely considered the dean of eyewitness research. In the presence of danger, he says, "we're wired for fight or flight. What helped for survival was not a quick recall of details."

The findings of Mr. Wells and his colleagues are finally gaining currency in the halls of criminal justice. In part that is due to the gradual acceptance of expert testimony on eyewitness identification.

Far more crucial, however, is the growing roster of convicts cleared by DNA evidence. In 1996, the U.S. Department of Justice released a report on the first 28 known cases of DNA exoneration. After studying those and 12 subsequent cases, Mr. Wells discovered that mistaken eyewitness testimony had played a part in about 90 percent of the convictions.

MISSING THE KEY DETAILS

Concerned about the high rate of eyewitness error in the DNA cases, U.S. Attorney General Janet Reno invited him to a meeting in early 1997. As a result of their conversation, the department's National Institute of Justice asked Mr. Wells and five fellow scholars to join a panel of law-enforcement officials, criminal-defense lawyers, and prosecutors created to write guidelines for handling eyewitness testimony.

The guide, published in October, gave scholars the opportunity to show that human memory is not a highly reliable tool for determining guilt in the courtroom. For example, contrary to popular belief, people under stress remember events no better than, and often less well than, they do under ordinary circumstances. Witnesses also perceive time as moving more slowly during traumatic events. That, in turn, leads them to overestimate how much time they had to notice details, a key factor of their credibility in court. And studies have found that witnesses to a crime are so distracted by the presence of a weapon—a phenomenon called "weapon focus"—that they remember little else with accuracy.

Researchers cannot ethically recreate the trauma of real crimes. But plenty of field research suggests that witnesses are apt to misidentify people.

Gary L. Wells: "Why should people make good eyewitnesses?" In times of danger, "we're wired for fight or flight. What helped for survival was not a quick recall of details."

For example, many studies have tested the ability of convenience-store clerks and bank tellers to recall customers they encountered in non-stressful situations. Around a third of the time, the employees wrongly identified faces from "lineups" that did not include the person they had actually met.

THE DETERIORATION OF MEMORY

In addition, all sorts of factors inhibit our ability to recognize and recall facial detail. For instance, psychologists have established that most of us have more difficulty recognizing people of a different race. And memory deteriorates very quickly over time.

Elizabeth F. Loftus, a psychologist at the University of Washington and a pioneer in research on false memory, has discovered that it's remarkably easy to alter one's recollection without realizing it. Human beings are highly susceptible to incorporating "post-event information"— newspaper articles, comments by police, conversations with other witnesses—into their recollections.

Witnesses also have been known to identify as criminals people they recognized from some other encounter, a process called "transference." In one bizarre example, an Australian psychologist and memory researcher named Donald Thomson was himself once identified by a rape victim as her attacker. Not only was his alibi airtight—he was being interviewed on live television at the time—but she had mistaken him for the rapist because she had seen his face on her television screen during the assault.

IMPROVING POLICE PROCEDURES

Of course, policymakers can't do much to improve the flaws in our memories. So scholars like Mr. Wells, who wanted to reduce eyewitness mistakes, began to focus on things that the justice system can control—particularly police procedures.

One of the biggest problems with eyewitness identification, researchers have found, is that uncertain witnesses are often prompted to finger the person whom police have detained, even when the suspect is not the same person they spotted at the scene. Witnesses viewing a lineup tend to assume that police have caught the person they saw. So they think their job is to find the face that most resembles the description they gave to police.

The police sometimes exacerbate that tendency by designing lineups poorly. Imagine a witness to a liquor-store robbery who says the robber was white, stocky, and bearded. Based on that description, the police identify a suspect and ask the witness to look at a lineup of live individuals or at a spread of photos (known as a "six-pack").

Too often, say researchers, the "distractor" faces used by police do not closely match the witness's description, or the suspect's photo looks different from the others. If the suspect stands out in any way—if his is the only color photo in the six-pack, for instance—the witness is far more likely to say, "That's the guy."

Lineups are also fraught with the possibility of mistaken identity, researchers report, because of our tendency to overlook differences in facial appearance among people not of our race. Not only are white witnesses, say, more likely to mistake one black suspect for another (and vice versa), but police officers may overestimate the degree to which the distractors they choose match the suspect's description.

Recently, Mr. Wells has raised the alarm about the way a witness's confidence can be manipulated. Witnesses are easily influenced during and after the lineup—by talking with other witnesses or police interviewers—to be more certain of their choice than their recall warrants. Police investigators, for example, may praise a witness for "picking the right guy" out of the lineup.

That taint frequently makes its way to the jury box. Understandably, jurors put a lot of stock in a witness who can point to the defendant and say, "He's the one. I'll never forget his face." But scholars have learned that the degree of confidence during trial is a poor predictor of a witness's accuracy. And, they warn, jurors ought to be particularly skeptical if they learn that a witness professed more confidence on the witness stand than in the squad room. Recall, they say, doesn't improve over time.

ASKING THE RIGHT QUESTIONS

Until recently, the criminal-justice system made little use of those findings. Defense lawyers, of course, have embraced and exploited them at least since the 1980's. But according to Brian L. Cutler, a psychologist at Florida International University, they have rarely been able to use the research to cross-examine eyewitnesses or police.

"Defense lawyers have no special training—they don't know what questions to ask," says Mr. Cutler. "If they do ask the right questions, how well-equipped are jurors to

As Expert Witnesses, Psychologists Have an Impact —but Only a Case at a Time

UNTIL a few years ago, when the U.S. Department of Justice invited six psychologists to help reshape police procedures for eyewitness identification, scholars had only one way to influence criminal justice: one defendant at a time. Many have themselves testified to educate juries about the pitfalls of witness memory.

Like a lot of his colleagues, Gary L. Wells, a psychologist at Iowa State University who testifies four or five times a year, got into that line of research in part to save innocent defendants from false imprisonment, and to force police to improve methods for interviewing witnesses and identifying suspects. "There was a time 20 years ago when I was so naive as to think that all I had to do was document the problem and the police would change their procedures," he says. But eventually he decided that "the courtroom was never the place to have that kind of impact."

"Judges are reluctant to tell police how to do their jobs," he says. And judges tend to hew to the established view that juries are the arbiters of witness credibility.

That has been changing slowly. In 1993, the U.S. Supreme court ruled in *Daubert* v. *Merrell Dow Pharmaceuticals, Inc.* that new federal rules of evidence permitted a broader standard for allowing expert psychological testimony. Since then, says Solomon Fulero, a psychologist at Sinclair Community College, in Dayton, Ohio, several convictions have been overturned because the trial judge had not allowed such experts to testify.

Still, there's a limit to the broad change that scholars can effect by testifying. According to Mr. Wells, there just aren't that many experts: About 50 to 75 psychologists testify in court regularly, and only about 25 of them actually do original research in the field.

Furthermore, their services can be pricey. While rates vary widely, the psychologists themselves report fees of up to $3,500 a case, although most will take some clients *pro bono.*

WITNESS CREDIBILITY

In general, the experts try to avoid challenging the credibility of individual witnesses or the conduct of the police officers who worked with them. "The goal of the defense is to cast doubt on the credibility of a particular witness. But that's not my job," says Mr. Fulero, who was invited to join the Justice Department's eyewitness-testimony panel because of his courtroom experience, not his scholarly *vitae.* What he can testify to, he explains, is that "eyewitnesses are not as accurate, over all, as the jurors believe them to be."

Unfortunately for defendants, that means the research doesn't always help their cause.

"The deep problem," says James M. Doyle, a Boston defense lawyer who served on the panel, "is that the research is all statistical and probabilistic, but the trial process is clinical and diagnostic." In other words, a jury expects the experts to say whether a witness is right or wrong, when all an expert can really do is explain how to assess the odds.

Mr. Wells echoes many of his colleagues when he says that he's not really in it for the money. He was among the half-dozen scholars who helped to fashion the new Justice Department guidelines for handling eyewitness testimony. If they are widely adopted, he says, "we have no business in the courtroom on this issue. My purpose is to make expert testimony unnecessary."

He may get his wish. According to participants, prosecutors on the Justice Department panel were concerned that quick-witted defense lawyers would use the new guidelines to impeach eyewitness testimony.

Mr. Doyle, who has co-written a lawyer's guide to the research, *Eyewitness Testimony*, calls that a reasonable fear. In the past, his colleagues have had difficulty incorporating the science into their cross-examination techniques, because they haven't taken the trouble to understand the research methods, he says. Now they won't have to.

On the other hand, he doubts that's a bad thing. "One thing police and defense lawyers share is that we don't really want to deal with innocent people. It's not necessarily easier or better for me to represent innocent people. I would just as soon the police did their jobs."

—D. W. MILLER

evaluate the questions?" Unfortunately, jurors cling to a belief that "the way memory works is a matter of common sense," he says. "It just isn't so."

"People expect it's like videotape, that we attend equally well to everything out there," says Roy S. Mal- pass, a psychologist at the University of Texas at El Paso who served on the Justice Department panel. In fact, he says, "we're highly selective."

No one knows how often eyewitness error leads to false convictions, but some scholars have taken a stab at the question. In their book *Mistaken Identification: The Eyewitness, Psychology, and the Law* (Cambridge University Press, 1995), Mr. Cutler and Steven D. Penrod, of the University of Nebraska at Lincoln, do some courtroom calculations: If just 0.5 percent of America's yearly 1.5 million convictions for serious crimes are erroneous—a rate suggested by some studies—then other research allows the authors to infer that well over half of those defendants, or around 4,500 innocent people, are convicted on false eyewitness testimony.

All that may change now that the nation's top law-enforcement officials have created new guidelines for police conduct. The Justice Department report, "Eyewitness Evidence: A Guide for Law Enforcement," reads like a primer on eyewitness research. Among other things, it instructs investigators who assemble a lineup to:

- Select "distractors" that match the witness's description, even simulating tattoos or other unusual features if necessary.
- Remind the witness that the suspect they saw may not even be in the lineup, and that the lineup is intended to clear the innocent as much as it is to identify the guilty.
- Avoid any comments that might influence the witness's selection.
- Ask for and record the witness's degree of certainty immediately.
- Photograph or film lineups to make the police more accountable to the defense.

Before they can take their new influence for granted, psychologists say, there is more to be done. For one thing, police officers and prosecutors need to be educated about the guidelines, which do not have the force of law. But Mr. Wells and others believe that both groups will embrace them once defense lawyers in the courtroom begin to hold the guidelines up as the gold standard of diligent police work.

NO DOUBLE-BLIND LINEUPS

The social scientists didn't win every battle. Despite their urgings, law-enforcement officials on the Justice Department panel batted down two key suggestions for improving police lineups. Research suggests that lineups are more accurate when they are double-blind—in other words, when the investigator in charge doesn't know which person is the suspect—and sequential—when the witness sees faces one at a time.

According to participants, police representatives nixed the former idea, because logistically it would be difficult to round up investigators who didn't know who the suspect was. More important, they said, it would be a tough sell to their fellow cops, because it smacks of mistrust and requires them to cede control of an investigation to someone else.

After scholars lost the battle to include double-blind procedures, participants say, they gave up on demanding sequential lineups. Without the first precaution, they explained, sequential lineups might be even more vulnerable to manipulation than simultaneous lineups are.

John Turtle, a panel member and a psychologist at the Ryerson Polytechnic Institute, in Toronto, believes that he has a high-tech solution to all those concerns. He has developed computer software that purports to take the bias out of the photo-spread lineups, which constitute about 80 percent of those in the United States and virtually all of those in Canada.

All a police investigator would need to do is scan a photo of the suspect into a computer and sit the witness down in front of the screen. The machine would then automatically choose photos of others who match the witness's description from a large database, and offer standardized, neutral instructions that wouldn't nudge the witness toward a particular response.

Psychologists deny they are imputing bad faith to police investigators. It's human nature, they say, to want your results to match your expectations. The scholars are simply urging police officers to treat their procedures for handling witnesses with all the care of scientific experiments. "Human memory is a form of trace evidence, like blood or semen or hair, except the trace exists inside the witness's head," says Mr. Wells. "How you go about collecting that evidence and preserving it and analyzing it is absolutely vital."

JUSTICE & ANTONIN SCALIA

The Supreme Court's most strident Catholic

Julia Vitullo-Martin

After being nominated as a Supreme Court Justice by President Ronald Reagan in 1986, Antonin Scalia faced down the Democratic-controlled Senate Judiciary Committee by refusing to discuss his views on any question likely to come before him as a sitting justice. Yet his confirmation hearings became a virtual lovefest. Scalia handled his interrogation so engagingly that the Senate voted ninety-eight to zero to confirm him. Reagan was said to have danced around the Oval Office, singing "Scalia/I've just picked a judge named Scalia," to the tune of *West Side Story*'s "Maria."

Reagan knew what he was getting. Scalia would soon establish himself as one of the most brilliant and belligerent conservatives ever to sit on the high court. The late Justice William Brennan's reputation as the most influential Supreme Court justice of his generation would shortly pass to Scalia, asserted Michael Greve, cofounder of the libertarian Center for Individual Rights, a public-interest law firm in Washington, D.C.

From today's perspective, in which Scalia has emerged as a reliable proponent of hard-right views on issues from property rights to the death penalty, his confirmation hearings seem to have happened in a parallel universe. Some senators even called Scalia by his nickname, Nino. It became clear that Nino was a man of many parts—Nino, the tennis player, opera singer, pianist, poker player, raconteur, man about town, father of nine. Potential enemies were declawed by his accomplishments and affability. Howard Metzenbaum, for example, an outspokenly liberal Ohio Democrat, announced that Scalia's conservatism was irrelevant and that all that mattered was his "fitness." Senator Edward Kennedy worried that Scalia might be "insensitive" on women's rights, but concluded that one could hardly "maintain that Judge Scalia is outside the mainstream."

His immigrant saga—the only child of a Sicilian father and a first-generation Italian-American mother—was lav-

ishly praised. Born in 1936, he spent his early childhood in Trenton, New Jersey, before the family moved to New York, when his father became a professor of Romance languages at Brooklyn College. He graduated first in his class from Saint Francis Xavier, a Jesuit high school in Manhattan, first in his class from Georgetown University, and cum laude from Harvard Law School. He went on to practice law from 1961 to 1967 with Cleveland's most prestigious firm, Jones, Day, Cockley, and Reavis—named after the city's first family of Virginia, became general counsel to the White House Office Telecommunications Policy, chaired the Administrative Conference of the United States, and became assistant attorney general in the U.S. Department of Justice's Office of Legal Counsel. In 1977, he joined the law faculty at the University of Chicago, from which he was appointed in 1982 to the nation's second most important court, the U.S. Court of Appeals for the D.C. Circuit.

Even the legal press was effusive about Scalia's Supreme Court confirmation. Tony Mauro in the *Legal Times* predicted that Scalia would become the court's "intellectual lodestar."

How, then, did this exemplar of charm and learning become what he is today—the scourge of the country's liberal establishment? FindLaw columnist Edward Lazarus, for example, recently questioned Scalia's integrity, arguing that his reputation as "a rigorous and thoroughly principled jurist" has always seemed to him "largely a myth." (Lazarus's own moral claim to fame: he betrayed the ethics of his Supreme Court clerkship by publishing the first and only insider account of the workings of the Court. But that's another story.) Ex-prosecutor and best-selling legal commentator Vincent Bugliosi's inflammatory charge is that "having Justice Antonin Scalia speak on ethics is like having a prostitute speak on sexual abstinence." Peter Laarman, minister at New York's Judson Memorial Church, gave a sermon naming Justices Scalia and Clarence Thomas as members of the "scary lunatic fringe occupying most of the seats of power."

Scoffing at the idea that our "maturing" society's "evolving standards of decency" might in and of themselves make the death penalty unconstitutional, Scalia said that the Constitution he interprets and applies is not living but dead.

But the pièce de résistance of liberal loathing can be found in a July 8, 2002, OpEd in the *New York Times* by Princeton professor Sean Wilentz. Wilentz attacked a speech Scalia had given at the University of Chicago Divinity School (and reworked for the conservative journal, *First Things*), arguing that the Eighth Amendment's prohibition of cruel and unusual punishment does not proscribe the death penalty. Scalia's remarks, wrote Wilentz, "show bitterness against democracy, strong dislike for the Constitution's approach to religion, and eager advocacy for the submission of the individual to the state. It is a chilling mixture for an American."

More important for Wilentz and his political allies, this is a chilling mixture for a chief justice—a job Scalia is rumored to want and that President George W. Bush is rumored to want him to have. While the chief is only first among equals, he has the crucial task of assigning opinions in which he is in the majority. A powerful, congenial chief such as Chief Justice Earl Warren—or William Rehnquist, for that matter—can mold the court in his image through persuasive deliberations and adept assignments. Scalia puts little effort into winning over those who disagree with him. Harvard Professor Lawrence Tribe once pointed out that Scalia's "vigor and occasional viciousness" in his written opinions may "alienate people who might be his allies in moving the Court to the right. I therefore hope he will keep it up." There's little reason to think that as chief Scalia wouldn't keep it up. After all, he recently attacked all his colleagues, asserting that the justices on the Court were no better qualified to rule on the right to die than nine people selected at random from a Kansas City phone book. He also took them on individually. He ridiculed Justice Stephen Breyer, for example, for writing a decision so vague that it gave trial courts "not a clue" as to how to carry it out. He mocked Justice David Souter for resorting "to that last hope of lost interpretive causes, that Saint Jude of the hagiography of statutory construction, legislative history."

Scalia can be particularly provocative, even shocking, on race. In a majority opinion on racially based jury selection, he attacked Justice Thurgood Marshall, saying that his dissent "rolls out the ultimate weapon, the accusation of insensitivity to racial discrimination—which will lose its intimidating effect if it continues to be fired so randomly." Given that Marshall knew far better than Scalia the reality of racial discrimination when he saw it—he was surely the only justice in the history of the Supreme

Court to have once been dragged to a river by a lynch mob—even years later Scalia's words seem intemperate and misplaced.

He can also be combative on issues that usually call for compassion. He says that the death penalty, for example, is not a "difficult, soul-wrenching question." Scoffing at the idea that our "maturing" society's "evolving standards of decency" might in and of themselves make the death penalty unconstitutional, Scalia said that the Constitution he interprets and applies is not living but dead. Or, as he prefers to put it, "enduring." It means today not what current society (much less the Court) thinks it ought to mean, but what it meant when it was adopted. Scalia has even affronted his conservative Catholic supporters. He's argued (correctly) that the pope's opposition to the death penalty expressed in *Evangelium vitae* is not "binding teaching" requiring adherence by all Catholics—though they must give it thoughtful and respectful consideration. When Cardinal Avery Dulles said he agreed with the pope's position, Scalia answered that this was "just the phenomenon of the clerical bureaucracy saying, 'Yes, boss.'"

What the pope has to say is irrelevant to him as a judge, says Scalia, since his own views on the morality of the death penalty have nothing to do with how he votes judicially. However, one's moral views do govern whether or not one can or should be a judge at all. "When I sit on a Court that reviews and affirms capital convictions," said Scalia, "I am part of 'the machinery of death.'" The Supreme Court's ruling is often the last step that permits an execution to proceed. Any judge who believes the death penalty immoral should resign, he says, rather than "simply ignoring duly enacted, constitutional laws and sabotaging death-penalty cases."

How, then, can Scalia continue to serve as a judge in a court that has repeatedly upheld abortion, which he regards as immoral? Capital cases, argues Scalia, are different from the other life-and-death issues the Court might hear, like abortion or legalized suicide. In these instances, it is not the state that is decreeing death, but private individuals whom the state has decided not to restrain. One may argue (as many do) that society has a moral obligation to interfere. That moral obligation may weigh heavily upon the voter, and upon the legislator who enacts the laws, Scalia argues, but a judge "bears no moral guilt for the laws society has failed to enact."

Ironically, despite Scalia's carefully drawn, if dubious, distinctions, Scalia's antagonist Wilentz accuses him of believing that Catholics, as citizens, would be unable to uphold views that contradict church doctrine. A shocked Wilentz says that Scalia "sees submission as desirable." This, Wilentz continues, is "exactly the stereotype of Catholicism as papist mind-control that Catholics have struggled against, and that John F. Kennedy did so much to overcome."

Obedience, for good or ill, is indeed an ongoing Scalia theme. He has joked more than once that the keys to being a good Catholic and a good jurist are the same: being strong enough to obey the relevant law. Still, he has not urged submission on American Catholic citizens.

Wilentz also writes that despite calling himself a strict constructionist—actually, he doesn't—Scalia wants to impose "a religious sense that is directly counter to the abundantly expressed wishes of the men who wrote the Constitution." This is not strict constructionism, says Wilentz. It "is opportunism, and it threatens democracy."

Is Wilentz right? Is Scalia an opportunist who threatens the very democracy whose Constitution he has sworn to uphold? Or is he a brace originalist, seeking to return to the principles of the American Founding Fathers that the Court discarded in the last fifty years?

The answer is not yet clear. Part of the anger Scalia arouses is a result of how successful he has been in restoring respect for the Constitution's actual words. Calling his approach textualism, Scalia argues that primacy must be given to the text, structure, and history of any document—Constitution or statute—being interpreted. Judges, he says are to eschew their own "intellectual, moral, and personal perceptions." Scalia says he takes the Constitution as it is, not as he wants it to be.

In effect, of course, this is an attack on much of twentieth-century jurisprudence, which has created a host of new constitutional rights by embracing such Holmesian ideas as the "balancing of competing interests" and Justice William Brennan's "living Constitution." This expanded vision of the Constitution gave judges enormous power to assert that their individual policy preferences and social goals—however unpopular—were also the law. As Scalia wrote in his solo, and prescient, dissent in the case recognizing the constitutionality of the now notorious Office of the Special Prosecutor: "Evidently, the governing standard is to be what might be called the unfettered wisdom of a majority of this Court, revealed to an obedient people in a case-by-case basis. This is not only not the government of laws that the Constitution established, it is not a government of laws at all."

Larry Kramer, a law professor at New York University, calls Scalia's belief that judges should renounce their own desires when interpreting the law "judicial asceticism." He argues that Scalia's "formalism, textualism, and originalism are only means: denial and self-control are the reasons."

If Scalia's first sin in the eyes of doctrinaire liberals is his textualism, make no mistake about the fact that his second sin is that he is a practicing Catholic—or, as commentators repeatedly mention, a "devout" Catholic. (How the devotion is known is not clear.) Of course, the sins of textualism and Catholicism are not unrelated—both reflect respect for the written word, an ordered universe, and an attachment to tradition. And both have a long contentious relationship with liberalism. Wilentz probably put his finger on something important when he wrote, "One senses that Mr. Scalia's true priority is to get secular humanists off the federal bench."

Certainly, there is something admirable in Scalia's allegiance to tradition and his stubborn refusal to pander on moral issues—both of which predictably incite his critics to excess. Harvard Law Professor Alan Dershowitz, for example, calls Scalia the "voice of Spanish clerical conservatism." The liberal *American Prospect* magazine scathingly refers to Scalia's "Jesuitical" logic. The editor of Salon.com wrote that defenders of the Bush v. Gore decision, in which Scalia played such a large role, "would have to perform feats of casuistry unseen since the days when Ignatius Loyola strode the earth to do so." Calling Scalia a cheap-shot artist, *Washington Post* columnist Richard Cohen maintains that the justice's mind is rigid on constitutional issues between church and state: "Anyone who thinks Scalia will give First Amendment issues a fair and reasoned hearing is, it seems, proceeding in a way Scalia would appreciate: solely on faith."

These knee-jerk liberal denunciations are appalling in a way, but while some of these comments might set off alarms for William Donohue and his Catholic League cohorts, they do not represent a revival of pure, nineteenth-century anti-Catholicism. No respectable attack was ever leveled at the Catholicism of Scalia's nemesis, Justice William Brennan. Generally thought by legal scholars (including Scalia) to have been the twentieth century's most influential justice, Brennan may well have also been the most loved. He was a brilliant, strategic, persuasive conciliator who more often than not won the day. He once said, "With five votes you can do anything around here." His "living Constitution" is both the dominant liberal constitutional concept and the polar opposite of Scalia's textualism.

Scalia, in contrast, goes out of his way to give speeches like his provocative 1996 "Fools for Christ's Sake" address at the Mississippi College of Law, a Baptist school. Most (perhaps all) of his critics missed the reference to Saint Paul and therefore misinterpreted the speech, but then Scalia pretty much knew they would. Baiting the opposition—whether outside or inside the Court—is basic to his temperament.

As a Catholic who grew up in working-class neighborhoods (even though his father was an academic), Scalia often reveals a different sensibility from his Brahmin peers. In a 1979 law review article he denounced "the Wisdoms and the Powells and the Whites," whose ancestors participated in the oppression of African Americans, and who as justice sought to correct the effects of that ancestral oppression at the expense of newer immigrants. In a 1987 dissent he defended the "unknown, unaffluent, and unorganized" workers ignored by proponents of affirmative action.

And, then, of course, there's abortion, by far the most divisive social issue of our time, and one that Scalia argues should be settled legislatively rather than judicially. Yet the conservative Rehnquist Court has signaled more than once that it's not going to reverse *Roe v. Wade*. It doesn't really matter to a majority of the Court that Scalia was probably correct when he said, "I do not believe—and for two hundred years, no one believed—that the Constitution contains a right to abortion." In *A Matter of Interpretation* (Princeton), his Tanner Lectures at Princeton, he cautions that creating new constitutional rights may trigger a majoritarian reaction. "At the end of the day," he notes, "an evolving Constitution will evolve the way the majority wishes." One has to wonder whether the 2002 elections giving the House, Senate, and (by extension, the Supreme Court) to the Republicans reflect, in part, this prediction come true.

Scalia's third sin is his shockingly bad temper, in print, toward his intellectual opponents. Some of his harshest language concerning his colleagues came in his criticism of *Roe*: "The emptiness of the 'reasoned judgment' that produced *Roe* is displayed in plain view by the fact . . . that the best the Court can do to explain how it is that the word 'liberty' must include the right to destroy human fetuses is to rattle off a collection of adjectives that simply decorate a value judgment and conceal a political choice."

That temper has regularly been directed at centrist Justice Sandra Day O'Connor, who often must be wooed as the crucial fifth vote in a conservative coalition. In dissenting from *Planned Parenthood v. Casey* (1992), Scalia questioned O'Connor's intelligence. "Reason finds no refuge in this jurisprudence of confusion," he wrote.

Such outbursts have been costly. For many years, O'Connor avoided signing majority opinions authored by Scalia, which meant that Chief Justice Rehnquist—who needed her vote—avoided assigning controversial opinions to Scalia.

Perhaps Scalia's most troubling sin is that he does not always hold himself to his own principles. He explains his judicial rigidity by saying that when "I adopt a general rule, and say 'This is the basis of our decision,' I not only constrain lower courts, I constrain myself as well. If the next case should have such different facts that my political or policy preferences regarding the outcome are quite opposite, I will be unable to indulge those preferences; I have committed myself to the governing principle." Such rules can embolden judges to be courageous when having to issue an unpopular ruling, such as one protecting a criminal defendant's rights. All around, an admirable position.

How then to explain *Bush v. Gore*, the 5-4 ruling that effectively handed the presidency to George W. Bush in 2000? Bush may well have won the election fair and square, but we'll never know for sure. This was the first time in American history that the Court decided a presidential election, and it did so by improbably concluding that Florida's diverse standards for counting votes constituted an equal protection violation under the Fourteenth Amendment. Scalia's respect for established precedents

and his disdain for catchall uses of the equal protection clause suddenly didn't seem to apply here—nor did his reverence for the separation of powers. As if the decision weren't mischievous enough, the Court also pronounced—amazingly—that "our consideration is limited to the present circumstances, for the problem of equal protection in election processes generally presents many complexities." Since when does the Supreme Court limit its rulings to present circumstances?

Ironically, Scalia's tightly argued dissent in *Casey* eerily foreshadows his own lead role in the scandal of *Bush v. Gore*: "The Imperial Judiciary lives," Scalia wrote. "It is instructive to compare this Nietzschean vision of us unelected, life-tenured judges—leading a Volk who will be 'tested by following,' and whose very 'belief in themselves' is mystically bound up in their 'understanding' of a Court that 'speak[s] before all others for their constitutional ideals'—with the somewhat more modest role envisioned for these lawyers by the Founders."

How can Scalia reconcile his principled views with his vote in *Bush v. Gore*? There aren't many convincing answers. His opponents claim Scalia acted as a ruthless, self-serving politician who put his own boy in power when it looked like the other side might win. Another possible explanation is that Scalia believes deeply something else he said in his *Casey* dissent, which is that *Roe* "fanned into life an issue that has inflamed our national politics in general, and has obscured with its smoke the selection of justices to this Court, in particular, ever since." In other words, the Court has embroiled itself in political issues that should be left to the people and their representatives—and that only a Republican administration would set the Court back on its right course. (It is not at all clear that this will happen.) Thus Scalia saw nothing wrong with the language he used in concurring with the Court's stay (by definition an emergency measure) halting the Florida vote recount. Continuing the manual count, wrote Scalia, would "threaten irreparable harm" to Bush "and to the country, by casting a cloud upon what he claims to be the legitimacy of his election." He may never have written a less convincing justification of one of his positions, but it makes some sense if understood in light of how far wrong he thinks the Court has gone.

Scalia has spent most of his career captivating others, who often let their affection for him overcome their distaste for some of his ideas. He is a social animal, and it is possible that his fury about being correct yet alone over several momentous issues has warped his judgment on others—on which he is probably not right. His wrath is born of his self-confidence in the face of universal opposition. Take two 1988 dissents, *Morrison* and *Mistretta*, which, in the words of Northwestern University Law Professor Thomas Merrill, showed Scalia to be "completely isolated" on the Court. Isolated he may have been, but he was also completely right.

Morrison v. Olson was the decision upholding the Independent Counsel Act. Scalia's colleagues thought he had pretty much lost it when he ferociously wrote, "The institutional design of the Independent Counsel is designed to heighten, not to check, all of the institutional hazards of the dedicated prosecutor; the danger of too narrow a focus, of the loss of perspective, of preoccupation with the pursuit of one alleged suspect to the exclusion of other interests." With unchecked discretionary powers and unlimited funds, the independent counsel would be accountable to no one and would be entirely focused on a single target. The office would encourage the worst tendencies in American democracy. "The context of this statute is acrid with the smell of threatened impeachment," wrote Scalia. Indeed.

The history of the Independent Counsel Act is replete with examples of prosecutorial abuse that would have made the Founders recoil. Scalia accurately predicted, "If the prosecutor is obliged to choose his case, it follows that he can choose his defendants. Therein is the most dangerous power of the prosecutor: that he will pick people that he thinks he should get, rather than cases that need to be prosecuted.... It is not a question of discovering the commission of a crime and then looking for the man who has committed it, it is a question of picking the man and then searching the law books, or putting investigators to work, to pin some offense on him."

Mistretta v. U.S., the other dissent that isolated Scalia, concerned a revolution in criminal sentencing that has gone almost unnoticed by most Americans. In 1984, Congress established the U.S. Sentencing Commission as an independent rule-making body to promulgate mandatory guidelines for every federal criminal offense. The act specifically rejected rehabilitation as a goal of imprisonment, and mandated instead "that punishment should serve retributive, educational, deterrent, and incapacitative goals." All sentences would become determinate (fixed), with no parole other than a small credit that could be earned by good behavior.

Indeed, the country has grappled with the gross injustices of federal sentencing. In the past, judges were able to use their discretion to minimize inequities in the law. No longer. Now judges are governed by this new branch of government, by what Scalia mockingly calls "a sort of junior-varsity Congress."

Scalia lost on *Mistretta*, but he eventually won on another crucial sentencing issue—victim impact statements. In the mid-1970s, the Supreme Court had begun requiring that defendants in capital cases be allowed to present "mitigating circumstances" during the sentencing phase of capital trials. Yet while defendants in particularly heinous crimes could present evidence about an abusive childhood, victims and their families had no standing to speak. The Supreme Court repeatedly said victim-impact statements created a constitutionally unacceptable risk of arbitrary and capricious decisions by juries. Worse, they would focus attention not on the moral guilt of the defendant's alleged harms to society but on the emotions and opinions of persons who were not parties to the crime. Scalia dissented, attacking the "recently invented" requirement of mitigating circumstances, asking why the jury could not also take into account "the specific harm visited upon society by a murderer." In 1991, in *Payne v. Tennessee*, the Court finally agreed and overturned the ban on victim-impact statements. Justice Marshall announced his retirement the same day—some said because his heart was broken.

This term the Court has ruled 5 to 4 on another sentencing issue—California's three-strikes law. Like victim-impact statements, added punishment for multiple offenses has a long tradition in the common law. Adopted by referendum in 1994, California's harsh law permits judges to treat crimes that would ordinarily be considered misdemeanors as third felonies. (Most states with three-strikes laws require the third strike to actually be a felony, usually a violent one.) The particular cases before the Court involved life sentences for two men whose third crimes were shoplifting—$1,200 worth of golf clubs in one case, and $154 worth of children's videotapes in the other.

Here was a case with Scalia's favorite elements: the direct voice of the majority expressed via referendum, state sovereignty via its law, and centuries of Anglo-Saxon tradition. All of these considerations were to be weighed in determining the punishment of two career criminals who had led astonishingly unproductive lives. What should society do with such people? It is a testament to the revolution Scalia has wrought that this case even came before the Court, much less that the Court upheld three strikes. No longer do courts cavalierly assume that the Constitution prevents Americans from protecting themselves against known repeat predators. We are reminded, again, that in most matters of criminal justice, Scalia is the people" champion—even if this decision was written by his protagonist, Justice O'Connor, leaving him to concur. This, in turn, reminds us of the conundrum of his role in *Bush v. Gore*. There he seemed to place the "irreparable harm" that a Florida recount would do to petitioner George W. Bush above the irreparable harm to citizens whose votes would not even be counted. Is Antonin Scalia an opportunist or an originalist? Perhaps he is both.

Julia Vitullo-Martin writes frequently for Commonweal, the Wall Street Journal, *and other publications. She is working on a book on the American Jury and Criminal Law.*

Courts asked to consider culture

An act defined as crime in USA may be common in other places. Should justice system take that into account?

By Richard Willing

Santeria priest Ernesto Pichardo thought it was a good thing when fellow members of the Church of the Lukumi Babalu Aye began to leave the bodies of sacrificed chickens near the trees and bushes of Hialeah, Fla., the congregation's hometown, during the 1980s.

Others did not. The City Council in the city of 240,000 people, 11 miles northwest of Miami, rejected the church's contention that the ritual scatterings were a vital part of the Santeria religion and of the Afro-Cuban culture on which it is based. The city prosecuted the church under a law banning animal sacrifices that stood until 1993, when the U.S. Supreme Court struck it down as religious discrimination.

The sacrifices continue, although Pichardo says church members still are occasionally hassled by authorities.

"I learned one thing," says Pichardo, who as an orite, or special priest, is empowered to conduct the sacrifices. "When you bring something forward that is outside the Judeo-Christian tradition, the dominant culture is going to cause you problems."

Immigrants with roots in Africa, Asia and other non-Western cultures are winding up in America's courts after being charged with crimes for acts that would not be offenses in their home countries. In recent years, U.S. courts have been asked to decide the fates of defendants involved in animal sacrifices, ritual mutilations and other customs of foreign cultures.

Some legal analysts and academics say the phenomenon should lead U.S. courts to allow defendants from non-Western backgrounds to raise a "cultural defense" when they are charged with certain crimes. Legal traditionalists blanch at the idea, and courts here traditionally have been reluctant to allow such defenses.

"We say that as a society we welcome diversity, and in fact that we embrace it," says Alison Dundes Renteln, a political science professor at the University of Southern California and author of *The Cultural Defense*, a book that examines the influence of such cases on U.S. courts. "In practice, it's not that easy."

Recent cases bear that out:

- In Fresno in 1995, Thai Chia Moua, a Hmong shaman originally from Laos, ordered a German shepherd puppy beaten to death on his front porch while he chanted over its body. Moua later explained that he wanted the puppy's soul to hunt down an evil spirit that was tormenting his wife. He pleaded guilty to animal cruelty. He was sentenced to probation and community service.

- In San Mateo, Calif., in 2000, Taufui Piutau was arrested for driving under the influence of kava tea, a mild euphoric popular in his native Tonga. A hung jury led to a mistrial.

- Chewers of khat, a leaf grown in East Africa and Yemen that produces a caffeine-like stimulant buzz, have been prosecuted in Michigan, New York, Georgia, Connecticut and Minnesota since the mid-1990s. Khat is legal in Great Britain, but the U.S. government classifies it as a controlled substance in the same category as LSD and Ecstasy.

- In Sanford, N.C., in 2003, city officials banned the slaughter of goats and other farm animals. Mexican agricultural workers who had settled in the town had begun killing goats for backyard barbecues and nailing their heads to nearby trees.

- In Lawrenceville, Ga., in March, Ethiopian immigrant Khalid Adem was charged with child cruelty after his 4-year-old daughter was found to have undergone female circumcision. The practice, in which portions of the female genitals are removed, is condemned by the United Nations and is banned under a 1995 U.S. law, but it is common in some African cultures.

Civil lawsuits

Culture clashes also are producing civil lawsuits that run in the other direction: Recently arrived immigrants have filed claims against airlines and fast-food restaurants over conduct that was offensive in the immigrants' cultures.

In 1988, the parents of Jasbir Singh, a Sikh, won $400,000 in court from Air Illinois after Singh, 26, was killed in a plane crash. An Illinois court ruled that the family was entitled to a larger-than-usual amount because Sikh custom would have required Singh to care for them in their old age.

Cultural claims have worked on occasion. In 1999, Mukesh Rai, a Carpenteria, Calif., pharmacist who is a vegetarian, accepted an undisclosed sum from Taco Bell after he mistakenly was served a beef burrito. Rai, a Hindu who had sued for

$144,000, claimed that he was offended on cultural and religious grounds. He said the incident led him to consult a psychiatrist and to journey to India for a purifying bath in the Ganges River. Similar lawsuits by non-religious vegetarians usually fail, legal analysts say.

U.S. courts have dealt with similar pressures before.

In the early 20th century, Renteln says, Orthodox Jewish immigrants from Eastern Europe and Catholics from Italy brought religious and cultural practices that clashed with U.S. customs. Practices such as contracted or underage marriages, she says, were not protected under U.S. law and largely were eliminated.

Renteln wants courts to recognize what she calls America's "evolving definition of diversity." She says cultural defenses should be considered when determining guilt. But she does not say that those who commit culture-based crimes should always be found not guilty.

"Courts can judge on a case-by-case basis," Renteln says.

"For instance, they could rule that it's OK for a Sikh man to wear a *kirpan* (a ceremonial dagger worn on or under the clothes) without endorsing female genital mutilation."

Legal traditionalists reject that notion. Michael Rushford, president of the Criminal Justice Legal Foundation, a conservative group, says that permitting cultural defenses would lead to a "legal relativism" in which "what's a crime for one person isn't for his neighbor.... The system we have is the best we can do to allow cultural differences without beating down basic human rights."

Religious aspect important

Courts have long been reluctant to accept cultural defenses. Exceptions have come when groups have been able to argue that their religious as well as cultural rights have been violated.

In a case now before a U.S. appeals court, Albuquerque-based adherents of Uniao de Vegetal, a Brazilian religion, are claiming that restricting their access to the

ayahuasca root violates a 1993 U.S. law that protects exotic religious practices. Tea brewed from the root produces a dreamlike state that is essential to their religion, the adherents say. The group won in federal trial court; the U.S. government has appealed.

Occasionally, lawyers have persuaded judges to go easy on defendants from other cultures.

In Brooklyn, N.Y., in 1989, Chinese-born Dong Lu Chen received probation for beating his wife to death with a claw hammer after she confessed to adultery. Chen's attorney, Stewart Orden, argued that the shame Chen felt was the result of his Chinese upbringing, and that it fed his frenzy.

"It was as much of a cultural explanation as cultural defense," says Orden, who says he has not used the strategy since the Chen case.

"Culture may not excuse (a crime), but it can certainly shed light on things we may have difficulty understanding. Why shouldn't a court listen?"

WHEN PROSECUTORS ERR, OTHERS PAY THE PRICE

Disciplinary Action Is Rare
After Misconduct of Mistakes

Milton Lantigua, a 20-year-old Dominican immigrant who helped his grandfather sell clothing from a van, insisted he was innocent when the police charged him with fatally shooting a man on a Bronx street in 1990. He was still insisting a year later, when the jury could not reach a verdict, and a year after that, when he was tried again, convicted and later sentenced to 20 years to life.

It was not until 1996, after Mr. Lantigua had served about five years in prison, that the criminal justice system came around to his view. A state appeals court reversed his conviction, saying that prosecutors in the Bronx had allowed their chief witness to perjure herself, and had failed to disclose the existence of a potential second witness who might have helped the defense.

New York State paid Mr. Lantigua $300,000 to settle a lawsuit over his wrongful conviction, but no prosecutors paid a professional price.

The Lantigua case is one of a handful of Bronx cases in the last 15 years in which serious misconduct or error by prosecutors has led to wrongful convictions and people sent to prison. District Attorney Robert T. Johnson and his aides say that none of their prosecutors have engaged in deliberate misconduct, and that the reversals—which they say are often made on minor, technical points—represent less than 1 percent of the hundreds of felony convictions won by the office each year.

Yet in all but one of the handful of cases, in which the misconduct and mistakes ranged from inappropriate closing arguments to the failure to disclose critical evidence, prosecutors escaped discipline. They were neither punished by their superiors nor publicly sanctioned by the State Supreme Court committee that investigates wrongdoing by lawyers. Many continued to receive merit raises and rise through the ranks.

In one heralded case, a day care teacher, Alberto Ramos, was convicted of raping a young girl and served seven years in prison before it was revealed that prosecutors had failed to disclose information that cast serious doubt on the girl's accusations. After Mr. Ramos's conviction was vacated, the city paid him a $5 million settlement in December, and his lawyer sharply questioned the Bronx's record in disciplining prosecutors. The lawyer, Joel B. Rudin, recently provided The New York Times with the internal personnel records of

The people of the State of New York, Respondent, v. Milton Lantigua, Appellant.

57249

SUPREME COURT OF NEW YORK, APPEALATE DIVISION, FIRST

said 'we'. I was by myself", the prosecutor per-mitted the statement to remain on the record without informing the court that it was perjured. As Court of Appeals noted in People v Pelchat (62 NY2d 97, 105), the prosecutor "is charged with the duty not only to seek convictions but also to see that justice is done." It hardly advances the interest of justice for a prosecutor to use testimony she

more than 70 Bronx prosecutors in cases in which courts cited errors, misjudgments and other forms of prosecutorial misconduct.

An examination of those records, and interviews with prosecutors, defense lawyers and defendants, offer a rare look at prosecutorial wrongdoing: how it happens, the costs that are paid—both human and financial—and what, if anything, is ever done to those responsible.

"Most of the time, when prosecutors withhold evidence, no one finds out about it," said Mr. Rudin, who took the Ramos case after a private investigator for the city discovered documents that pointed to Mr. Ramos's innocence. "It took a freak accident to expose it."

Misconduct by prosecutors has become a national concern in recent years, highlighted last month in a United States Supreme Court decision to throw out a Texas inmate's death sentence because prosecutors had deliberately withheld critical evidence. In a study last year, the Center for Public Integrity, a group that monitors government ethics issues, reported that from 1970, there had been more than 2,000 cases of prosecutorial misconduct in the United States that resulted in dismissed charges, reversed convictions or reduced sentences.

In the Bronx, Mr. Johnson and his staff said, prosecutors are constantly striving to ensure fairness for defendants, citing hundreds of cases they dismiss each year because of problems with evidence or other factors. "In thousands of cases, some mistakes are inevitable," Mr. Johnson said in a statement. "Where there is an allegation or finding of prosecutorial misconduct," he added, "we deal with it on an individual basis with the assistant involved." In some cases, his aides said, a lecture to the offending prosecutor was considered sufficient. In others, prosecutors resigned or left the office for private practice before the reversals were handed down.

"Not one of them involves a finding of deliberate or intentional shielding or concealment of evidence," Mr. Johnson's deputy, Barry Kluger, said of the reversals. "They were technical rulings or a slip of the tongue." The aides emphasized that several of the cases involving reversals because of prosecutors' errors were tried before Mr. Johnson was elected in 1989.

It is not known whether the performance of Bronx prosecutors is any worse than that of others. The Times reviewed dozens of Bronx cases since 1989 in which a conviction was reversed at least in part because of prosecutorial misconduct or error. What follows is an examination of cases that reveal the human dimensions of a problem that seldom receives a public airing.

A Key Witness Withheld

It was after midnight on June 27, 1990, when Felix Ayala was found bleeding on a Bronx street from a fatal shot to the head, after what the police said was an argument among several men. About a month later, a woman who said she had witnessed the killing from a bedroom window was being driven around the neighborhood by the police when she pointed out Milton Lantigua as the man who had fired the gun. Mr. Lantigua was charged and jailed in the shooting.

The woman, Frances Rosario, became the chief witness against him, even though an appeals court would later say that her trial testimony was "confusing, inarticulate, vague, frequently inaudible and extremely hesitant."

One curiosity was that she repeatedly spoke as if she had been with someone else at the time of the killing, using "we" rather than "I" in recalling what she had seen. But when asked about the discrepancy during cross-examination, she told the jury: "I was probably nervous and I said 'we.' I was by myself."

After Mr. Lantigua's first trial ended in a hung jury, prosecutors offered him a deal, he recalled: plead guilty to a lesser charge of weapons possession, and be sentenced only to time served—an extraordinary outcome for a man who had been accused of murder. "They would let me go," he said.

He refused the offer, he said, because he was not guilty of anything. He was retried, convicted of second-degree murder and sentenced to 20 years to life in prison.

But in the meantime, new questions about the reliability of the prosecution's key witness, Ms. Rosario, had emerged. A new defense lawyer, Joel S. Cohen, obtained an affidavit in which she recanted her testimony that Mr. Lantigua had been involved in the shooting. In a hearing, a prosecutor revealed that Ms. Rosario had told the prosecution that she had in fact been with a man, identified only as Jo-Jo, on the night of shooting.

And as an appeals court would later rule, the prosecution let Ms. Rosario testify falsely that she had been alone.

That ruling, handed down in 1996 by the Appellate Division of State Supreme Court, threw out Mr. Lantigua's conviction, saying he had been denied a fair trial because of errors, and conduct by prosecutors that it called "especially egregious." In strong language, the court said the prosecution's failure to disclose the existence of the potential new witness had denied the defense the opportunity to investigate what that witness might have observed, or to meaningfully cross-examine Ms. Rosario on "her whereabouts, her view of the unfolding events, any distractions caused by the presence of another person, and her general credibility."

The ruling cited the failure of the trial prosecutor, Sophia Yozawitz, to correct Ms. Rosario's testimony that she had been alone during the shooting. "The prosecutor permitted the statement to remain on the record without informing the court that it was perjured," the court said, adding that a prosecutor "is charged with the duty not only to seek convictions but also to see that justice is done." The court also found that Ms. Yozawitz had distorted evidence during her summation to the jury, which also warranted reversal.

Irving Cohen, the lawyer for Mr. Lantigua who negotiated a $300,000 settlement with New York State and is representing him in a civil-rights lawsuit against New York City, said the ruling revealed a lack of oversight and discipline in the district attorney's office. "I think the case was given to an assistant district attorney who, because of her lack of training and supervision in that office, was dedicated to getting a conviction without looking at the case in a critical way," he said.

Ms. Yozawitz left the district attorney's office before the conviction was reversed. Reached by telephone, she said she had been unfairly portrayed in the ruling, but could not comment because of Mr. Lantigua's pending lawsuit. "Otherwise," she said, "I wouldn't stop speaking."

In an earlier proceeding, she contended that Ms. Rosario had been credible, and that the potential new witness, Jo-Jo, would have corroborated the identification. His existence, she said, was not the kind of exculpatory information that prosecutors are obliged to turn over to the defense.

Senior aides to the district attorney offered a broad defense of their office's actions, noting that a judge had found Ms. Rosario's recantation not credible. Ms. Yozawitz's failure to correct Ms. Rosario's testimony that she had been alone was an honest mistake, they said.

Mr. Lantigua, who is now 33, suggests he has paid too great a price for the prosecution's errors. "They don't want to say they made a mistake," he said.

Evidence Left in a File

Alberto Ramos was 21 and had no criminal record when he took a part-time job in January 1984 as a teacher in the city-financed Concourse Day Care Center on East Mount Eden Avenue in the Bronx. A month later, a 5-year-old girl whose class he supervised during a 15-minute nap period accused him of raping her in a bathroom.

Mr. Ramos was actually one of five men charged, over three months, of raping or sexually abusing children at city day care centers in the Bronx. In the midst of a national fervor to aggressively prosecute sex abuse of children, he was convicted of first-degree rape and sentenced to 8 1/3 to 25 years in prison.

Even before the sentencing, he started a campaign to overturn his conviction, bringing numerous motions and appeals in state and federal courts, but to no avail.

Diana Farrell was a fast-rising 29-year-old prosecutor when she landed the Ramos case a month before the trial. She presented powerful testimony to jurors: the girl took the stand and re-enacted the rape, using dolls. A classmate testified that she had seen Mr. Ramos go into the bathroom with the 5-year-old. Medical records showed that the girl, who was first examined two days after the alleged incident, had vaginal bruising. Perhaps the strongest testimony came from a doctor who had examined the girl and concluded that she had been abused because she could provide "such an accurate description of everything that happened."

It took the jury less than a day to convict. But it took much longer for the remarkable turn of events that would eventually free Mr. Ramos.

Four years after Mr. Ramos went to prison, the city hired a private investigator, Anthony Judge, to help defend it against a civil suit brought by the girl's mother. He asked to see the case file of the Human Resources Administration, which had investigated the incident before Mr. Ramos was indicted.

"I was astounded to read what I read," Mr. Judge said in a recent interview. In the file were documents that the agency had sent Ms. Farrell in a manila envelope at the end of the trial. The documents showed inconsistencies in the girl's story: she had told social workers that Mr. Ramos did nothing but tape her mouth. Teachers had noted that before the alleged abuse, the girl showed extensive knowledge about sexual acts, was seen placing dolls "in an intercourse position" and masturbated frequently in class, according to the documents.

Neither the jury nor the defense in Mr. Ramos's trial ever saw those documents, because the prosecution never turned them over, a judge later ruled. All but two of the documents were later discovered in Ms. Farrell's file. But in an interview, Ms. Farrell said she never saw them and did not know how they got there. She said she had seen a statement from a day care teacher and a document that mentioned the girl's masturbating and sexual knowledge. She did not turn these over to the defense, she said, because she did not think they qualified as exculpatory evidence.

The private investigator shared the documents with Mr. Ramos's mother in 1991, after the city settled with the girl's mother. Mr. Ramos hired Mr. Rudin, who was representing three of the other men accused of sex abuse in the day care centers. And in June 1992, Mr. Ramos's conviction was vacated in a State Supreme Court ruling that found that the prosecutor had failed to turn over evidence during his trial that could have led to his acquittal.

"The greatest crime of all is an unjust conviction," Judge John P. Collins said. "It is truly a scandal which reflects unfavorably on all participants in the criminal justice system."

Shortly after the ruling, the State Supreme Court's Departmental Disciplinary Committee, which looks into complaints of wrongdoing by lawyers, opened an investigation into Ms. Farrell's conduct during the trial. The Bronx district attorney asked the committee to hold off its investigation pending an appeal of the reversal. In 1993, Ms. Farrell resigned because of personal reasons, she said.

In 1994, an appeals court panel affirmed the decision vacating the conviction, and the disciplinary committee proceeded with its investigation.

The committee's procedures and findings are usually kept secret unless a decision is made to take public action, like censuring, suspending or disbarring a lawyer. The panel questioned Ms. Farrell several times, then dropped the investigation, said Ms. Farrell and officials in the district attorney's office.

"If they thought I had done something improper, there would have been a letter, a censure," said Ms. Farrell, who is retired. "I know I've done nothing wrong."

Mr. Rudin questioned why the committee did not allow him to present evidence about the case, aside from a transcript of the appeals hearing.

All four of the other Bronx sex-abuse cases were eventually overturned. Mr. Ramos's $5 million check arrived at his lawyer's office in the mail on Dec. 5, but he is angry that prosecutors were never seriously disciplined. "They had in their possession a lot of favorable evidence that would have helped me greatly," said Mr. Ramos, who is now 41, "and they just chose to keep it under the table."

Crossing a Fine Line

Not all examples of prosecutorial misconduct involve failing to turn over critical evidence or allowing jurors to hear false testimony. But the consequences of even lesser violations can be serious: convictions may be reversed, even some that may be supported by the evidence.

Three times over the career of William E. Racolin, another Bronx prosecutor, he was cited by appeals courts for violations. Two of the cases were reversed in the mid-1980's, and the third in 1992. In each ruling, judges found problems with his cross-examination tactics, his summation, or both. In the third case, People v. Butler, a judge cited errors by Mr. Racolin in his summation.

The decision cited, for example, inflammatory comments by Mr. Racolin during his summation, including, "It's a tragedy for good people to have to listen to defendant's contentions." After the defense objected, he continued, "And it is pure, unadulterated hogwash."

The defendant, Kevin Butler, who was convicted of fatally shooting Ismael Quiles in 1988, later pleaded guilty to manslaughter and is still serving his prison sentence, said Martin Lucente, the lawyer who represented Mr. Butler in his appeal.

"There are many, many fine lines that a prosecutor has to face," said Mr. Racolin, 59, who is retired. "If you're going to try to impeach the evidence that is presented by the defense, it is almost impossible not to make a mistake." An official in the prosecutor's office said that after the reversal in the Butler case, the only one of the three involving Mr. Racolin to occur during Mr. Johnson's tenure as district attorney, "Mr. Racolin was reprimanded by his supervisor, and based on the totality of his performance, including this case, he received no pay increases for the next two years."

Mr. Racolin recalled in an interview that he was spoken to after the reversal, although he said he did not remember being denied pay increases. Regardless, he said, he always strove to respect the rights of defendants, and did not think his mistakes were significant enough to warrant reversal.

Whoever is right, it is clear that prosecutors in Mr. Johnson's office feel perceptions of prosecutorial abuses are exaggerated. "The term 'prosecutorial misconduct' is very broad," Mr. Johnson said, "and could run the gamut from an inadvertent error to an intentional abuse, and rarely have we seen a flagrant abuse which would be subject to appropriate administrative action."

But critics question whether prosecutors' offices in the Bronx and around the country are understating the seriousness of the problem and the need for more discipline. "It's so infrequent," said Bennett L. Gershman, a Pace Law School professor and former assistant Manhattan district attorney, "that you have to say that these offices have an ethos or culture where they don't want to deter their lawyers from being aggressive, being champions of the victims."

UNIT 5
Juvenile Justice

Unit Selections

Key Points to Consider

- What reform efforts are currently under way in the juvenile justice system?

- What are some recent trends in juvenile delinquency? In what ways will the juvenile justice system be affected by these trends?

- Is the departure of the juvenile justice system from its original purpose warranted? Why or why not?

 **Links: www.dushkin.com/online/**
These sites are annotated in the World Wide Web pages.

Gang Land: The Jerry Capeci Page
http://www.ganglandnews.com
Institute for Intergovernmental Research (IIR)
http://www.iir.com
National Criminal Justice Reference Service (NCJRS)
http://virlib.ncjrs.org/JuvenileJustice.asp
Partnership Against Violence Network
http://www.pavnet.org

Although there were variations within specific offense categories, the overall arrest rate for juvenile violent crime remained relatively constant for several decades. Then, in the late 1980s something changed, bringing more and more juveniles charged with a violent offense into the justice system. The juvenile justice system is a twentieth century response to the problems of dealing with children in trouble with the law or children who need society's protection.

Juvenile court procedure differs from the procedure in adult courts because juvenile courts are based on the philosophy that their function is to treat and to help, not to punish and abandon the offender. Recently, operations of the juvenile court have received criticism, and a number of significant Supreme Court decisions have changed the way that the courts must approach the rights of children. Despite these changes, however, the major thrust of the juvenile justice system remains one of diversion and treatment, rather than adjudication and incarceration, although there is a trend toward dealing more punitively with serious juvenile offenders.

This unit's opening essay, "Sentencing Guidelines and the Transformation of Juvenile Justice in the 21st Century," makes the argument that the past decade witnessed dramatic changes to juvenile justice in America, and that these changes are altering the focus and administration of juvenile justice as it enters the twenty-first century.

"A Century of Revolutionary Changes in the United States Juvenile Court Systems" points out that today's juvenile court is so different from the original court, and more similar to the criminal courts, than at any prior time in the past century. This turnabout raises the question as to whether a separate juvenile court is any longer needed. In spite of numerous studies casting doubt on DARE's effectiveness, "DARE Program: Sacred Cow or Fatted Calf?" points out that these programs continue through the country.

The next article in this unit by Judge James Gray, "The Peer Court Experience," provides insight into a unique court run by teenagers, which currently exits in 46 states. Concluding this section, Corrie Pikul reports on a new public service ad campaign reminding men that sex with a minor is a crime, in "Isn't She a Little Young?"

Sentencing Guidelines and the Transformation of Juvenile Justice in the 21st Century

As we enter the 21st century, many states have introduced fundamental changes to their juvenile justice systems. The changes focus on jurisdictional authority, especially transfer to adult court; sentencing guidelines and options; correctional programming; interagency information sharing; offender confidentiality; and victim involvement. At the same time, attention has turned increasingly to prevention, early intervention, rehabilitation, and the use of specialized courts. Because of their special significance in the historical context of the juvenile court, this article focuses on the emergence of sentencing guidelines to identify underlying trends and issues in the transformation of juvenile justice. In so doing, the article argues that the considerable attention given by policy makers and researchers to transfer rather than other changes provides a distorted picture of current juvenile justice practice.

DANIEL P. MEARS
The Urban Institute

The past decade witnessed dramatic changes to juvenile justice in America, changes that have altered the focus and administration of juvenile justice as it enters the 21st century (Butts & Mitchell, 2000; Feld, 1991; Harris, Welsh, & Butler, 2000). In contrast to the philosophical foundation and practice of the first juvenile courts, punishment and due process today constitute central features of processing. These emphases, which run counter to the rehabilitative *parens patriae* ("state as parent") foundation of the first juvenile courts, emerged in the 1960s with a series of U.S. Supreme Court decisions. In cases such as *In re Gault*, the Supreme Court recognized that juvenile courts served not only a rehabilitative function but also a punishment function, and that consequently due process rights and procedures should figure more prominently in juvenile proceedings (Feld, 1999). In recent years, the transition has become more pronounced, with states enacting sweeping legislative changes affecting all aspects of the juvenile justice system (National Criminal Justice

Association, 1997; Torbet et al., 1996; Torbet & Szymanski, 1998).

It is important to recognize, however, that the changes have not been entirely or even primarily focused on punishment. One would not know this from a review of research, the bulk of which has examined patterns, correlates, and effects of transfer (for a review, see Butts & Mitchell, 2000). The focus is understandable—transfer provides an easily identifiable symbol for debates about the merits of maintaining two separate juvenile and adult systems (Feld, 1999; Hirschi & Gottfredson, 1993). Indeed, why have a juvenile justice system if youth are being sent into adult courts? But the fact is that only about 1% of all formally processed delinquency cases ultimately are transferred (Snyder & Sickmund, 1999, p. 171).

Focusing solely on transfer ignores the fact that other equally, if not more significant, transformations have occurred in juvenile justice. These include enactment of sentencing guidelines; creation of blended sentencing options for linking the juvenile and criminal justice systems; enhanced correctional programming, with an increasing emphasis on treatment; greater interagency and cross-jurisdiction cooperation and information sharing; reduced confidentiality of court records and proceedings; and increased participation of victims in juvenile justice processing (Fagan & Zimring, 2000; Guarino-Ghezzi & Loughran, 1996; National Criminal Justice Association, 1997; Torbet et al., 1996). In addition, states increasingly are turning their attention to prevention, early intervention, rehabilitation, and the use of specialized courts to address juvenile crime (Butts & Harrell, 1998; Butts & Mears, 2001; Cocozza & Skowyra, 2000; Coordinating Council on Juvenile Justice and Delinquency Prevention, 1996; Cullen & Gendreau, 2000; Howell, 1995; Lipsey, Wilson, & Cothern, 2000; Rivers & Anwyl, 2000).

It is apparent that juvenile justice has been evolving along many dimensions. With all of these changes, the question arises: What, if any, are the common trends and issues underlying these different changes? To answer this question, I examine sentencing guidelines, showing that they reflect many of the major trends and issues in juvenile justice. I focus on guidelines because typically they apply to all juvenile offenders and embody a range of goals, thus reflecting many of the conflicts and tensions inherent in attempts to modify the focus and administration of juvenile justice. By contrast, transfer laws, which have received much more attention in the research literature, focus only on select age groups and offenders and have the delimited purpose of punishing and deterring offenders.

The primary goal of this article, in short, is to use an analysis of sentencing guidelines to highlight a range of critical underlying trends and issues in juvenile justice. A secondary goal is to show that research on transfer laws provides little insight into juvenile justice as it is practiced today and, in the absence of research on or attention to other reforms, can provide a distorted picture of current practice. To achieve these goals, I begin by briefly describing the history of the juvenile court and the emergence of juvenile sentencing guidelines. I then use this discussion to identify key trends and issues in juvenile justice.

FOUNDATION OF THE JUVENILE JUSTICE SYSTEM

Juveniles have not always been viewed the same way throughout U.S. history. For example, in the 18th century, juvenile offenders were treated as adults and received the same types of punishments. During the 19th century, a movement began that focused on the unique, less-than-adult capacities and needs of youth. This movement highlighted the need for a specialized sanctioning process, one that emphasized rehabilitation and deemphasized punishment.

The result of this movement was the development of the first U.S. juvenile court in Cook County, Illinois, in 1899. By 1925, juvenile courts were established in all but two states, with most courts defining juveniles as individuals who were aged 17 years or younger. (For histories of the juvenile court, see Platt [1977], Bernard [1992], Feld [1999], and Butts and Mitchell [2000].)

These new youth-centered courts were grounded in the doctrine of parens patriae. The guiding rationale was that states had an obligation to intervene in the lives of children whose parents provided inadequate care or supervision. Juvenile court interventions were to be benevolent and in the "best interests" of the child.

For this reason, court processing entailed fundamentally different notions of procedural and substantive justice. Unlike adult court proceedings, juvenile court proceedings were to be informal and conducted on a case-by-case basis, with the aim of improving the lives of children through individualized treatment and varying dispositional options, ranging from warnings to probation to confinement.

The basis for intervening in the lives of juvenile offenders derived not from criminal law but civil law, further highlighting the focus on helping youth rather than sanctioning them for their crimes. Similarly, the philosophy of parens patriae clearly suggested that the courts had an obligation to help youth who committed crimes or who clearly needed help. As a result, juvenile courts could use coercive means to help youth, even when relatively minor crimes had been committed or when there was insufficient basis for determining that a crime in fact was committed.

The potential for abuse of this discretionary authority is evident in critiques of the juvenile court (see Feld, 1999). Indeed, as many scholars have shown, the transition to establishing a juvenile justice system was not motivated entirely by benevolent concerns. Under the guise of providing social services and crime control, juvenile courts could, for example, be used instead to provide a form of social control over "undesirable classes," including minorities, immigrants, and indigents (Butts & Mitchell, 2000).

By the 1960s, deep-rooted concerns arose about the procedural and substantive unfairness of juvenile court proceedings, leading the U.S. Supreme Court, through a series of decisions, to emphasize greater procedural parity with criminal court proceedings. The result was an increasingly criminal-like juvenile court. This trend, coupled with tougher transfer provisions in the 1990s, led to considerable debate about the merits of having two separate court systems, one for juveniles and one for adults (Feld, 1999).

JUVENILE SENTENCING GUIDELINES: AN OVERVIEW

The early juvenile court emphasized individualized, offender-based treatment and sanctioning. Indeed, almost every justification of the juvenile court rests on the notion that the most appropriate and effective intervention for youth is one that takes into account their particular needs and resources. Ironically, despite the establishment of this view more than 100 years ago, recent research provides considerable empirical support for it—the most effective interventions are those premised on addressing the specific risk, needs, and capacities of youth (Cullen & Gendreau, 2000; Lipsey, 1999).

Under the Office of Juvenile Justice and Delinquency Prevention's (OJJDP's) Comprehensive Strategy for Serious, Violent, and Chronic Juvenile Offenders (Howell, 1995; Wilson & Howell, 1993), states have been encouraged to adopt individualized sanctioning and to emphasize risk and needs assessment. Many have responded by enacting guideline systems that are modeled to a considerable extent on the Comprehensive Strategy.

In some states, these guideline systems are voluntary, in others there are incentives to use them, and in still others they are required. In each instance, the guidelines typically are offense-based and outline a sequence of increasingly tougher sanctions, while at the same time emphasizing rehabilitative interventions when appropriate.

In 1995, for example, Texas enacted what it termed the Progressive Sanctions Guidelines. The Guidelines outline seven tiers of sanctioning, with each linked to the instant offense and the offender's prior record. Once the appropriate level of sanctioning is established, courts are encouraged to include additional, nonpunitive interventions. Although the Guidelines are voluntary, Texas documents the extent to which county-level sanctioning deviates from the recommendations of the Guidelines (Texas Criminal Justice Policy Council, 2001). Similar approaches have been implemented in other states, including Illinois, Kansas, Nebraska, New York, Utah, Virginia, and Washington (Corriero, 1999; Demleitner, 1999; Fagan & Zimring, 2000; Lieb & Brown, 1999; National Criminal Justice Association, 1997; Torbet et al., 1996).

State guideline systems often identify their goals explicitly. In Texas, for example, the Progressive Sanction Guidelines are used to "guide" dispositional decision making in providing "appropriate" sanctions and to promote "uniformity" and "consistency" in sentencing (Dawson, 1996). At the same time, the Guidelines are seen as furthering the newly established and explicitly stated goal of the Texas Juvenile Justice Code—namely, punishment of juveniles. But they also promote rehabilitative sanctioning by encouraging appropriate treatment and interventions for each recommended sanction level. In addition, the Guidelines implicitly promote certain goals, including public safety through incapacitation of the most serious or chronic offenders and reduced crime through get-tough, deterrence-oriented sanctioning.

Other states have followed similar paths. For example, Washington established sentencing guidelines aimed directly at reducing the perceived failings of a system founded on practitioner discretion (Lieb & Brown, 1999). The guidelines focus not only on offense-based consider-

ations but also on the juvenile's age, with younger offenders receiving fewer "points" and thus more lenient sanctions. Similarly, Utah has enacted sentencing guidelines focusing on proportionate sentencing, early intervention, and progressively intensive supervision and sanctioning for more serious and chronic offenders (Utah Sentencing Commission, 1997).

Because many states increasingly are adopting sentencing guidelines and because the guidelines focus on all youth rather than simply those who may be transferred, an examination of them can help to identify underlying trends and issues emergent in juvenile justice. By contrast, a focus on transfer, typical of most research on recent reforms, provides relatively little leverage to do so. Transfer laws typically focus on "easy cases," those in which the seriousness of the offense largely vitiates, rightly or wrongly, concerns many would have about individualized or rehabilitative sanctioning. Any resulting debate therefore centers on extremes: Should we retain or eliminate the juvenile court?

But a broader issue in juvenile justice is how to balance individualized, offender-based sanctioning with proportional and consistent punishment. These issues, among several others, are a consideration in almost every case coming before the juvenile court. It is appropriate, therefore, to focus on a recent reform, such as sentencing guidelines, that typically target, in one manner or another, all youth and that reflects attempts to shape the entire juvenile justice system. For this reason, the remainder of this article uses a focus on sentencing guidelines to identify key trends and issues in the transformation of juvenile justice.

JUVENILE SENTENCING GUIDELINES: TRENDS AND ISSUES IN THE TRANSFORMATION OF JUVENILE JUSTICE IN THE NEW MILLENNIUM

Balancing Multiple and Conflicting Goals

The motivation for transforming juvenile justice has come from many sources. Scholars cite a range of factors, including the desire to address violent crime, inconsistency and racial/ethnic disproportionality in sentencing, financial burdens faced by counties versus states, and public support for get-tough and rehabilitative measures (Bazemore & Umbreit, 1995; Bishop, Lanza-Kaduce, & Frazier, 1998; Butts & Mitchell, 2000).

As suggested by the different motivations for reform, a key trend in juvenile justice is the move toward balancing multiple and frequently competing goals, only one of which includes the punitive focus associated with transfer (Bazemore & Umbreit, 1995; Guarino-Ghezzi & Loughran, 1996; Mears, 2000). Today, many juvenile justice codes and policies focus on retributive/punitive sanctioning (through get-tough sanctions generally), incapacitation, deterrence, rehabilitation, individualized as well as consistent and proportional sentencing, and re-storative sanctioning.

Reduced crime is a broad goal underlying many but not all of these more specific goals. For example, get-tough sanctions are viewed as a primary mechanism to instill fear and achieve specific or general deterrence (i.e., reduced offending among sanctioned or would-be of-fenders) or to reduce crime through temporary incapaci-tation of offenders. In many instances, retribution serves as the primary focus of sanctioning, irrespective of any potential crime control impact.

Some goals, like rehabilitation, serve as steps toward enhancing the lives of juveniles, not simply reducing their offending. Others, such as restorative sanctioning, focus on reintegrating offenders into their communities while at the same time providing victims with a voice in the sanctioning and justice process. Still others, including proportional and consistent sentencing, focus primarily on fairness rather than crime control. That is, the motiva-tion is to provide sanctions that are proportional to the crime and that are consistent within and across jurisdic-tions so that juveniles sanctioned by Judge X or in County X receive sanctions similar to those administered by Judge Y or in County Y.

Historically these different goals, including what might be termed intermediate goals leading to reduced crime, have overlapped considerably with those of the criminal justice system (Snyder & Sickmund, 1999, pp. 94–96). In general, though, criminal justice systems have given greater weight to punishment than rehabilitation, whereas juvenile justice systems generally have favored rehabilitation more than punishment.

In reality, the goals in each system are diverse, as are the weightings given to each goal. Indeed, the diversity of goals and their weighting can make it difficult to deter-mine how exactly the two systems differ, especially if we focus only on new transfer laws (see, however, Bishop & Frazier, 2000). But one major difference between the two is that juvenile justice systems—as is evident in their sentenc-ing guideline systems—are actively struggling to balance as wide a range of goals as possible. By contrast, most crim-inal justice systems have veered strongly toward retribu-tion and incapacitation (Clark, Austin, & Henry, 1997).

Giving Priority to Punishment Through Offense-Based Guidelines and Changes in Discretion

Most state guideline systems use offense-based criteria for determining which types of sanctions to apply (Cool-baugh & Hansel, 2000). Once the punishment level has been established, the court is supposed to consider the needs of the offender and how these may best be ad-dressed. However, these needs frequently are only vaguely specified and rarely assessed. One result is that priority implicitly and in practice may be given to punish-ment.

This priority can be reinforced through various mech-anisms that place greater discretion in the hands of pros-ecutors rather than judges. For example, laws that stipulate automatic sanctions for certain offenses do not eliminate discretion; instead, they shift it to prosecutors, who can determine whether and how to charge an offense (Feld, 1999; Mears, 2000; Sanborn, 1994; Singer, 1996). Consequently, in practice, many guideline systems make punishment a priority not just for youth who may be transferred but for all youth referred to juvenile court.

Sentencing guidelines have not gone unopposed. For example, research on the Texas Progressive Sanction Guidelines indicates that many judges resisted enactment of the Guidelines and then, once they became law, re-sisted using them (Mears, 2000). One reason is their belief that offense-based criteria provide too limited a basis for structuring decision making. Thus, even though compli-ance with the Guidelines is voluntary, some judges feel that the Guidelines symbolize too narrow a focus, one that draws attention from factors they believe are more important, such as the age and maturity of the youth and their family and community contexts. Such concerns have been expressed about adult sentencing guidelines (e.g., see Forer, 1994). One difference with juvenile sentencing guidelines is that, despite the views of opponents, they generally state explicitly that there are multiple goals as-sociated with sanctioning and that practitioners should consider a range of mitigating factors (Howell, 1995).

Balancing Discretion Versus Disparity and Consistency, and Procedural Versus Substantive Justice

In stark contrast to the early foundation of the juvenile court, many states today are intent on eliminating dispar-ity and inconsistency in sentencing (Feld, 1999; Torbet et al., 1996). The widespread belief, evident in many sen-tencing guidelines, is that (a) judicial discretion causes disparity and inconsistency and (b) that offense-based systems can eliminate or reduce these problems. Both be-liefs prevail despite the fact that little empirical evidence exists to support them (Mears & Field, 2000; Sanborn, 1994; Yellen, 1999).

But the fact that such strategies may not work does not belie that underlying trend toward discovering ways to promote fairness and consistency in sentencing. Nor does it belie the fact that, as with adult sanctioning, there likely will continue to be an ongoing tension between the use of discretion and the need to have sanctions that are rela-tively similar for different populations and within and across jurisdictions.

This tension is captured in part by the distinction in the sociology of law between procedural and substantive jus-tice. From the perspective of procedural justice, fairness emerges from decisions that are guided by established rules and procedures for sanctioning cases that exhibit specific characteristics. By contrast, from the perspective of substantive justice, fairness emerges from decisions that are guided by consideration of the unique situational context and characteristics of the defendant (Gould, 1993; Ulmer & Kramer, 1996).

In recent years, and as exemplified by the creation of offense-based sentencing guidelines, juvenile justice systems increasingly are focusing on procedural justice. In the case of transfer particularly, the Supreme Court and state legislatures have attempted to ensure that there is procedural parity with adult proceedings. Yet despite the increased proceduralization, for most cases facing the juvenile courts, substantive justice also remains a priority, especially when sanctioning first-time and less serious offenders. In these instances, states have devised strategies, outlined in their guidelines, that promote diversion, rehabilitation, and treatment.

Maintaining the View That Most Youth Are "Youth," Not Adults

Public opinion polls show that whereas most people consistently support rehabilitative sanctioning of youth, they also support punitive, get-tough measures for serious and violent offenders (Roberts & Stalans, 1998). Moreover, even when the public supports transferring youth to the adult system, they generally prefer youth to be housed in separate facilities and to receive individualized, rehabilitative treatment (Schwartz, Guo, & Kerbs, 1993).

The apparent contradiction likely constitutes the primary reason that wholesale elimination of the juvenile justice system has not prevailed. In the debate about abolishing the juvenile court, this fact frequently is omitted, perhaps because so much attention has centered on changes in transfer laws. Indeed, were one to focus solely on recent trends in transfer, one might conclude that an eventual merging of juvenile and adult systems is inevitable (Feld, 1999).

Yet the focus and structure of juvenile sentencing guidelines, which explicitly call for rehabilitation and early intervention, suggest otherwise. In contrast to get-tough developments in the criminal justice system (Clark et al., 1997), most states—even those without guideline systems—have struggled to maintain a focus not only on the most violent offenders but also on efficient and effective intervention with less serious offenders.

This trend is reflected in the proliferation of alternative, or specialized, courts, including community, teen, drug, and mental health courts (Butts & Harrell, 1998; Office of Justice Programs, 1998; Santa Clara County Superior Court, 2001). These courts focus on timely and rehabilitative sanctioning that draws on the strengths of families and communities and the cooperation and assistance of local and state agencies.

Some authors suggest that these courts threaten the foundation of the juvenile court (Butts & Harrell, 1998). But specialized courts can be viewed as symbolic of the reemergence of the juvenile justice system as historically conceived—namely, as a system designed to intervene on an individualized, case-by-case basis, addressing the particular risks and needs of offenders (Butts & Mears, 2001). Indeed, to this end, many guidelines promote diversion of first- and second-time, less serious offenders from formal processing to informal alternatives available through specialized courts.

Limited Conceptualization and Assessment of the Implementation and Effects of Changes in the Juvenile Justice System

One last and prominent trend in juvenile justice bears emphasizing—the lack of systematic attention to conceptualizing and assessing the implementation and effects of recently enacted laws. A focus on sentencing guidelines illustrates the point: Few states have systematically articulated precisely what the goals of the guidelines are, how specifically the guidelines are expected to achieve these goals, or what in fact the effects of the guidelines have been (Coolbaugh & Hansel, 2000; Fagan & Zimring, 2000; Mears, 2000).

One example common to many guidelines is the focus on consistency. Several questions illustrate the point. What exactly does *consistency* mean? Is it identical sentencing of like offenders within jurisdictions? Across jurisdictions? Does it involve similar weighting of the same factors by all judges or judges within each jurisdiction in a state? Across states? Apart from definitional issues, does consistency lead to reduced crime or increased perceptions of fairness? If so, how? What precisely are the mechanisms by which increased consistency would lead to changes in crime or perceptions of fairness? The failure to address these questions means that it is impossible to assess whether there has been more or less consistency resulting from guideline systems.

Similar questions about many other aspects of recent juvenile justice reforms remain largely unaddressed, with two unfortunate consequences. First, as noted above, it is impossible to assess the effects of the reforms without greater clarity concerning their goals and the means by which these goals are to be reached. As a result, it is difficult if not impossible to make informed policy decisions, including those focusing on maintaining or eliminating the juvenile justice system (Schneider, 1984; Singer, 1996). Second, without conceptualization and assessment of the effects of recent reforms, there is an increased likelihood that research on delimited aspects of juvenile justice systems will be generalized into statements about entire systems, even though there may be little to no correspondence between the two.

CONCLUSION

Recent changes to juvenile justice systems throughout the United States indicate a trend toward developing more efficient and effective strategies for balancing different and frequently competing goals. This trend is evident in recent juvenile sentencing guidelines. As the above discussion demonstrates, guidelines focus on more than transferring the most serious offenders to the criminal justice system. They also focus on balancing competing goals, reducing discretion and promoting fair and consistent sanctioning, and tempering procedural with substantive justice. More generally, guidelines aim to preserve the notion that youth are not adults.

One result of such trends is increasing interest in alternative administrative mechanisms for processing youthful offenders. Specialized "community," "teen," "drug," "mental health," and other such courts have been developed to do what the original juvenile court was supposed to do—provide individualized and rehabilitative sanctioning. But the "modern" approach involves doing so in a more timely and sophisticated fashion, and in a way that draws on the cooperation and assistance of local and state agencies as well as families and communities.

In the new millennium, juvenile justice thus involves more than an emphasis on due process and punishment. It also involves substantive concerns, including a range of competing goals, a belief in the special status of childhood, and the desire to develop more effective strategies for preventing and reducing juvenile crime.

By focusing on sentencing guidelines, these types of issues become more apparent, highlighting the need for researchers to look beyond transfer laws in assessing recent juvenile justice reforms. Indeed, there is a need for research on many new and different laws, polices, and programs in juvenile justice, most of which remain unassessed. As we enter the new millennium, it will be critical to redress this situation, especially if we are to move juvenile justice beyond "juvenile" versus "adult" debates and to develop more efficient and effective interventions.

REFERENCES

Bazemore, G., & Umbreit, M. (1995). Rethinking the sanctioning function in juvenile court: Retributive or restorative responses to youth crime. *Crime & Delinquency, 41,* 296–316.

Bernard, T. J. (1992). *The cycle of juvenile justice.* New York: Oxford University Press.

Bishop, D. M., & Frazier, C. E. (2000). Consequences of transfer. In J. Fagan & F. E. Zimring (Eds.), *The changing boundaries of juvenile justice: Transfer of adolescents to the criminal court* (pp. 227–276). Chicago: University of Chicago Press.

Bishop, D. M., Lanza-Kaduce, L., & Frazier, C. E. (1998). Juvenile justice under attack: An analysis of the causes and impact of recent reforms. *Journal of Law and Public Policy, 10,* 129–155.

Butts, J. A., & Harrell, A. V. (1998). *Delinquents or criminals? Policy options for juvenile offenders.* Washington, DC: The Urban Institute.

Butts, J. A., & Mears, D. P. (2001). Reviving juvenile justice in a get-tough era. *Youth & Society, 33,* 169–198.

Butts, J. A., & Mitchell, O. (2000). Brick by brick: Dismantling the border between juvenile and adult justice. In C. M. Friel (Ed.), *Criminal justice 2000: Boundary changes in criminal justice organizations* (Vol. 2, pp. 167–213). Washington, DC: National Institute of Justice.

Clark, J., Austin, J., & Henry, D. A. (1997). *"Three strikes and you're out": A review of state legislation.* Washington: DC: National Institute of Justice.

Cocozza, J. J., & Skowyra, K. (2000). Youth with mental health disorders: Issues and emerging responses. *Juvenile Justice, 7,* 3–13.

Coolbaugh, K., & Hansel, C. J. (2000). *The comprehensive strategy: Lessons learned from the pilot sites.* Washington, DC: Office of Juvenile Justice and Delinquency Prevention.

Coordinating Council on Juvenile Justice and Delinquency Prevention. (1996). *Combating violence and delinquency: The national juvenile justice action plan.* Washington, DC: Office of Juvenile Justice and Delinquency Prevention.

Corriero, M. A. (1999). Juvenile sentencing: The New York youth part as a model. *Federal Sentencing Reporter, 11,* 278–281.

Cullen, F. T., & Gendreau, P. (2000). Assessing correctional rehabilitation: Policy, practice, and prospects. In J. Horney (Ed.), *Criminal justice 2000: Policies, processes, and decisions of the criminal justice system* (Vol. 3, pp. 109–175). Washington, DC: National Institute of Justice.

Dawson, R. O. (1996). *Texas juvenile law* (4th ed.). Austin: Texas Juvenile Probation Commission.

Demleitner, N. V. (1999). Reforming juvenile sentencing. *Federal Sentencing Reporter, 11,* 243–247.

Fagan, J., & Zimring, F. E. (Eds.). (2000). *The changing borders of juvenile justice.* Chicago: University of Chicago Press.

Feld, B. C. (1991). The transformation of the juvenile court. *Minnesota Law Review, 75,* 691–725.

Feld, B. C. (1999). *Bad kids: Race and the transformation of the juvenile court.* New York: Oxford University Press.

Forer, L. (1994). *A rage to punish: The unintended consequences of mandatory sentencing.* New York: Norton.

Gould, M. (1993). Legitimation and justification: The logic or moral and contractual solidarity in Weber and Durkheim. *Social Theory, 13,* 205–225.

Guarino-Ghezzi, S., & Loughran, E. J. (1996). *Balancing juvenile justice.* New Brunswick, NJ: Transaction.

Harris, P. W., Welsh, W. N., & Butler, F. (2000). A century of juvenile justice. In G. LaFree (Ed.), *Criminal justice 2000: The nature of crime: Continuity and change* (Vol. 1, pp. 359–425). Washington, DC: National Institute of Justice.

Hirschi, T., & Gottfredson, M. R. (1993). Rethinking the juvenile justice system. *Crime & Delinquency, 39,* 262–271.

Howell, J. C. (1995). *Guide for implementing the comprehensive strategy for serious, violent, and chronic juvenile offenders.* Washington, DC: Office of Juvenile Justice and Delinquency Prevention.

Lieb, R., & Brown, M. E. (1990). Washington state's solo path: Juvenile sentencing guidelines. *Federal Sentencing Reporter, 11,* 273–277.

Lipsey, M. W. (1999). Can rehabilitative programs reduce the recidivism of juvenile offenders? An inquiry into the effectiveness of practical programs. *Virginia Journal of Social Policy and Law, 6,* 611–641.

Lipsey, M. W., Wilson, D. B., & Cothern, L. (2000). *Effective intervention for serious juvenile offenders.* Washington, DC: Office of Juvenile Justice and Delinquency Prevention.

Mears, D. P. (2000). Assessing the effectiveness of juvenile justice reforms: A closer look at the criteria and impacts on diverse stakeholders. *Law and Policy, 22,* 175–202.

Mears, D. P., & Field, S. H. (2000). Theorizing sanctioning in a criminalized juvenile court. *Criminology, 38,* 101–137.

National Criminal Justice Association. (1997). *Juvenile justice reform initiatives in the states: 1994–1996.* Washington, DC: Office of Juvenile Justice and Delinquency Prevention.

Office of Justice Programs. (1998). *Juvenile and family drug courts: An overview.* Washington, DC: Author.

Platt, A. M. (1977). *The child savers: The invention of delinquency.* Chicago: University of Chicago Press.

Rivers, J. E., & Anwyl, R. S. (2000). Juvenile assessment centers: Strengths, weaknesses, and potential. *The Prison Journal, 80,* 96–113.

Roberts, J. V., & Stalans, L. J. (1998). Crime, criminal justice, and public opinion. In M. Tonry (Ed.), *The handbook of crime and punishment* (pp. 31–57). New York: Oxford University Press.

Sanborn, J. A. (1994). Certification to criminal court: The important policy questions of how, when, and why. *Crime & Delinquency, 40,* 262–281.

Santa Clara County Superior Court. (2001). *Santa Clara County Superior Court commences juvenile mental health court.* San Jose, CA: Author.

Schneider, A. L. (1984). Sentencing guidelines and recidivism rates of juvenile offenders. *Justice Quarterly, 1,* 107–124.

Schwartz, I. M., Guo, S., & Kerbs, J. J. (1993). The impact of demographic variables on public opinion regarding juvenile justice: Implications for public policy. *Crime & Delinquency, 39,* 5–28.

Singer, S. I. (1996). Merging and emerging systems of juvenile and criminal justice. *Law and Policy, 18,* 1–15.

Snyder, H. N., & Sickmund, M. (1999). *Juvenile offenders and victims: 1999 national report.* Washington, DC: Office of Juvenile Justice and Delinquency Prevention.

Texas Criminal Justice Policy Council. (2001). *The impact of progressive sanction guidelines: Trends since 1995.* Austin, TX: Author.

Torbet, P., Gable, R., Hurst, H. IV, Montgomery, I., Szymanski, L., & Thomas, D. (1996). *State responses to serious and violent juvenile crime.* Washington, DC: Office of Juvenile Justice and Delinquency Prevention.

Torbet, P., & Szymanski, L. (1998). *State legislative responses to violent juvenile crime: 1996–97 update.* Washington, DC: Office of Juvenile Justice and Delinquency Prevention.

Ulmer, J. T., & Kramer, J. H. (1996). Court communities under sentencing guidelines: Dilemmas of formal rationality and sentencing disparity. *Criminology, 34,* 383–407.

Utah Sentencing Commission. (1997). *Juvenile sentencing guidelines manual.* Salt Lake City, UT: Author.

Wilson, J. J., & Howell, J. C. (1993). *Comprehensive strategy for serious, violent, and chronic juvenile offenders: Program summary.* Washington, DC: Office of Juvenile Justice and Delinquency Prevention.

Yellen, D. (199). Sentence discounts and sentencing guidelines. *Federal Sentencing Reporter, 11,* 285–288.

Correspondence concerning this article should be addressed to Daniel P. Mears, The Urban Institute, 2100 M Street, Washington, D.C. 20037; phone: (202) 261-5592; fax: (202) 659-8985; e-mail: dmears@urban.org. The views in this article were those of the author and do not necessarily reflect those of The Urban Institute, its board or trustees, or its sponsors. The author gratefully acknowledges the constructive comments of the anonymous reviewers.

Daniel P. Mears, Ph.D., is a research associate in The Urban Institute's Justice Policy Center. His research focuses on the causes of crime and effective ways to prevent and intervene with crime and justice problems. He has conducted research on delinquency, juvenile and criminal justice programs and policies, domestic violence, immigration and crime, correctional forecasting, and drug treatment in prisons. Recent publications include articles in Criminal Justice and Behavior, Criminology, Journal of Research in Crime and Delinquency, Law and Society Review, *and* Sociological Perspectives.

A Century of Revolutionary Changes in the United States Court Systems

By Charles Lindner

Introduction

The first juvenile court in the United States was created in the city of Chicago in 1899. It was revolutionary in the sense that it removed juveniles from the jurisdiction of the adult criminal court and established a court exclusively for children.

Originally, the philosophy underlying the early juvenile court was the doctrine of parens patriae, manifested in "the best interests of the child." Accordingly, unlike the adult criminal court, treatment and protection of the child was accorded greater importance than punishment. In order to promote these goals, all due process rights of juveniles were waived, for at least in theory, the juvenile would be protected by a benign and benevolent judge.

In the 1960s and 1970s, a number of United States Supreme court rulings essentially reshaped the court process. Known as the due process model, juveniles were given rights essentially comparable to those providing legal protection to adults in the criminal court. Nevertheless, the concept of treatment and protection of the juvenile remained a major concern of the court.

The controlling model of the juvenile court shifted again in the mid-1980s. Consistent with the nationwide movement towards more punitive sentencing and due to increases in young-sters' crimes rates, the juvenile courts of the United States similarly shifted to increased sanctions. Similar to the "just deserts model" of the adult courts, the philosophy of the juvenile courts were not only concerned with the "best interests of the child," but now also gave consideration to the "protection of the community."

This article will review the creation of juvenile courts, the revolutionary changes which have reshaped the court system and current practices.

Living Conditions of Children in Large Cities in the 1800s

In the 1800s, life was brutal for children of impoverished families, especially those living in large cities. Families lived in overcrowded tenement apartments, without such amenities as indoor toilets, bathtubs or showers. It was not unusual for a single apartment to house several families, each having a single room and the use of a shared kitchen. In the absence of government funded welfare programs, some had to turn to the paltry handouts of private charitable agencies.

Life was especially difficult for the children of the poor. Many were encouraged to leave home and live on the street, as the families often neither had support nor room for their children. Many children under the age of ten left school to earn money by selling newspapers, running errands, rag-picking or petty thefts. Some went "junking" which was to find discarded wood, metal, rags and other materials and objects to sell to junk dealers for pennies. Many were encouraged by their family and friends to earn money through minor criminal acts, such as shoplifting or stealing coal for heating. For impoverished young women, prostitution was sometimes made necessary to support the family and to survive.

Conditions were especially harsh for immigrant families. Not only did most arrive without funds or resources, but their lives were made more difficult because of language difficulties, inadequate educations, a lack of relevant job skills, and culturally endorsed practices of having large numbers of children. Robert Ernst (1965: 52-3) provided a vivid portrait of conditions in New York City during the mid-1800s.

Life in the slums was a continual struggle against illness and death. The high incidence of disease in New York was directly related to the sanitary condition of tenement dwellers, of whom a large number were the foreign born or their children. In the crowded immigrant quarters quarantine was an impossibility, and communicable diseases erupted into epidemic proportions.

Jacob A. Riis (1890: 150-1), writing contemporaneously, found an army of homeless boys all over the city of New York. In answer to the question of where they came from, he stated:

> Some are orphans, actually or in effect … Sickness in the house, too many mouths to feed … There is very little to hold the boy who has never known anything but a house in a tenement. Very soon the wild life in the streets holds him fast, and thenceforward by his own effort there is no escape.

Over the years, reform groups sought to ameliorate the conditions of the poor, often by progressive legislation. This included a number of private charitable organizations, many of which were religiously oriented. However, in the absence of governmental welfare programs, there were simply too many poor and too few dollars.

Many reforms were specifically focused on children. A major attempt to rehabilitate troubled juveniles was the reform school movement. Juvenile correctional facilities were initially opened in the first half of the nineteenth century throughout the United States. Subsequently, state and municipal governments administered these institutions for juvenile delinquents "and by 1890, almost every state outside the south had a reform school, and many jurisdictions had separate facilities for male and female delinquents" (Krisberg and Austin, 1978: 21).

There were a number of precursors to the creation of a juvenile court, all of which were intended to improve the living conditions of youths from troubled families. The Houses of Refuge, the first of which was established in New York City in 1925 (Folks, 1902), were residential facilities intended to be benevolent and protective of the wayward children, many of whom were living in the street. In actuality, life in the Houses of Refuge was not easy and discipline was quite harsh:

Placing offenders on a diet of bread and water or depriving them of meals altogether were milder forms of discipline, but were coupled with solitary confinement if a severe punishment was deemed necessary. Corporal punishments, used alone or in combination with other corrections, consisted of whipping with cat-o'-nine tails or menacing with a ball and chain. The worst offenders were shipped off to sea (Bartollas & Miller, 2001: 241-243).

The philosophy of the Houses of Refuge was to prevent juveniles from becoming delinquent because of the influences of the street, and "reforming them in a family-like environment" (Siegel & Senna, 2000: 438). Although, most of the children were status offenders and had not committed a criminal act, the

Houses of Refuge often utilized a jail model with strict rules and harsh punishments, including corporal punishment. Within a short time, a number of cities built similar Houses of Refuge. Unfortunately, although originally a reformist move, the Houses of Refuge turned conservative and were no longer considered in the forefront of reform. They instead incorporated the system of contract labor, the cell system, and the use of corporal punishment (Folks, 1902).

Another experiment, beginning in the second half of the 19th century and continuing for about 75 years was the "placing out movement" or the "orphan train movement." The plan of Charles Loring Brace, head of the Children's Aid Society, was to send orphans and dependent and neglected children to the Midwest, so as to escape the poverty, crime and pollution of New York City. Juveniles were transported by train, in groups of 20 to 40, to cities in the western states, where arrangements had been made for a large public meeting in the local school or town hall, so that the residents of the area could choose which children, if any, would be given shelter in their homes. In some cases, this might include several siblings of the same family (Holt, 1992; Folks, 1902; Brace, 1880). There was great interest by the farmers in taking children into their homes for extra laborers. Others housed the children out of a sense of charity, while some simply wanted the love and companionship that only a child could offer. The program was ended in 1929, after about 100,000 children had been shipped to the West (Folks, 1902). Many of the children benefited greatly, for instead of living on the street, in a public facility or in a reform school, they were given the opportunity to live with a family. Some were adopted by the families with whom they lived. Many enjoyed stable homes, obtained an education, learned the discipline of work, and went on to successful careers. But some children worked unrelentingly at difficult tasks, and some children ran away from the homes in which they were placed.

Reformers were also active in establishing juvenile detention homes. Even prior to the creation of a juvenile court, reformers struggled to develop detention homes for juveniles as a substitute for co-mingling juveniles and adults in jails or police lockups. This lessened the likelihood of their being victimized by adult inmates. In addition, the reduced contact of juveniles and adult offenders diminished the opportunity for juveniles to learn criminal attitudes or skills (Flexner, 1910).

Despite the humane concept inherent in the removal of juveniles from adult jails, there was critical resistance to the construction and maintenance of detention homes. The concept of a separation of juveniles from adults was new and its potential benefits were not fully understood. Some critics viewed the practice as excessively lenient and unnecessarily expensive. For example, in Chicago the original law creating a juvenile court provided that juveniles could not be confined with adults pending their hearings, bur funds were not allocated to pay for detention costs. As a result, the costs of detention were originally borne by contributions from private persons (Plarr, 1977; Bowen, 1925).

For a number of years after the turn of the century, detention homes were maintained in different ways. In New York City, homes were run by the Society for the Prevention of Cruelty to

Children. In some cities, the detention center was maintained by the municipality, in others by private organizations, while other cities had no detention homes at all. Eventually, detention centers were recognized as essential to the protection of juveniles and were established in all large cities.

The Early Relationship of Probation and the Juvenile Court

One of the dominant forces supporting the creation and growth of the juvenile court was the development of a probation system. The probation system was especially important to the first juvenile court as probation officers supervised the youngsters and provided other services to the court. As other juvenile courts were developed nationwide, they too relied on probation for administration.

The juvenile court movement accelerated the growth of probation, serving as an integral part of many juvenile court programs. As a result, probation for adults did not expand as quickly (Dressler, 1969). This phenomenon was also attributable to the public's greater willingness to exculpate juvenile offenders while punishing adult criminals. During the early years of the Chicago juvenile court, officials in the system were magnanimous in their praise of the probation service. As contemporaneously stated by one of the first juvenile court judges:

"And then, of course, as we have recognized from the very beginning, we need the probation officer. The probation officer is the right arm of the court; it cannot do without him or her (Mack, 1925: 315).

Reasons for the Creation of a Juvenile Count

As noted, there was significant opposition to the origin of a juvenile court. Some believed that it was unnecessary in that it would duplicate the role of the adult criminal courts, that it would be unnecessarily expensive, and that it would serve to "mollycoddle" juveniles (Whitman, 1916; N.Y.S Probation Commission, 1918).

One of the basic reasons for the creation of a juvenile court was to remove children from the harshness of criminal court sanctions. Punishment is the raison d'etre for criminal courts in accordance with a retributive theory of justice. In recognition of the malleability of juveniles and their immaturity, it was the belief of reformers that they should not be punished with the same harshness as adults. In the juvenile court, it was presumed that judges would be benign, and that the court would substitute protection and rehabilitation for brutal punishment.

Another reason was to reduce co-mingling between adults and juveniles. This would lessen their exposure to criminal attitudes and skills. In addition, it was believed that the stigmatization of the child would be reduced if he or she was processed behind closed doors in the juvenile court. Unlike the criminal court, the proceedings and records would not be open to the public, so as to reduce the negative labeling of the child.

Finally, reformers were generally dissatisfied with reformatories, many of which were considered to be brutal and harsh in their treatment of juveniles, and most important, failed to achieve the goal of rehabilitation. It was believed that commitments to these facilities would be reduced through a juvenile court which focused on extensive rehabilitative services, and the ability to make non-incarcerative referrals through a network of social services.

The Creation of the Juvenile Court

The first juvenile court was established in the city of Chicago effective July 1, 1899. The enabling legislation was named "An Act to Regulate the Treatment and Control of Neglected, Dependent and Delinquent Children." The Illinois Juvenile Court Act of 1899 applied only to children under the age of 16 who were dependent, neglected and/or delinquent. It also provided for jurisdiction over children under the age of eight who were found "peddling or selling any article or singing or playing any musical instrument upon the streets or giving any public entertainment" (Illinois statute 1899, Section 131).

The Act further provided for a separate courtroom for juvenile hearings and prohibited the detention of children under 12 years of age in jails and police stations. Most importantly, this law also authorized the appointment of probation officers whose duty it would be to:

… make such investigations as may be required by the court: to be present in court in order to represent the interest of the child when the case is heard; to furnish the court such information and assistance as the judge may require, and to take charge of any child before and after trial as may be directed by the court (Illinois Statute 1899, Section 131).

Although diverted from the punitiveness of the criminal court, the juvenile court system significantly increased court jurisdiction over troubled children. A 1913 study of juvenile arrests in New York City reported that 50 percent of the arrests made in the district were for non-crimes like begging, setting bonfires, fighting, gambling, jumping on streetcars, selling papers, playing with a water pistol and similar minor non-criminal acts (Collier & Barrows, 1914). Nasaw (1985: 23) noted that "there appeared to be little rhyme or reason in the causes for arrest. Some of the children's crimes involved junking, petty thievery and playing with or on private property, but there were many more that were victimless." Therein, a great deal of non-criminal juvenile misbehavior which was not controlled by the adult criminal court, was now subject to juvenile court control.

The primary force behind the legislative passage of the Act were a group of female activists who believed that juveniles should neither be confined with adults nor subject to criminal court jurisdiction, but instead should be tried in a special juvenile court which would be guided by a philosophy of the "best interests of the child." These women were successful in the establishment of a juvenile detention center several years before the creation of the court. Years later, Platt (1977) would sarcastically name these women as "the childsavers" believing that their intentions were designed to enrich themselves, and at the same time exercise control over the juveniles, most of whom were poor and/or the children of immigrants.

The basic philosophy underlying the creation of the court was the doctrine of "parens patriae," carried over from English common law. Under this doctrine the king had the responsibility of protecting children, and others who could not care for themselves. Transported to America, the role of the king was replaced by the judiciary. Framed by the doctrine of "parens patriae," the role of the juvenile court was to act in the best interests of the child. Unlike the criminal court, whose role was to punish the transgressor, the theory underlying the juvenile court was to protect the juvenile offender through the provision of treatment and rehabilitation. Even in those serious cases where the juvenile was remanded to a reform school, it was perceived as rehabilitative in that the experience should result in improved behavior.

Innovative Practices of the Early Juvenile Court

A number of modifications of criminal court practices and procedures were put into place in the early juvenile court to accomplish the stated goals of treatment and rehabilitation of the juvenile. The major changes included:

1. A change from a punishment ideology to a treatment-oriented philosophy. No longer were juveniles to be subjected to trial and incarceration with adults, nor to the harsh punishments of a criminal court. Juveniles because of their immaturity should not be held accountable for their acts in the same way as adults.

2. The concept of parens patriae as manifested by the "best interests of the child" would prevail. At least in theory, and in contrast to the criminal court, these concepts held the court responsible for the welfare and protection of the child while at the same time giving the court virtual control of the child through the elimination of nearly all due process rights conferred on juveniles when under criminal court jurisdiction.

   Among other due process rights, juveniles were denied the right to appointed counsel, to an appeal, to a jury trial and to the confrontation and cross examination of witnesses. Similarly, court decisions were based on the preponderance of the evidence rather than the higher standard of proof of beyond a reasonable doubt as used in the adult criminal court. It was believed that due process protections were not necessary as the court was a quasi-civil court rather than a criminal court. In addition, legal protections were not considered necessary as the welfare of the child would be safeguarded by a kindly and benevolent judge, who was more interested in the rehabilitation of the child, than in punishment.

3. In the absence of prosecutors and defense attorneys, the juvenile court carried on its work with great informality and flexibility and acted as a social service function rather than in a legal manner. The two principal actors in the process were the judge and probation officer, and they exercised total control over the court process.

4. To further disassociate the juvenile court from the criminal court, a euphemistic nomenclature was adopted which was less criminally oriented. This terminology continues today. The Chart 1, is illustrative of the alternative language.

CHART 1

Adult Criminal Court Terminology	Juvenile Court Terminology
Criminal	Delinquent Child
Crime	Delinquent Act
Arrest	Take Into Custody
Arraignment	Preliminary Hearing
Trial	Hearing
Conviction	Hearing Adjudication or Finding of Fact
Sentencing	Dispositional Hearing

5. A tenet of the early juvenile court was that they were more interested in the needs of the child, than the deeds of the child. The original court, therefore, considered the act as a symptom of the underlying causal factors.

The First Sixty Years of the Juvenile Court

The concept of a juvenile justice system spread throughout the nation, "and by 1925 juvenile courts existed in virtually every jurisdiction in every state" (Siegel & Senna, 2000: 445). Then as now, there was great diversity between the juvenile courts in different states:

Some jurisdictions established elaborate juvenile court systems, whereas others passed legislation but provided no services. Some courts had trained juvenile court judges; others had non-lawyers sitting in juvenile cases. Some courts had extensive probation departments; others had untrained probation personnel (Siegel & Senna, 2000: 445).

Because children lacked due process protections, including the important right to appointed counsel, justice was often overlooked. Despite the rhetoric, fairness was often ignored in many juvenile court proceedings, and children were sometimes adjudicated delinquent on the whim or caprice of a judge. Without counsel, juveniles were often unable to express themselves, were intimidated by the judge, and were entirely subject to the domination of the court. In a court without due process, each judge acted with the absolute power of a king.

Often court decisions were solely at the discretion of the judge. It was not unusual to have a child who committed a social wrong, receive a longer period of incarceration than a child whose act would have been criminal were he an adult. In many instances, juveniles received harsh sentences rationalized by the court's duty to protect, treat and rehabilitate the child. For example, a child might be committed to a training or reform school, not to punish the child, but to change his behavior. Unfortunately, a disposition allegedly in the best interests of the child was hardly different from the harsh punishments imposed by the reform school administrators.

Great diversity also marked juvenile institutions. Some maintained a lenient treatment orientation, but others relied on harsh physical punishments, including beatings, straightjacket restraints, immersion in cold water, and solitary confinement in a dark cell with a diet of bread and water (Siegel & Senna, 2000: 445).

Over the years, it became clear that the early promises of the juvenile court reformers were not being fulfilled. Forceful criticisms of the injustices of the juvenile court system were expressed by lawyers, academicians and reformers, in addition to investigative committees of private and governmental child care agencies.

Paul Tappan, a law professor, was illustrative. He was critical of those reformers who believed that all children could be "saved" by the court. He instead warned that it was necessary for the courts to be more realistic in their goals. He was also critical of many of the extra-legal practices of the court, stating that the juvenile court of the time was characterized by an absence of due process protections, resulting in unofficial treatment in more than half of the cases. Specifically, he criticized the absence of counsel, the secrecy surrounding privacy of hearings and decisions, the denial of a jury trial, the disregard of the rules of evidence, the denial of the right to appeal, the informality of procedures, and a failure to make and preserve adequate records. He concluded his indictment of the juvenile court by noting that:

The state's purpose may not be punitive, as the courts have tirelessly repeated, but the deprivations to the child and his parents are no less real because they are benignly inspired. The child enjoys no constitutional protection against incarceration or supervision disproportionate to the seriousness of his misconduct (Tappan, 1962: 159).

Others similarly criticized the lack of justice and fair play in the juvenile court, despite its benign and benevolent goals. The court was censured for its permissive, social agency type organization. Dunham wrote that:

When, however, the juvenile court fails directly to advert to the fact that a particular illegal act has been committed by the child and, in its zeal to "treat" the child, completely glosses over this matter, the final disposition of the child's case is very likely to seem to him confusing and even unjust. (Dunham, 1964: 347).

As criticisms grew the United State Supreme Court began to radically change the juvenile court laws throughout the nation. Using language, even stronger than many other critics of the court, Justice Abe Forras took issue with the parens patriae concept underlying the very foundation of the juvenile court's practices. In the case of Kent v. United States, [383 U.S. 541, at 556 [1966] he forcefully criticized the lack of legal protections afforded juveniles, stating:

There is evidence, in fact, that there may be grounds for concern that the child receives the worst of both worlds: that he gets neither the protection accorded to adults nor the solicitous care and regenerative treatment postulated for children.

Moreover, in writing the majority opinion, Justice Fortas argued that the rehabilitative orientation of the juvenile court

was" not an invitation to procedural arbitrariness" (383 U.S. 541, at 541). The Supreme Court was warning the juvenile court to either provide adequate treatment or substantial due process protections, if it were to continue its operations.

The Second Revolution of the Juvenile Court System

A second revolution began in the middle of the 1960s and provided juveniles with many of the due process rights enjoyed by adults. Kent v. United States, 383 U.S. 541 (1966) initiated the process. In this case the United States Supreme Court held that a formal waiver hearing was required before a case could be transferred from the family to the criminal court. Although not providing many rights for juveniles, it did serve to commence the restoration of due process rights for juveniles.

In the following year, the Supreme Court ruled on the case of In re Gault, 387 U.S. 1 (1967), possibly the most important of juvenile cases. Noting the injustices suffered by juveniles without due process protections, Justice Fortas, who had previously written the majority decision in the Kent case, wrote that "under our Constitution, the condition of being a boy does not justify a kangaroo court" (387 U.S. 1, at 28, 1967). The importance of In re Gault lies in the rights given to juveniles which included: right to the notice of the charges; right to counsel; right to confront and cross-examine witnesses; and the privilege against self-incrimination.

In the case of In re Winship, 397 U.S. 358 (1970), the Supreme Court continued the expansion of juvenile rights by mandating that the juvenile court follow the highest criminal court standard of "beyond a reasonable doubt" to establish guilt, rather than the civil court standard of the" preponderance of the evidence."

The trend of providing additional rights to juveniles was temporarily interrupted with the Supreme Court rulings in McKiever v. Pennsylvania, 403 U.S. 528 (1971), and Schall v. Martin, 104 S. Ct. 2403 (1984). In McKiever, the Court ruled that due process protections do not give juveniles a right to a jury trial, although a state can grant this right if it desires. Similarly; it ruled in Schall, that juveniles could be held in preventive detention, if they present a serious risk to society to commit a new crime. The basis for the Supreme Court's ruling was the belief that adults have a right to liberty whereas juveniles only have a right to custody. As a result, it is not unreasonable to hold a juvenile for his own protection.

A number of other important cases contributed to the due process rights of juveniles. In Breed v. Jones, 421 U.S. 519 (1975) the Supreme Court ruled that children in the juvenile court are protected against double jeopardy. In Thompson v. Oklahoma, 487 U.S. 815 (1988), the Supreme Court ruled that the execution of a person who was below the age of 16 when the crime was committed is unconstitutional. In Stanford v. Kentucky; 492 U.S. 109 S. Ct. 2969 (1989) the Supreme Court held that the imposition of the death penalty on a juvenile who committed a crime between the ages of sixteen and eighteen was not unconstitutional.

The second revolution of the juvenile justice system, served to grant children in the juvenile court almost all of the same due process rights of adults,

The Third Revolution

With the United States Supreme Court granting due process rights to juveniles in the 1960s and 1970s, almost comparable to the rights of adults in the criminal court, the doctrine of parens patriae was seriously diminished, although not totally discarded. From a legal standpoint the original mold of the juvenile court was now broken. While the non-punitive, benevolent, and rehabilitative goals of the court remanded in place, the legal process governing the court was now similar to the criminal court.

A third revolution of the juvenile court took place in the 1980s. Replicating the adult criminal court's move towards harsher and more punitive sentences, the juvenile court similarly adopted a "control model." While, the early court primarily focused on treatment and the protection of the child, the control model also advocates the protection of society. For example, the Family Court Act of the State of New York, which previously provided that the purpose of the Court was to "consider the needs and best interests of the child" was amended to include" the need for protection of the community" (EC.A., See. 301.1). As noted by Trojanowicz and Morash (1992: 181-3), "There is a growing trend to revise juvenile justice statutes that have traditionally emphasized rehabilitation as the primary purpose of court intervention."

Examples of this trend include:

1. All states now have waiver provisions by which certain juveniles can be tried in the adult criminal court for very serious crimes. When in the adult court, the juvenile receives all of the due process rights of an adult, but faces more punitive sanctions than in the juvenile court.
2. A number of states now permit juveniles of 16 or 17, who are tried in the adult criminal court, to face the death penalty. In Stanford v. Kentucky, 492 U.S. 361 (1989), the Supreme Court ruled that the imposition of capital punishment on a juvenile who committed a murder between the ages of 16 and 18 is permissible.
3. Some stares have moved to "determinate sentencing" both for adults and juveniles. Unlike earlier sentencing in the juvenile court, which was extremely flexible and usually based on the juvenile's treatment needs, "determinate sentencing" provides fixed forms of sentences for offenses. The terms of these sentences are generally set by the legislature rather than determined by judicial discretion (Barrollas, 1999).
4. A significant number of states have increased their sanctions in sentencing juvenile delinquents. As found by Feld (1988: 821), "in at least ten states, preambles to the juvenile law have been changed to focus on public safety; punishment; and individual accountability' as objectives." The Office of Juvenile Justice and Delinquency Prevention (1999) reported that:

During the 1980s, the public perceived that serious juvenile crime was increasing and that the system was too lenient with offenders. Although there was substantial misperception regarding increases in juvenile crime, many states responded by passing more punitive laws. Some laws removed certain classes of offenders from the juvenile justice system and handled them as adult criminals in criminal court. Others required the juvenile justice system to be more like the criminal justice system and to treat certain classes of juvenile offenders as criminals but in the juvenile court.

The juvenile court has moved virtually full circle horn a rehabilitative and treatment-oriented focus to a concentration on accountability and punishment, Albanese (1994: 185) commented on the changed philosophy of the juvenile court, remarking that:

> ... the last hundred years has seen the process of juvenile justice undergo a complete and cyclical change: from the treatment of all juveniles as adults to the invention of the juvenile court and the rehabilitative model to the due process model to where we are now almost back to where we started. It is ironic, but in the 1990s we are closer to treating juveniles as adults than at any time since the turn of the century.

Today's juvenile court is so different from the original court, and more similar to the criminal courts than at any prior in the past century. This turnabout is causing many to ask whether a separate juvenile court is any longer needed.

In McKeiver v. Pennsylvania, 403 U.S. 528 (1971), Justice Blackmun writing for the majority warned that:

If the formalities of the criminal adjudicative process are to be superimposed upon the juvenile court system, there is little need for its separate existence. Perhaps that ultimate disillusionment will come one day, but for the moment we are disinclined to give impetus to it.

As the juvenile courts increasingly mirror the adult criminal courts, Justice Blackmun's concerns become increasingly important. Whether or not the juvenile court has been made obsolete by these revolutionary changes is a crucial question that must be answered.

References

Albanese, J.S. (1994). Dealing With Delinquency: The Future of Juvenile Justice, 2nd ed. Chicago: Nelson-Hall.

Bartollas, C. (1999). Juvenile Delinquency, 5th ed. Boston: Allyn & Bacon.

Bartollas, C. & Miller, S.J. (2001). Juvenile Justice in America, 3rd ed., New Jersey: Prentice-Hall.

Bowen, J.T. (1925). The Early Days of the Juvenile Court. In, The Child, The Clinic and the Court. N.Y.: Johnson Reprint Corp.

Brace, C.L. (1880). The Dangerous Classes of New York, and Twenty Years Among Them, 3rd ed. N.Y.: Wynkoop & Hallenback.

Breed v. Jones, 421 U.S. 519 (1975).

Collier, J. & Barrows, E. (1914). The City Where Crime is Play: A Report by the People's Institute. New York, pp. 14–18.

Dressler, D. (1969). Practice and Theory of Probation and Parole (2nd ed.) New York: Columbia University Press.

Dunham, W.H. (1958). The Juvenile Court: Contradictory Orientations in Processing Offenders. From: Cavan, ed., Readings in Juvenile Delinquency. New York: J.P. Lippincott, Co.

Ernst, R. (1965). Immigrant Life in New York City, 1825–1863. Port Washington, N.Y.: Ira J. Friedman, Inc.

Family Court Act of the State of New York, Section 301.1, N.Y.: Looseleaf Publications.

Feld, B.C. (1988). The Juvenile Court Meets the Principle of Offense: Punishment, Treatment, and the Difference it Makes. Boston University Law Review, 68:5, (Nov.) pp. 821–915.

Flexner, B. (1910) The Juvenile Court as a Social Institution. The Survey (Feb).

Folks, H. (1902). The Care of Destitute, Neglected, and Delinquent Children. N.Y.: Macmillan.

Holt, M.I. (1992). The Orphan Trains: Placing Our in America. Lincoln, Nebraska: The University of Nebraska Press.

Illinois Statute 1899, Section 131.

In re Gault, 387 U.S. 1 (1967): Citing Justice Forras.

In re Winship, 397 U.S. 358 (1970).

"Juvenile Justice: A Century of Change" (December 1999). 1999 National Report Series. Juvenile Justice Bulletin. Office of Juvenile Justice and Delinquency Prevention, U.S. Department of Justice.

Kent v. United States, 383 U.S. 541 (1966), Citing Justice Fortas.

Krisberg, B. & Austin, J. (1978). The Children of Ishmael. Palo Alto, CA

Mack, J.W. (1925). The Chancery Procedure in the Juvenile Court. The Child, The Clinic and the Court. N.Y.: New Republic.

McKeiver v. Pennsylvania, 403 U.S. 203 (1972), Citing Justice Blackmun.

Nasaw, D. (1985). Children of the City: At Work and At Play. Garden City, N.Y.: Anchor Press/Doubleday.

New York State Probation Commission for the Year 1917, Eleventh Annual Report (1918). Albany, N.Y.: J.B. Lyon Co.

Platt, A.M. (1977). The Child Savers: The Invention of Delinquency, 2nd ed. Chicago, IL: University of Chicago Press.

Riis, J.A. (1997). How The Other Half Lives. New York, N.Y.: Penguin Classics.

Schall v. Marrin, 104 S.Ct. 2403 (1984).

Siegel & Senna (2000). Juvenile Delinquency: Theory, Practice and the Law. 7th ed. Belmont, CA.: Wadsworth.

Stanford v. Kentucky, 492 U.S. 109 S. Ct. 2969 (1989).

Tappan, P.W. (1962). Justice for the child: The Juvenile Court in Transition, edited by Rosenheim, Margaret Kenny. New York: The Free Press of Glencoe.

Thompson v. Oklahoma, 102 S. Ct. 2687 (1988).

Trojanowicz, R.C. & Morash, M. (1992). Juvenile Delinquency, Concepts and Control, 5th ed. New Jersey: Prentice Hall.

Whitman, C.S. (1916). 9th Annual New York State Probation Commission.

Charles Lindner *is a Professor at the John Jay College of Criminal Justice.*

From *Perspectives,* Vol. 38, No. 2, Spring 2004, pp. 24-29. Copyright © 2004 by American Probation and Parole Association. Reprinted by permission.

DARE Program: Sacred Cow or Fatted Calf?

By Julia C. Mead

HAMPTON BAYS

"Are you ready to rock?" Police Officer Theresa Tedesco shouted into the microphone. In thunderous unison, 300 sixth graders at Hampton Bays Elementary School shouted back, "Yes!"

Parents and some grandparents packed the bleachers and lined up along the walls for the Jan. 23 ceremony put on for graduates of DARE, the Drug Abuse Resistance Education program. The students turned cartwheels, performed a rap song and took turns reciting lines in skits they wrote themselves. The first-place finishers in an essay contest each read their winning submissions.

The essays, like the hand-drawn posters hung on the gym walls, offered variations on a single theme: that tobacco, illegal drugs and violence are dangerous. It's the central message that thousands of students across Suffolk are taught each year in the DARE program.

Suffolk is not alone. The DARE America curriculum, developed two decades ago by members of the Los Angeles Police Department, has been adopted by 80 percent of all schools nationwide. It puts uniformed officers in elementary and middle-school classrooms to teach about the dangers of tobacco, alcohol, controlled or illegal drugs and violence. The officers also propose ways to help students resist the temptation to experiment or to act out aggressions, and they provide warnings about the consequences if they don't.

But there's a catch: numerous studies across the country, including one in Suffolk two years ago, cast doubt on DARE's effectiveness. Its graduates are no less likely to use drugs than other children, the studies have concluded.

Nevertheless, the program remains enormously popular. So popular, in fact, that any suggestion that it be replaced with a more effective or less expensive program tends to raise howls of protest from parents, school officials and the police.

As a result, Suffolk lawmakers girding to do battle with a projected $250 million budget shortfall in 2005 are reluctant to take any overt jab at DARE, even though it costs the police department nearly $3 million a year.

"We suspect that there are gaping holes in the program and that it may not be cost-effective, but legislators are politicians," said one Suffolk legislator, who spoke on the condition that his name not be used. "No one's going to risk their political future by doing anything other than standing up with the parents. Parents vote."

Other legislators said that asking school districts to help bear the cost of DARE has never been more than talk. "The schools are up against a rock and a hard place already," said Joseph Caracappa, the Legislature's presiding officer. "And it would just shift the tax burden from one district to another."

Steve Levy, the new county executive, was elected on a reform platform that called for a soup-to-nuts evaluation of all county spending and promised aggressive change wherever he found waste and inefficiency. Although the police department's budget is squarely in his crosshairs, Mr. Levy declined last week to say that DARE was.

What Mr. Levy would say was that within a month his staff would begin looking at ways to use DARE officers for other police work during school vacations.

He also said that the new police commissioner, Richard Dormer, would help evaluate DARE itself for possible improvements and that civilian teachers might be used in parts of the program. "We're believers in the concept, but we have to find the best implementation," Mr. Levy said. "It will likely stay in place through the rest of this school year as it is. If there are changes, they'll take place in September."

In an echo of a recommendation made two years ago by a countywide study, he said those changes could include moving some DARE officers out of elementary schools and into high schools. The program might also be extended to both the lower and higher grades. "We may have to experiment to find the best age bracket," he said.

Most Suffolk schools customize DARE America's curriculums and pick and choose which grades to use them in. Some, like Hampton Bays, use the program only in one grade, typically the fifth or sixth.

Dr. Lee Koppelman, the executive director of the Long Island Regional Planning Board, said the board's 2001 study looked at schools across Suffolk and at the incidence of drug abuse among DARE graduates. It concluded, as studies elsewhere have, that the program was ineffective in the long term.

"You can't have a 10-week session in sixth grade and expect it to have enduring, lifelong qualities," Dr. Koppelman said. "We found it was generally effective while the students were in the program, but in terms of lasting impact, it didn't measure up. If I had my druthers, it would be taught from fifth through 12th grade. That would be a real opportunity to address addictive behavior."

Asked what became of his study, he replied, "Nothing."

Mr. Dormer, the new police commissioner, was noncommittal about DARE, saying only that he planned to evaluate the program with one eye on the 2005 budget.

DARE America has countered criticisms by revamping its curriculum for middle-school students, compacting what was a 17-week course into 10 weeks and trying to make it more realistic, said Sgt. Enrico Annichiarico, the head of the Suffolk Police Department's DARE office. He supervises 28 officers, 6 of them with teaching degrees, who work in about 180 schools.

Sergeant Annichiarico said the new curriculum placed emphasis on the seventh and ninth grades, which he called a sign that DARE America was "keeping up with the times" and was responding to criticism about not addressing the needs of older students who are more at risk.

Bemoaning the lack of any frank public discussion of DARE's shortcomings, Dr. Koppelman said its widespread popularity was "part of the problem."

School administrators like DARE because it allows them to send out an anti-drug message at no cost to their districts. Police departments pay most of the costs, and the local P.T.A. typically covers the incidentals, like the DARE T-shirts given to every graduate and for pizza for the graduation party.

"It really is a good deal for the district," said Marc Meyer, the acting principal of Hampton Bays Elementary School. Mr. Meyer, like officials in other districts, said he had heard about but had not read studies critical of DARE. "I have to admit that my view is skewed because I love the program," he said.

Other school officials said they had never studied its effectiveness and had no intention to do so. "We've never discussed that," said George Leeman, the Hampton Bays school board president. "We've always supported its continuation."

Parents say they like DARE because they believe their children's enthusiasm is a sign that they are getting the "Just Say No and Mean It" message.

Dorothy and John Capuano, whose daughter Amanda, 11, graduated from the Hampton Bays DARE program on Jan. 23, said that the program helped students resist peer pressure, encouraging them to think about the possible consequences of drug and alcohol use and to choose positive alternatives, like sports.

"It puts in the kids' faces what can happen if they make bad choices," Mrs. Capuano said. "Some parents don't know how to do that."

Her husband said: "We both quit smoking 10 years ago, and we talk to our kids about the mistakes we made. But I also tell them that, because we didn't have DARE when I was a kid, we didn't know that we had choices."

They conceded their daughter was probably too young to experience real temptation. "But it's a good influence," Mr. Capuano said. "It's another opportunity for her to make a good decision."

Besides, his wife added, "The kids think it's cool to be in DARE."

Police officials are equally enthusiastic about DARE. "Putting a uniformed officer into the school helps build relationships with the kids, with the community," said David Hegermiller, the chief of the Riverhead Town Police Department. "Police departments certainly do get a lot of public relations mileage out of that."

Although he was aware of the criticism of DARE, he and other police officials called the program the one "proactive thing" that departments can do to fight violence and drug and alcohol use. Everything else, they said, amounts to reactive mopping up after the damage has been done.

"The parents go crazy if anyone talks about stopping it," Chief Hegermiller said. "They like the contact between the officer and the kids, too, but when I talk about putting officers in the schools in some other capacity, they start screaming. It doesn't make sense to me because I see them as the same thing."

But Dr. Koppelman said he found that DARE's message and its widespread popularity provide little more than a false sense of security and an unearned opportunity for parents, the police and educators to be self-congratulatory.

"The kids like it because they get recognition and having a police officer in the classroom is a novel thing," he said. "And parents whose kids don't have drug problems to begin with think that DARE is responsible. But the real serious problem is that behind all the fun and recognition and hoopla is a valid concept that hasn't been allowed to work because it isn't pounded into these children throughout the educational process. Like anything else, it wears off."

THE PEER COURT ExperiencE

BY JAMES P. GRAY

WITHOUT QUESTION, numbers of things with our young people are not going well in our society today. Even worse, in several well-publicized situations our local government organizations have not only been unresponsive, but sometimes they have been a part of the problem. However, our citizens, parents and taxpayers should be aware that many things are going right, too. One of those successful and helpful programs is peer court *(also known as youth court or teen court).*

We started our peer court in Orange County, California in 1994. The purpose was to provide an institutional means for our young people to focus upon ethics, individual responsibility, the long-range importance in their lives of getting accurate information and making intelligent decisions based upon it, and the fact that they are important role models for others, especially their younger siblings.

Orange County's Peer Court is a diversion program that presents real juvenile court cases that are carefully screened by the probation department to high school "jurors." The juvenile subject must admit the truth of the charged offense and, along with his/her parents, waive their rights to confidentiality. They personally appear at a high school outside of their own school district (so that no one present knows them) with at least one parent. A jury of students at the host high school is impaneled after short questioning to determine if they can be fair and impartial. A probation officer reads a statement of facts about the case, and then the subject and parent are sworn and given an opportunity to make a statement about themselves, their backgrounds, the offense, or anything they feel would be important for the jury to know about the situation. A sitting county judge presides over each of the sessions, and also asks questions; however the program is designed for most of the questioning to be done by the high school jurors. After enough questions are asked to enable the jurors to feel that they have received suffi-

cient information, the jury retires along with a volunteer adult attorney advisor to deliberate and reach a recommended sentence to give to the judge. The attorney advisor tries to keep the jury focused, but does not participate in the deliberations.

When the jury returns, the judge reviews the recommendations and tries to incorporate them into the sentence. If the juvenile subject completes the sentence within four months, the underlying offense is dismissed. The only sanction for a failure to complete the sentence is to refer the underlying offense back to the district attorney for prosecution. Obviously, the district attorney must exercise appropriate discretion in making this decision; however, that office has stated that it will consider the subject's failure of the diversion program as a "factor in aggravation" in whether or not to proceed. We stress that these are serious matters. Even though juvenile records are still sealed for most purposes, there are always exceptions and the risks of having a criminal conviction should not be taken lightly.

Peer court sentences can include virtually anything except incarceration or the payment of a fine. They frequently include community service, such as picking up trash in a park, graffiti removal, and/or working with the sick, injured or elderly at local medical institutions; individual and/or family counseling; restitution to the victims of the offense; completion of alcohol and/or other drug abuse programs; writing letters of apology to the victims of the offense and/or parents, or essays about what they have learned from this experience; being ordered to attend school regularly, and attend all classes; and participating as a juror at a future peer court session.

One of the critical issues in our program is the screening and selection of the offenses. Many of them are shoplifting or other petty theft, receiving stolen property, graffiti or other vandalism, trespass, "simple" alcohol, marijuana or other drug offenses, and driving a motor vehicle without a license and/or taking a parent's car without permission. We never accept cases involving dangerous weapons, and only rarely do we accept offenses dealing with violence. Exceptions to this have been cases like a juvenile male who assaulted another male because he had insulted his girlfriend, as long as there were no injuries.

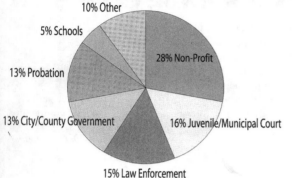

Who Administers Youth Court

- 10% Other
- 5% Schools
- 13% Probation
- 13% City/County Government
- 15% Law Enforcement
- 28% Non-Profit
- 16% Juvenile/Municipal Court

Source: National Youth Court Center

Without a doubt it would be less costly and time consuming to have the Probation Department implement a diversion program without peer court. However, even though we have a history of success with the individual juvenile subjects and their parents, the real impact of our program is to pursue those "teachable moments" not only with the subjects themselves, but also with the jurors and other high school students in the audience. (A total of 4174 young people either participated in or observed our Peer Court in the 2001–2002 school year.) For example, when our jurors ask a parent one of our "sample" questions like "Why don't you know who your child's friends are?" both the parents as well as all of the young people in the audience start to focus upon the fact that young people actually expect a parent to parent. We have had jurors ask the subjects if they want their younger siblings to smoke marijuana. When they say "no," people focus on the fact that if the older sibling smokes, no matter what is said, the younger sibling will probably follow the lead of the older. As a result, the students realize that they are mentors for their younger brothers and sisters, and the examples they set are important. These are valuable lessons that are often not learned elsewhere.

Peer court makes distinctions between a friend and an acquaintance. We ask questions like, "Would friends request a person to shoplift an item and give it to them?" "Does it matter who you choose as friends?" "If your friends tend to ditch classes, smoke marijuana or shoplift, how successful do you think they will be in later life?" "If you hang out with them, what are the chances that you will end up doing the same things, with the same results?" On the other hand, "If you surround yourselves with friends who work and study hard and are successful, don't you think that this will increase your chances of being successful as well?" Other questions are asked like "Don't you realize that if you do something positive that this will have a gratifying effect upon the people who love you, and that the same thing is also true in reverse?" "How do think your

parents are feeling having strangers tell you how they should raise you," and "How disappointed do you think they feel that you are in trouble?" "Did you ever think about this before you shoplifted that tape cassette from the store?" These questions are particularly probative when the parents sitting next to their child are in tears.

Petty theft is a big problem with young people. We frequently ask the subjects if they have ever had something stolen from them. If so, we ask how they felt when the theft was first discovered. And then we will say something like, "Tell the truth—didn't you want to throttle the person who took that item from you? Do you think your victim felt any differently? Is that what you want to inflict upon other people?" We also ask the subject if he/she is a thief. Yes it is true that they stole something on that particular occasion, but did their parents raise them to be a thief? After a few more questions, we center the discussion onto the fact that it really is easy to steal, and most often it can be done without anyone discovering who did it. However, people like us don't do that. Why? Not because of possible punishment, but because "I am better than that!" Even though no one else will know, I myself will, and that is not who I am. Numbers of times, our judge has had placed a $20 dollar bill at the back of the assembly hall, saying that it is that judge's money. If anyone takes it that would, of course, be stealing, but this time there will be no legal consequences. Nevertheless, we expect that our students there are better than that. So far, the money has always been there at the end of each session.

We focus upon other matters of behavior by our young people as well, such as courtesy and respect. For example, we are still old fashioned enough to believe that a man does not sit down before first helping his mother to be seated. If one of our male subjects sits down first, we take the time to make both mother and son stand up again and do it the respectful way. Or our judges will make the comment that they are sorry the subject does not take these proceedings more seriously—because if they did, they would tuck in their shirt, or wear more appropriate attire, etc. before coming to our peer court session.

We also have some problem areas. When the subject, or even the subject's parent, does not take our proceeding seriously; saying, for example, that this is a waste of time, or that our sanctions are not appropriate, we simply will agree with them, saying that this program is not meant for them. Then we refer the matter back to the district attorney for prosecution. In addition, although this can get touchy, if a parent appears to be inappropriately defending the subject and enabling the anti-social behavior to continue, we have been known to ask the parent to depart, and require the subjects to defend their conduct themselves. Similarly, if a subject fails our program and the district attorney does not prosecute, that word gets out among the students quickly and our program loses credibility. As a result, if the subjects say in any way that they are not guilty of the offense, or do not think it can be proved, we send it back. As we tell them, we are not running a railroad. That means that neither the probation department nor the district attorney can send us cases for which proof is lacking. If they do that, they will undercut our credibility and our program.

We always try to end our sessions on a positive note. In appropriate cases, we tell the subjects that we believe this never will happen again, and that there is simply no reason why they cannot enjoy happy, successful and satisfying lives. We schedule four cases in a two-hour session. By the time we have handled the four hearings, at least two of the juries have usually returned with their recommended sanctions, and then by the time we have handled those sentencings, the other two juries have returned. We also encourage an "open forum" atmosphere in which the young people ask questions of the judge. Many questions show a heightened interest in the judicial process.

Once everything has been completed and the students are dismissed, the subjects and their parents have a conference with our probation officer in which logistical questions are answered, and court documents are signed. During this time, our judges often speak privately with the subjects and parents, giving encouragement and recommendations. This has been found to furnish positive reinforcement to all of the parties.

We are now holding sessions in 13 of our county's high schools. We have deeply benefited from the efforts of our team, which is comprised of members of the Orange County Constitutional Rights Foundation, Department of Education, Probation Department, District Attorney's Office and Superior Court. Most of the participants are volunteers, including all of our judges, on-scene probation officers, host high school officials, attorney advisors, and student ROTC bailiffs. Each of our high schools has been adopted by a law firm, which graciously supplies young attorneys to act as our advisors.

The results of our program have been gratifying. For example, the no-show rate for the sessions has consistently been below ten percent. Of the 207 subjects who went through the peer court sessions in the 2001–2002 school year, only 12 failed to complete the ordered sentences and that their cases were referred back to the district attorney for prosecution. Obviously, if the "success" rate were 100 percent, we would not be taking serious enough cases. So we are pleased with those results.

In addition, since the educational component is one of the major reasons for the program, we are pleased with the statistics taken from a survey of 516 of the students who participated as jurors, bailiffs or observers. After observing the sessions, 74 percent of the participants and 60 percent of the observers agreed that peer court is an effective way to reduce youth crime; 83 percent of the participants and 70 percent of the observers agreed that peer court is an effective way for students to learn about the legal system; 80 percent of the participants and 60 percent of the observers agreed that peer court is an excellent alternative to the formal court/juvenile justice system; and 74 percent of the participants and 56 percent of the observers agreed that Peer Court is an effective way to keep youth from committing other crimes in the future. In addition to these statistics, there are numerous individual comments on the surveys about consequences and individual responsibility and pride.

Preliminarily, of course, this survey verifies the old maxim that people who get involved in a program get more out of it. However, youth crime is a difficult area in which to get positive results. Combining the results of this survey with our observations tells us that our peer court program is contributing to an ethical dialogue and focus that otherwise appear to be lacking. It is one thing for adults to admonish our young people, and an-

other for them to hear it from their peers. In addition, the program is assisting our young people in developing sophistication about life that is hard to develop or define. For example, in one of our cases that involved the shoplifting of some cough syrup, one of the jurors asked the subject if he was addicted to the alcohol in the syrup. After a few more questions, it became ap-

Youth Court Provides the Community

- An early intervention and prevention program
- An option on the continuum of juvenile services
- A way to hold juvenile offenders accountable
- A means for educating youth on the legal and judicial system/ Builds competencies
- A meaningful forum for youth to practice and enhance skills
- An avenue for building ties between youth and their community

Source: National Youth Court Center

parent that the answer was yes. In another case, where one of the shoplifting subjects stated that his career objective was to become a firefighter, after recommending that this offender perform a suitable number of hours picking up trash at a county park, the jurors recommended that he serve the remainder of his community service at a fire station. In each session, we see further examples of the increased sophistication of our student jurors, and it is a rewarding sight to see.

One of the biggest pitfalls in these sessions is the adults becoming too dominant. The program is designed for peers to listen to the problems of their peers, and to render peer justice. To the degree that the judges begin to preach, or to take too much control, then we undercut our own program. However, the probation department does give judges some access to confidential information not possessed by the jurors, such as prior arrests, truancy, parental problems, etc. So when the questioning begins to lag, or starts to go in an inappropriate direction, it is the responsibility of the judge to bring the discussion back on track. The trick is not to overdo it.

The involvement of the Department of Education has brought an added benefit. They have put together a curriculum package that teaches about government, the justice system, advocacy, and the importance of acquiring accurate information, and then incorporates our peer courts into the curriculum as a field trip and practical learning experience. This allows the peer court concept to be extended beyond our 13 high schools, and adds some real life experience to the educational process. In addition, at some time in the future, we hope to create several video programs of simulated peer court sessions, which also can be used for instructional purposes.

Nationally, the youth/peer/teen court movement is strong. According to the National Youth Court Center website (www.youthcourt.net) as of the end of July 2003, there were close to 900 youth court programs in 46 states and the District of Columbia. Most of them are diversion programs like ours. Otherwise, there are many differences among the programs. A few have their juries decide guilt or innocence, and many use youth prosecuting and defense attorneys and judges. Most youth courts hold their session in courtrooms; however, we have chosen to hold ours in the schools. In doing that, we give away a little of the sanctity of the courtroom, but gain a great deal in student attendance. In my view; it is clearly worth the trade. We also feel that those programs that use youth attorneys sometimes result in the best attorney carrying the day, instead of focusing upon and emphasizing the subject's responsibility for his/her actions.

We are proud of our peer court program. If anyone would like to have some further information, please feel free to contact Mr. Greg Ronald at the Orange County Probation Department at (714) 935-6647, or Ms. Gwen Vieau at the Constitutional Rights Foundation of Orange County at (949) 440-6757, ext. 137, or at **gvieau@crfoe.com**. We have found that the concept of young people delivering justice to their peers works. Our young people are confronting and addressing the impact of their behavior upon their victims, their families and themselves, and along the way are learning critical citizenship, knowledge and skills. We believe that something good is happening here and thought you would like to hear about it.

James P. Gray is a Judge of the Superior Court in Orange County, California

"Isn't she a little young?"

A new public service ad campaign in Virginia uses billboards and bar coasters to remind men that sex with a minor is against the law. But will it work?

By Corrie Pikul

JULY 26, 2004—The Rock Falls Tavern in Richmond, Va., is a typical neighborhood bar: There's pizza, a pool table and a regular after-work crowd. It's comfortable in its predictability—which is why, when strange new postcards appeared in racks last week, patrons took notice.

"So when I saw my buddy going after this young girl," the postcards read in black type, printed above the address for the statutory rape section of the Virginia Department of Health's Web site, "I knew I couldn't just sit there. Isn't she a little young?"

The Tavern has allowed advertisers to offer postcards in the past—but to sell a product, not dissuade men from pursuing underage girls. Chip Dell, the Tavern's general manager, who says he "doesn't allow people under the age of 21 into the bar area after 9 p.m.," has mixed feelings about the cards. "I agree with the sentiment behind them, but I don't know how effective they're going to be," he says. He just put out the cards about a week ago, but he's already received feedback from the regulars: "They mostly joke—say things like, 'I need to send this to my buddy and make sure his wife gets it!'—to get their buddy in trouble."

The postcards are part of a public awareness campaign sponsored by the Virginia Department of Health. Similar "Isn't she a little young?" messages will appear on 225,000 coasters, postcards and napkins in nearly 150 bars and retail stores in northern Virginia, Richmond and Roanoke. People who don't frequent bars like the Rock Falls Tavern or SJ's Lakeside Tavern on Lakeside Avenue will still have a chance to see the messages—in giant type, on outdoor

billboards in central and northern Virginia. The billboards—which include the warning "Sex with a minor. Don't go there"—will be up until the end of July; the bars will keep materials on hand until they run out.

Under Virginia's statutory rape laws it's illegal for an adult 18 or older to have sex with someone age 15 to 17—but the Virginia Department of Health isn't targeting the high school senior and her college boyfriend (although, for obvious reasons, the department can't actually say this). Nor is this campaign targeted at the other extreme of the spectrum: pedophiles or disturbed adults with sexual fetishes for young children. "We agreed that people who are going after children 12 and under are not going to be fazed by a billboard campaign," says Rebecca Odor, the Department of Health's director for violence prevention. (In Virginia, it's a felony for an adult to have a sexual relationship with a 13- or 14-year-old child.)

Rather, says Robert Franklin, the department's male-outreach coordinator for sexual violence prevention, who helped initiate the $85,000 campaign, "Our goal is to bring awareness to the issues of statutory rape and sexual coercion."

What really worries the Virginia Department of Health is teen pregnancy and how it relates to sex with minors, technically called statutory rape. "The push for the campaign came from seeing the numbers of teens becoming pregnant by older men," Franklin says. "The campaign is aimed at reducing the number of young girls who have had children fathered by older men."

"Statutory rape is a significant public health problem nationwide," says Georges

Benjamin, executive director of the American Public Health Association. "A large percentage of births from young women can be from older men." He cites several studies, including a 1997 study that indicated that at least half of all babies born nationally to minor women were fathered by adult men. "The fact that Virginia is trying to do something about this is commendable," Benjamin says.

It is estimated that in 2000 the state of Virginia "had a total of 104 births to 14- and 15-year-olds that the age of the fathers would have made their engaging in sex a felony," Franklin says. (The number can only be estimated because just 28 percent of mothers age 14 to 15 reported the age of the baby's father.)

"A girl at 13 or 14 doesn't have the same decision-making skills, self-confidence, maturity or experience as an older woman and is thus more susceptible to bribery and intimidation," says Michelle Oberman, a law professor at Chicago's DePaul University who has written extensively about statutory rape laws. "This makes her prey to a guy who doesn't consciously want to violently rape a woman, but wants sexual intimacy."

All states have laws against sex with a minor, but those laws vary from state to state—and few states vigorously enforce them. "Numerous studies tell us that a good number of teens under 15 are sexually active—and it's something we just know [from anecdotal evidence]," Oberman says. "If we really had a vigorous enforcement of statutory rape laws, we'd have no room in our jails."

When dealing with teen pregnancy and sex with minors, state departments of health tend to focus their energy and finances on raising young girls' awareness and teaching them ways to protect themselves; a male-focused campaign is a new approach. "In the past, a 13-year-old girl was being asked to stand up to an adult," says Franklin. "We said to ourselves, 'Why aren't we talking to the men?' Not that we don't need to do education for young women on victimization, but we need to start talking to the men as well."

But will men listen? After all, the campaign is competing against a media culture saturated with images fetishizing young (and youthful-looking) women. MTV even titled its "satirical" movie about a high school football star who is accused of the statutory rape of his 16-year-old girlfriend "Jailbait," while teen queen Hillary Duff's 18th birthday is eagerly awaited by online fans (the first online "legality countdown" was, of course, the Olsen twins').

One of the goals of the campaign is to urge men to start talking to each other about the reality of statutory rape—to remind each other that dating underage girls is against the law. "If he hears it from enough of his friends, hopefully he'll change his behavior," Odor says. Billboards and bar props seemed like the best way to reach groups of men when they might be meeting up with friends or going out for the night.

Dr. Rev. Darius Beechaum, who runs a men's support group (and provides individual counseling for men) in Richmond thinks Virginia's statutory rape campaign is a positive effort, but questions the heavy focus on male responsibility. Sex with a minor is a topic that occasionally comes up in his groups, he says. "You have these younger ladies that look older, act older, say that they're older. The attitude expressed by men in my group is, if she looks the age, then I guess she is."

And Beechaum isn't sure that men involved with a minor will be open to discussing their personal life with friends. "If a man is engaged in a sexual activity with someone younger, no one knows about it. He won't really take that person out in public—he'll visit her at home, keep their relationship a secret."

Currently, a special provision in federal law requires states to take active measures against statutory rape. Any state that accepts welfare funds from the Administration for Children and Families (and all 50 states do) must submit a plan that establishes numerical goals to reduce out-of-wedlock pregnancies and births. The "Isn't she a little young?" campaign is part of Virginia's federally mandated plan to tackle the statutory rape issue.

The blueprint for this campaign was a pilot project conducted by the health department last year in the Tidewater region on the eastern edge of Virginia. (Tidewater is home to numerous military bases, including the world's largest naval base, in Norfolk.) According to Franklin, 46 percent of men interviewed after the campaign ran remembered seeing the campaign slogan ("Isn't she a little young?") somewhere.

For a campaign intended to catch the attention of libidinous men in their 20s, the images in the billboards and bar materials are noticeably chaste—as likely to be advertising insurance services as notions of propriety. Odor says this wasn't always the case. In fact, the original ideas proposed by the American Institutes for Research, the agency that created the campaign, were much spicier and featured pictures of seductive young women. "Sex sells, so that was the first thing that came out of American Institutes for Research," Odor says. (The AIR is prohibited by contract from talking publicly about the campaign.)

But the Virginia Department of Health felt such ads would be perpetuating the objectification of women. "We had to put a stop to that from a philosophical perspective," Odor says. Plus, when prototypes of the ads with women's faces were tested in focus groups, the men often ended up debating "whether or not she looks old enough to consent," Odor says. Instead, the agency decided to go with the simple lettering and shadowy silhouettes that crop up alongside Virginia highways today.

"It's a very innovative take on this issue," says Kristina Vadas, the sexual assault outreach counselor at Richmond's YWCA. "Most statutory rape programs target young girls, and say, 'Here are ways to protect yourself.' They put the responsibility on young people to resist adults. I think that going to the root of the problem—adults who are preying on young teens—is a much more appropriate way to go about it."

Not everyone believes in the campaign as much as Vadas. "The overall message over this campaign is that sex with a minor is against the law, and I'm not sure that's what drives men to be or not to be with women," says Adrienne Verrilli, director of communications at SIECUS, the Sexuality Information and Education Council of the United States. "There are a lot of other factors that contribute to a relationship between an underage woman and an older man."

Jamie Shuttleworth, a director of account planning at advertising agency Foote Cone Belding—who has extensive experience with male-targeted campaigns for brands like Coors and John Deere—worries that using a threatening tone in an ad (like the one taken by the "Don't go there" campaign) might be alienating. "The logical human reaction is to say, 'That doesn't apply to me.' It may get the point across, but it may also be easy to dismiss," Shuttleworth says.

And the "Don't go there" creators are already fighting an uphill battle, says Benjamin. "People's behaviors don't change very easily," he says. "The biggest problem with public health campaigns is that they aren't usually adequately financed. You can't get these kinds of ads into prime time. It is difficult to be competitive with the consumer advertising community because of the amount of money they have compared to the amount of money we have."

They're still going to try, Franklin says. "Sure, one billboard isn't gonna work—people see something like 30,000 sexually explicit images a day or a week, and here I am throwing up one message to counter that. But we've got to start somewhere."

About the writer: Corrie Pikul is an editorial fellow at Salon.

UNIT 6
Punishment and Corrections

Unit Selections

Key Points to Consider

- How does probation differ from parole? Are there similarities?

- Discuss reasons for favoring and for opposing the death penalty.

- Should college-level education be available to inmates?

 **Links: www.dushkin.com/online/**
These sites are annotated in the World Wide Web pages.

American Probation and Parole Association (APPA)
http://www.appa-net.org

The Corrections Connection
http://www.corrections.com

Critical Criminology Division of the ASC
http://www.critcrim.org/

David Willshire's Forensic Psychology & Psychiatry Links
http://members.optushome.com.au/dwillsh/index.html

Oregon Department of Corrections
http://www.doc.state.or.us/links/welcome.htm

In the American system of criminal justice, the term "corrections" has a special meaning. It designates programs and agencies that have legal authority over the custody or supervision of people who have been convicted of a criminal act by the courts. The correctional process begins with the sentencing of the convicted offender. The predominant sentencing pattern in the United States encourages maximum judicial discretion and offers a range of alternatives, from probation (supervised, conditional freedom within the community) through imprisonment, to the death penalty.

Selections in this unit focus on the current condition of the U.S. penal system and the effects that sentencing, probation, imprisonment, and parole have on the rehabilitation of criminals.

The lead article, "Kicking Out the Demons by Humanizing the Experience" is an interview with Anthony Papa, an artist and activist who uses his art to promote prison and drug war reform. Convicted under the Rockefeller drug laws, Papa spent 12 years in Sing Sing Prison. The essay that follows, "Trends in State Parole" asserts that the more things change in the parole system, the more they stay the same.

Any answer to the question "What do we get from imprisonment?" has to recognize that U.S. imprisonment operates differently than in any other democratic state in the world. This point is made in Todd R. Clear's essay, "The Results of American Incarceration." The following essay, "Correctional Boot Camps: Lessons From a Decade of Research," points out that boot camps as an alternate sanction have had difficulty meeting these correctional objectives: reducing recidivism, prison populations, and operating costs. Differing perspectives on the utility of the death penalty are found in the essay entitled "Do We Need the Death Penalty?" Which view do you hold?

"Prison Programs That Produce," which follows next, discusses the role religion played over the centuries in efforts to rehabilitate criminals. Following is a short article, "Encouraging Students to Pursue Careers in Community Corrections," wherein the author asserts probation and parole are worthy career options. Next, why Texas leads the nation in executions is examined by Joseph Rosenbloom in "The Unique Brutality of Texas."

Kicking Out the Demons by Humanizing the Experience— An Interview With Anthony Papa

"I want to write directions, 'How to be an agent of change and transformation.' Take posters and place them all over in public places. You know, educate."
Anthony Papa, April 30, 2002

by Preston Peet

May 1, 2002

Anthony Papa is an accomplished artist and ardent activist living and working in NYC, using his art to promote prison and Drug War reform. After being set up, then arrested in a drug sting operation in 1985, he received two concurrent sentences of 15 years to life in New York State's Sing Sing prison for his first offense under the Rockefeller Drug Laws' mandatory minimum sentencing guidelines. After gaining widespread attention through the harrowing and beautiful paintings he was creating from inside his prison cell, he received clemency after serving 12 years from NY Governor George Pataki in 1997. Papa, a friendly, intelligent, and very articulate man, graciously took time to sit down for a long and illuminating discussion with Drugwar.com, covering such topics as his art, the benefits of art for rehabilitation of prisoners, who the real targets of the War on Drugs really are and why the War continues, and some of the efforts he and friends are making to instigate positive changes in the system.

P- Have you seen the NORML ads out on the streets yet? What do you think of that idea?

AP- I think it's a great idea, putting the Mayor on the spot, but I don't think it's going to change anything.

P- You don't think it's going to change much, but you're not opposed to the idea of putting the Mayor's face out there?

AP- They should, he smoked pot. See, the whole problem with the War on Drugs is they demonize drugs, and they target specific populations and individuals, disenfranchise and marginalize blacks and Latinos, who always
get pinned for these drug crimes, yet the majority of users are white individuals. That's the whole beef man. I think it's positive to use the media in a creative way, to use the arts, to enlighten people as to what the real issues are. Like with this installation we did at the Drug War Race and Party on 4-20, 'Faces of the Drug War— American Dreams, American Tragedy,' what I try to do is humanize the experience through the creative arts. This is what I do with my art. I have two websites, www.15yearstolife.com, and www.prisonzone.com, where you can take a tour in prison through the web with my friend Chris Cozzone's photography and my art. My own website, 15yearstolife.com, is basically a site that people from around the world come into. They come not necessarily because they want to know about it, they come by chance because of the art. The art drew them in, and that's what I do with the art. The whole thing with my art now, I'm not into the scene of showing my art in galleries because I'm not with those politics man. At first it's a big deal, you get a show, you sell some work, you know, every artist's dream. I've been through that, I did it, it's gone. I just don't like the politics involved. I like to freewheel, do what I like to do with no limitations. That's the greatest thing for me.

P- You were arrested in 1985 for passing an envelope of cocaine. Was it a setup, or were you just unlucky?

AP- It was a sting operation. What had happened in 1984 was I was married, had a child, was self-employed with a radio business in the South Tremont section of the Bronx. I belonged to a bowling team in Westchester County. Business was slow, my car kept breaking down,

so I kept showing up late to the leagues. So one of my teammates asked me what was going on. I told him about my car, he asked why didn't I fix it, and I told him I couldn't, things were slow. He said, "Do you want to make some money? I know somebody." He introduced me to this guy who was a drug dealer, dealing in the bowling alleys in Westchester. So to make a long story short, the guy asked me if I wanted to deliver an envelope, to Mt. Vernon from NYC. He'd give me $500, and said it might become a steady thing. At first I said no, I'm not into that.

P- You pretty much knew it was drugs then?

AP- Yeah, I knew what it was about. A couple months went by, he came back around Christmas time and asked me again. Now things were really bad financially, so I asked him what I had to do. He said I just had to deliver this package to Mt. Vernon. I did, brought it to Mt. Vernon NY and walked into a sting operation. Twenty narcotics officers came out from everywhere. The individual who actually set me up was working for the police. He had three sealed indictments against him, so what his thing was, the more people he got involved, the less time he was supposed to get. So he reached out for everybody he knew. For me it was a bad mistake and afterwards I did everything wrong. I got this shyster lawyer. They offered me a cop-out to three to life because they knew I wasn't dealing the drugs, that I was just the courier, a mule. I didn't take it because I was desperate, didn't want to leave my wife and kid and wound up listening to this attorney, going to trial, and ended up with two 15 year to life sentences.

P- You get a worse sentence if you fight it , right?

AP- Yeah, in NY State. The Rockefeller Drug Laws were enacted in 1973. The legislative intent was to catch the drug kingpins and curb the drug epidemic. They're a dismal failure. We're going to the 30 year anniversary on May 8th of this year. The kingpin is still out there, the prisons are bursting at the seams. Of 72,000 in prison, 24,000 are incarcerated under the Rockefeller Drug laws. The prison population in 1973 was 12,500, now it's 72,000. 94 percent of those incarcerated under these Rockefeller Drug Laws are black and Latino. Marginalized, disenfranchised individuals, they come from 7 inner city neighborhoods in NYC, 75 percent of those individuals are non-violent offenders.

P- Wait a minute. How many come from those 7 inner city neighborhoods?

AP- Seventy Five percent come from 7 communities in NYC, and 94 percent of them are black and Latino. So there's definitely racism involved in these issues. From my perspective, I was in prison for 12 years under the Rockefeller Drug Laws, sentenced 15 years to life. The only way I survived it was my discovery of my art. From there I transcended the negativity of the imprisonment

through the art. It became for me meaning, gave me purpose in life and helped me maintain my humanity, my self-esteem, which is very essential in order to positively interact with society upon release. I met an individual who turned me onto painting, and it created this positive but crazy energy, but a crazy energy in a socially acceptable way.

P- Ok, let me come back to that. Did you use drugs personally at the time of your arrest?

AP- I did. I was a casual user, I never really used cocaine, I smoked pot and drank. Couldn't afford hard drugs, coke, stuff like that, but yeah, I was a drug user at the time.

P- In your case, prison turned you onto creating art, which is obviously a positive result of your imprisonment. Are you the exception, or the rule?

AP- I say there's plenty of individuals in prison who experience what I experienced because of the existential nature of imprisonment. What I mean by that is there's something mystical about spending a lot of time in a 6 by 9 cell. You get to discover who you are. So for me, I pull this artist that lay dormant inside. There's plenty of individuals who do that. That's why in prison, I believe in a restorative approach of justice as opposed to a punitive approach. Where punitive approach is strictly a terrible approach because it sleeps in the shadows of life itself. To lock them up type of mentality that doesn't think of the future of the incarcerated individual as opposed to restorative justice which maintains an individual yet allows him or her to hold onto their self-esteem which is very important.

P- That could lead to rehabilitation.

AP- Right. Rehabilitation exists only if you have the programs available to someone to take advantage of, to turn their lives around.

P- You earned two degrees, one in paralegal studies, and another Behavioral Sciences, as well as earning a graduate degree in ministry from the NY Theological Seminary while in prison. How does that education help you now in spreading your message?

AP- Oh, tremendously, because it gives me credibility when I speak. In reference to say, my job. I'm a legal assistant for a patent trade firm, Fish and Neave. I've been here 5 years. The reason I got the job was because I was prepared. I had a college education and a graduate degree so it made things easier for me to be released and to interact with society. I think also that my education, especially in my theological background, well, I studied liberation theology.

P- Which is?

AP- Which is a theology which is sort of created in third world countries as opposed to white man theology. It's a main belief of my liberation theology that you can talk about the bible, you can talk about tradition all you want, if there's no tangible change or challenge to the principalities, to the powers that be, nothing is going to happen, no change is going to occur. We believe in the hands on, the hermeneutical approach, the study of the nucleus of liberation theology. What it talks about is practical change practical use of problems and challenge in a way that's tangible, not just talking about the issues, but reacting and taking care of business in a positive and tangible way. This has helped me with my art. What really turned me onto art is when I studied art at first, I got into the French impressionists, and then somebody told me art is nice, but there's more to art than pretty beach scenes and frilly white dresses. I said, what do you mean? I was into Manet, Monet, all these French impressionist artists, and he says art can be used for political purposes. He sent me a book about the Mexican muralist, Diego Rivera, who used art showing the oppressors against the oppressed, basically challenging the powers that be. So I took that and used my art. In prison I became a political artist. I saw the artist in his role as a social commentator.

P- *What do think of current art, and in that I include music, film, literature, as well as fine arts. Do you find that those artists using their art to promote a message, such as yourself, are not given as much attention, nor funding, as those artists who create the emptiest of art, art without any message whatsoever?*

AP- You're exactly right. There's a body of art out there, a collection of artists who are political artists, who use art as a vehicle for social commentary, which is what I think art is for, yet because of the politics involved, they are not getting the grants, from foundations, they're just considered part of the elite as the handful of artists are who paint diabetic art. By that I mean sugar and spice, sweet stuff kind of art. I just went to the Whitney Biennial, and I was amazed at the crap they showed there. I didn't see one political piece in the whole show. There is a problem of breaking out with your art and getting discovered if you are going to use your art in a political context. In society today, mainstream artists really don't do that way.

P- *Yeah, my girlfriend overheard a conversation between two guys on the bus the other day, where one was telling the other how he hates it when a musician tries to "get all political, it's just a song." She was struggling not to light into this guy.*

AP- That's what art is for, to use it as a vehicle to get that social message out. I think it is very important. You really interact with society that way. I think it's positive. Film makers, musicians, visual artists, performance artists, all can be positive in using their art to promote social change.

P- *So what's the deal with the new anti-art policies in the NY State prison system? Why do you think they were initiated, and do you think it a smart move to stifle positive creativity in people locked in cages?*

AP- On March 29, 2002, Glen Goord, the Commissioner of Corrections for NY State made a declaration where he prohibited the sale of art by prisoners, doing away with a yearly art show, the Correction On Canvas exhibit that was in existence for 35 years in the NY State prison system. Every year prisoners had the opportunity to show and sell their work at this exhibit that was run by the State Senate and the Department of Corrections in the legislative office building in Albany. Fifty percent of the proceeds went to crime victims.

P- *To a crime victims' fund, or to those specific individuals hurt by the artist/criminals?*

AP- A crime victims' fund. What happened was that Goord made a statement that it wasn't worth the anguish that crime victims would feel for the little money that they raised through the show, allowing prisoners to profit from their art. Behind the scenes it was a political issue that started when Pataki took office in 1995. At that time 100 percent of the profits went to the prisoners, so an agreement was worked out where 50 percent of the money raised would go to a crime victims. It worked for almost 7 years, but last year, a mass murderer who killed something like 11 prostitutes and chopped up their bodies was allowed to show his work in the annual show that is run by the State Senate and the Corrections Dept. The Daily News got a hold of it and blew it up into a big story. An assembly man from Schenectady took hold of the issue and from there the politics went into overdrive. A year later, because of 1 individual, 72,000 individuals were punished. When I heard about it, from my point of view I was really angry because I was in that show for 12 years. I know how important art is for prisoners. I actually have a ribbon on my wall that I got in 1997 for best donated work.

When I got clemency from the Governor, I donated 15 pieces of art, and won this ribbon. I took it very personally, and started this campaign to challenge the Commissioner's decision. I got the NYCLU involved. They've taken the case, which is in the early stages of litigation. The NY Times came out with a beautiful editorial, Newsday is supposed to come out with one, as well as the Christian Science Monitor. We have a major rally planned May 8, also challenging the Governor on both the Rockefeller Drug Laws, and have a petition going around demanding that the show be reinstated and the ability of prisoners be allowed to sell their art be reinstated. The petition is up on my website. I actually got a call from this woman who was so angry that Goord used crime victims as the reason for his decision, a woman whose son and daughter were both murdered and was appalled that Goord was using someone like her for the excuse to take away the art show. I actually hooked her up with a Christian Science Monitor. This is what we've been doing with this issue, and a lot of people are angry. We're challenging the Governor and not the Commissioner, since that's an appointed position, we're challenging the Governor as voters, saying we the voters of NY demand you reinstate it, because it is a political year, he's up for reelection. Hopefully something will happen in a positive way. But artist prisoners are the lowest of the low. No one cares about prisoners. So what if you take away art and music programs? They're in prison, it's there for punishment, but these same people don't realize that these are the same individuals that you have to return to society.

P- You touched on this a little earlier. Do you feel that prisons are at all concerned with rehabilitation?

AP- Not at this point. It used to be a concern, but all it is now is warehousing individuals because I was there, I know personally, and I speak from that viewpoint. If prisons were meant to rehabilitate, every step of the way would be rehabilitative in value and therapeutic.

P- You took your own initiative?

AP- Yeah, I took it upon myself to take advantage of what was available. In 1995 they cut out college education, they did away with Pell and Tap, because again, politicians used crime as a political issue, where first federal money was taken away, then state followed.

P- So prisoners in prison now are not getting an education?

AP- There's a small movement in NY State where there's volunteers, colleges working at Bedford Hills for woman, and at Sing Sing for men, instructors work on a volunteer basis and it is run strictly on private donations.

P- Which would you say is more damaging to individuals and society as a whole—drug use, or the War on Drugs?

AP- I would say the War on Drugs. We've been involved with drug use for thousands of years. It's nothing new, we've dealt with it, there's always going to be an inkling for an individual to escape reality. so we can't control it in that capacity. But I think by creating the War on Drugs, which is a War on People not on Drugs, it's a bigger problem, because the black market exists. What it has become now is a vehicle to fuel the prison-industrial complex. Money raised from State, local and federal level through people's misery. By creating this fictitious war it's caused all sorts of problems. Now we've become comfortable with locking up non-violent offenders. NY State for example, 90 percent of the prisons upstate are in Republican territory where they fight each other to build the next prison. They have become a commodity, prisons. What happens is they keep them filled with non-violent offenders. In 1995, when Clinton's Crime Bill was passed it was a big mistake, because it gave millions of dollars to states to build

prisons. Advocates spoke out against this, because when these prisons are built you're going to have to keep them filled. And what do you fill them with? Drug users. Drug users today are like communists in the McCarthy era. It's a stigma, they demonize drug use.

P- Do you have a position on decriminalization or legalization?

AP- At this point if we tried legalization right now, we wouldn't do it, it wouldn't work. I think we should try out decriminalization first, as a society, see how that works, especially with marijuana. Hard drugs are always going to be a problem. Personally I think we have the right to self-medication. I believe in harm reduction, that theory. Some people will always be addicted to drugs, but let's make it easy for them, let's give them treatment. Let's do it the right way.

P- You're talking about the option for treatment, not mandated treatment.

AP- Right. I don't believe in mandated treatment at all. But again, when you put it all together in the big picture, it becomes part of the War on Drugs, which fuels the prison-industrial complex, because there's more money involved when you mandate. That's the whole story on that.

P- And they keep people in the system.

AP- It's a constant, vicious cycle that continues because of the monetary gain made into the whole issue.

P- Do you see any shift among police and politicians in how them themselves are perceiving the way?

AP- My personal point of view, 5 years ago, when I first got out of prison there wasn't a lot going on in the form of politicians taking stances, because it was a sure fire way to look soft on crime, which is advocating for say, reduced sentencing, or against the Rockefeller Drug Laws. But in the 5 years we've been out here, me working with my organization, the William Kunstler Fund for Racial Justice, and other groups, like the Drug Policy Awareness Project, which teaches people about the war through art and education. Through the efforts of groups like these, people are beginning to understand there's a significant problem. But they look at it in a different way. Why? Because these groups and what we do, we humanize the experience, we don't demonize the experience. We tell people that these are human beings that deserve second chances. Then we have the issue of mandatory minimum sentencing, which was really enacted with the Rockefeller Drug Laws in 1973, and they in turn became the catalyst for the federal government to make the mandatory minimum sentencing the laws in the federal government, and went to all 50 states where there's some form of mandatory minimum sentencing. It really got out of hand. It took the judges ability to look at totality of the facts of each case, where everybody is just pigeonholed by the weight itself. My case for instance, the judge didn't want to sentence me to 15 years to life, but he had no choice because I went to trial and lost. Under mandatory sentencing he could give me in my case 15 years to life, and could of sentenced me to 25 years to life, but he sentenced me to two 15 years to life sentences because it was my first offense.

P- *15 years to life? For your first offence?*

AP- Right, first offence, non-violent, no criminal record at all.

P- *Not even a smudge on your record?*

AP- I have a violation, but that's not a criminal record. I had a stolen license plate on my car I'd borrowed from my boss. 5 years earlier he's forgotten he put it in his trunk and called the police to report it stolen. 5 years later he found it and gave it to me. I got a $25 fine for that. I'd also actually gotten another violation for a joint back in 1973, again not a criminal offense, but a violation.

P- *You were arrested in 1985?*

AP- I was arrested in 1985.

P- *You did 12 years? Then Gov. Pataki gave you clemency in 1997?*

AP- Yeah. I painted my way out of prison I like to say, when in 1995, my self portrait that I did in 1988 while sitting in my cell one night. First I looked in the mirror and saw this individual who was going to be spending the most productive years of his life in a cage.

P- *How old were you?*

AP- I was 30 years old when I went into prison. I picked up this canvas and painted this self portrait titled 15 years to life, where 7 years later it wound up in a show at the Whitney Museum of American Art as part of a retrospective of Mike Kelly's work.

P- *Where did you keep your art?*

AP- I kept it in my cell. At a certain point where they made it a rule where they said we couldn't keep too much art in our cells. They were constantly making rules. It was a platonic view of the artist, they didn't like artists in prison because they were too individual, they weren't part of the collective. Which was against that whole rap about behavior modification, where the individual goes out you become part of the collective, they train you the way they want, but I wasn't about that. My art helped me transcend that. They had these rule where we couldn't keep finished pieces of art in our cells. I met this girl through an art show that every year I went into at this church. She became the keeper of my art. Every time I finished a piece I would send it out to her and she would keep it for me. A lot of work I have I wasn't able to finish because they forced me to send it

out, like one piece called metamorphosis, with barbwire and hands reaching out that turn into butterflies. I wasn't able to finish that one, because one day this lieutenant by my cell. I used to paint with a nail, hanging the painting on the nail. This piece was a huge, 40 by 50 piece, the biggest I ever did. He told me I had to get rid of it because it was a risk that I could use it to escape. I asked what he meant, and he said I could easily put a hole through the wall. I said, "but lieutenant, if I wanted to go to the other side of the wall, all I had to do was open my cells door, and open the guy's cell door and go in his cell. He said, "no, no, I don't care it's got to go."

P- *What, you were going to escape from one cell to the next?*

AP- That was the mentality. As a matter of fact, the first ribbon I ever won, in 1986, the first year I went into the Corrections on Canvas exhibit, I won a blue ribbon, my first time trying and I won it. I worked hard. I was a watercolorist, and I won for this piece called, "Pink Bathroom Sink." When I got the ribbon, well, when I got the package at the package room, I got a catalogue, and a letter from a Senator congratulating me on winning first prize, over 5,000 people viewed your piece, congratulations, blah, blah, blah, but when I looked in the package the ribbon wasn't there. I called the guard, and asked him where my ribbon was. He said, "you can't have it." I asked "what do you mean I can't have it?" He said you can't have it because it's blue, and blue isn't allowed. Now, blue is a color considered contraband, blue orange gray, these were colors that police uniforms were made of.

P- *They must have had a lot of faith in your artistic abilities to think you'd be able to create a police uniform and make your escape using a 2 inch blue ribbon.*

AP- Yeah, with a two inch ribbon I was going to try to weave this uniform. So I tried to explain to the guard but he didn't want to hear it. He called the sergeant, who said he'd go check on it with his superiors, and I figured cool, I'll get the ribbon no problem. But he came back and said, "look, you can't have it because it's blue." What eventually happened was I wrote the Senator who sent me the ribbon, who wrote me back. I'd told him I'd grieved it. There's a process where a prisoner can write a grievance, sort of like a process where you let some steam off. Prisoners rarely win, but in this case I figured I had to win. The Senator wrote back and asked me to let him know what happened with my grievance because they might have to change the color of the ribbon.

P- *And did they?*

AP- No, eventually someone came to their senses. The grievance hearing didn't happen, it didn't get to that point. I got the ribbon after a while. The ribbon was given by a guard to the hobby shop teacher to give to me because I was too low on the ladder for him to personally give me my ribbon. That's the kind of mentality you deal with in prisons.

P- So, do you see any shift in how politicians and police perceive and/or wage the War on Drugs?

AP- I do see a shift especially among the black and Latino caucus in the NY State Assembly, not in the Senate, not among the Republicans. Maybe some, but not a lot, of moderate Republicans. I lobby a lot in Albany, and there's a different opinion behind closed doors as to these drug laws. "Yeah, these are terrible laws, I don't support them," but they can't go out and support changes because they'd loose their constituency but behind the doors they all know it doesn't work right. But now there's a lot of black and Latino caucuses especially that support a change in the Rockefeller Drug Laws. For the first time in 30 years, we have the Governor, the Senate, and the Assembly that all want change, but at the end of the last session that couldn't come to an agreement, at this point there's a stalemate on it, which is why it is so important for us activists and advocates to go out and protest, to raise out voices and make a lot of noise to let them know we're still involved in this issue.

P- Now aren't they on the one hand moving towards small reforms and on the other trying to increase penalties for things like marijuana?

AP- It's always about that. The Governor wants to change the Rockefeller Drug Laws, in some ways, really watered down. I'd rather have no changes at all. They want to do away with parole, they want to increase penalties for marijuana. Politicians never want to give up anything for free. They always something for something.

P- Do you really think that it would be political suicide even today if a politician stood up and said flat out, "these laws are fucked up, let make some changes"? I mean among their voters. Their financial backers are probably going to be upset at this kind of stance, but there does seem to be a lot of groundswell among the common people that the War is wrong.

AP- It depends on their constituency and where you live. If you live in redneck Republican territory where everybody is conservative, if a politician came out suddenly, like say Dale Volker, a staunch Republican who is all for the Rockefeller Drug Laws, who has 9 prisons in his district, the 59th NY Senate District. This is why he supports the Rockefeller Drug Laws. Let's say he came out and was opposed to the Rockefeller Drug Laws, his constituency wouldn't be too happy.

P- Because he's got all those prisons.

AP- Right, He would probably loose his office. But let's say someone from like the South Bronx, from an area like that, where drugs are prevalent so people know about the issue, it's not going to hurt the politician that much to advocate for changing the drug laws.

P- Plus people in those areas see a lot of families broken apart.

AP- Exactly. So I think there's a difference now. I think that since the Senate, the Assembly, and the Governor all want change, I think it's different than it was 5 years ago when no one wanted change. I think then it would have been total political death. Right now I think it's really not, it's a smart issue to get involved with, but politics are politics. Some people are just not going to do it because of their politics.

P- Do you yourself hold any political affiliation?

AP- I'm a registered Democrat. I was actually registered for 5 years but couldn't vote because I was on parole. I just got off parole in February, so now is the first time I'm going to be able to vote coming up so I'm definitely going to exercise that right.

P- Now, I know that Bush and his ilk are talking about ratcheting up the War on Drugs, and already have in many ways. But under Clinton we also had this huge explosion in the prison population and in the Drug Laws. He himself might not have admitted inhaling, but he at least held the marijuana in his hand and put it to his lips. Do you see much of a difference between the Democrats and the Republicans on this issue?

AP- On the federal level? I think basically there's not too much difference, because we're talking about politics across the board, so politicians are afraid of supporting change at that level. There's some, like Democrats who support some change in mandatory minimum sentencing laws, but at the federal level I don't think there's much difference.

P- Do you have any ideas on how to build more and stronger ties between the different ethnic communities on this issue? I know that in NY, well actually, most all of the conferences and events on the Drug War, with the notable exception of Drug War Awareness Project's recent party on 4-20, that there are almost all white faces in the audience, and almost all white faces up on stage speaking and presenting. Very rarely do I see blacks and Latinos at these events. Do you have any ideas on how to bridge the cultural divides, or whatever it is that's keeping the communities apart?

AP- Well, in my experience, in the places that I've gone to in reference to conferences, I've seen a majority of black and Latinos, with whites, so I don't know the audiences you're talking about.

P- That's precisely what I'm talking about. The places I'm going to, as a white guy, I see mainly white folk, but you, a Latino, see mainly blacks and Latinos. How do we get these groups together, to work together?

AP- I really can't answer that.

P- No ideas?

AP- I think it's a universal issue that everyone should be involved with because the War on Drugs, although clearly racist in many ways, has no class barriers, no color barriers. It affects everybody. The prosecutorial tools that were created to curb the drug epidemic then in turn those laws are used against the average citizens who doesn't even use drugs, like exclusionary rules, the 4th Amendment, search and seizure...

P- Asset Forfeiture.

AP- Yeah, forfeiture laws, these are all tools that prosecutors use. They use them beyond their intended purposes. They go to the average citizen, where you can even lose your home for something like a marijuana cigarette.

P- Do you focus your efforts mainly in NY State, or do you also work on national efforts for reform?

AP- I work with the Kunstler Fund for Racial Justice mainly on the Rockefeller Drug Laws, and at the federal level I work with groups like FAMM, (Families Against Mandatory Minimum Sentencing), I've been to Washington DC and lobbied on Capitol Hill. Because the Rockefeller Drug Laws really touched me on a personal level, that's my main area of concentration. Plus, I live in NY. I've been involved with different groups, November Coalition, FAMM, groups that do work more on a national level.

P- Ok. Does being an ex-con hinder you in any way, say in your work as a legal assistant?

AP- Oh, a lot. For instance, let's say in this community here, this job. There's a lot of people here with PhD's, attorneys, people from sort of the higher echelons of society, went to the best schools. What I've calmed down

is promoting what I'm about here at the firm. At first people used to hear about me and knew I was an artist. But they really didn't know what kind of artist, so when I exposed myself and they saw the art and heard the story that I was in prison, it created a stigma.

P- Just like that?

AP- Just like that. It's a stigma I'll live with all my life. They look at me different, maybe they won't even say hi to me. That's some people. Not all people, but a majority of people in this firm. I think it's a stigma. My next door neighbor doesn't know I'm an ex-prisoner. I'm always paranoid. I've been living there in this private house, with a little Italian couple who love me, yet they don't know my past. I remember when people would be coming over to do interviews, with all their production equipment, and I used to freak out because I have a small apartment and all this stuff would be out in the hall, and there's a knock on the door. Who is it but my landlord. She asked what was going on and I told her they were making a film about my art. She said, "ooh, can I see it when it's done?" I said sure, but I never showed it to her. Things like that. I always live with this stigma, carrying a Scarlet Letter as I call it. It's universal the stigma I carry, it tainted me, but it also gave me courage and strength to go on in a positive way. I use it as a tool now. Because what happens when you do an extraordinary amount of time, many people want to put it aside and go on with their life. But with me, I use it as a vehicle to become who I am, this activist involved in change, positive change and transformation to make things better for people still inside and people outside, yet still wear this Scarlet Letter, that label as a convicted felon.

P- One last question. Do you find it a bit ironic that you served 12 years in prison under the Rockefeller Drug laws, and now you work in the Rockefeller Center?

AP- I work at Rockefeller Center. I think it's very appropriate that I help stage rallies at 50th and 5th at the Rockefeller Center. Everything has evolved around the Rockefeller Center, so this is the place for me to be.

Trends in State Parole

The More Things Change, the More They Stay the Same

BY TIMOTHY A. HUGHES, DORIS JAMES WILSON AND ALAN J. BECK, PH.D.

At YEAR-END 2000 more than 652,000 adults were under state parole supervision, up from 509,700 ten years earlier. During the year 441,600 adults entered parole supervision and 432,200 exited. Although prison release rates dropped sharply early in the decade, the number under parole supervision grew exponentially (averaging ten percent per year) before peaking in 1992. At the same time, despite a decade of reform and change, including enhancements in sentencing, added restrictions on prison releases and experimentation with community supervision and monitoring, parolee success rates remained unchanged. Among state parole discharges, 42 percent successfully completed their term of supervision in 2000, 45 percent successfully completed their term in 1990.

These findings and others appeared in *Trends in State Parole, 1990–2000*, a special report issued by the Bureau of Justice Statistics in October 2001. The report not only documents the nature and extent of growth of state parole populations but presents statistics on parole success and failure. The report, updated specially for *Perspectives*, underscores the complex interaction between incarceration and post-release supervision policies.

Growth in parole linked to incarceration trends

Changes in sentencing laws and prison release policies, as well as the increased likelihood of a conviction and incarceration if arrested, spurred the growth of the prison population in the 1980s and early 1990s. Since 1980 incarceration rates have soared but are now beginning to stabilize. At mid-year 2001, the rate of incarceration in federal or state prisons and local jails was 690 inmates per 100,000 adult U.S. residents up from 458 in 1990. However, the 1.1 percent growth in the number of prison inmates for the 12 months ending June 30, 2001 was significantly lower than the 5.8 percent average annual increase since 1990. It was also the lowest annual rate recorded since 1972.

A consequence of the growth in imprisonment is a corresponding change over time in the number of people under community supervision. Of the people who are admitted to prison, most return to the community at some point—either released from prison by completing their sentence, by discretionary parole or by mandatory parole. In general, parole is a period of conditional supervision after serving time in prison. Discretionary parole exists when a parole board has authority to conditionally release prisoners based on a statutory or administrative determination of eligibility. Mandatory parole generally occurs in jurisdictions using determinate sentencing statutes in which inmates are conditionally released from prison after serving a specified portion of their original sentence minus any good time earned. About 95 percent of all inmates currently in state prison will be released, and 80 percent will have a period of parole or post-custody supervision.

The number of adults under state parole supervision more than tripled between 1980 and 2000 (from 196,786 to 652,199). While growth in the state parole population had nearly stabilized by yearend 2000, the largest increase occurred between 1980 and 1992. During this period, the number of adults on parole grew ten percent annually. After 1992, following more than a decade of rapid growth, annual increases in the number of adults on state parole slowed dramatically, increasing at an average annual rate of 0.7 percent **(Figure 1)**.

From 1990 to 2000, the state parole population grew at a slower rate than the state prison population. During this period, parolees increased 30 percent, compared to a 75 percent increase in state prisoners. On average, the parole population increased 2.6 percent per year, while the prison population rose 5.7 percent per year. The lower rate of growth in parole supervision reflects changes in sentencing and parole release policies that have resulted in increasing lengths of stay in prison and declining prison release rates. However, growth in the prison population has slowed since 1995 and recent data suggest

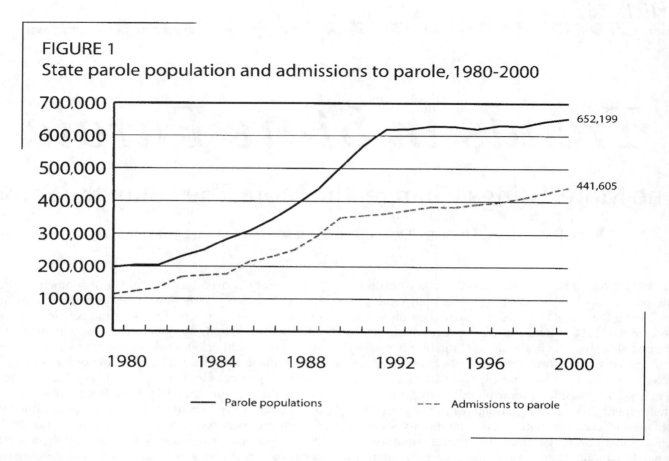

FIGURE 1
State parole population and admissions to parole, 1980-2000

652,199

441,605

——— Parole populations   - - - Admissions to parole

that the population has stabilized. Underlying the dramatic slow down in the rate of growth in state prison populations has been a rise in the number of prison releases. In the last six months of 2000, the state prison population actually dropped by 0.1 percent, the first measured decline since 1972. In the last 12 months ending June 30, 2001, the number under state jurisdiction increased 0.4 percent. **(Figure 2)**.

States reduced the discretion of parole boards

Trends in state parole populations have been affected by a movement from discretionary release toward mandatory parole release and by the enactment of truth-in-sentencing legislation. Historically, most state inmates were released to parole supervision after serving a portion of an indeterminate sentence based on a parole board decision. In 1977, 69 percent of offenders released from state prison were released by a parole board. Good time reduction and other earned time incentives permitted officials to individualize the amount of punishment or leniency an offender received and provided a means to manage the prison population.

This discretion led to criticism that some offenders were punished more harshly than others for similar offenses and to complaints that overall sentencing and release laws were lenient on crime. By 1989, eight states

(California, Florida, Illinois, Indiana, Maine, Minnesota, Oregon and Washington) had abolished discretionary parole and in 20 others, the majority of prison releases were through expiration of sentence or mandatory parole release.

Continuing the shift away from release by a parole board, an additional eight states (Arizona, Delaware, Kansas, Mississippi, North Carolina, Ohio, Virginia and Wisconsin) abolished discretionary parole in the 1990s. Most of the remaining states further restricted parole by setting specific standards offenders must meet to be eligible for release. As a result, parole boards are no longer the dominant mechanism by which inmates are released from state prison. More inmates are now released by state statutes that mandate release after inmates serve a specified portion of their sentence. After 1980, mandatory parole increased from 19 percent of releases from prison to 39 percent in 2000, while discretionary parole decreased from 55 percent to 24 percent.

In absolute numbers, releases by state parole boards peaked in 1992 (at 170,095), dropping to 136,130 in 2000 **(Table 1)**. Mandatory parole releases steadily increased, from 26,735 in 1980 to 116,857 in 1990. By 1995 the number of mandatory releases exceeded the number of discretionary releases. In 2000, 221,414 state prisoners were released by mandatory parole, an 89 percent increase from 1990. The number of annual releases via mandatory parole is

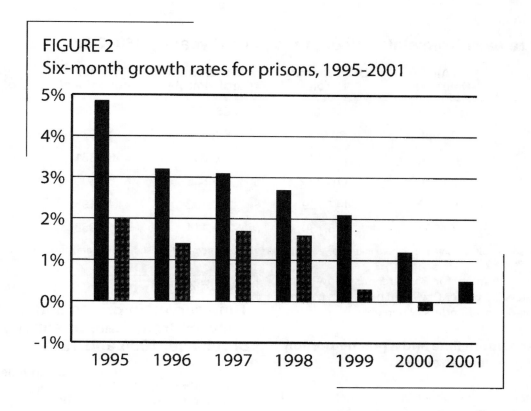

FIGURE 2
Six-month growth rates for prisons, 1995-2001

expected to continue to grow over the next several years. Instead of entering prison faced with an uncertain sentence suggestive of a rehabilitative model of criminal justice, more and more inmates are virtually guaranteed a release date upon admission to prison.

Growth in releases expected as inmates complete enhanced sentences

Several factors influenced the flow of offenders from prison to parole supervision, such as fluctuations in prison release rates, an increase in elapsed time served by offenders, and changes in release policies. Prison release rates declined from 37 percent in 1990 to 32 percent in 2000. Though this is a modest percentage difference, when applied to the growing number of inmates in prison at some time during the year, the drop implies at least 90,000 fewer releases in 2000 as a result of the five percent drop in the annual release rate since 1990. Nevertheless, the number of prisoners released from state prison has grown from 405,400 in 1990 to an expected 595,000 in 2001. (See box, State Prison.)

While violent offenders accounted for most of the growth among those in prison, drug offenders comprised an increasing percentage of prison releases as well as entries to parole. Nearly 33 percent of state prison releases in 1999 were drug offenders (up from 26 percent in 1990 and 11 percent in 1985) **(Figure 3)**. In contrast to drug offenders, the release of violent offenders has remained stable, while property offenders have dropped sharply.

Approximately 24 percent of releases were violent offenders in 1999 (compared to 26 percent in 1990), and 31 percent were property offenders (down from 39 percent).

State Prison	
Year	**Releases***
1990	**405,400**
1995	**455,100**
1999	**543,000**
2000	**571,000**
2001 (projected)	**595,000**
*Excluding escapees, AWOL's and transfers.	

Drug law violators increasing among parole entries

Between 1990 and 1999, annual releases from state prison to parole supervision grew by an estimated 78,900 inmates. Drug offenders accounted for 61 percent of that increase, followed by violent offenders (23 percent), and public-order offenders (15 percent). The number of property offenders released to parole declined from 1990 to 1999. Among the nearly 424,000 entries to parole in 1999,

TABLE 1

Method of release from state prison, for selected years, 1980–2000

YEAR	All Releases	Discretionary Parole	Mandatory Parole Parole	Other conditional	Expiration of sentence
1980	143,543	78,602	26,735	9,363	20,460
1985	206,988	88,069	62,851	15,371	34,489
1990	405,374	159,731	116,857	62,851	51,288
1992	430,198	170,095	126,836	60,800	48,971
1995	455,140	147,139	177,402	46,195	66,017
2000	570,966	136,130	221,414	66,958	110,441

Note: Based on prisoners with a sentence of more than one year who were released from state prison. Counts are for December 31 of each year.

drug offenders accounted for 35 percent, followed by property offenders (31 percent), violent offenders (24 percent) and public-order offenders (9 percent).

Offenders serve more time and a greater portion of their sentence before release

Reflecting statutory and policy changes that required offenders to serve a larger portion of their sentence before release, all offenders released for the first time in 1999 served on average 49 percent of their sentence, up from 38 percent in 1990. Among all state inmates released from prison for their first time on their current offense (first releases), the average time served in prison increased from 22 months in 1990 to 29 months in 1999. Released inmates had also served an average of five months in local jails prior to their admission to prison. Overall, released inmates had served a total of 34 months in 1999, compared to 28 months in 1990. Of the four major offense categories, violent offenders served the highest percentage of their sentence (55 percent) in 1999, followed by public-order (51 percent), property (46 percent) and drug offenders (43 percent).

Much of the increase in time served is likely due to the enactment of the truth-in-sentencing standards that in general specify a portion of the sentence an offender must serve in prison. By the end of 2000, the federal truth-in-sentencing standard that requires that Part 1 violent offenders serve not less than 85 percent of their sentence in prison before becoming eligible for release had been adopted by 29 states and the District of Columbia. Part 1 violent offenses, as defined by the Federal Bureau of Investigation's Uniform Crime Reports, include murder, non-negligent manslaughter, rape, robbery and aggravated assault.

By adopting this standard, states could receive truth-in-sentencing funds under the Violent Offender Incarceration and Truth-in-Sentencing (VOITIS) incentive grant program as established by the 1994 Crime Act. VOITIS

TABLE 2

Time served in prison and jail for first releases from State prison, by method of release, 1990 and 1999

Type of release and offense	Mean time served	
	1990	1999
Discretionary release	29 months	35 months
Violent	49 months	59 months
Property	25 months	31 months
Drug	20 months	28 months
Public-order	18 months	21 months
Mandatory release	27 months	33 months
Violent	41 months	47 months
Property	23 months	30 months
Drug	20 months	27 months
Public-order	19 months	25 months
Expiration of sentence	31 months	36 months
Violent	44 months	52 months
Property	27 months	30 months
Drug	21 months	29 months
Public-order	28 months	25 months

Note: Based on prisoners with a sentence of more than one year. Excludes persons released from prison by escape, death, transfer, appeal or detainer.

grants can be used by states to build or expand prison capacity. States not adopting the federal standard may have other truth-in-sentencing policies that specify a certain percentage of the sentence to be served prior to release.

At year-end 2000, nearly three-quarters of the parole population was in states that met the federal 85 percent standard. Nine of the ten states with the largest parole

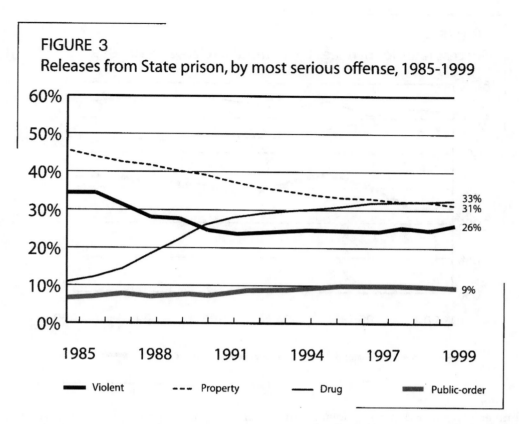

FIGURE 3
Releases from State prison, by most serious offense, 1985-1999

Legend: ■ Violent --- Property — Drug ■ Public-order

populations in 2000 met the federal truth-in-sentencing standard for violent offenders. Texas, with the second largest parole population, required violent offenders to serve 50 percent of their sentence before becoming eligible for release.

The result of longer lengths of stay due to truth-in-sentencing (in combination with the increased average age of prison admissions) has been an aging of the parole population. The average age of prisoners released to parole increased from 31 years in 1990 to 34 years in 1999. An estimated 109,300 state prisoners paroled in 1999 (26 percent of all entries to parole) were age 40 or older. This was more than double the number of prisoners age 40 or older who entered parole in 1990.

Inmates released by a parole board serve longer than mandatory parolees

Contrary to the widespread perception that reliance on parole board discretion implies early release, data from 30 states participating in BJS's National Corrections Reporting Program reveal that offenders released by parole boards actually serve more time in prison than other parolees. Overall, prisoners released in 1999 by discretionary parole for the first time on the current sentence had served an average of 35 months in prison and jail, while those released through mandatory parole had served 33 months **(Table 2)**. In 1990, and in every other year during the 1990s, the average time served by discretionary re-

leases exceeded the time served by mandatory parole releases. The largest disparities appear among violent prisoners released in 1999—those released through discretionary parole served an average 59 months, those released through mandatory parole served 47 months.

Though time served by discretionary releases exceeded the time served by mandatory releases, discretionary releases served a smaller percentage of their prison sentences before release. In 1999 discretionary releases served 37 percent of their total prison sentence (up from 34 percent in 1990); mandatory releases served 61 percent of their sentence (up from 55 percent).

Re-releases an increasing portion of parole entries

Among all parole entries, the percentage that had been re-released rose between 1990 and 1999. Re-releases are persons leaving prison after having served time either for a violation of parole or other conditional release or for a new offense committed while under parole supervision. In 1990, 27 percent of entries to parole were re-releases; in 1999, 45 percent were re-releases. During 1999 an estimated 192,400 re-releases entered parole, more than double the 94,900 re-releases in 1990.

These data highlight the significant number of individuals cycling through our nation's prisons. Underlying the dramatic growth in state prison populations has been a rise in parole violators returned to prison. Between 1990

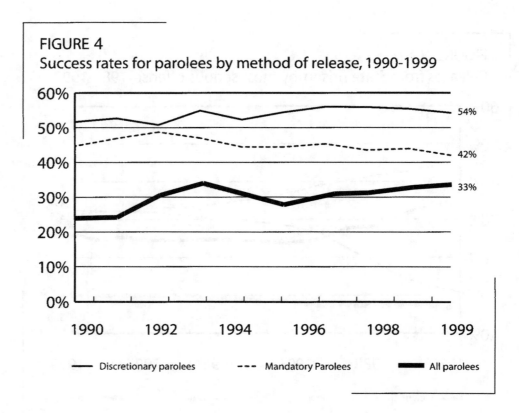

FIGURE 4
Success rates for parolees by method of release, 1990-1999

— Discretionary parolees   - - - Mandatory Parolees   ▬ All parolees

and 2000, the number of returned parole violators increased 52 percent (from 133,900 to 203,600), while the number of new court commitments increased 8 percent (from 323,100 to 350,400). As percent of all admissions to prison, parole violators totaled 35 percent in 2000. As a consequence, these previously released offenders, who have failed under parole supervision in the past, represent a growing portion of subsequent parole entries.

After having been returned to prison for a parole or conditional release violation, re-releases served on average 13 months in prison in 1999. From 1990 to 1999 their average time served in prison following re-admission increased by two months.

Success rates stable despite changes in release policies

A comparison of the rates of success on parole reveals a complex relationship between the methods of parole (discretionary or mandatory), the type of offender (first release or re-release) and the length of time served. Success rates also vary by other risk factors, including age, gender and type of offense.

Despite dramatic changes in the criminal justice system over the last decade, the outcomes of parole supervision remained relatively consistent with the levels observed in 1990. Of the 410,613 discharges from State parole in 1999, 42 percent successfully completed their term of supervision, 43 percent were returned to prison or jail, and ten percent absconded (**Figure 4**). In 1990, 45 percent

of state parole discharges were successful. Between 1990 and 1999 the percent successful among state parole discharges has ranged from 42 percent to 49 percent, without any distinct trend.

A successful discharge occurs when the offender is released by the parole authority after completing the term of conditional supervision. Unsuccessful discharges include revocations of parole, returns to prison or jail and absconders. Parolees who are transferred to other jurisdictions and those who die while under supervision are not included in the calculation of success/failure rates.

Success rates highest among parole board releases and first releases

In every year between 1990 and 1999, state prisoners released by a parole board had higher success rates than those released through mandatory parole. Among parole discharges in 1999, 54 percent of discretionary parolees were successful compared to 33 percent of those who had received mandatory parole. Between 1990 and 1999 the percent successful among discretionary parolees varied between 50 and 56 percent, while the percent successful among mandatory parolees ranged between 24 and 33 percent.

Success rates also varied by type of release. In every year during the 1990s, first releases to state parole were much more likely to have been successful than re-releases. Among state parole discharges in 1990, 56 percent of first releases successfully completed their supervi-

TABLE 3

Percent successful among parole discharges in California and all other states, 1995–1999

YEAR	California	Parole in all other States		
	All Parole	**All**	**Mandatory**	**Discretionary**
1995	22.7%	52.8%	64.0%	54.2%
1996	23.8%	56.6%	71.6%	55.8%
1997	22.8%	55.9%	67.2%	55.8%
1998	24.3%	54.5%	65.7%	55.2%
1999	25.2%	53.3%	63.9%	53.9%

Note: Based on prisoners with a sentence of more than one year who were released from State prison.

sion, compared to 15 percent of re-releases. Of offenders exiting parole in 1999, 63 percent of first releases were successful, compared to 21 percent of re-releases.

Among parole discharges in 1999 that had been released from prison for the first time on their current offense, mandatory parolees had a higher success rate (79 percent) than discretionary parolees (61 percent). Discretionary parolees in 1999 who had been re-released from prison were more likely to be successful (37 percent) than mandatory parolees (17 percent).

Success rates higher if California is excluded

The size and make-up of California's parole population, combined with the low percent of successful terminations (25 percent in 1999), affect the national rate of success for parole discharges **(Table 3)**. When data from California are removed from the analysis, the comparative rates of success for discretionary and mandatory parole change dramatically.

Overall, California accounted for nearly 30 percent of all state parole discharges during 1999. Discretionary parole, though available as a method of release, is rarely used in California. In 1999 more than 99 percent of California's parole discharges had received mandatory parole. When California data are excluded, the success rate for all parole discharges rises to 53 percent (from 42 percent), and the rate for mandatory parolees increases to 64 percent (from 33 percent) in 1999. In states other than California, success rates are found to be higher among prisoners released through mandatory parole than by a parole board.

Nevertheless, the differences in outcomes vary by type of release. Parole boards achieve significantly higher suc-

cess rates when releasing offenders who have previously violated parole. In 1999 37 percent of discretionary parolees who had been re-released were successful, compared to 17 percent of mandatory releases. Throughout the decade, success rates among discretionary re-releases were at least twice those of mandatory re-releases.

Half of all revoked parolees returned for technical violations

During 2000 more than 203,000 offenders were returned to prison for parole violations.

Based on interviews of inmates in state prison in 1997, approximately half of those returned annually are technical violators without a new sentence. Among technical violators, seven percent had an arrest for a new offense, 36 percent had a drug violation (including a positive test, possession, or failure to participate in treatment), 50 percent had absconded or failed to report to a parole office, and 40 percent had some other violation of parole (including failure to maintain employment, to pay fines, fees or restitution, having contact with known felons, or possessing a gun). Since violators often have more than one reason for revocation, the total of all reasons exceeded 100 percent.

As a consequence of the growing number of admissions for parole violations and the longer length of stay for the most serious of these violators, nearly a quarter of all state inmates in 1997 reported having been on parole at the time of the offense for which they were serving time. Nearly 70 percent of these violators reported having been arrested or convicted of a new offense. The percent with new offenses was higher among inmates in prison than among those returned each year, due to the longer time served by violators with new offenses.

Findings have implications for prison and paroling authorities

The changing characteristics of offenders entering parole may have important implications for developing policies and programs to adequately assist offenders when they return to the community. Such changes underscore the need to have pre-release treatment programs and adequate follow-up for drug offenders who represent the largest portion of the growth in parole entries. Though the largest source of growth in state prison populations has been the increased numbers of violent offenders entering prison and staying longer once incarcerated, drug offenders represent a major portion of those inmates cycling through prisons annually.

Other changes, including the aging of parole entries, increased length of time in prison, and statutorily-mandated release, have implications for strategies to transition offenders from prison to community supervision. A growing proportion of offenders both in prison and on parole are middle aged. In part, the aging of the prison and parole populations is due to longer lengths of stay in prison combined with higher numbers of returns to prison.

The expected reductions in recidivism due to age are offset by the growing percent of older inmates who previously violated parole. Since mandatory release policies may not permit an assessment of risk when inmates who previously failed are re-released, the risk of failure would be significantly higher for this new group of older inmates. The opportunity to conduct adequate risk assessments is undercut by statutory release requirements that replace the judgments of parole boards.

Regardless of the amount of discretion to determine who gets released and when, parole failure rates remain high and unchanged for nearly a decade. Correctional authorities have relatively little time to address the often complex array of problems inmates bring with them to prison and on to parole. A third of all released prisoners serve 12 months or less. On average, inmates released from prison spend nearly three years incarcerated and about two years on parole. Along with their criminal records, many have extensive histories of drug and alcohol abuse, mental illness, homelessness, illiteracy, joblessness and domestic violence. These factors are strongly related to success or failure following prison release and must be addressed if parole success rates are to be improved.

Despite efforts to improve public safety through incapacitation and enhanced punishment, the vast majority (95 percent) of today's inmates will be released. While a sudden wave of prison releases is not expected the number of inmates released annually will continue to grow. Without new efforts and added resources directed to community supervision, the flow back to prison will likely remain steady and troubling.

The report from which this article was derived, *Trends in State Parole, 1990–2000* (October 2001, NCJ 184735), can be viewed online at: http://www.ojp.usdoj.gov/bjs/.

Timothy A. Hughes *and* **Doris James Wilson** *are statisticians at the Bureau of Justice Statistics and work in the Corrections Statistics Program Unit.*

Allen J. Beck, Ph. D. *is the chief of the unit, which is responsible for the collection and analysis of all national-level data on incarcerated and community-based populations.*

From *Perspectives*, Summer 2002, pp. 26-33. © 2002 by the American Probation and Parole Association. Reprinted by permission.

The Results of American Incarceration

Any answer to the question "What do we get from imprisonment?" has to recognize that U.S. imprisonment operates differently than it does in any other democratic state in the world.

By Todd R. Clear

Let's begin with a little thought experiment. Today, there are 1.3 million federal prisoners; over 2 million citizens are incarcerated in state prisons and local jails. Imagine that those numbers grow methodically for the next generation. By the time people born today reach their thirtieth birthday, there will be over 7 million prisoners and, if local jails are counted, more than 10 million locked up on any given day. How are we to react to such daunting numbers?

First, let's agree that the experiment seems unrealistic. This kind of growth would result in about 2 percent of the population incarcerated on any given day. Taken as a percentage of males aged 20–40 (most of those behind bars are from this group), the proportion locked up would be stupefying.

A rational person might say, "State and local governments have trouble affording today's prisons and jails, so how could they pay for such a mind-boggling expansion? What kind of society could justify locking up so many of our young men?"

After a bit more thought, that person might also say, "Well, if we are going to do it, then at least we will eliminate a lot of crime."

This is perhaps a disturbing thought experiment, but it is not a far-fetched one.

The 'war' on crime

To illustrate, go back a full generation, to the beginning of the 1970s. Richard Nixon is president, and we are having a bit of a "war" on crime (puny, by today's standards). Crime rates seem disturbingly high,

and the nightly news seems dominated by stories about disorder in the streets.

Imagine, for a moment, attending a futurist seminar, and the speaker has turned his attention to the topic of social control. He has said a few words about the coming days of electronic surveillance through bracelets on people's ankles and wrists, pictures and home addresses of convicted criminals displayed for all to see at the touch of a keyboard, detention in an offender's home enforced by threat of prison, chemical testing of a person's cells—detectable from saliva left at the scene of a crime—instead of fingerprints to prove guilt at trial, and so on. The audience would rightfully have been a bit awed by the prospect.

Then he makes the most stunning prediction of all. He says, "In the next 30 years, the prison population is going to grow by 600 percent. Instead of today's 200,000 prisoners, we will have more than 1.3 million."

Anyone who heard such predictions in the early 1970s would have been more than a bit skeptical. But they have all come true.

Any answer to the question, "What do we get from imprisonment?" has to begin with a frank recognition that incarceration in the United States today operates differently than in any other modernized or democratic state in the world, and that this phenomenon has resulted from very recent changes in U.S. penal policy. Today, we lock up our fellow citizens at a rate (700 per 100,000) that is between 5 and 10 times higher than in comparable industrial democracies.

A Washington, D.C., prison reform group, the Sentencing Project, has offered these comparisons: European states such

as Germany, Sweden, France, the Netherlands, and Switzerland have incarceration rates of less than 100 per 100,000, one-seventh of ours. The big lock-up states—England, Spain, Canada, and Australia—have prison/jail rates of between 100 and 200, or one-fourth of ours. Our only competitors are Russia and South Africa, with prison-use levels that are 90 and 60 percent of ours, respectively.

That is not the whole story. Our world leadership in the use of prison is a fairly recent accomplishment. U.S. prison population statistics go back to 1925, when there were about 100,000 prisoners. Between 1925 and 1940, a period of fairly substantial immigration and U.S. population growth, the number of prisoners doubled. During the years of World War II, the prison population dropped by about a third. (Most observers think this drop was due to the large number of young men in the armed forces and unavailable for imprisonment). Between 1945 and 1961, the number of prisoners grew by 68 percent, to a high of about 210,000 in the early 1960s, staying more or less stable into the 1970s.

Social scientists looked at these numbers and saw a pattern of profound stability. In 1975, two researchers from Carnegie-Mellon University, Alfred Blumstein and Jacqueline Cohen, argued that after accounting for such factors as war, immigration, and changes in youth population, there had been a "homoeostatic" level of stability in punishment for the first three-quarters of the twentieth century. That theory no longer applies. Between 1971 and 2002, the number of prisoners grew by an astounding 600 percent. Why did everything change?

- Today, the United States locks up its citizens at a rate (700 per 100,000) that is between 5 and 10 times higher than in comparable industrial democracies.
- In European states such as Germany, Sweden, France, the Netherlands, and Switzerland, incarceration rates are under 100 per 100,000.
- The big lockup states—England, Spain, Canada, and Australia—have prison/jail rates of between 100 and 200, or one-quarter of ours.
- The only competitors for prison and jail use are Russia and South Africa, with levels that are 90 and 60 percent of ours, respectively.
- Since the 1990s, almost all the growth in the prison population has been due to longer sentences, not more crime or prisoners.
- In effect, the U.S. anomaly in prison use results mostly from the policies we enact to deal with crime, much less than from crime itself.

Why the growth in crime?

It is easy to say that prison populations grew because crime—or at least violent crime—grew. But this view turns out to be simplistic. In their recent book, *Crime Is Not the Problem*, UCLA criminologists Franklin Zimring and Gordon Hawkins point out that several countries have violent crime rates that rival ours, yet use prison less readily than we do. Moreover, those European countries with low rates of incarceration seem to have property crime rates that are not so different from ours.

Besides, the growth of the U.S. prison population has been so consistent for a generation that nothing seems to affect it much. Since 1980, for example, prison populations grew during economic boom times and recessions alike; while the baby boomers were entering their crime-prone years and as they exited those years; and as crime dropped and while it soared.

Today's nationally dropping crime rates—a trend in some big cities that is almost a decade long—suggest that prison growth has helped make the streets safer. But when we take the long view, aside from burglary (which has dropped systematically for 20 years), today's crime rates are not very different than at the start of the big prison boom in the 1970s. Since then, crime rates went up for a while, down for a while, back up again, and are now (thankfully) trending downward. Prison populations, by contrast, went only one way during this entire period: up.

Blumstein and Department of Justice statistician Allen Beck have studied trends in criminal justice since the 1980s to better understand what accounts for the recent growth in the prison population. They argue that you can divide the growth into three distinct periods. In the late 1970s and early 1980s, prisons grew because crime was growing and more criminals were being sentenced to prison. In the 1980s into the beginning of the 1990s, prison growth was partly due to crime rates, but it was much more a product of greater numbers of criminals being sentenced to prison and of longer terms for those sentenced there.

By the 1990s and into the early 2000s, the story has changed, and almost all of the growth in the prison population is due to longer sentences, not more crime or more prisoners. In effect, the U.S. anomaly in the use of prison is a result mostly of the policies we enact to deal with crime, and much less of crime itself.

A street's-eye view

But all of this exploration looks for broad patterns. What about the view from the streets? John DiIulio of the University of Pennsylvania, former codirector of the White House Office on Faith-Based Initiatives, once observed, "A thug in jail can't shoot my sister?" Isn't it apparent on its face that a person behind bars is someone from whom the rest of us are pretty safe?

Yes, but that may not be the most effective way to deter crime. The irony is that while people who are behind bars are less likely to commit crimes, that may not mean those crimes are prevented from occurring.

Drug crime is the obvious example. Almost one-third of those sent to prison are punished for drug-related crimes, and one prisoner in four is serving time for a drug crime. In most of these cases, the criminal activity continued without noticeable interruption, carried out by a replacement. One of the recurrent frustrations of police work is to carry out a drug sweep one day, only to see the drug market return in a matter of hours. Locking up drug offenders is not an efficient strategy for preventing drug crime.

This line of analysis can be misleading, though, because most drug offenders are not specialists in drug crime. Analyses of criminal records show that people in prison who are serving time for drug-related activity typically have arrests and/or convictions for other types of offenses. Doesn't locking them up for drugs prevent the other

crimes from happening? At least some other crime is prevented, but not as much as might be thought.

A few years ago, Yale sociologist Albert Reiss reported that about half of all criminal acts are perpetrated by young offenders acting in groups of two or more. Rarely are all of the members of the group prosecuted for the crime. This discovery led to a string of studies of what has been referred to as "co-offending," the commission of crimes by multiple offenders acting in concert. When one person out of a group is arrested and imprisoned, what impact does the arrest have on the crimes the group had been committing? A lot rides on the nature and behavior of criminal groups.

Much research is now under way to better understand how crimes are committed by offenders acting alone and in a group. It would be convenient if criminal groups had stable leaders and were systematic in the way they planned criminal activity. If so, arresting the leaders might break up the groups, and strategies of deterrence might reduce the likelihood of criminal actions. Neither characteristic applies.

Criminologist Mark Warr of the University of Texas has studied the way young males form co-offending groups and engage in criminal acts. He reports that leadership is sporadic and often interchangeable, that criminal actions are spontaneous, and that co-offending groups are loosely formed and vary over time. His findings suggest that well-respected strategies of targeted prosecution and focus on leaders of criminal activity are likely to have diminishing returns in crime prevention. As Rutgers University's Marcus Felson has argued, this analysis of dynamic, spontaneous, loosely organized criminal activity applies not simply to some youth but to most gang behavior. Arresting one person in the network and sending him to prison is far from a guarantee that the crime that person was involved in will stop.

Are crime and punishment connected?

None of this is to argue that imprisonment prevents no crime. Professor David W. Garland of New York University School of Law, one of the most widely respected social critics of imprisonment, puts it well when he says that only the naive would claim that prisons and crime are unrelated. But even if it is recognized that crime and prisons are connected, under close scrutiny, we can find various reasons why wildly growing rates of imprisonment might not lead willy-nilly to wildly reducing rates of crime. Said another way, we can find explanations for the fact that the period in which incarceration has grown so much has not been matched by a corresponding drop in crime.

A new literature is emerging about the unintended consequences of incarceration. Prison populations, for example, are drawn predominantly from the ranks of poor people from minority groups. Today, one in eight black males aged 25–29 is locked up; this rate is almost eight times higher than for white males. Estimates reported by the Department of Justice indicate that of black males born today, 29 percent will go to prison for a felony offense, while currently 17 percent of all African-American males have spent time in prison. These rates are about six times higher than for white males.

Patterns of racial segregation mean that imprisonment also concentrates residentially. James Lynch and William Sabol, researchers from the Urban Institute, have estimated that in some very poor neighborhoods in Washington, D.C., and Cleveland, Ohio, upwards of 18–20 percent of adult males are locked up on any given day. New York City's Center for Alternative Sentencing and Employment Services reported that in 1998, in two of Brooklyn's poorest Council Districts, one person went to prison or jail for every eight resident males aged 20–40.

These high rates of incarceration, concentrated among poor minority males living in disadvantaged locations, are a new phenomenon that results from a generation of prison population growth in the United States. Social scientists are beginning to investigate whether this socially concentrated use of prison sentences has long-term effects on such factors as neighborhood order, family structure, and child development.

One can imagine, for example, that a neighborhood where a large proportion of parent-age men are missing is a neighborhood that would grapple with a number of problems, from family stability to child supervision. My own research with my colleagues Dina Rose and Elin Waring seems to suggest that high incarceration rates produce socially destabilizing results that may be a factor in sustaining high rates of crime.

The prison is a blunt social instrument, while crime is a much more nuanced social problem. Given what we know about crime, it should not surprise us that so much prison has provided so little in the way of broad public safety.

When trying to weigh the benefits of prison, perhaps we are used to asking the wrong question. We tend to ask about whether prison is a good idea compared to alternative sentencing. In today's America, this may be a fascinating question but it is not a very meaningful one. The more appropriate question would be, "Given our experience with incarceration over the last century, what might we expect from further increases in its use; what might happen if we began to cut back in its use?" This question, which we might perhaps save for another day, would recognize the political reality that U.S. prison rates are going to be internationally out-of-scale for a long time. The only question we face is, how much?

Todd R. Clear is Distinguished Professor in Community Justice and Corrections at John Jay College of Criminal Justice in New York City.

Correctional Boot Camps: Lessons From a Decade of Research

Dale G. Parent

In response to rising rates of serious crime, many correctional systems established boot camps as an alternative sanction that might reduce recidivism, prison populations, and operating costs. Despite a decade of popularity with policymakers and the public, boot camps have had difficulty meeting these objectives.

The National Institute of Justice (NIJ) sponsored an analysis of research conducted over a 10-year period beginning in the late 1980s. This analysis concluded that—

- Boot camps generally had positive effects on the attitudes, perceptions, behavior, and skills of inmates during their confinement.
- With limited exceptions, these positive changes did not translate into reduced recidivism.
- Boot camps can achieve small *relative* reductions in prison populations and modest reductions in correctional costs under a narrow set of conditions (admitting offenders with a high likelihood of other wise serving a conventional prison term and offering discounts in time served to those who complete boot camps).

The surveyed research identified three factors largely responsible for the failure of boot camps to reach goals related to prison population and recidivism:

- Mandates to reduce prison populations through early release made volunteering for boot camps unnecessary as a means of shortening sentences.
- Lack of a standard boot camp model.
- Insufficient focus on offenders' reentry into the community.

The camps' disciplined structure and therapeutic programs eliminated idleness and created a safer environment, which in turn improved inmate attitudes and behavior. Such structure, coupled with a therapeutic orientation, may apply to other correctional programs, especially those that target youthful offenders.

Why boot camps?

As the name implies, correctional boot camps are in-prison programs that resemble military basic training. They emphasize vigorous physical activity, drill and ceremony, manual labor, and other activities that ensure that participants have little, if any, free time. Strict rules govern all aspects of conduct and appearance. Correctional officers act as drill instructors, initially using intense verbal tactics designed to break down inmates' resistance and lead to constructive changes.

Three generations of camps. Boot camps proliferated in the late 1980s and early 1990s. By 1995, State correctional agencies operated 75 boot camps for adults, State and local agencies operated 30 juvenile boot camps, and larger counties operated 18 boot camps in local jails. [1]

The camps evolved over time. Early research findings shaped subsequent boot camp policies and the design and operation of new programs.

Although first-generation camps stressed military discipline, physical training, and hard work, second-generation camps emphasized rehabilitation by adding such components as alcohol and drug treatment and prosocial skills training. Some also added intensive postrelease supervision that may include electronic monitoring, home confinement, and random urine tests. A few camps admitted females, but this proved somewhat controversial (see "Females in Boot Camps"). Recently, some boot camps, particularly those for juveniles, have substituted an emphasis on educational and vocational skills for the military components to provide comparable structure and discipline. [2]

After the mid-1990s, the number of boot camps declined. By 2000, nearly one third of State prison boot camps had closed—only 51 camps remained. The average daily population in State boot camps also dropped more than 30 percent. [3]

Boot camps' goals. Boot camps had three main goals: reducing recidivism, reducing prison populations, and reducing costs.

FEMALES IN BOOT CAMPS

Some boot camp programs began accepting eligible female inmates in the early 1990s, but concerns soon emerged about whether the boot camp strategy is appropriate for women.

Findings from the limited research on female boot camp participants and their high dropout rate clearly indicate that this population faces unique problems. A 1992 study[a] noted that the programs were designed for males and did not accommodate women's special needs or problems.

• **Female inmates are more likely to have children and be the sole parent for those children**. Boot camps often restricted, or even banned, visitation, creating difficult situations for mothers and their children. Also, the programs did not teach parenting skills.
• **Female inmates are more likely to have a history of physical or sexual abuse**. Although female inmates were four to five times more likely than male inmates to have been victims of physical or sexual abuse, most camps had no programs to help them cope with or avoid victimization. Derogatory boot camp tactics tended to retraumatize domestic violence victims.
• **Female inmates are more likely to have a different history and pattern of drug use than males**. Most substance abuse treatment used therapies designed for males.
• **Female inmates are more likely to have been unemployed before imprisonment**. Boot camps did little to prepare women for employment after release.

Female inmates at boot camps reported high stress levels, which may be why they tended to drop out of boot camp at a higher rate than male inmates. Stress stemmed from a physical training regimen designed for males; drill instructors' "in your face" tactics; lack of other female participants, often leading to isolation within the camp; and cross-gender supervision.
A 1998 study[b] described features of successful prison programs for females, most of which were absent from boot camps. These features include the following:

• Using women staff members as role models.
• Addressing participants' prior victimization by building self-esteem and emphasizing empowerment and self-sufficiency.
• Using nonaggressive program management styles.

Notes
[a]MacKenzie et al. 1996.
[b]Morash, Bynum, and Koons 1998.

Camps were expected to reduce recidivism by changing inmates' attitudes, values, and behaviors and by addressing factors that increase the likelihood of returning to prison (such as lack of job skills, addiction, and inability to control anger). Camps were expected to reduce prison populations by shortening time served. Reduced length of stay was expected to reduce costs.

Reducing recidivism—an unmet goal

NIJ evaluation studies consistently showed that boot camps did not reduce recidivism regardless of whether the camps were for adults or juveniles or whether they were first-generation programs with a heavy military emphasis or later programs with more emphasis on treatment. Most of the research suggested that the limitations of boot camps prevented them from reducing recidivism or prison populations, even as they achieved other goals. These limitations mostly resulted from—

• *Low "dosage" effects.* The length of stay in boot camps—usually from 90 to 120 days—was too brief to realistically affect recidivism.
• *Insufficient preparation of boot camp inmates for reentry into the community.* Many boot camps provided little or no postrelease programming to prepare graduates to lead productive lives. In addition, the intensive supervision common to later generations of boot camps meant heightened surveillance levels for boot camp graduates. These factors combined to magnify the high rates of return for technical parole violations.
• *Conflicting or unrealistic goals or mandates set by State legislatures.* For example, most boot camp programs sought to reduce prison populations. Shorter programs more effectively meet this goal, but they also lower dosage effects and reduce the likelihood that treatment programs will work, thereby potentially increasing recidivism.
• *The absence of a strong underlying treatment model.* Pragmatism and local politics often affected boot camp structure more than theory and research results. In fact, this lack of consistent design and approach made controlled scientific analysis difficult (see "Researching the Research: A Thumbnail Review").

RESEARCHING THE RESEARCH A THUMBNAIL REVIEW

The author reviewed boot camp studies to determine the effects of these camps on participants and whether their goals were achieved or even achievable. The first published boot camp study (1989) informed practitioners about existing programs and called for rigorous evaluations.[a] Subsequent research included—

- A multisite evaluation of boot camps in several States.[b]
- Studies of camps receiving funds under the Violent Crime Control and Law Enforcement Act of 1994.[c]
- A multisite process and evaluation study of three juvenile boot camps.[d]
- Evaluations funded by State and local governments.[e]

Although study findings were remarkably consistent, some of the methods of deriving results and conclusions illustrate the difficulties in researching phenomena as complex as correctional boot camps.

Designing for the Differences

Most evaluations compared boot camp graduates with non-boot camp correctional inmates. One problem with this approach was that differences could have stemmed from differences among members of the two groups, rather than from boot camp effects. Researchers tried to match group members on important variables and to control statistically for known differences. A few evaluations used random assignment of eligible subjects, lowering the possibility of differences among groups.

Estimating Elusive Cost Savings

Most studies that examined boot camps' cost impact multiplied the estimated charges attributed to the boot camp in person-days of confinement by the average operating costs for each person-day of confinement. However, this approach may overstate cost savings because staffing costs will not vary unless changes in confinement person-days are large enough to allow the actual closing of facilities. Small population reductions avert marginal costs only. Moreover, States vary in how they determine costs, making comparisons across States problematic.

Counting Hypothetically Empty Beds

Some findings about boot camps, especially those involving the impact on prison populations, are hypothetical because they are derived from simulations and calculations based on projections, rather than on actual results.

For example, a key element used to determine boot camp impact on required prison bed space was the probability that boot camp entrants would have been imprisoned if the boot camp did not exist. Modeling in one study showed that the probability of imprisonment for boot camp entrants would have to be very high to reach a "break-even" point of overall prison population.[f] If the probability of imprisonment for boot camp entrants was not high enough, the camp's existence would actually *increase* prison population.

For the probability of imprisonment factor to fall below a break-even (thereby hypothetically reducing the prison population), correctional officials needed to select offenders who were *already sentenced*. If judges selected boot camp participants before sentencing, this would not reduce the prison population according to these calculations.

Untangling Findings and Results

Many studies had ambiguous findings. Although NIJ's multisite evaluation[g] found no difference overall in recidivism between boot camp graduates and the comparison groups, three of the eight sites may have had lower recidivism. These sites had better treatment services, longer program duration, and more intensive postrelease supervision.

However, some of the other five boot camps also had these components, and the apparent reason for lower recidivism in two of the three sites was different from the third. Evaluators admitted they could not "untangle the particular effects of each program component on recidivism."[h] Focusing on what they could prove, they concluded that "the core elements of boot camp programs-military—style discipline, hard labor, and physical training—by themselves did not reduce offender recidivism." Finally, they speculated that for programs to affect recidivism, "it is likely that some mixture of rehabilitation and intensive followup supervision plays an important role."[i]

Notes

[a]See Parent 1989.
[b]See MacKenzie and Souryal 1994.
[c]Parent et al. 1999; Zhang 1999; MacKenzie et al. 2001; Lewis et al. 1998; Austin 2000.
[d]Peters et al. 1997.
[e]Flowers et al. 1991.
[f]Parent 1994.
[g]MacKenzie and Souryal 1994; MacKenzie et al.1995.
[h]MacKenzie and Hebert 1996, p. 293.
[i]Ibid.

Adult recidivism. A multisite evaluation sponsored by NIJ could not establish a difference in recidivism between adult boot camp graduates and comparison group members, although the research indicated that more treatment services, longer programs, and intensive postrelease supervision may lower recidivism. [4]

Other research on adult boot camps in Georgia and Illinois found no difference in recidivism.[5] An evaluation of Washington's Work Ethic Camp[6] (WEC) actually found higher recidivism, from high rates of revoked parole. Most of these were technical violations.[7] One study found that Oregon adult boot camp graduates had significantly lower recidivism than the comparison group, but results were flawed because camp dropouts were excluded from the analysis.[8]

Juvenile recidivism. Results from juvenile boot camp studies are similar: Random-assignment evaluations in California and Indiana and a multisite evaluation sponsored by the Office of Juvenile Justice and Delinquency Prevention (OJJDP) found no significant differences in recidivism rates between boot camp participants and comparison groups. In some cases, boot camp graduates had higher rates of recidivism.[9]

Improving behavior— a success story

Boot camps were almost universally successful in improving inmates' attitudes and behavior during the course of the program; they also produced safer environments for staff and residents, presumably due to their highly structured atmosphere and activities.

Several studies indicated that adult boot camp participants had better attitudes about their confinement experiences and had improved their prosocial attitudes more than comparison group members.[10] One study concluded that inmates in adult boot camps had increased self-esteem, reduced antisocial attitudes, increased problem-solving skills, improved coping skills, and improved social support.[11] In other studies, boot camp inmates improved their self-esteem and standardized education scores in reading and math more than comparison group members.[12]

Anxiety and depression declined to a greater degree among juveniles in boot camps than among those in comparison facilities.[13] Dysfunctional impulsivity (the inability to control one's impulses) increased among youths in comparison facilities but decreased among boot camp participants. Social attitudes improved among youths in boot camps, but worsened among those in comparison facilities.

Reducing prison population— mixed results

NIJ-sponsored boot camp researchers agree that correctional boot camps might achieve small *relative*[14] reductions in prison populations. Boot camps could reduce the number of prison beds needed in a jurisdiction, which would lead to modest reductions in correctional costs.

NIJ's multisite study[15] concluded that adult boot camp programs in Louisiana and New York reduced their need for prison beds. Two other studies[16] found that WEC and an Illinois camp reduced prison bed-space requirements.[17] Researchers also concluded that juvenile boot camps reduced the needed number of correctional beds in South Dakota and Oregon.[18]

However, restrictive entry criteria for boot camp participants often made it impossible to reduce prison populations. For example, some jurisdictions required that boot camp inmates be nonviolent offenders convicted of their first felony. This small pool of eligible candidates typically serves short prison terms before parole. These inmates had little incentive to volunteer for boot camps that would not shorten their terms. When inmates sentenced to longer prison terms were recruited, however, a reduction in time served became a compelling incentive.

Efforts to meet the recidivism goal may work against meeting population and cost reduction goals. For example, lengthening a boot camp term to add more treatment programs in order to reduce the chances of recidivism would shorten the discount in time served and, thus, not reduce the population or prison bed costs.[19]

Conclusions

Correctional practitioners and planners might learn from boot camps' failure to reduce recidivism or prison populations by considering the following:

- Building reintegration into the community into an inmate's individual program and reentry plans may improve the likelihood he or she will not commit a new offense.
- Programs that offered substantial discounts in time served to those who completed boot camps and that chose candidates sentenced to serve longer terms were the most successful in reducing prison populations.
- Chances of reducing recidivism increased when boot camp programs lasted longer and offered more intensive treatment and postrelease supervision, activities that may conflict with the goal of reducing population.

Efforts to achieve multiple goals are likely the overall cause of boot camps' conflicting results. Program designers are urged to determine which options are best for their jurisdictions; for example, they may consider whether to implement more treatment programs or move inmates out of the system more rapidly. These decisions affect costs, as prison bed-space savings go up or down.

Other correctional programs are adopting some of the important elements of boot camps—for example, carefully structured programs that reduce idleness—to increase safety and improve conditions of confinement for younger offenders.[20] However, in recent years, some jurisdictions facing rising costs have responded by cutting programs. One lesson for policymakers from 10 years of boot camp research is that curtailing programs may lead to increased violence, misconduct, and serious management problems.

Notes

1. Camp and Camp 2001a, 2001b.
2. Gransky et al. 1995.
3. Camp and Camp 2001a.
4. MacKenzie and Souryal 1994; MacKenzie et al. 1995.
5. See Flowers et al. 1991; Austin 2000.
6. See Austin 2000.
7. Prosecutors often decide against trying offenders on new crimes because parole officials can revoke parole for technical violations. If revocations and returns for technical violations are reduced, new convictions may increase.
8. The program had a 52-percent failure rate. See Austin 2000.
9. See Bottcher and Isorena 1994; Austin 2000; Zhang 1999; Peters et al. 1997.
10. See MacKenzie and Souryal 1994.
11. See Austin 2000.
12. Clark et al. 1994; Bottcher and Isorena 1994; Peters et al. 1997.
13. MacKenzie et al. 2001.
14. Boot camps were unlikely to lower *absolute* prison population levels. The camps opened during a time when major changes in sentencing policies and practices caused prison populations to soar. Even at the height of their popularity, the total capacity of boot camps was minuscule compared to the total prison population.
15. See MacKenzie and Piquero 1994, pp. 222-249; MacKenzie and Souryal 1994. A later study of the New York network of boot camps reached the same conclusion: see Clark et al. 1994.
16. See Parent et al. 1999; Austin 2000.
17. See Austin 2000.
18. See Parent et al. 1999.
19. Ibid.
20. OJJDP's Performance-based Standards project seeks to improve conditions by establishing standards for correctional facilities and programs. More information may be found at http://www. performance-standards.org/.

References and Further Reading

Austin, J. 2000. *Multisite Evaluation of Boot Camp Programs: Final Report*. Washington, D.C.: George Washington University, Institute on Crime, Justice, and Corrections.

Bottcher, J., and T. Isorena. 1994. "LEAD: A Boot Camp and Intensive Parole Program: An Implementation and Process Evaluation of the First Year." NCJ 150513. Washington, D.C.: California Youth Authority and U.S. Department of Justice, National Institute of Justice.

Camp, C.G., and G.M. Camp. 2001a. *The 2000 Corrections Yearbook: Adult Corrections*. Middletown, Connecticut: Criminal Justice Institute.

Camp, C.G., and G.M. Camp. 2001b. *The 2000 Corrections Yearbook: Jails*. Middletown, Connecticut: Criminal Justice Institute.

Clark, C.L., D.W. Aziz, and D.L. MacKenzie. 1994. *Shock Incarceration in New York: Focus on Treatment*. Program Focus, NCJ 148410. Washington, D.C.: U.S. Department of Justice, National Institute of Justice.

Flowers, F.T., T.S. Carr, and R.B. Ruback. 1991. *Special Alternative Incarceration Evaluation*. NCJ 132851. Washington, D.C.: Georgia Department of Corrections and U.S. Department of Justice.

Gransky, L.A., T.C. Castellano, and E.L. Cowles. 1995. "Is There a 'Second Generation' of Shock Incarceration Facilities?" In J.O. Smykla and W.C. Selka (eds.), *Intermediate Sanctions Sentencing in the 1990s*. Cincinnati, Ohio: Anderson Publishing, pp. 89-111.

Hunter, R.J., V.S. Burton, J.W. Marquart, and S.J. Cuvelier. 1992. "Measuring Attitudinal Change of Boot Camp Participants." *Journal of Contemporary Criminal Justice* 8(4): 283-298.

Lewis, R.A., M. Jones, and S. Plant. 1998. *National MultiSite Process Evaluation of Boot Camp Planning Grants: An Analysis of Correctional Program Planning*. San Francisco: National Council on Crime and Delinquency and the U.S. Department of Justice, National Institute of Justice.

MacKenzie, D.L. 1991. "The Parole Performance of Offenders Released From Shock Incarceration (Boot Camp Prisons): A Survival Time Analysis." *Journal of Quantitative Criminology* 7(3): 213-236.

MacKenzie, D.L., R. Brame, D. McDowall, and C. Souryal. 1995. "Boot Camp Prisons and Recidivism in Eight States." *Criminology* 33(3): 327-357.

MacKenzie D.L., A.R. Grover, G.S. Armstrong, and O. Mitchell. 2001. *A National Study Comparing the Environments of Boot Camps With Traditional Facilities for Juvenile Offenders*, NCJ 187680. Washington, D.C.: U.S. Department of Justice, National Institute of Justice.

MacKenzie, D.L., and E.E. Hebert, eds. 1996. *Correctional Boot Camps: A Tough Intermediate Sanction*. Research Report, NCJ 157639. Washington, D.C.: U.S. Department of Justice, National Institute of Justice.

MacKenzie, D.L., and A. Piquero. 1994. "Impact of Shock Incarceration Programs on Prison Crowding." *Crime and Delinquency* 40(2): 222-249.

MacKenzie, D.L., and J.W. Shaw. 1990. "Inmate Adjustment and Change During Shock Incarceration: The Impact of Correctional Boot Camp Programs." *Justice Quarterly* 7: 125-150.

MacKenzie, D.L., L.A. Elis, S.S. Simpson, and S.B. Skroban. 1996. "Boot Camps as an Alternative for Women." In D.L. MacKenzie and E.E. Hebert (eds.), Correctional Boot Camps: A Tough Intermediate Sanction. Research Report, NCJ 157639. Washington, D.C.: U.S. Department of Justice, National Institute of Justice.

MacKenzie, D.L., and C. Souryal. 1994. *Multisite Evaluation of Shock Incarceration*. Research Report, NCJ 150062. Washington, D.C.: U.S. Department of Justice, National Institute of Justice.

Morash, M., T. Bynum, and B. Koons. 1998. *Women Offenders: Programming Needs and Promising Approaches*. Research in Brief, NCJ 171668. Washington, D.C.: U.S. Department of Justice, National Institute of Justice.

Parent, D. 1989. *Shock Incarceration: An Overview of Existing Programs*. Issues and Practices, NCJ 114902. Washington, D.C.: U.S. Department of Justice, National Institute of Justice.

Parent, D. 1994. "Boot Camps Failing To Achieve Goals." *Overcrowded Times* 5(4): 8-11.

Parent, D., B.S. Snyder, and B. Blaisdell. 1999. Boot Camps' *Impact on Confinement Bed Space Requirements*. Final Report, NCJ 189788. Washington, D.C.: U.S. Department of Justice, National Institute of Justice.

Peters, M., D. Thomas, and C. Zamberlan. 1997. *Boot Camps for Juvenile Offenders*. Program Summary, NCJ 164258. Washington, D.C.: U.S. Department of Justice, Office of Juvenile Justice and Delinquency Prevention.

Zhang, S.C. 1999. *An Evaluation of the Los Angeles County Juvenile Drug Treatment Boot Camp*. Final Report, NCJ 189787. San Marco: California State University and the U.S. Department of Justice, National Institute of Justice.

About the Author Between 1988 and 1997, Dale G. Parent, a Senior Associate at Abt Associates Inc., conducted studies of correctional boot camps for the National Institute of Justice.

From *National Institute of Justice Journal*, June 2003, pp. 1–10. Published by the Office of Justice/U.S. Department of Justice.

DO WE NEED THE DEATH PENALTY?

It Is Just and Right

By Dudley Sharp

There is nothing quite like hanging out with your best friend. Jenny Ertman, 14, and Elizabeth Peña, 16, shared their hopes and dreams with each other. Like millions of other teenagers, they liked to have fun, to laugh and smile. One summer evening in Houston, Texas, they shared their last moments on earth together—their own murders.

They were late returning home and took a shortcut through the woods, next to some railroad tracks. They ran into a gang initiation. They were both raped: orally, anally, and vaginally. The gang members laughed about the virgin blood they spilled. When they had finished, they beat and strangled the girls. But Jenny and Elizabeth wouldn't die. With all their strength, with their souls still holding on to the beautiful lives before them, they fought for life.

The gang worked harder. The girls were strangled with belts and shoelaces, stomped on and beaten. Their dreams disappeared as life seeped away from their broken bodies.

Their parents are left to visit empty rooms, to cry upon the beds of their daughters and think what could have been. How beautiful Elizabeth would have been in her prom dress. Her corsage was replaced by the flowers on her grave.

And Jenny's future children, would their grandparents have spoiled them? You know the answer. The immutable joy of grandchildren's laughter was silenced by the cruel selfishness of murder.

WHY THE DEATH PENALTY

Sometimes, the death penalty is simply the most appropriate punishment for the vile crime committed. In such cases, jurors are given the choice between a death sentence and a variety of life sentences, depending upon the jurisdiction. It is never easy for juries to give a death sentence. Neither hatred nor revenge is part of their deliberations. The search for justice determines the punishment.

The murder of the innocent is undeserved. The punishment of murderers has been earned by the pain and suffering they have imposed on their victims. Execution cannot truly represent justice, because there is no recompense to balance the weight of murder. For some crimes, it represents the only just punishment available on earth.

Today, much more than justice is part of the death penalty discussion. Opponents are relentlessly attacking the penalty process itself. They insist that it is so fraught with error and caprice that it should be abandoned. At the very least, they say, America should impose a national moratorium so the system can be reviewed.

The leading salvo in those claims is that 101 innocent people have been released from death row with evidence of their innocence. The number is a fraud. Unfortunately, both the international media and, most predictably, the U.S. media have swallowed such claims and passed them along to the public.

Even many of our elected officials in Washington have blindly accepted those numbers. Sen. Patrick Leahy, chairman of the Senate Judiciary Committee, has said: "What we know is that nearly 100 innocent people have been released from death row since 1973."

The source for these claims is the Death Penalty Information Center (DPIC), the leading source of antideath penalty material in the United States. Richard Dieter, head of the DPIC, has admitted, in the June 6, 2000, *ABA Journal*, that his group makes no distinction between the legally innocent ("I got off death row because of legal error") and the actually innocent ("I had no connection to the murder") cases. Although the DPIC has attempted to revise its standards for establishing innocence, none of the various contortions even suggests actual innocence.

As everyone knows, the debate is about the actually innocent. To strengthen their case, death penalty opponents have broadened their "innocent" count by cases that don't merit that description. On June 20, for example, the Florida Commission on Capital Cases released its review of 23 death sentence cases that the DPIC had called into question. Its conclusion was that in only 4 of those cases were there doubts as to guilt.

Though the DPIC claims that 101 cases were released from death row with evidence of innocence, the actual number is closer to 30. That is 30 cases out of 7,000 sentenced to death since 1973. It appears that the death penalty may well be this country's most accurate criminal sanction, when taking into account the percentage of actual innocent convicted (0.4 percent) and the thoroughness of preventing those allegedly innocent from being executed (100 percent).

Of all the world's social and governmental institutions that put innocents at risk, I can find only one, the U.S. death penalty, that has no proof of an innocent killed since 1900. Can you think of another?

SAVING INNOCENT LIVES

Two other factors weigh into the innocence consideration. First, the death penalty remains the most secure form of incapacitation, meaning that executed murderers do not harm and murder again. Living murderers do, quite often. This is unchallenged. Second, although the deterrent effect of capital punishment has been unjustifiably maligned, the evidence is overwhelming that the potential for negative consequences deters or alters behavior. History and the social sciences fully support that finding.

Three major studies were released in 2001, all finding for the deterrent effect of the death penalty. One, out of Emory University, finds that "each execution results, on average, in 18 fewer murders—with a margin of error of plus or minus 10."

Another, out of the University of Houston, found that a temporary halt to executions in Texas resulted in an additional 90–150 murders, because of the reduction in deterrence. One author, Professor C. Robert Cloninger, states: "[Our] recent study is but another of a growing list of empirical work that finds evidence consistent with the deterrent hypothesis. It is the cumulative effect of these studies that causes any neutral observer to pause."

Death penalty opponents want us to believe that the most severe criminal sanction—execution—deters no one. However, if reason is your guide and you remain unsure of deterrence, you are left with the following consideration. If the death penalty does deter, halting executions will cause more innocents to be slaughtered by giving murderers an addi-

tional opportunity to harm and murder again. If the death penalty does not deter, executions will punish murderers as the jury deems appropriate, preventing them from harming any more victims. Clearly, ending or reducing executions will put many more innocents at risk.

Another major factor in the debate was introduced in a study headed by James Liebman, a professor at Columbia University Law School. *A Broken System: Error Rates in Capital Cases* revealed that there was a 68 percent reversal rate in death penalty cases from 1973 to 1995. The error rate within that study has not been publicly discussed.

Professors Barry Latzer and James Cauthen of John Jay College of Criminal Justice found a 25 percent error within the study's calculations, bringing the reversal rate down to 52 percent. Unfortunately, they had to accept the accuracy of Liebman's assessments, because he refused to release his database. Case reviews in Florida, New Jersey, Utah, and Nevada have provided specific cause to challenge his data. Florida challenges any assessment of error in 33 percent of the cases identified by Liebman, suggesting that the national "error" rate may be closer to 35 percent.

But even that number is suspect. The Supreme Court has stated that the death penalty system receives super due process. This means that the courts are extraordinarily generous in granting reversals in death penalty cases. In fact, the appellate courts are twice as likely to reverse the sentence in death penalty cases as they are the conviction.

Traditionally, death penalty opponents have stated that racism and poverty determine who receives the death penalty. Those arguments persist. What they fail to reveal is that white murderers are twice as likely to be executed as black murderers and are executed 12 months faster.

Some claim that the race of the victim determines the sentence. While those who murder whites dominate death row, it is also true that, overwhelmingly, whites are the victims in robberies, rapes, burglaries, and car-jackings, which make up the majority of death penalty crimes.

No one disputes that the wealthy have an advantage in avoiding a death sentence. The United States executes about 0.1 percent of its murderers. Is there any evidence that it is less likely to execute the wealthier ones, based on the ratio of wealthier to poorer capital murderers? Surprisingly, no.

THE JUSTICE FACTOR

This brings me back to where I started: justice. Some say that executions show a contempt for human life, but the opposite is true. We would hope that a brutal rape may result in a life sentence. Why? We value freedom so highly that we take freedom away as punishment. If freedom were not valued, taking it away would be no sanction.

Life is considered even more precious. Therefore, the death penalty is considered the severest sanction for the most horrible of crimes. Even murderers tell us that they value life (their own) more than freedom. That is why over 99 percent of convicted capital murderers seek a life sentence, not a death sentence, during the punishment phase of their trials.

Even some of those traditionally against capital punishment have decided that some crimes are justly punished with death. Timothy McVeigh's 2001 execution was thought a just punishment by 81 percent of the American people, reflecting an all-time high of support. When 168 innocents were murdered, including 19 children whom McVeigh described as "collateral damage," the collective conscience of the American people reached an overwhelming consensus. A Gallup poll, released on May 20, shows that 72 percent supported the death penalty, with nearly half those polled saying the sanction is not imposed enough.

Why didn't I invoke the murder of 3,100 innocents on September 11? Because the murder of one Jenny Ertman is enough—much too much. Which one of the murdered innocents was more valuable than another? Was one child blown apart in Oklahoma City not enough? Was a father forever lost on September 11 not enough? A son? A granddaughter?

Is it the numbers, at all? No, it is the realization that those innocent lives, so willfully ripped from us, represent individuals who contributed to someone's life and happiness. The sheer numbers of murders committed each year may numb us beyond what an individual murder can. But that is only because we must shield ourselves from the absolute horror represented by one innocent murdered. It is a matter of emotional self-preservation.

Often, in the most horrible of times, we find that the goodness in people stands out. At one point during the attack, Jenny was able to escape and run away. Elizabeth's cries brought Jenny back in a fruitless attempt to aid her friend. Love, friendship, and devotion overcame fear.

Of the six attackers who brutalized these girls for over an hour, five received the death penalty. The sixth was too young to prosecute for death. And why did five separate juries give death? Justice.

DUDLEY SHARP is vice president of Justice for All, a criminal justice reform organization in Houston, Texas. Web sites include www.jfa.net, www.prodeathpenalty.com, and www.murdervictims.com.

It Is Immoral and Ineffective

by Steven W. Hawkins

When the Supreme Court struck down death penalty laws in 1972, former Justice Potter Stewart compared the arbitrariness of the death penalty to the freakishness of being struck by lightning.

Thirty years later, were he still alive, Justice Stewart would probably appreciate his choice of words. In the past five years, an average of 78 people a year have been executed in the United States; in 1995, according to the National Center for Health Statistics, 76 Americans were struck by lightning.

Americans who support the death penalty think it should be reserved for the worst of the worst. The reality of capital punishment, however, shows that it is reserved for racial minorities, people who are retarded or mentally ill, and those who cannot afford to hire a good attorney. It is also all too often reserved for people who are factually innocent of the crime for which they were convicted and sentenced to be executed.

Doubt that the death penalty is racist? Consider this: 55 percent of the inmates who make up America's death row population are people of color (43 percent of death row inmates are black). Two of every three juvenile offenders on death row are people of color, as are a majority of retarded inmates.

Furthermore, the race of the victim plays a role in who ends up on death row. Nationwide, just half of murder victims are white, yet four out of every five people executed in the United States have died for killing white people.

SIGNS OF RACISM

Of course, the numbers do not paint a complete picture. Racial minorities have been the victims of particularly cruel and vindictive wrongful prosecutions, particularly in the South. Consider the case of Clarence Brandley, who spent 10 years on death row in Texas for a crime he did not commit.

Brandley was the head janitor at a high school where a young white female student was found strangled. When police arrived at the crime scene and saw Brandley, a black man, and another janitor, who was white, one officer reportedly declared, "One of you is gonna hang for this. Since you're the nigger, you're elected." Brandley was freed from prison when all charges against him were dropped after a Department of Justice and FBI investigation uncovered trial misconduct.

Doubt that the death penalty is reserved for people who are retarded or mentally ill? Since executions were allowed to resume in 1976, we've executed 44 mentally retarded inmates. (And that is a conservative number. Many inmates are not evaluated for mental retardation before they are executed.)

These 44 inmates include Morris Mason of Virginia who, on his way to the death chamber, turned to a prison worker and I said. "You tell Roger [another death row inmate] when I get back, I'm going to show him I can play basketball as good as he can." Ricky Rector of Arkansas separated his pecan pie from his last meal and left it on the windowsill of his prison cell. He wanted to eat it after the execution.

Doubt that the death penalty discriminates against those who cannot afford a good attorney? Consider the case of Ronald Keith Williamson, who was convicted in Oklahoma and sentenced to death for murder and rape in 1988.

Williamson's conviction was tossed out because of ineffectiveness of counsel; a federal appellate court wryly noted that his attorney failed to investigate and present to the jury the fact that another man had confessed to the rape and murder. It was a case of you get what you pay for—the attorney had received only $3,200 for his defense. Later, DNA evidence would exonerate Williamson.

Of course, that is just the tip of the iceberg. We've seen capital murder suspects represented by drunken. lawyers, sleeping lawyers, biased lawyers, inexperienced lawyers, lawyers who were later disbarred, and lawyers who would be institutionalized due to mental illness.

Aden Harrison Jr., a black man, had as his court-appointed counsel 83-year-old James Venable, who had been an imperial wizard of the Ku Klux Klan for more than 15 years. Judy Haney's court-appointed lawyer was so drunk during the trial in 1989 that he was held in contempt and sent to jail. The next day, both client and attorney came out of the cellblock and the trial resumed. George McFarland's attorney slept through much of the trial. He objected to hardly anything the prosecution did, and every time he opened his eyes, a different witness was on the stand.

THE IMPORTANCE OF THE TRIAL ATTORNEY

As Supreme court Justice Ruth Ginsburg put it, "People who are well represented at

A RACIST JUDGMENT

- Capital punishment is reserved for racial minorities, people who are retarded or mentally ill, and those who cannot afford a good attorney.
- All too often, it is reserved for people who are factually innocent of the crime.
- Fifty-five percent of the inmates who make up America's death row population are people of color.
- Two of every three juvenile offenders on death row are people of color, as are a majority of retarded inmates.
- Furthermore, the victim's race plays a role in who ends up on death row. Just half of murder victims are white, yet four out of every five of those executed have died for killing white people.

trial do not get the death penalty. I have yet to see a death penalty case among the dozens coming to the Supreme Court on eve-of-execution stay applications in which the defendant was well represented at trial."

Doubt that the death penalty ensnares innocent Americans in its complicated legal web? More than 100 people have been freed from death row due to actual innocence, while close to 800 people have been executed. This means that for every eight people we are executing, one person is completely exonerated.

Think of it this way. What if a prescription drug cured eight of every nine people who took it but killed the ninth? What if an airline carrier successfully completed eight of every nine flights it launched, but the ninth resulted in mechanical failure?

What if you are able to successfully reboot your computer eight of every nine tries, but the rest of the time, it crashes and destroys your document? As a society that depends upon a functioning criminal justice system, should we have confidence when that same justice system sends innocent people to death row?

As Supreme Court Justice Sandra Day O'Connor put it, "If statistics are any indication, the system may well be allowing some innocent defendants to be executed. More often than we want to recognize, some innocent defendants have been convicted and sentenced to death."

Kirk Bloodsworth of Maryland and Clyde Charles of Louisiana should know. Bloodsworth spent nine years in prison—two on death row—before DNA testing of old evidence proved him innocent of the only crime for which he had ever been arrested, the brutal rape and murder of a nine-year-old girl. While he was in prison, his mother passed away, and Bloodsworth was forced to view the body while wearing shackles. The real child predator and killer remains unidentified.

Charles spent 19 years at Angola in Louisiana, one of the country's most notorious prisons. He fought for 9 years to get DNA testing done. The results proved that Charles could not have committed the crime, and he was released.

His children grew into adults while he was in prison, and both his parents died; he also caught tuberculosis and developed diabetes. The same DNA test that exonerated Charles identified the real criminal—who had since been tested for committing other crimes against innocent victims while the wrong man was in jail.

Some death penalty proponents quibble over the number of people who have been found to have been factually innocent. The exact number isn't really what's important. What's important is that not one of us—death penalty opponents or proponents—would conclude that executing even one innocent person constitutes acceptable criminal justice policy in the United States.

WHO IS LISTENING?

Arguments against the death penalty are easy to make, but is anyone listening? The bad news is that most Americans continue to support capital punishment in theory. The good news is when you start to probe, there is a growing sense of unease and ambivalence.

For example, 80 percent of voters want to abolish or significantly reform the death penalty system. Sixty-nine percent of voters are more worried about executing an innocent person than executing the guilty. And 64 percent of voters—including 50 percent of Republican voters—want to suspend executions until issues of fairness can be resolved.

The fact is that people are beginning to respond to concerns about the system. Across the United States, a healthy and vibrant moratorium movement is gathering steam. Elected bodies in 73 municipalities have passed resolutions in favor of a moratorium.

Two governors, Republican George Ryan in Illinois and Democrat Parris Glendening in Maryland, have each declared a moratorium. Some 14 states have debated moratorium legislation; in New Hampshire, the legislature passed a bill abolishing the death penalty, only to see it vetoed by the governor.

In Nevada and Maryland, bills imposing a moratorium passed one chamber, only to be defeated in the other. In New Mexico, a bill to abolish the death penalty failed in the Senate by one vote. Next year, as legislatures across the nation convene for their 2003 session, we can expect many more moratorium bills to be debated—as well as bills calling for outright abolition.

Let's face it. The death penalty experiment in America has been tried and found wanting. It is time for the lethal injection gurney to go the way of the stake, the guillotine, and the gallows. It is time to relegate this gruesome practice to the dustbin of history. Our common decency demands no less.

STEVEN W. HAWKINS is executive director of the National Coalition to Abolish the Death Penalty, located in Washington, D.C. NCADP was founded in 1976 and is the only fully staffed national organization devoted specifically to abolishing the death penalty. For more information, please visit www.ncadp.org.

PRISON PROGRAMS THAT PRODUCE

Religion was important in efforts to rehabilitate criminals in the eighteenth and nineteenth centuries. It is now considered a new method of altering the careers of chronic offenders.

By Alfred Himelson

In 1974, criminal rehabilitation programs were no longer seen as effective vehicles for reducing recidivism. Most research evaluations of a wide variety of programs indicated meager or no results in reducing the number of convicts returning to prison. The coup de grace came from sociologist Robert Martinson's article in *Public Interest*, "What Works—Questions and Answers About Prison Reform." Martinson, backed up by statistics, questioned the effectiveness of many categories of rehabilitation programs and also rued the poor methodological quality of the studies. According to Martinson, "It is possible that some of our treatment programs are working to some extent, but our research is so bad it is incapable of telling."

The resulting disillusionment with criminal rehabilitation might have been less shattering if the original designers of these programs in the 1950s and '60s had not with little evidence made grandiose claims for what they might accomplish. Claims of success rates of 80 percent were not uncommon. Careful evaluation usually indicated little or no difference between program subjects and a matched group of inmates who hadn't participated in this form of rehabilitation.

The lack of results coupled with the rising U.S. crime rate led correctional administrators to state publicly that it was time to stop relying on rehabilitation to solve the problem of high rates of recidivism and move on to other means. It appeared that the 100-year-old criminal rehabilitation movement was moribund, if not quite ex-

pired. But two events that occurred in the 1980s led to its partial revival.

The first was the development of a new statistical technique. Many studies prior to the introduction of meta-analysis showed modestly successful results but because of small sample size did not reach the level of statistical significance. In meta-analysis, by assessing the outcomes of a larger number of similar studies, it was possible, according to David B. Wilson of George Mason University, to "focus on the size and direction of effects across studies rather than the statistical significance of individual effects."

Looked at this way, the results indicated a modest degree of success for vocational, educational, behavior modification, and other programs. Program practitioners still have a tendency to make grandiose claims about the success of particular rehabilitation programs. The real results of well-conceived and researched programs now indicate that we should typically expect program subjects to have 10 to 15 percent less recidivism than nonprogram subjects with comparable backgrounds.

The second event was the introduction of various forms of cognitive-behavioral treatment. These, according to clinical psychologist James McGuire, include social skills training, social problem solving, rational-emotive therapy, and reasoning programs. They replaced nonbehavioral treatment that had earlier been one of the mainstays of prison rehabilitation efforts. Included in this latter category were Freudian-oriented programs and watered-down

versions that defined inmates as "sick" and ascribed their emotional illness to foul-ups in childhood development.

These kinds of programs ordinarily had two strikes against them. The first was the scarcity in the prison setting of competent analytic therapists or group leaders. The second problem stemmed from the nature of the inmate prison culture, which was strongly opposed to having most criminals defined as emotionally ill. Due to this opposition, many or most of the unwilling participants in this mode of treatment would not accept the definition of their "problems" assigned by therapists. Without a meeting of the minds (either full or partial) between the therapist and inmate, this variety of treatment was destined to fail. Research results showed this to be the case.

RELIGIOUS REHABILITATION PROGRAMS

It is ironic that religion, which was important in efforts to rehabilitate criminals at the end of the eighteenth century and for most of the nineteenth century, is now being seriously considered as a new method of altering the careers of chronic offenders. In these earlier periods of the American experience, the inmate was seen as a sinner; the cure for his wickedness was to expose him, voluntarily or involuntarily, to massive doses of Scripture. Discipline was enforced with an iron hand, with physical

The Importance of a Religious Foundation

- In early America, the inmate was seen as a sinner and the cure for his wickedness was to expose him to massive doses of Scripture.
- Discipline was enforced with an iron hand, with physical punishment frequently applied to those who broke the rules.
- Penitentiary staff often included clergymen or ex-clergymen drawn to the possibility of saving souls.
- After the Civil War, secular professionals emerged as the preferred bearers of knowledge and scientifically derived techniques.
- The progenitor in modern times for turning the prison into a religious community was the faith-based Humaita Prison in Brazil.
- The Prison Fellowship Ministry established by Charles Colson is doing similar work in the United States.
- This religious-based work has been challenged by secular groups, such as Americans United for Separation of Church and State.

punishment applied to those who broke the roles. The penitentiary staff often included clergymen or ex-clergymen drawn to the work by the possibility of saving souls.

The situation changed after the Civil War. Secular professionals emerged as the preferred bearers of knowledge and scientifically derived techniques. They were believed to be able to solve many social problems—among them, high rates of criminal recidivism.

Religion, while never absent from the prison setting, became subservient to secular efforts. It was relegated to the role of ameliorating harsh conditions within the prison. Organizations such as the Salvation Army provided chaplains, conducted religious classes, and provided spiritual and economic resources for former inmates and their families. By the 1930s, however, despite all the good work they had done, they were likely to be perceived as sanctimonious soul savers—not a serious force for rehabilitation. Other prison ministries were then and still are active in providing religious classes, seminars, and necessary religious items such as pulpits and Bibles. Some of these organizations train people to become prison chaplains.

The revived interest in using religion as a rehabilitative tool was in part a by-product of two events that occurred in the 1970s. The first, previously mentioned, was the disillusionment with current criminal rehabilitation efforts. The second event might be viewed as the Third Great Awakening in the history of America. The first of these occurred in the middle of the eighteenth century; the second, in the early decades of the nineteenth; and the third in the last quarter of the twentieth century.

Each of these "awakenings" was accompanied by heightened religious fervor and increasing emphasis on evangelicalism or fundamentalism. Representative of the Third Awakening was the appearance of the Kairos movement (Greek for moment of opportunity). Typically, 30 to 50 men from the outside come into the prison and meet with 30 to 60 prisoners. There are lengthy sessions and presentations about the nature of Christianity. Members of the Kairos offer what they see as unconditional love. This movement started in Florida more than two decades ago and has spread to many states and countries.

THE PRISON AS A RELIGIOUS COMMUNITY

Starting in 1974, the progenitor for turning the prison into a religious community was the faith-based Humaita Prison in Brazil. Byron Johnson, director of the Center for Research and Urban Civil Society at the University of Pennsylvania, who studied this institution, has stated, "Humaita has received national and international recognition for a number of correctional innovations, such as (1) turning over completely the day-to-day operations of the prison to religious volunteers rather than paid correctional staff, (2) saturating the prison environment with religious programming and instruction, and (3) promoting family visits, spiritual mentoring, and work release."

Johnson found that those released from Humaita had a three-year recidivism rate of 16 percent compared to 36 percent for another Brazilian prison that stressed vocational training (both rates are low). The apparent success of Humaita has encouraged the establishment of similar programs in the United States and Great Britain. Four states (Kansas, Iowa, Minnesota, and Texas) have created programs similar but not identical to Humaita. Among the most ambitious is the Prison Fellowship Ministry (PFM)—run project at the Carol Vance, a 378-bed prison in Richmond, Texas

(PFM was created by former convict and born-again Christian Charles Colson). The program consists of three phases. Two take place mostly within the prison, the third in the community.

According to Johnson, phase 1 lasts for 12 months and centers on "building in inmates a spiritual and moral foundation from which the rest of the program is based. A heavy emphasis is placed on biblical education as well as GED tutoring, substance abuse prevention, and life skills." In phase 2, the inmates continue their previous efforts while becoming involved with community service outside the prison.

There is now an emphasis on developing leadership roles. The Kairos is offered periodically. Phase 3 is the postrelease component of the program. The subject receives help in finding housing and employment, and mentoring continues. A connection is established between the ex-offender and local churches. To be considered a graduate of the PFM program, the Innerchange Freedom Institute (IFI), the subject has to have completed 16 months in the IFI unit, with 6 or more months in aftercare, held a job, and been active in a church for 3 months prior to graduation.

How much was accomplished by such total immersion in religious study and participation, bolstered by other means of individual development such as education and vocational skills? According to the preliminary evaluation by Johnson and David Larson, 17.3 percent of the IFI graduates were arrested during two-year follow-up, compared with 35 percent for a matched comparison group. The figure for incarceration was 8 percent for the IFI graduates and 20.3 percent for the matched group.

However, if one includes all IFI participants (graduates and nongraduates), there was no advantage for the IFI subjects. The IFI group had 36.2 percent arrested and 24.3 percent incarcerated. The matched comparison group had 35 percent arrested and 20.3 percent incarcerated. One puzzling finding was that "participants graduating from IFI with less than 16 months in the program had lower arrest and incarceration rates than graduates who had 16 or more months in the program."

The Kainos experiment (Greek for new beginning), which operated briefly in four British prisons, was a variant of the previously discussed American and Brazilian programs. The project began in 1996. In it, a portion of the prison was taken over by the Kainos Community, a Christian charity. Security was still maintained by prison officers. All inmates in the wings were volunteers, including non-Christians. They signed an agreement to abide by a set of rules that included attending courses and being polite to all staff, visitors, and other inmates.

By 2001 the Kainos was having difficulty maintaining its programs in the British prison system. The Prison Service terminated several of its wings. Why became a controversial question. The Prison Service said that it wouldn't be legitimate to monetarily support the Kainos or other religion-based interventions. According to the London *Daily Telegraph*'s sources, the real reason was pressure from Muslims and members of other faiths.

But there was another factor weakening the program's position. In 2001, the British Home Office published the results of an evaluation of the Kainos' success in reducing recidivism. The researchers claimed that there was no significant difference in reconviction rates between those in or not in the program.

LEGAL CHALLENGES

The PFM programs in several states have been legally challenged. In one suit, an inmate at the Newton Correctional Facility in Newton, Iowa, charged that money earned by the prison through inmate phone calls was used to fund the faith-based program. Barry Lynn, executive director of Americans United for Separation of Church and State, was quoted as saying that preferential treatment was given to prisoners willing to undergo religious conversion and indoctrination. An additional charge was that better living facilities and greater access to parole applications were provided to inmates in these faith-based programs. These challenges bring into focus the question of whether legal or inmate welfare considerations will predominate.

The results from other studies of the influence of religion show benefits from prison ministry efforts for some inmates but not others. Young and associates conducted a 14-year follow-up of 185 former PFM subjects and compared them with a cohort of 2,289 former inmates. They found lower rates and longer time to recidivism among PFM women (white or black) and white PFM men in low-risk categories. The program had no impact for high-risk males or among black males of all risk categories.

In Israel, the Orthodox religious kibbutz is the setting for an integrated attempt to change the lives of convict-addicts. (The kibbutz is a democratic commune that stresses a unique set of norms and values but does not emphasize isolation from the rest of the country.) The story begins with the release of inmates to the Shaar Hatikvah facility (currently located in Beersheba), where they reside for three months. Those graduating from this phase move into a halfway house or room with two college students. The next goal is placement in a kibbutz, where they are immersed in a way of life that emphasizes both Torah study and hard work. Fragmentary results from this program look promising.

POSSIBLE PITFALLS FOR RELIGIOUS REHABILITATION EFFORTS

We have already mentioned one potential obstacle to the operation of these new varieties of religious programs, namely, legal-constitutional challenges. A second potential problem of a different kind is less apparent. More than 60 years ago, Donald Clemmer described the inmate culture as being defined by a set of norms that emphasize noncooperation with the staff and solidarity with other inmates. While the importance of the norms and values that inmates bring into the prison is now recognized, Clemmer's analysis is still relevant.

These oppositional norms have limited the effectiveness of earlier prison rehabilitation efforts that called for self-disclosure and the revelation of what happens between inmates. Religious programs for the most part seemed exempt from this inmate opposition. These programs were seen as something apart from the hypocritical "square" world—and were one way for inmates to search for meaning in their lives. Inmates are often attracted to the revelatory, prophetic, and ethical teachings of religion as well as to the guilt-reducing power of prayer and observance. The Kairos fits well into this context, as did such venerable organizations such as the Salvation Army and the multitude of prison ministries.

Programs such as the Kainos in Great Britain and the PFM efforts in several states (where a portion of the prison is operated by the program) are sometimes opposed by the inmate culture, which may view them as alliances between the prison and religious staffs in order to make inmates more docile. This possibility merits further study.

CONCLUSION

Expectations for what criminal rehabilitation can accomplish have ranged from the grandiose optimism of the 1950s and '60s to the limited optimism of the present. Many rehabilitation programs do have success, but it is likely to be limited to 10 to 15 percent when compared with similar prisoners not exposed to these environments. Many sorts of pro grams seem to have some impact.

Traditional efforts such as academic education and vocational training often produce positive results in well-conceived projects. Research evaluation of secular-oriented programs indicates that the cognitive-rational-emotive efforts appear to be the most successful in reducing recidivism. The evaluation of religious programs shows some positive results. Further research and methodological refinement are necessary before a more definitive answer can be given on their degree of importance.

A final note. One problem in assessing results from all rehabilitation programs is in comparing volunteers with non-volunteers. While every attempt is made in competent studies to find a matched comparison group not exposed to the program—no matter how well the match is made—the fact that inmates volunteer for a program may indicate some real difference from nonvolunteers. The best way to deal with this dilemma is to use random assignment of inmates who volunteer into an experimental group and a control group. Lacking this resource, the alternative is to arbitrarily place inmates in the test groups. Requiring participation and using coercion to accomplish this may drastically reduce the program's effectiveness.

Alfred Himelson is emeritus professor of sociology at Cal State, Northridge.

Encouraging Students to Pursue Careers in Community Corrections

By John M. Paitakes, Ph.D

Based upon my six years of teaching experience in criminal justice it is apparent that many undergraduate criminal justice students are not fully aware of the career opportunities in probation and parole. I have found that they are not usually aware of all the functions and roles of a probation or parole officer, nor are they aware of how to apply for these positions. Therefore, I have made it part of my responsibilities as an educator to make students more aware of the career opportunities in the areas of community corrections. This can only increase the professionalism of these positions.

Probation and parole be become increasingly more professional career opportunities in the past ten years. Almost all states require applicants to possess a four-year degree in either criminal justice or a related discipline. An increasing number of applicants possess master's degrees, and a significant number, once hired, pursue advanced degrees.

One of my goals as a former probation officer, and now educator, is to make students more aware of the positions, functions and career opportunities available in community corrections. I do not believe that probation and parole have marketed themselves effectively in the past.

I would like to share with the readers some of the techniques and methods I utilize in my classes to heighten the awareness of students for these positions. I believe these methods can help students aspiring to enter these fields. In addition, agency personnel can also benefit. The agency can use the student to take on the project they may not have had time to address. I believe these methods, utilized over a period of time, will increase and enrich the pool of students seeking positions in probation and parole. In addition, prospective employees will be much more informed about these important and challenging career opportunities.

There are a number of techniques the educator can implement in his/her criminal justice courses to increase the students knowledge and awareness of community corrections careers:

Internships

At Seton Hall University, we offer a three-credit course "Community Experience." This is an elective which provides a semester-long internship opportunity. Most of these internship opportunities are non-paid, although some are. The student may select their own criminal justice agency with approval of the professor, or the professor will assist them in securing a placement. They must work eight hours a week at the selected agency for a total of 120 hours. The host agency must offer a pre-career opportunity and correlate it to college level skills. During this time, the student must maintain a journal describing the duties and skills utilized each day they work at the site. In addition, the student must complete a term paper describing the agency, its historical development, organizational structure (formal and informal), and major agency functions; as well as the skills and knowledge gained, and any impact on the student's career choice.

The site supervisor must complete an evaluation of the student's performance during the tenure of the internship. This can be a win-win experience for both the student and the agency. The student gains first-hand knowledge and experience in a specific agency. The agency is give the opportunity to showcase their agency to potential applicants.

I have referred students to probation and parole agencies for the experience of seeing what the practitioner actually does as compared to the theoretical of literature review. A number of these students have secured positions in probation and parole as a result of their community experience course.

Service Learning

Service learning is less extensive and can be incorporated in many criminal justice courses. It involves the student completing 25 hours of service to a criminal of juvenile justice agency.

In my Juvenile Delinquency class, I offer service learning as an alternative to a 15-page paper. Similar to community experience, it provides the student with a mini exposure to a certain component of criminal justice. For example, students have worked with probation departments in their intake units, with juvenile probation officers as a ride along, and with the family court staff. Similar to community experience, they are required to submit a short term paper and are evaluated by agency staff.

This is an excellent experience for both the student and the agency employer. This experience can lead to a community experience for credit course of open up a career field for students taking advantaged of this experience. The employer gets the opportunity to market their agency.

Volunteering

Volunteering in a probation or parole agency is another means for a student to gain knowledge about the field they may be interested in pursing. I encourage students who may not be able to complete 120 hours of an internship, or are not in a class that offers service learning, to simply volunteer. They are advised to make an appointment with the agency director or supervisor and indicate that they would like to find out more about the function and role of a probation or parole officer position. At this interview, the student and agency representative should agree on a mutually acceptable schedule and time frame (i.e., 3 months, 4 months, etc.). This alternative benefits both student and agency. It broadens the student's perception of the work done by the agency and can improve the public image of the agency for a very small cost. In addition, the agency may be able to have the student take on a project that they just never had enough time to address (i.e., some type of research project).

Guest Speakers

As a former probation officer and currently an alternate parole board member, I believe it is very important to integrate the theoretical and the practical aspects of criminal justice for optimum student learning. For example, texts relating to community corrections will describe the roles, functions and duties of a probation or parole officer, which are generally quite thoroughly presented. However, to enhance the information provided, it is very informative to invite a practitioner such as a chief probation officer of a parole officer to a class to describe their respective duties and functions. Students should be given the opportunity to question and discuss issues with these practitioners. I have found representatives from agencies are usually more than willing and quite enthusiastic about speaking to a college class regarding their positions and agencies. This also is a win-win for both students and agencies. Student learn first-hand from the agency personnel about the field. Employers are given the opportunity to showcase their agency and also expand the pool of applicants.

Career Center

The vast majority of colleges and universities have a career center. Their overall goals are to inform and present some of the numerous job opportunities for students. In addition, many will offer a variety of assessments to assist students in career decisions. They will also assist students in seeking placements for internships, and dependent on their staff and resources, engage in other functions assisting students in career decision making.

We are very fortunate at Seton Hall University to have a comprehensive service oriented career center staffed by highly motivated and resourceful personnel. I work very closely with their staff in helping to plan career fairs for criminal justice students, always making sure to include representative of probation and parole and also making sure to have representatives from the three major components of the criminal justice system, law enforcement, courts, and corrections.

In addition, my faculty colleagues and I work closely with career center staff sharing information on agencies providing internships, hiring and new positions created. Our career center offers a variety of workshops addressing resume writing, interviewing techniques, testing and a number of other job-related preparation issues.

Conclusion

One of my purposes of preparing this article was to share some of the methods I utilize to present information on community corrections careers to our future generation of employees. Having recently completed 35 years in community corrections, I reflected how meaningful and significant humanitarian contribution by helping to reshape people's lives. Therefore, I felt it was important to share the methods I use to enhance and further professionalize community corrections.

The techniques I have described are of benefit to both personnel contemplating careers in community corrections and to current agency personnel. I have discussed several methods that prospective employees and students can utilize to learn more about and network with professionals in the field. Agency personnel can benefit by creating additional opportunities for positive public experiences for their agencies. This is always welcomed, especially in probation and parole. In addition, using students of criminal justice as interns and assigning special projects as part of their internships can be beneficial to the agency and ultimately, the student. The agency can assign a research project, which they haven't had time in the past to complete, to the student intern. The agency gains the data and the student enhances his/her research abilities.

Creative techniques and methods utilized by educators in cooperation with community corrections agencies can only enhance probation and parole in the future.

Notes

(For further information regarding any of these methods or other information presented in this article, Dr. John Paitakes may be contacted at Seton Hall University, Dept. of Criminal Justice, 400 South Orange Avenue, South Orange, NJ 07079. (973) 275-5886, or e-mail at Paitakjo@shu.edu)

John M. Paitakes, Ph.D., is a Senior Faculty Associate with the Department of Criminal Justice at Seton Hall University, South Orange, NJ.

The Unique Brutality of Texas

Why the Lone Star State leads the nation in executions

by Joseph Rosenbloom

GATHERING DUST IN TEXAS GOVERNOR RICK Perry's inbox is a clemency petition from Joe Lee Guy, a death-row inmate. The petition declares that "the integrity of Guy's capital trial was severely compromised." Considering how horrendously the wheels of Texas justice turned for Guy, the petition's claim seems, if anything, understated.

In 1994, Guy was sentenced to death for his role, the year before, in the robbery of a grocery store and the murder of its proprietor, Larry Howell. Guy was the unarmed lookout for two other men, Ronald Springer and Thomas Howard. Springer supplied the .22 caliber pistol that Howard used to shoot Howell. Springer and Howard received life sentences.

Guy's involvement in the crime was never in question, but something went terribly wrong in his legal defense. Frank SoRelle, the investigator hired by the defense, developed a "relationship" with Howell's elderly mother, who was seeking Guy's execution, and SoRelle eventually inherited her $750,000 estate. The work performed by SoRelle and Guy's lawyer was woefully inadequate: The sentencing jury never heard important mitigating evidence, such as the fact that Guy grew up poor and neglected by a gambling-addicted mother, and that he was hampered by extremely limited intelligence.

When the circumstances of Guy's case came to light years after his conviction, it was more than even the Texas Board of Pardons and Paroles could stomach. The board reviews clemency appeals in death-penalty cases and recommends "yes" or "no" to the governor (who may grant clemency only if the board recommends it). The board almost never votes "yes" in a case where a death row inmate seeks clemency; it's done so just four times since 1990. But in January, the board unanimously urged Perry to commute Guy's sentence to life.

Despite that extraordinary vote, however, Perry is withholding a decision until all federal appeals are exhausted. That Perry is ducking the question speaks volumes about the political climate around the issue of capital punishment in Texas. At a time when many other states have been questioning their death-

penalty systems, the Texas political establishment has expressed no such doubts.

Is it any surprise, then, that the state's death penalty machinery has been steaming right along?

A Democrat turned Republican, Perry was lieutenant governor during the gubernatorial tenure of George W. Bush, and he became governor in January 2001, when Bush took office as president. During Bush's six years in Austin, Texas executed 152 people—a modern-day record for a governor. Since then, 82 more have been put to death—a rate that approaches Bush's. The numbers on Perry's watch would almost certainly have been higher if a Supreme Court ruling two years ago had not prevented the execution of 38 death-row inmates in Texas because of mental-retardation claims.

Why Texas continues to execute people at much the same clip seems rooted not so much in public opinion (polls show that the proportion of Texans favoring capital punishment approximates the national average) as in the state's peculiar political and judicial circumstances. Conservative Republicans have consolidated their power over all the state's main political institutions, including the judiciary. Judges, who are elected in Texas, know that any decision appearing to offer leniency in a capital case could cost them dearly in the next Republican primary.

If capital-defense lawyers are at a disadvantage in many states because of a lack of resources available to them next to what prosecutors have at their disposal, the imbalance is particularly striking in Texas, experts say. Robert O. Dawson, a professor of criminal law at the University of Texas School of Law, decries the "disparity of resources" in capital cases Texas-style. "Why is that? Because it's hard to sell [criminal defense] politically. I think that's a wrongheaded political judgment," Dawson says.

Among the 38 states that have capital punishment, Texas is far and away the modern-day leader in implementing it. Although it has 7.6 percent of the nation's total population, Texas carried out 35 percent of the nation's executions between 1976 and last month—putting to death 321 of 909 condemned prisoners, according to the Death Penalty Information Center in Washington. Virginia was a distant second with 91 executions. And since 2002, the record is still more lopsided, with Texas responsible for 42 percent of the nation's total. As executions have emptied death-row prison cells, moreover, Texas juries have quickly filled them back up. The state's death-row population has held steady (in the 450 range) since the late 1990s.

As an executioner of juvenile offenders, Texas also stands out not just in this country but around the globe. Since 1998, the state has put to death eight offenders who were under 18 at the time of their crime—nearly half the worldwide total of 17, according to Amnesty International.

How Texas handles death penalty cases has attracted international scrutiny of another kind. In March, the International Court of Justice (World Court) held that the United States had violated the rights of Mexican nationals on death row in nine states, including Texas. Of the 52 inmates now covered by the opinion, 15 are in Texas prisons. At the time of the Mexicans' arrests, they were not notified of their right to meet with their government's consular representatives, as the Vienna Convention on Consular Relations requires, the court said. It ordered the United States to remedy the violations of the treaty, which this country signed in 1963, by undertaking an "effective review" of the Mexicans' convictions and sentences.

The ruling brought this retort from Governor Perry's spokesman: "Obviously the governor respects the World Court's right to have an opinion, but the fact remains [that the court has] no standing and no jurisdiction in the state of Texas."

There is some logic, however tortured, to Perry's position. Treaties signed by the United States are binding on the states under the federal Constitution, but it is also true that the World Court lacks enforcement power. The United States ignored the court's order in a consular-notification case and allowed Arizona to execute two German brothers in 1999.

By openly defying the court's authority, however, Perry is burnishing his tough-on-crime credentials. That may pay political dividends in Texas, but it leaves him little room to maneuver on consular notification. Perry's chest-thumping contrasts with how Oklahoma Governor Brad Henry, another death-penalty supporter, dealt with one of the Mexicans covered by the court's order. In May, Henry commuted the death sentence of Osbaldo Torres to life without parole.

Perry's death penalty posture is not at odds with the Republican-dominated Texas Legislature. Strengthened by legislative redistricting, the coP gamed a majority of seats in the House (where Republicans outnumber Democrats 88 to 62) in 2002 for the first time since Reconstruction and tightened its grip on the Senate (where the margin favors Republicans 19 to 12). Now, the Republicans have a lock on the legislature and occupy every statewide office.

In 2003, the last time the legislature met in a regular biennial session, it rejected a bill to establish a consular notification procedure. Proposals to authorize the governor to impose a moratorium on executions and create a death-penalty study commission were bottled up in committee.

One death-penalty proponent who has gained influence due to the rightward tilt is state Representative Terry Keel. A Republican, ex-sheriff, and former county prosecutor, Keel became chairman of the Criminal Jurisprudence Committee in the Texas House of Representatives last year.

A bill that Keel helped quash would have allowed Texas juries in capital cases to impose, as an alternative to a death sentence, a penalty of life imprisonment without the possibility of parole. Only two of the 38 death-penalty states, Texas and New Mexico, do not offer juries that choice. Keel opposed the measure on the grounds that "incarcerating the most violent of criminals for life, with no hope of parole, places corrections employees in inexcusable danger," as he wrote in a newspaper column, although the point is widely disputed by corrections experts. "The system of justice [in Texas] is sound. I believe we have a high level of integrity," Keel told a newspaper reporter last summer.

WHERE KEEL SEES SOUNDNESS AND INTEGRITY, other observers see deep flaws. One who has an upclose view is Charlie Baird, a former judge on the Texas Court of Criminal Appeals who now sits as a visiting judge in criminal trials and appeals. According to Baird, a critical weakness of the Texas judiciary is the lack of meaningful appellate review. The deliberations of the state appeals court in capital cases are typically "exceedingly poor" and "devoid of any kind of critical legal reasoning," Baird says.

All judges in Texas are elected. Baird was one of the last two Democrats to serve on the criminal appellate court. After eight years on the court, which hears all death-penalty appeals in Texas, he lost his bid for re-election in 1998. The other Democrat retired the same year.

When judges run for re-election, the death penalty is rarely an issue—unless there is a contest about who is most for it. All nine members of the Texas Court of Criminal Appeals are conservative Republicans, and eight of them are former prosecutors with little or no experience as capital defenders, sources say. The court's rate of affirming death sentences is "probably the highest" of any appellate court in the nation, Baird says. "When I was there, [the court] had such a results oriented ideology that no matter what issue was raised on appeal, [the judges] were going to affirm the conviction and sentence."

To illustrate what's wrong with the appellate judiciary in Texas, critics point especially to two well-publicized cases that eventually reached the U.S. Supreme Court, *Banks v. Dretzke* and *Miller-El v. Cockrell*. In the first, Delma Banks Jr. was convicted of fatally shooting a 16-year-old boy and stealing his car near the northeast Texas town of Nash. But it turned out that prosecutors had withheld evidence that would have allowed Banks to discredit two key witnesses against him, including the fact that one of them was a paid police informant. The Texas Court of Criminal Appeals found that Banks' appeal had come too late. But in February, the Supreme Court found otherwise—and unanimously granted Banks the right to appeal.

In the second case, a jury sentenced Thomas Miller-El to death for the robbery and murder of a Holiday Inn employee. The trial of Miller-El, an African American, was held in a Dallas County court in 1986. Miller-El's lawyer objected that the prosecutors had used racially discriminatory tactics to select the jury, which the lawyer said resulted in 10 of the 11 African Americans eligible to serve on the jury being excluded. The Texas appellate court rebuffed Miller-El's claim. Last year, by an 8-to-1 vote, the Supreme Court sided with the Texas defendant, finding that Miller-El had been denied the right to a fair trial.

Another weakness of Texas justice is the quality of capital-defense representation. "I think at the heart of the problem in Texas is that [capital-defense representation] is underfunded," says Andrea Keilen, deputy director of the Texas Defender Service, a death-penalty research and consulting organization that brings appeals on behalf of some of the state's death-row inmates.

A critical weakness of the Texas judiciary is the lack of meaningful appellate review in death-penalty cases.

In Texas, judges appoint lawyers on a case-by-case basis from a list of "qualified" counsel. Lawyers' fees vary widely from county to county. The amount provided to defend indigents in capital cases is typically much lower in rural areas. In Fort Bend County, for example, the fees lawyers are paid to try such cases are as low as $200 a day. Investigators earn a maximum of $600 per case, and the total sum for experts is $750.

The maximum available for a habeas-corpus appeal to the Texas Court of Criminal Appeals is $25,000, which must pay lawyers, investigators, and experts. A habeas appeal is time-consuming. It requires the defense team to go beyond the trial record and seek out any possible factor—such as new evidence of a convicted offender's innocence or prosecutorial misconduct during the trial—that might justify further appellate review.

"The competent attorneys are not drawn to the cases because they know they're going to lose money, or they're going to lose the case because they don't have the money to do a proper investigation or something else that's necessary to win the case," says Keilen.

Unlike California and Florida, two other states where capital trials are common (but executions are not), Texas has no statewide public defender system. There are public-defender offices in Dallas, El Paso, and Wichita Falls, but they handle only a fraction of the death-penalty cases even in their own cities. The lack of a significant public-defender system puts capital defenders—many of whom are solo practitioners—at a disadvantage against the organized corps of death-penalty specialists that are common in prosecutors' offices.

Many lawyers appointed to represent death-row inmates in habeas petitions to the Texas Court of Criminal Appeals are "unqualified, irresponsible or overburdened and do little if any meaningful work for the client," a study by the Texas Defender Service concluded two years ago. One lawyer approved by the court as "qualified," for example, had been disciplined for dereliction of duty to his client. Five qualified lawyers proved ineligible because they already held jobs that created potential conflicts of interest. One lawyer named as qualified was dead.

Although the Joe Lee Guy case was not singled out in the report, its particulars echo these findings. Besides having an ill-trained and self-serving investigator, Guy had the misfortune of being assigned a lawyer, Richard Wardroup, whose record at the State Bar of Texas would show numerous reprimands and suspensions between 1985 and 2000, including sanctions for misrepresenting to a client that he had filed a suit, missing deadlines to seek a new trial and to appeal, failing to act competently as a lawyer, and otherwise neglecting his clients.

What's more, Wardroup's drug and alcohol use was "pervasive" during the period that he was Guy's lawyer, and he "did approximately three to four lines of cocaine" while driving to Guy's trial one morning, says a sworn affidavit of the lawyer's former secretary, Regina Young.

Wardroup was appointed as Guy's appellate lawyer but was suspended from practice while the appeal was pending. The appellate brief filed by a substitute lawyer also "did not address [investigator] SoRelle's actions or his relationship with Mrs. Howell," according to Guy's clemency petition.

SoRelle's bizarre role as Guy's investigator did not come to light until pro bono lawyers from Minneapolis tackled the case in early 2000 and appealed to a federal court. Guy's execution, which Texas had scheduled for June 28 of that year, was stayed by a federal judge just 15 days earlier. The possibility remains that the federal courts, if not Governor Perry, will rectify the injustices in Guy's case. Whether Texas will do the same in the case of its death-penalty system is another question altogether.

JOSEPH ROSENBLOOM *is a* Prospect *senior correspondent.*

Glossary

A

Abet   To encourage another to commit a crime.

Accessory   One who harbors, assists, or protects another person, although he or she knows that person has committed or will commit a crime.

Accomplice   One who knowingly and voluntarily aids another in committing a criminal offense.

Acquit   To free a person legally from an accusation of criminal guilt.

Adjudicatory hearing   The fact-finding process wherein the court determines whether or not there is sufficient evidence to sustain the allegations in a petition.

Administrative law   Regulates many daily business activities, and violations of such regulations generally result in warnings or fines, depending upon their adjudged severity.

Admissible   Capable of being admitted; in a trial, such evidence as the judge allows to be introduced into the proceeding.

Affirmance   A pronouncement by a higher court that the case in question was rightly decided by the lower court from which the case was appealed.

Affirmation   Positive declaration or assertion that the witness will tell the truth; not made under oath.

Aggravated assault   The unlawful attack by one person upon another for the purpose of inflicting severe or aggravated bodily injury.

Alias   Any name by which one is known other than his or her true name.

Alibi   A type of defense in a criminal prosecution that proves the accused could not have committed the crime with which he or she is charged, since evidence offered shows the accused was in another place at the time the crime was committed.

Allegation   An assertion of what a party to an action expects to prove.

American Bar Association (ABA)   A professional association, comprising attorneys who have been admitted to the bar in any of the 50 states, and a registered lobby.

American Civil Liberties Union (ACLU)   Founded in 1920 with the purpose of defending the individual's rights as guaranteed by the U.S. Constitution.

Amnesty   A class or group pardon.

Annulment   The act, by competent authority, of canceling, making void, or depriving of all force.

Antisocial personality disorder   Refers to individuals who are basically unsocialized and whose behavior pattern brings them repeatedly into conflict with society.

Appeal   A case carried to a higher court to ask that the decision of the lower court, in which the case originated, be altered or overruled completely.

Appellate court   A court that has jurisdiction to hear cases on appeal; not a trial court.

Arbitrator   The person chosen by parties in a controversy to settle their differences; private judges.

Arraignment   The appearance before the court of a person charged with a crime. He or she is advised of the charges, bail is set, and a plea of "guilty" or "not guilty" is entered.

Arrest   The legal detainment of a person to answer for criminal charges or civil demands.

Autopsy   A postmortem examination of a human body to determine the cause of death.

B

Bail   Property (usually money) deposited with a court in exchange for the release of a person in custody to ensure later appearance.

Bail bond   An obligation signed by the accused and his or her sureties that ensures his or her presence in court.

Bailiff   An officer of the court who is responsible for keeping order in the court and protecting the security of jury deliberations and court property.

Behavior theory   An approach to understanding human activity that holds that behavior is determined by consequences it produces for the individual.

Bench warrant   An order by the court for the apprehension and arrest of a defendant or other person who has failed to appear when so ordered.

Bill of Rights   The first 10 amendments to the U.S. Constitution that state certain fundamental rights and privileges that are guaranteed to the people against infringement by the government.

Biocriminology   A relatively new branch of criminology that attempts to explain criminal behavior by referring to biological factors which predispose some individuals to commit criminal acts. *See also Criminal biology.*

Blue laws   Laws in some jurisdictions prohibiting sales of merchandise, athletic contests, and the sale of alcoholic beverages on Sundays.

Booking   A law-enforcement or correctional process officially recording an entry-into-detention after arrest and identifying the person, place, time, reason for the arrest, and the arresting authority.

Breathalizer   A commercial device to test the breath of a suspected drinker and to determine that person's blood-alcohol content.

Brief   A summary of the law relating to a case, prepared by the attorneys for both parties and given to the judge.

Burden of proof   Duty of establishing the existence of fact in a trial.

C

Calendar   A list of cases to be heard in a trial court, on a specific day, and containing the title of the case, the lawyers involved, and the index number.

Capital crime   Any crime that may be punishable by death or imprisonment for life.

Capital punishment   The legal imposition of a sentence of death upon a convicted offender.

Career criminal   A person having a past record of multiple arrests or convictions for crimes of varying degrees of seriousness. Such criminals are often described as chronic, habitual, repeat, serious, high-rate, or professional offenders.

Case   At the level of police or prosecutorial investigation, a set of circumstances under investigation involving one or more persons.

Case law   Judicial precedent generated as a by-product of the decisions that courts have made to resolve unique disputes. Case law concerns concrete facts, as distinguished from statutes and constitutions, which are written in the abstract.

Change of venue   The removal of a trial from one jurisdiction to another in order to avoid local prejudice.

Charge   In criminal law, the accusation made against a person. It also refers to the judge's instruction to the jury on legal points.

Circumstantial evidence   Indirect evidence; evidence from which a fact can be reasonably inferred, although not directly proven.

Civil law   That body of laws that regulates arrangements between individuals, such as contracts and claims to property.

Clemency   The doctrine under which executive or legislative action reduces the severity of or waives legal punishment of one or more individuals, or an individual exempted from prosecution for certain actions.

Code   A compilation, compendium, or revision of laws, arranged into chapters, having a table of contents and index, and promulgated by legislative authority. *See also Penal code.*

Coercion   The use of force to compel performance of an action; the application of sanctions or the use of force by government to compel observance of law or public policy.

Common law   Judge-made law to assist courts through decision making with traditions, customs, and usage of previous court decisions.

Commutation   A reduction of a sentence originally prescribed by a court.

Complainant   The victim of a crime who brings the facts to the attention of the authorities.

Complaint   Any accusation that a person committed a crime that has originated or been received by a law enforcement agency or court.

Confession   A statement by a person who admits violation of the law.

Confiscation   Government seizure of private property without compensation to the owner.

Conspiracy   An agreement between two or more persons to plan for the purpose of committing a crime or any unlawful act or a lawful act by unlawful or criminal means.

Contempt of court   Intentionally obstructing a court in the administration of justice, acting in a way calculated to lessen its authority or dignity, or failing to obey its lawful order.

Continuance   Postponement or adjournment of a trial granted by the judge, either to a later date or indefinitely.

Contraband   Goods, the possession of which is illegal.

Conviction   A finding by the jury (or by the trial judge in cases tried without a jury) that the accused is guilty of a crime.

Corporal punishment   Physical punishment.

Corpus delicti (Lat.)   The objective proof that a crime has been committed as distinguished from an accidental death, injury, or loss.

Corrections   Area of criminal justice dealing with convicted offenders in jails, prisons, on probation, or parole.

Corroborating evidence   Supplementary evidence that tends to strengthen or confirm other evidence given previously.

Crime   An act injurious to the public, which is prohibited and punishable by law.

Crime Index   A set of numbers indicating the volume, fluctuation, and distribution of crimes reported to local law enforcement agencies for the United States as a whole.

Crime of passion   An unpremeditated murder or assault committed under circumstances of great anger, jealousy, or other emotional stress.

Criminal biology   The scientific study of the relation of hereditary physical traits to criminal character, that is, to innate tendencies to commit crime in general or crimes of any particular type. *See also Biocriminology.*

Criminal insanity   Lack of mental capacity to do or refrain from doing a criminal act; inability to distinguish right from wrong.

Criminal intent   The intent to commit an act, the results of which are a crime or violation of the law.

Criminalistics   Crime laboratory procedures.

Criminology   The scientific study of crime, criminals, corrections, and the operation of the system of criminal justice.

Cross examination   The questioning of a witness by the party who did not produce the witness.

Culpable   At fault or responsible, but not necessarily criminal.

D

Defamation   Intentional causing, or attempting to cause, damage to the reputation of another by communicating false or distorted information about his or her actions, motives, or character.

Defendant   The person who is being prosecuted.

Deliberation   The action of a jury to determine the guilt or innocence, or the sentence, of a defendant.

Demurrer   Plea for dismissal of a suit on the grounds that, even if true, the statements of the opposition are insufficient to sustain the claim.

Deposition   Sworn testimony obtained outside, rather than in, court.

Deterrence   A theory that swift and sure punishment will discourage others from similar illegal acts.

Dilatory   Law term that describes activity for the purpose of causing a delay or to gain time or postpone a decision.

Direct evidence   Testimony or other proof that expressly or straightforwardly proves the existence of fact.

Direct examination   The first questioning of witnesses by the party who calls them.

Directed verdict   An order or verdict pronounced by a judge during the trial of a criminal case in which the evidence presented by the prosecution clearly fails to show the guilt of the accused.

District attorney   A locally elected state official who represents the state in bringing indictments and prosecuting criminal cases.

DNA fingerprinting   The use of biological residue found at the scene of a crime for genetic comparisons in aiding the identification of criminal suspects.

Docket   The formal record of court proceedings.

Glossary

Double jeopardy   To be prosecuted twice for the same offense.

Due process model   A philosophy of criminal justice based on the assumption that an individual is presumed innocent until proven guilty.

Due process of law   A clause in the Fifth and Fourteenth Amendments ensuring that laws are reasonable and that they are applied in a fair and equal manner.

E

Embracery   An attempt to influence a jury, or a member thereof, in their verdict by any improper means.

Entrapment   Inducing an individual to commit a crime he or she did not contemplate, for the sole purpose of instituting a criminal prosecution against the offender.

Evidence   All the means used to prove or disprove the fact at issue. *See also Corpus delicti.*

Ex post facto (Lat.)   After the fact. An *ex post facto law is a criminal law that makes an act unlawful although it was committed prior to the passage of that law. See also Grandfather clause.*

Exception   A formal objection to the action of the court during a trial. The indication is that the excepting party will seek to reverse the court's actions at some future proceeding.

Exclusionary rule   Legal prohibitions against government prosecution using evidence illegally obtained.

Expert evidence   Testimony by one qualified to speak authoritatively on technical matters because of her or his special training or skill.

Extradition   The surrender by one state to another of an individual accused of a crime.

F

False arrest   Any unlawful physical restraint of another's freedom of movement; unlawful arrest.

Felony   A criminal offense punishable by death or imprisonment in a penitentiary.

Forensic   Relating to the court. Forensic medicine would refer to legal medicine that applies anatomy, pathology, toxicology, chemistry, and other fields of science in expert testimony in court cases or hearings.

G

Grand jury   A group of 12 to 23 citizens of a county who examine evidence against the person suspected of a crime and hand down an indictment if there is sufficient evidence. *See also Petit jury.*

Grandfather clause   A clause attempting to preserve the rights of firms in operation before enactment of a law by exempting these firms from certain provisions of that law. *See also Ex post facto.*

H

Habeas corpus (Lat.)   A legal device to challenge the detention of a person taken into custody. An individual in custody may demand an evidentiary hearing before a judge to examine the legality of the detention.

Hearsay   Evidence that a witness has learned through others.

Homicide   The killing of a human being; may be murder, negligent or nonnegligent manslaughter, or excusable or justifiable homicide.

Hung jury   A jury which, after long deliberation, is so irreconcilably divided in opinion that it is unable to reach a unanimous verdict.

I

Impanel   The process of selecting the jury that is to try a case.

Imprisonment   A sentence imposed upon the conviction of a crime; the deprivation of liberty in a penal institution; incarceration.

In camera (Lat.)   A case heard when the doors of the court are closed and only persons concerned in the case are admitted.

Indemnification   Compensation for loss or damage sustained because of improper or illegal action by a public authority.

Indictment   The document prepared by a prosecutor and approved by the grand jury that charges a certain person with a specific crime or crimes for which that person is later to be tried in court.

Injunction   An order by a court prohibiting a defendant from committing an act, or commanding an act be done.

Inquest   A legal inquiry to establish some question of fact; specifically, an inquiry by a coroner and jury into a person's death where accident, foul play, or violence is suspected as the cause.

Instanter   A subpoena issued for the appearance of a hostile witness or person who has failed to appear in answer to a previous subpoena and authorizing a law enforcement officer to bring that person to the court.

Interpol (International Criminal Police Commission)   A clearing house for international exchanges of information, consisting of a consortium of 126 countries.

J

Jeopardy   The danger of conviction and punishment that a defendant faces in a criminal trial.

Judge   An officer who presides over and administers the law in a court of justice.

Judicial notice   The rule that a court will accept certain things as common knowledge without proof.

Judicial process   The procedures taken by a court in deciding cases or resolving legal controversies.

Jurisdiction   The territory, subject matter, or persons over which lawful authority may be exercised by a court or other justice agency, as determined by statute or constitution.

Jury   A certain number of persons who are sworn to examine the evidence and determine the truth on the basis of that evidence. *See also Hung jury.*

Justice of the peace   A subordinate magistrate, usually without formal legal training, empowered to try petty civil and criminal cases and, in some states, to conduct preliminary hearings for persons accused of a crime, and to fix bail for appearance in court.

Juvenile delinquent   A boy or girl who has not reached the age of criminal liability (varies from state to state) and who commits an act that would be a misdemeanor or felony if he or she were an adult. Delinquents are tried in Juvenile Court and confined to separate facilities.

L

Law Enforcement Agency   A federal, state, or local criminal justice agency or identifiable subunit whose principal functions are the prevention, detection, and investigation of crime and the apprehension of alleged offenders.

Libel and slander   Printed and spoken defamation of character, respectively, of a person or an institution. In a slander action, it is usually necessary to prove specific damages caused by spoken words, but in a case of libel, the damage is assumed to have occurred by publication.

Lie detector   An instrument that measures certain physiological reactions of the human body from which a trained operator may determine whether the subject is telling the truth or lying; polygraph; psychological stress evaluator.

Litigation   A judicial controversy; a contest in a court of justice for the purpose of enforcing a right; any controversy that must be decided upon evidence.

M

Mala fides (Lat.)   Bad faith, as opposed to *bona fides, or good faith.*

Mala in se (Lat.)   Evil in itself. Acts that are made crimes because they are, by their nature, evil and morally wrong.

Mala prohibita (Lat.)   Evil because they are prohibited. Acts that are not wrong in themselves but which, to protect the general welfare, are made crimes by statute.

Malfeasance   The act of a public officer in committing a crime relating to his official duties or powers, such as accepting or demanding a bribe.

Malice   An evil intent to vex, annoy, or injure another; intentional evil.

Mandatory sentences   A statutory requirement that a certain penalty shall be set and carried out in all cases upon conviction for a specified offense or series of offenses.

Martial law   Refers to control of civilian populations by a military commander.

Mediation   Nonbinding third-party intervention in the collective bargaining process.

Mens rea (Lat.)   Criminal intent.

Miranda rights   Set of rights that a person accused or suspected of having committed a specific offense has during interrogation and of which he or she must be informed prior to questioning, as stated by the Supreme Court in deciding *Miranda v. Arizona in 1966 and related cases.*

Misdemeanor   Any crime not a felony. Usually, a crime punishable by a fine or imprisonment in the county or other local jail.

Misprison   Failing to reveal a crime.

Mistrial   A trial discontinued before reaching a verdict because of some procedural defect or impediment.

Modus operandi   A characteristic pattern of behavior repeated in a series of offenses that coincides with the pattern evidenced by a particular person or group of persons.

Motion   An oral or written request made to a court at any time before, during, or after court proceedings, asking the court to make a specified finding, decision, or order.

Motive   The reason for committing a crime.

Municipal court   A minor court authorized by municipal charter or state law to enforce local ordinances and exercise the criminal and civil jurisdiction of the peace.

N

Narc   A widely used slang term for any local or federal law enforcement officer whose duties are focused on preventing or controlling traffic in and the use of illegal drugs.

Negligent   Culpably careless; acting without the due care required by the circumstances.

Neolombrosians   Criminologists who emphasize psychopathological states as causes of crime.

No bill   A phrase used by a grand jury when it fails to indict.

Nolle prosequi (Lat.)   A prosecutor's decision not to initiate or continue prosecution.

Nolo contendre (Lat., lit.)   A pleading, usually used by a defendant in a criminal case, that literally means "I will not contest."

Notary public   A public officer authorized to authenticate and certify documents such as deeds, contracts, and affidavits with his or her signature and seal.

Null   Of no legal or binding force.

O

Obiter dictum (Lat.)   A belief or opinion included by a judge in his or her decision in a case.

Objection   The act of taking exception to some statement or procedure in a trial. Used to call the court's attention to some improper evidence or procedure.

Opinion evidence   A witness's belief or opinion about a fact in dispute, as distinguished from personal knowledge of the fact.

Ordinance   A law enacted by the city or municipal government.

Organized crime   An organized, continuing criminal conspiracy that engages in crime as a business (e.g., loan sharking, illegal gambling, prostitution, extortion, etc.).

Original jurisdiction   The authority of a court to hear and determine a lawsuit when it is initiated.

Overt act   An open or physical act done to further a plan, conspiracy, or intent, as opposed to a thought or mere intention.

P

Paralegals   Employees, also known as legal assistants, of law firms, who assist attorneys in the delivery of legal services.

Pardon   There are two kinds of pardons of offenses (1) the absolute pardon, which fully restores to the individual all rights and privileges of a citizen, setting aside a conviction and penalty, and (2) the conditional pardon, which requires a condition to be met before the pardon is officially granted.

Parole   A conditional, supervised release from prison prior to expiration of sentence.

Penal code   Criminal codes, the purpose of which is to define what acts shall be punished as crimes.

Penology   The study of punishment and corrections.

Peremptory challenge   In the selection of jurors, challenges made by either side to certain jurors without assigning any reason, and which the court must allow.

Perjury   The legal offense of deliberately testifying falsely under oath about a material fact.

Glossary

Perpetrator   The chief actor in the commission of a crime, that is, the person who directly commits the criminal act.

Petit jury   The ordinary jury composed of 12 persons who hear criminal cases and determines guilt or innocence of the accused. *See also Grand jury.*

Plaintiff   A person who initiates a court action.

Plea bargaining   A negotiation between the defense attorney and the prosecutor in which the defendant receives a reduced penalty in return for a plea of "guilty."

Police power   The authority to legislate for the protection of the health, morals, safety, and welfare of the people.

Postmortem   After death. Commonly applied to an examination of a dead body. *See also Autopsy.*

Precedent   Decision by a court that may serve as an example or authority for similar cases in the future.

Preliminary hearing   The proceeding in front of a lower court to determine if there is sufficient evidence for submitting a felony case to the grand jury.

Premeditation   A design to commit a crime or commit some other act before it is done.

Presumption of fact   An inference as to the truth or falsity of any proposition or fact, made in the absence of actual certainty of its truth or falsity or until such certainty can be attained.

Presumption of innocence   The defendant is presumed to be innocent and the burden is on the state to prove his or her guilt beyond a reasonable doubt.

Presumption of law   A rule of law that courts and judges must draw a particular inference from a particular fact or evidence, unless the inference can be disproved.

Probable cause   A set of facts and circumstances that would induce a reasonably intelligent and prudent person to believe that a particular person had committed a specific crime; reasonable grounds to make or believe an accusation.

Probation   A penalty placing a convicted person under the supervision of a probation officer for a stated time, instead of being confined.

Prosecutor   One who initiates a criminal prosecution against an accused; one who acts as a trial attorney for the government as the representative of the people.

Public defender   An attorney appointed by a court to represent individuals in criminal proceedings who do not have the resources to hire their own defense council.

R

Rap sheet   Popularized acronym for record of arrest and prosecution.

Reasonable doubt   That state of mind of jurors when they do not feel a moral certainty about the truth of the charge and when the evidence does not exclude every other reasonable hypothesis except that the defendant is guilty as charged.

Rebutting evidence   When the defense has produced new evidence that the prosecution has not dealt with, the court, at its discretion, may allow the prosecution to give evidence in reply to rebut or contradict it.

Recidivism   The repetition of criminal behavior.

Repeal   The abrogation of a law by the enacting body, either by express declaration or implication by the passage of a later act whose provisions contradict those of the earlier law.

Reprieve   The temporary postponement of the execution of a sentence.

Restitution   A court requirement that an alleged or convicted offender must pay money or provide services to the victim of the crime or provide services to the community.

Restraining order   An order, issued by a court of competent jurisdiction, forbidding a named person, or a class of persons, from doing specified acts.

Retribution   A concept that implies that payment of a debt to society and thus the expiation of one's offense. It was codified in the biblical injunction, "an eye for an eye, a tooth for a tooth."

S

Sanction   A legal penalty assessed for the violation of law. The term also includes social methods of obtaining compliance, such as peer pressure and public opinion.

Search warrant   A written order, issued by judicial authority in the name of the state, directing a law enforcement officer to search for personal property and, if found, to bring it before the court.

Selective enforcement   The deploying of police personnel in ways to cope most effectively with existing or anticipated problems.

Self-incrimination   In constitutional terms, the process of becoming involved in or charged with a crime by one's own testimony.

Sentence   The penalty imposed by a court on a person convicted of a crime, the court judgment specifying the penalty, and any disposition of a defendant resulting from a conviction, including the court decision to suspend execution of a sentence.

Small claims court   A special court that provides expeditious, informal, and inexpensive adjudication of small contractual claims. In most jurisdictions, attorneys are not permitted for cases, and claims are limited to a specific amount.

Stare decisis (Lat.)   To abide by decided cases. The doctrine that once a court has laid down a principle of laws as applicable to certain facts, it will apply it to all future cases when the facts are substantially the same.

State's attorney   An officer, usually locally elected within a county, who represents the state in securing indictments and in prosecuting criminal cases.

State's evidence   Testimony by a participant in the commission of a crime that incriminates others involved, given under the promise of immunity.

Status offense   An act that is declared by statute to be an offense, but only when committed or engaged in by a juvenile, and that can be adjudicated only by a juvenile court.

Statute   A law enacted by, or with the authority of, a legislature.

Statute of limitations   A term applied to numerous statutes that set limits on the length of time after which rights cannot be enforced in a legal action or offenses cannot be punished.

Stay   A halting of a judicial proceeding by a court order.

Sting operation   The typical sting involves using various undercover methods to control crime.

Subpoena   A court order requiring a witness to attend and testify as a witness in a court proceeding.

Subpoena *duces tecum*   A court order requiring a witness to bring all books, documents, and papers that might affect the outcome of the proceedings.

Summons   A written order issued by a judicial officer requiring a person accused of a criminal offense to appear in a designated court at a specified time to answer the charge(s).

Superior court   A court of record or general trial court, superior to a justice of the peace or magistrate's court. In some states, an intermediate court between the general trial court and the highest appellate court.

Supreme court, state   Usually the highest court in the state judicial system.

Supreme Court, U.S.   Heads the judicial branch of the American government and is the nation's highest law court.

Suspect   An adult or juvenile considered by a criminal agency to be one who may have committed a specific criminal offense but who has not yet been arrested or charged.

T

Testimony   Evidence given by a competent witness, under oath, as distinguished from evidence from writings and other sources.

Tort   A breach of a duty to an individual that results in damage to him or her, for which one may be sued in civil court for damages. Crime, in contrast, may be called a breach of duty to the public. Some actions may constitute both torts and crimes.

U

Uniform Crime Reports (U.C.R.)   Annual statistical tabulation of "crimes known to the police" and "crimes cleared by arrest," published by the Federal Bureau of Investigation.

United States Claims Court   Established in 1982, it serves as the court of original and exclusive jurisdiction over claims brought against the federal government, except for tort claims, which are heard by district courts.

United States district courts   Trial courts with original jurisdiction over diversity-of-citizenship cases and cases arising under U.S. criminal, bankruptcy, admiralty, patent, copyright, and postal laws.

V

Venue   The locality in which a suit may be tried.

Verdict   The decision of a court.

Vice squad   A special detail of police agents, charged with raiding and closing houses of prostitution and gambling resorts.

Victim and Witness Protection Act of 1984   The federal VWP Act and state laws protect crime victims and witnesses against physical and verbal intimidation where such intimidation is designed to discourage reporting of crimes and participation in criminal trials.

Victimology   The study of the psychological and dynamic interrelationships between victims and offenders, with a view toward crime prevention.

Vigilante   An individual or member of a group who undertakes to enforce the law and/or maintain morals without legal authority.

Voir dire (Fr.)   The examination or questioning of prospective jurors in order to determine his or her qualifications to serve as a juror.

W

Warrant   A court order directing a police officer to arrest a named person or search a specific premise.

White-collar crime   Nonviolent crime for financial gain committed by means of deception by persons who use their special occupational skills and opportunities.

Witness   Anyone called to testify by either side in a trial. More broadly, a witness is anyone who has observed an event.

Work release (furlough programs)   Change in prisoners' status to minimum custody with permission to work outside prison.

World Court   Formally known as the International Court of Justice, it deals with disputes involving international law.

SOURCES

The Dictionary of Criminal Justice, Fourth Edition, © 1994 by George E. Rush. Published by McGraw-Hill/Dushkin, Dubuque, IA 52001.

Index

Index

Test Your Knowledge Form

We encourage you to photocopy and use this page as a tool to assess how the articles in *Annual Editions* expand on the information in your textbook. By reflecting on the articles you will gain enhanced text information. You can also access this useful form on a product's book support Web site at *http://www.dushkin.com/online/*.

NAME: DATE:

TITLE AND NUMBER OF ARTICLE:

BRIEFLY STATE THE MAIN IDEA OF THIS ARTICLE:

LIST THREE IMPORTANT FACTS THAT THE AUTHOR USES TO SUPPORT THE MAIN IDEA:

WHAT INFORMATION OR IDEAS DISCUSSED IN THIS ARTICLE ARE ALSO DISCUSSED IN YOUR TEXTBOOK OR OTHER READINGS THAT YOU HAVE DONE? LIST THE TEXTBOOK CHAPTERS AND PAGE NUMBERS:

LIST ANY EXAMPLES OF BIAS OR FAULTY REASONING THAT YOU FOUND IN THE ARTICLE:

LIST ANY NEW TERMS/CONCEPTS THAT WERE DISCUSSED IN THE ARTICLE, AND WRITE A SHORT DEFINITION:

We Want Your Advice

ANNUAL EDITIONS revisions depend on two major opinion sources: one is our Advisory Board, listed in the front of this volume, which works with us in scanning the thousands of articles published in the public press each year; the other is you—the person actually using the book. Please help us and the users of the next edition by completing the prepaid article rating form on this page and returning it to us. Thank you for your help!

ANNUAL EDITIONS: Criminal Justice 05/06

ARTICLE RATING FORM

Here is an opportunity for you to have direct input into the next revision of this volume.
We would like you to rate each of the articles listed below, using the following scale:

1. **Excellent: should definitely be retained**
2. **Above average: should probably be retained**
3. **Below average: should probably be deleted**
4. **Poor: should definitely be deleted**

Your ratings will play a vital part in the next revision.
Please mail this prepaid form to us as soon as possible.
Thanks for your help!

RATING	ARTICLE
	1. What Is the Sequence of Events in the Criminal Justice System?
	2. The Road to September 11
	3. Global Trends in Crime
	4. The FBI's Cyber-Crime Crackdown
	5. Toward a Transvaluation of Criminal 'Justice': On Vengeance, Peacemaking, and Punishment
	6. Enough Is Enough
	7. Trust and Confidence in Criminal Justice
	8. Dirty Bomber? Dirty Justice
	9. Evidence of Failure
	10. Ordering Restitution to the Crime Victim
	11. Pickpockets, Their Victims, and the Transit Police
	12. Telling the Truth About Damned Lies and Statistics
	13. Violence and the Remaking of a Self
	14. Prosecutors, Kids, and Domestic Violence Cases
	15. Strengthening Antistalking Statutes
	16. The NYPD's War On Terror
	17. Racial Profiling and Its Apologists
	18. Too Close for Comfort, Negotiating with Fellow Officers
	19. Ethics and Criminal Justice: Some Observations on Police Misconduct
	20. Community Policing: Exploring the Philosophy
	21. The Blue Plague of American Policing
	22. Educating and Training the Future Police Officer
	23. Jury Consulting on Trial
	24. You As An Expert Witness. Are You Ready?
	25. Jury Duty: When History and Life Coincide
	26. Looking Askance at Eyewitness Testimony
	27. Justice & Antonin Scalia
	28. Courts Asked to Consider Culture
	29. When Prosecutors Err, Others Pay the Price
	30. Sentencing Guidelines and the Transformation of Juvenile Justice in the 21st Century
	31. A Century of Revolutionary Changes in the United States Juvenile Court Systems
	32. DARE Program: Sacred Cow or Fatted Calf?
	33. The Peer Court Experience

RATING	ARTICLE
	34. Isn't She a Little Young?
	35. Kicking Out the Demons by Humanizing the Experience—An Interview With Anthony Papa
	36. Trends in State Parole
	37. The Results of American Incarceration
	38. Correctional Boot Camps: Lessons From A Decade of Research
	39. Do We Need the Death Penalty?
	40. Prison Programs that Produce
	41. Encouraging Students to Pursue Careers in Community Corrections
	42. The Unique Brutality of Texas, Why the Lone Star State Leads the Nation in Executions

(Continued on next page)

ANNUAL EDITIONS: CRIMINAL JUSTICE 05/06

BUSINESS REPLY MAIL
FIRST CLASS MAIL PERMIT NO. 551 DUBUQUE IA

POSTAGE WILL BE PAID BY ADDRESEE

McGraw-Hill/Dushkin
2460 KERPER BLVD
DUBUQUE, IA 52001-9902

NO POSTAGE
NECESSARY
IF MAILED
IN THE
UNITED STATES

ABOUT YOU

Name   Date

Are you a teacher? ☐   A student? ☐
Your school's name

Department

Address   City   State   Zip

School telephone #

YOUR COMMENTS ARE IMPORTANT TO US!

Please fill in the following information:
For which course did you use this book?

Did you use a text with this ANNUAL EDITION?   ☐ yes ☐ no
What was the title of the text?

What are your general reactions to the *Annual Editions* concept?

Have you read any pertinent articles recently that you think should be included in the next edition? Explain.

Are there any articles that you feel should be replaced in the next edition? Why?

Are there any World Wide Web sites that you feel should be included in the next edition? Please annotate.

May we contact you for editorial input?   ☐ yes ☐ no
May we quote your comments?   ☐ yes ☐ no